WORLD HISTORY 1914-80

WORLD HISTORY
1914~80

Peter Neville

Heinemann Educational Books

Title-page illustration:
Soviet missiles in Finland (Keystone).

Cover illustrations (clockwise):
Nazi motor cycle and sidecar detachment, Berlin, 1939
  (Keystone).
*Churchill, Roosevelt and Stalin at the Yalta Conference,
  1945* (Keystone).
Poverty in the Third World (Oxfam)
Prototype Fast Reactor, Dounreay, Scotland (United
  Kingdom Atomic Energy Authority and Keystone).
Troops haul a field gun out of the Flanders mud, August 1917
  (Popperfoto).

Heinemann Educational Books Ltd
22 Bedford Square, London WC1B 3HH

LONDON   EDINBURGH   MELBOURNE
AUCKLAND   HONG KONG   SINGAPORE
KUALA LUMPUR   NEW DELHI   IBADAN
NAIROBI   JOHANNESBURG   EXETER (NH)
KINGSTON   PORT OF SPAIN

© Peter Neville, 1982
First published 1982

British Library Cataloguing in Publication Data

Neville, Peter
  World history 1914–80.
  1. History, Modern – 20th century
  I. Title
  909.82   D421

  ISBN 0-435-31670-2

Filmset and printed in Great Britain by
BAS Printers Limited, Over Wallop, Hampshire

Preface

Words and phrases that may cause difficulty are marked in the text with an asterisk(*) and are explained under the heading Keywords at the end of each chapter.

Although in 1978 the government of China announced a new system of transliterating from the Chinese to the Western alphabet, this method is not yet in general use in the West. Therefore, names that were well-known before 1978 retain their traditional spelling, such as Mao Tse-tung and Peking, while names that sprang to prominence after 1978 are spelt in the new way, so that Teng Hsiao-ping becomes Deng Xiaoping.

Acknowledgements

The author is grateful to Professor Northedge, London School of Economics, Dudley Woodgett, Head of the History Department, St George's College, Weybridge, and Mr R. C. Hart, who read and commented on the manuscript.

The author and publishers wish to thank the following for permission to reproduce illustrations:

Associated Press: Fig. 17.4.
BBC Hulton Picture Library: Figs. 1.2, 3.2, 5.2, 5.4, 6.1, 14.2 and 16.5.
Fox Photos: Figs. 7.1 and 7.3.
Imperial War Museum: Figs. 2.4, 2.5, 12.4, 12.8 and 13.2.
Keystone Press Agency: Figs. 2.3, 6.5, 7.4, 7.5, 8.3, 8.4, 9.2, 9.3, 11.2, 11.4, 11.7, 12.2, 12.5, 12.6, 13.1, 14.1, 14.4, 15.2, 16.1, 16.3, 17.3, 17.5, 17.7, 17.8, 18.2, 18.3, 18.4, 19.2, 19.3, 19.4, 20.3, 20.4, 21.1, 21.2, 21.3, 21.4, 22.2, 22.4, 22.5, 23.1, 23.2, 23.3, 23.4, 24.1 and 24.3.
Library of Congress: Figs. 4.2 and 9.5.
The Low Trustees and the *Evening Standard*: Figs. 13.3 and 13.4.
Mansell Collection: Figs. 2.2, 4.1 and 6.3.
Museum of the City of New York: Fig. 8.1.
Peter Newark's Western Americana: Figs. 3.1, 8.2, 9.4, 17.1, 17.2 and 17.6.
Novosti Press Agency: Figs. 1.3, 5.3, 10.1, 12.7 and 20.2.
Oxfam: Fig. 24.2.
Popperfoto: Figs. 4.3, 7.2, 9.1, 20.1 and 22.3.
Punch: Figs. 1.5, 5.5, 11.6 and 15.3.
Roger-Viollet: Fig. 6.4.
Society for Cultural Relations with the USSR: Figs. 10.2 and 10.3.
Sport and General Press Agency: Fig. 10.4.

Maps by Reg Piggott.

Acknowledgement is also due to all those who have given permission to reproduce extracts.

Contents

1 Europe in 1914

In 1914 Europe was, as it is today, the most densely populated continent in the world. It contained approximately 420 million of the world's 1,600 million people, although this figure would also include Asiatic Russia. But there the resemblance ends because the European society that existed before 1914 was, in most respects, very different from the one we know today. It is true that there had been important technical changes in the previous fifty years – such as the telephone, the aeroplane (Bleriot had flown the Channel in 1909) and the motor car – but as yet these changes had made only a limited impression on everyday life. Most Europeans still worked on the land and lived in villages where they remained for most of their lives.

There were nonetheless new and dynamic influences at work in society. Trade unionism was becoming an important force, and in Britain and Germany the foundations of the modern welfare state were laid in the period before 1914. The grip of the Christian religion was still strong, but it was starting to weaken. In France, for example, there had been a great struggle between Church and State over control of the schools that resulted in a victory for the latter. Napoleon's Concordat with the Pope, which made Catholicism the official religion in France, was cancelled by the French government. This was an indication of the way the established order would be challenged in Europe after 1918. In 1914 the old order still seemed to dominate, but its serenity was to prove an illusion.

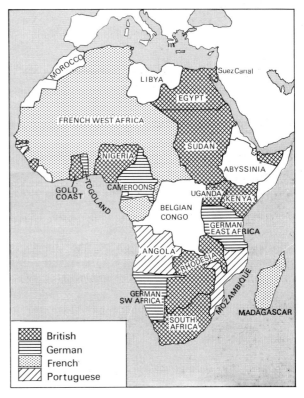

Fig. 1.1   European possessions in Africa, 1900.

Imperialism*

We have started our story of the twentieth century in Europe because in 1914 it was still very much the centre of world affairs. In one sense this book is about how Europe ceased to be the centre of the world and was replaced as the dominant influence by the great flanking powers, Russia and the United States. But at the beginning of the century nobody could have foreseen this development as the European powers still ruled over the larger part of the earth's surface. Fig. 1.1 shows the size of their colonial* empires in Africa. Why did the European powers become imperialist and seize so much territory in the closing quarter of the nineteenth century? The scale of the land grab is indicated in Table 1.1.

Table 1.1 The growth of empire, 1871–95

Country	Territory seized (millions of sq. km (sq. miles))		Population increase (millions)
Britain	9.6	(4.5)	66
France	7.5	(3.5)	26
Germany	2.6	(1.0)	13
Belgium	2.3	(0.9)	8.5
Italy	0.429	(0.185)	0.75

The urge to build an empire is an old one, but it seemed to be particularly strong in Western European countries at that time.

There were a number of motives behind this process:

1. *Raw materials.* All the European powers needed raw materials like cotton, rubber, silk, etc. Many of these could only be obtained in the colonial territories.

2. *Markets.* These were needed to sell their manufactured goods.

3. *Tradition of empire.* This was strong in countries like Britain, France and Holland.

4. *Military needs.* Britain, for example, wanted naval bases in Cyprus and the Cape.

5. *Religious zeal.* Missionaries, such as David Livingstone, felt it was their duty to take the Christian gospel to countries like Africa.

6. *Desire to increase national prestige.* Great imperialists, for example, Cecil Rhodes, Milner and Marshal Lyautey, felt it was their mission to bring Rhodesia, South Africa and Morocco under British and French rule.

7. *The 'white man's burden'.* Much of the drive behind imperialism was provided by the feeling that the white man was superior to other races and had a mission to civilize them and *perhaps* prepare them for self government.

Imperialism was therefore the result of many factors, as the historian David Thomson says: 'It was not just that trade followed the flag, but that the flag accompanied the botanist and buccaneer, the Bible and the bureaucrat, along with the banker and the businessman.'[1]

Sometimes colonies were obtained by accident, and their conquest was not always a matter for great enthusiasm. Even the British Prime Minister Disraeli, later a great imperialist, commented dryly in 1852 that 'these wretched colonies will all be independent in a few years and are millstones round our necks'.

Quite often there were disputes between the colonial powers, as we shall see, but underneath the surface powerful forces were stirring, based on the belief of the subject peoples that they had the right to rule themselves. A few perceptive people had noticed these stirrings. One of them was the American Negro leader W. E. B. du Bois who wrote at the turn of the century: 'The problem of the twentieth century is the problem of the colour line – the relation of the darker to the lighter races of men in Africa and Asia, in America and the islands of the sea.' The defeat of Russia by Japan, an Asian power, in the war of 1904–5 was already pointing the way towards this 'revolt against the West'.

The 'mighty continent', 1914

The next section deals with what was happening inside the 'mighty continent', the decline of which forms such an important part of the history of the twentieth century. Five great countries dominated it in these years: Britain, Germany, France, Russia and Austria–Hungary.

Britain

Britain, as we have seen, was a great colonial power, but it had other problems too in 1914. On the other side of the Irish Sea the issue of independence or Home Rule had exploded once more. The largely Catholic south of Ireland wanted Home Rule, the largely Protestant north wanted union with Britain. Both sides seemed prepared to fight over it, and the Liberal government under Herbert Asquith was caught in the middle.

Then there were the trade unions, flexing their muscles in the years 1912–14 and demanding better conditions and pay for their members. Newer still was the suffragette movement under Mrs Pankhurst and her daughters. The suffragettes were prepared to go to prison to get women the vote, and even to die – as Emily Davison did, by throwing herself under the King's horse at the Derby in 1913 (Fig. 1.2).

The Liberal government between 1906–14 was a great reforming administration. It had introduced old age pensions, health insurance, and unemployment benefits, but it was also facing new forces that many of its leaders found difficult to understand.

Germany

Britain's traditional security was challenged by the new German Empire created by the defeat of France

Fig. 1.2 Suffragette Emily Davison throws herself under the King's horse at Epsom race course in 1913.

miserable existence, dependent on the whims of the weather and the harvest. There was, too, a growing proletariat or urban working class as Russia began to industrialize in the 1880s and 1890s. This had side effects that worried the government, such as the growth of trade unionism and the Marxist parties. Political violence was common in Russia. The Tsar had lost his grandfather and his prime minister to political assassins. He had, therefore, some reason to hope that a foreign war might distract the attention of his people from domestic complaints, and allow him to pose as the champion of the Slavs*.

in the war of 1870–71. Under its Kaiser (Emperor) William II (1888–1918) the new Germany proved to be a turbulent addition to the European state system. It was a curious mixture: it had an emperor and a parliament with a socialist* majority; it had the strongest army in Europe, yet wanted to build a large navy. Colonial ambitions clashed oddly with Germany's position as the greatest land power in Europe. By 1914 the German military leaders were in a restless mood, and the government was growing worried about the increasing size of the socialist vote. In 1914 Army Commander-in-Chief von Moltke told Foreign Secretary von Jagow that a war that summer would be as good a time as any. Germany was led by men in a hurry who were 'individually and as a group . . . as ill-equipped to lead this great machine as a seventeenth-century coachman would be to drive a Mercedes–Benz'.[2]

France

The French Republic was the product of military defeat in 1871, and its leaders never forgot the loss of the two provinces of Alsace and Lorraine to Germany. The internal history of France before 1914 was a story of fierce political struggle between the Right, representing the Church, the army and the rich, and the Left, representing the socialists, the working class and the anti-clericals. In between floated the great mass of French peasants whose instincts were conservative and who would usually vote the way the parish priest wanted.

At the turn of the century, France was deeply split by the famous Dreyfus case, when a Jewish army

Fig. 1.3 A peasant sowing grain in tsarist Russia.

Russia

Far off to the east was the sprawling mass of the Russian Empire with its huge population. Since 1613 it had been ruled by the Romanov family, and the last of the Tsars, Nicholas II, began his reign in 1894. Russia was an autocracy*, most power lying with the Emperor and his immediate advisers. At this time they were generally men of low calibre, although one, the strange holy man Gregori Rasputin, had a certain claim to fame (see p. 11). The Tsar had granted a duma or parliament in 1905, but took little notice of what it said. Effective opposition was forced underground and was represented by the Social Revolutionaries (the Peasant Party), the Mensheviks and the Bolsheviks. The latter were to play a big part in the history of modern Russia.

In 1914 Russia was still a backward country with a mainly peasant population (Fig. 1.3). Although freed from slavery in 1861, the peasants still lived a

officer was wrongly accused and sent to prison for selling military secrets to the Germans. Later it was the victim of a wave of strikes as the parties of the Left showed their disapproval of the middle-class government. The general mood of the country though was peaceful and far from sympathetic to military leaders like Foch, anxious to revenge the defeats of 1870–71. France was noted above all for its culture as the home of writers Hugo and Zola, and painters Degas, Gauguin, and Toulouse Lautrec. If France's squabbling politicians were a joke in more stable countries its writers, painters and sculptors were not.

Austria–Hungary

The last of the great European powers in 1914 was also the most complicated. Like Russia, it had an ancient royal family, the House of Habsburg, which had kept the throne of the empire since the fifteenth century. This empire was a great hotchpotch of different races including Poles, Czechs, Slovaks, Ruthenes, Croats, Serbs, Hungarians and Germans. From 1867 the last two dominated what became known as the Dual Monarchy. The Emperor, Francis Joseph, who became Emperor in 1848, then became King of Hungary. This pleased the Hungarians, but did little to satisfy the other races of the empire. The imperial government in Vienna, therefore, began to fear the rising tide of Slav nationalism in eastern Europe, in an area called the Balkans. The government was corrupt and inefficient, and its military power was in sharp decline as Austria–Hungary's allies found to their cost. A German general was to remark ruefully that friendship with Austria–Hungary was like 'being shackled to a corpse'.

There were also smaller powers inevitably involved in the struggles of their larger neighbours: Italy, anxious to improve her second class status by seizing more colonial territory; the Turkish Empire, once great, but now confined largely to its Middle Eastern lands, and in the hands of the revolutionary 'Young Turks'; and lastly Serbia, a small independent Slav power that had offended others by defeating them in the Balkan wars of 1912–13.

The Slav peoples of the Austro–Hungarian empire looked to Serbia for encouragement, while Serbia similarly looked for encouragement from them. The seeds of the coming war were to lie in the desire of the Vienna government to teach the upstart Serbs a lesson.

Europe stands to arms

In their foreign affairs as well as their domestic ones,

the European powers were the victims of considerable tensions and anxieties. These tensions were, at least in part, the result of the Bismarckian alliance system which first appeared in 1879. Otto von Bismarck was the man who had united Germany, and then wanted to protect his new creation. He did this by forming an alliance block with Austria–Hungary, Russia and Italy. France was out in the cold, Britain uninterested, but this did not worry Bismarck. He believed that if he could keep on good terms with Russia and Austria, then all would be well, for a vengeful France would have no ally.

His plan had one major flaw. Austria and Russia were always likely to quarrel in the Balkans and then he would have to choose between them. The Balkans, Bismarck said, were not 'worth the bones of a Pomeranian grenadier', but he predicted that the next war would start there. Only the clever diplomacy* of the 'Iron Chancellor' had prevented a flare up in this area before his fall in 1890.

The *Ententes*

Soon after Bismarck's fall his fears were realized. In 1893 France and Russia made a military agreement; the Russians were angry that Bismarck had refused them a financial loan, but this had been expected. Britain, too, was to become involved in this complex system of alliances. It felt endangered by the ambitious expansion of the German navy in the 1890s and isolated by its unpopularity during the war against the Boers* in South Africa (1899–1902). The result was the *Entente Cordiale* of 1904 with France. This was a colonial agreement recognizing French rights in Morocco and British rights in Egypt. There was no military agreement between them, but obviously the 1904 *Entente* brought the two countries closer together.

Then came the 1907 *Entente* with Russia making the Triple *Entente*. This time Persia was the bone of contention, and it was divided into Russian and British 'spheres of influence'. Once again, there was no promise of military assistance on either side. But the logic of the agreements was plain for all to see: Europe was now divided into two armed camps.

The three crises, 1905–11

This division sharpened the ill-feeling that already existed and made any crisis a potential cause of war. The decade before 1914 saw three such crises, each bringing the continent a little nearer to the brink.

Morocco, 1905 and 1911

Two of the crises were to take place in Morocco, which was generally accepted in these years as being within the French sphere of influence. In 1905 the German Kaiser William II paid a visit to Tangier and made a provocative speech that seemed to dispute the French position in Morocco. He went so far as to warn the French government that 'we know the road to Paris and we can get there again if needs be. They should remember that no fleet can defend Paris'. Britain supported France in the dispute, which merely resulted in an international conference that confirmed France's position in Morocco. Still dissatisfied, the Germans tried again in 1911 by sending a gunboat called the *Panther* to the Moroccan port of Agadir (Fig. 1.4). It was supposed to be protecting German rights, but this claim fooled no one. The British Chancellor of the Exchequer Lloyd George warned Germany against this action in a strong speech, and the Germans backed down. Germany's blustering tactics did obtain part of the French

Fig. 1.4   This cartoon shows France and Morocco protesting at the arrival of the German gunboat Panther *at Agadir in 1914, while Britain looks disapprovingly at Germany.*

Congo, but failed to split the Anglo–French alliance as it had hoped.

Bosnia–Hercegovina, 1908

The third and most serious crisis arose in Bosnia–Hercegovina, then part of the Turkish Empire. Since 1878 this area had been administered by Austria–Hungary, although remaining under the overall control of the Turkish Sultan. Believing that possession was nine-tenths of the law, the Austrians then seized Bosnia–Hercegovina in 1908. The Russians protested angrily, but were in no position to act. Their ally France would not fight and the Russian army was still recovering from its humiliating defeat in 1904–5. The Austro–Hungarians, by contrast, had Germany's full support, and Chancellor Bulow told them that their 'humiliation would be our humiliation'. So Austria–Hungary kept the two provinces, although its behaviour was clearly illegal. This crisis had two unfortunate effects:
1. It encouraged the war party in Vienna.
2. It made Russia more determined to fight next time.

The Balkan wars that followed in 1912–13 only made the situation more tense. Germany's allies, Turkey and Bulgaria, were defeated while Austria's hated neighbour Serbia finished on the winning side both times.

The powder keg

All this time the great powers were building up their armies for a possible trial of strength. As one side increased its armies, so did the others. Britain and Germany also found themselves in their own private naval race. In the beginning the Royal Navy had a great advantage in numbers, but this disappeared with the invention of the dreadnought, a revolutionary new battleship. Both powers began to build dreadnoughts as quickly as they could.

All the major countries stepped up arms production and recruitment especially in the years 1900–14 (Table 1.2), e.g. in 1913 France lengthened the period of military service from two to three years.

Table 1.2 Standing armies and populations, 1914

Country	Army	Population
France	846,000	41,500,000
Germany	812,000	58,500,000
Austria–Hungary	424,000	51,400,000
Russia	1,300,000	153,800,000

War planning

To a considerable degree foreign policy was dictated by war plans. This was particularly true of Germany and its Schlieffen Plan – named after Count Alfred von Schlieffen, the Chief of Staff of the German army up to 1905. Germany's major problem was having to fight a war on two fronts, against France in the west and Russia in the east. Schlieffen's answer was to mount a knockout blow in the west, removing the French from the war in only six weeks. Then the Germans could turn east and deal with the slow-moving Russians. There was one major snag in this plan: the Germans did not want to attack across the heavily-fortified frontier with France, so they intended to march through neutral Belgium. This act would infringe the treaty of 1839 safeguarding Belgium's neutrality and would bring Britain into the war if its government honoured its promise.

If the plan worked it would win the war for Germany and it was assisted by France's own plans for war. The Germans knew that the French Plan 17 involved a mad dash into Alsace–Lorraine to regain the lost provinces. The German army would be there waiting, and the effect would be like pushing a swing door. The harder the French pushed in Alsace–Lorraine, the easier it would be for the Germans to push through Belgium and attack them from the rear.

Germany planned to leave some soldiers in the east to guard the frontier with Russia, France's ally. Russia, for its part, had promised to send two armies into eastern Germany within two weeks of the outbreak of war. Her problem was mobilization. Could she get her slow-moving cumbersome army there in time?

The Russians also had to consider the likely behaviour of Austria–Hungary, their enemy and Germany's friend. The Austro–Hungarians were obsessed by the desire to 'smash the Serbs' and planned only a defensive campaign against the Russians. Britain, as we have noted, was not involved in any of these military agreements. But there was one significant exception. In 1912 the British navy had promised to protect France's Channel coastline if the French navy would look after the Mediterranean sea. The government would, therefore, feel under some obligation to help France in the event of war.

This then was Europe in 1914, a powder keg just waiting for someone to apply the match. If war was not inevitable, it was always likely as an American observer noted on a visit in 1914. 'Militarism run stark mad', was how he described the situation.

Fig. 1.5 'The Triumph of "Culture"', which appeared in Punch *on 26 August 1914, condemned the German invasion of Belgium.*

Sarajevo, 28 June 1914

The match was applied, as might have been expected, in the Balkans. On 28 June 1914 the heir to the Austrian throne, the Archduke Franz Ferdinand, was due to pay a visit to the town of Sarajevo, the capital of Bosnia. On that day he and his wife were assassinated by Gavrilo Princip, a Serbian nationalist, and the Austrians had the excuse for which they had been waiting. An impossible ultimatum was sent to the Serbs, expressly designed to make acceptance impossible, but safe in the knowledge of German support. The Kaiser gave Austria a 'blank cheque' and said that he would appear at her side like a 'knight in shining armour'. To everyone's surprise the Serbs accepted almost all the points in the ultimatum, excepting the Austrian demand that their officials should help look for the Archduke's murderers. Even Kaiser William admitted that with the Serb reply 'every ground for war disappears'.

But the Austrians were in no mood to argue, and on 28 July 1914 they declared war on Serbia. The intricate web of alliances then dragged in all the other powers except the Italians, who anyway disliked the Austrians, and the British, who anxiously discussed what to do. Two Liberal cabinet ministers resigned rather than support the war, but in the end the

German invasion of Belgium was decisive. On 4 August the government decided that 'gallant little Belgium' was an issue worth fighting for, and declared war on Germany (Fig. 1.5).

Europe's rush to war, 1914

28 June	Murder of Franz Ferdinand in Sarajevo.
5 July	Germany assures Austria of support in the event of war with Russia (the 'blank cheque').
23 July	Austrian ultimatum to Serbia.
28 July	Austria declares war on Serbia.
30–31 July	Russia starts mobilization.
1 August	German declaration of war on Russia. France starts to mobilize.
3 August	Germany declares war on France.
4 August	Germany invades Belgium, explaining to Britain that this is only in response to France's warlike plans. Britain declares war on Germany, which regards Anglo–Belgian treaty as a 'scrap of paper'.

What the historians say

There has been a lot of controversy about why the First World War started. Here are some of the things historians have said about it:

In 1914 Germany fought a two-front war and fought it successfully until 1918. Germany could have gone on defending herself indefinitely. That a two-front war could not be fought was a false assumption, but it was one which absolutely dictated Germany's policy. – A. J. P. Taylor[3]

Among the numerous men who had to make decisions there was no outstanding personality – no Cavour, Bismarck, or Disraeli. – Bernadotte E. Schmitt[4]

Once Austria declared war on Serbia, Europe moved helplessly according to a determinist Fate; and that fate lay in the military timetables of each nation, above all Germany's. – Corelli Barnett[5]

Keywords

imperialism: the urge to dominate other countries by military or economic means.

colonial: from colony – meaning land ruled by another country, e.g. British India.

socialist: one who believes that the state should own the means of production, i.e. industry, agriculture and commerce.

autocracy: absolute rule by an emperor or king.

Slav: the race of East European peoples inhabiting countries such as Russia, Poland, Bulgaria, Czechoslovakia and Yugoslavia.

diplomacy: the art of maintaining relations with foreign countries.

Boers: descendants of early Dutch settlers in South Africa.

2 'The War to End Wars', 1914-18

The war that began in August 1914 was not expected to last long. In Britain it was generally believed that it would be over by Christmas, and William II confidently told his departing soldiers that they would be home 'before the leaves fell'. The character of the war was quite different from that expected by military experts in all the countries involved.

The failure of the Schlieffen Plan

We saw in Chapter 1 how the German leaders were bound hand and foot by the demands of their military plans. They *had* to defeat France within six weeks regardless of whether the French actually wanted a war or not (to justify their attack the Germans had to pretend that France had violated their air space!). In the event they were to come very close to achieving their objective (Fig. 2.1).

Fig. 2.1   The Schlieffen Plan.

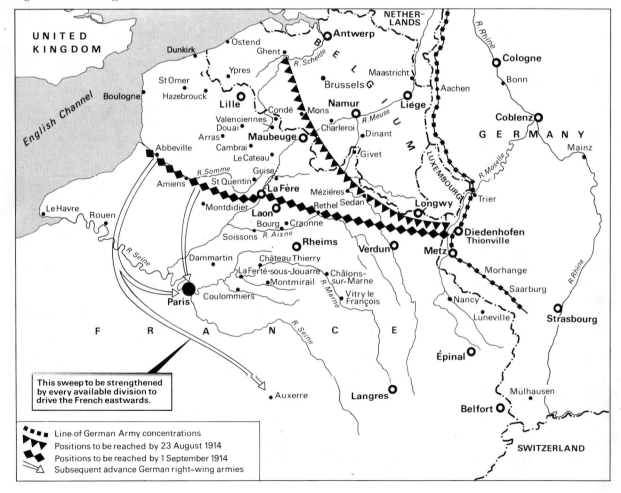

This sweep to be strengthened by every available division to drive the French eastwards.

- ▪▪▪▪ Line of German Army concentrations
- ▼▼▼ Positions to be reached by 23 August 1914
- ◆◆◆ Positions to be reached by 1 September 1914
- △ Subsequent advance German right–wing armies

At first all seemed to go well for the German armies, although the resistance of the Belgians was tougher than they expected. Then things started to go wrong for a variety of reasons. The German Commander-in-Chief von Moltke was a long way from the front and this allowed local commanders to make decisions without reference to him first. For this reason the German armies did not move west as Schlieffen intended, but eastwards. This allowed the French and British to attack their communication lines.

Then the Russians surprised the Germans by arriving early in east Prussia. Some forces had to be sent east to deal with them. The German infantry was very tired, and in the end von Moltke lost his nerve and ordered a general retreat to the River Aisne. Shortly afterwards he had a nervous breakdown and had to be replaced. The Battle of the Marne was, therefore, an Allied victory, even though the Germans had come within 40 km (25 miles) of Paris. Its effect was spoiled by the failure to follow up the German retreat and in the end the Germans were left in occupation of a large part of northern France and virtually the whole of Belgium.

The German Army began to dig defensive lines of trenches, so did the Anglo-French forces, and in the end these stretched from the Channel to the Swiss frontier. Their construction was to be followed by a complete stalemate on the western front that lasted for almost four years. Neither side could think of a way of breaking through. This may seem strange nowadays but it was the result of two basic facts of military life:

1. In 1914 the main attacking force of armies was the cavalry, as had been the case in the nineteenth century. But this attacking arm was to prove quite useless in battle.
2. The battlefield was dominated by the machine gun and its ally, barbed wire. The machine gun made infantry attacks virtually impossible, and the barbed wire would entangle any soldiers fortunate enough to reach the enemy lines.

There was, in addition, powerful artillery on both sides that could pin down advancing troops and make it impossible for them to move. Obviously horsemen were totally ineffective against such defensive weapons, and only when the British invented the tank was an attacking weapon available to counter the 'queen of the battlefield', the machine gun. Quite why the deadly merits of the machine gun should have been overlooked in this way was a mystery. There was plenty of evidence from the American Civil War and the Russo–Japanese War about its performance.

In the beginning, everyone, particularly the French, believed in the effectiveness of frontal assaults with the bayonet. Before the war men like Ferdinand Foch had dominated the thinking of the French army: 'All attacks are to be pressed to the extreme . . . to charge the enemy with the bayonet in order to destroy him . . . this result can only be obtained at the price of bloody sacrifice.' Such tactics were to cost the French army a million casualties before the year 1914 had ended.

The war on the eastern front, 1914–15

The Russian intervention in eastern Germany in August 1914 played a crucial role in the German defeat on the Marne, but it did them little good. The Russian armies demonstrated their traditional technical backwardness (even sending out uncoded messages which told the Germans their plans!), and suffered the consequences. Two crushing defeats at Tannenburg and the Masurian lakes hurled their forces back over the frontier, and never again were they able to secure a foothold on German territory. The eastern front then settled down. There was more movement over the great tracts of Polish, Hungarian and Russian land involved, but the results were no more decisive. Where the Russians faced German troops, as at Gorlice–Tarnów in 1915 they did badly. Where they fought the Austro–Hungarian army they did well, as their brother Slavs were reluctant to fight hard against Russian troops. For a long time it was believed that the Russian army was severely handicapped by a shortage of shells, but modern research has shown this to be false. The historian, Norman Stone, says that the 'shell was exaggerated as a feature of Russian defeats in the spring and summer of 1915. The German's artillery superiority on the eastern front was no greater, and indeed was usually smaller, than the Western powers' artillery superiority in France, which got them nowhere.'[1] A more significant reason for Russian defeats was incompetent leadership. Many high ranking officers owed their position to nothing other than the favour of the royal family.

Meanwhile what happened to little Serbia? This was, after all, the reason why Russia and Austria–Hungary were fighting each other. It should of course have been easy for Austria–Hungary as a great power to defeat the Serbs. This did not prove to be the case, and in 1914 the Serbs were able to drive the Austrians out of their country. When the Austrians returned in October 1915 they did so with German and Bulgarian help. Even then many Serbian troops retreated into Greece to continue the struggle. No one could pretend, however, that 1915 had been a good year for the Allies in the east.

Gallipoli, 1915–16

By now the Turks had also come into the war on the side of Germany and its allies. Their relative weakness seemed to offer an opportunity too good to be missed. Could not the *Entente* powers seize the straits into the Black Sea and link Russia with the west? So reasoned Winston Churchill and other 'easterners' in Britain, i.e. those who thought the war could be won in the east rather than on the western front. It was a promising idea, but its execution was bungled. First the Turks were warned of Anglo–French intentions by a naval attack and then they were allowed too much time to prepare their land defences. The result was a disaster. The Allied troops could not get off the beaches of Gallipoli, and in 1916 they were all evacuated. The Australian and New Zealand Army Corps (Anzac) suffered particularly heavy losses in the assault.

Churchill was rightly made the scapegoat for the Gallipoli fiasco and sacked from his job at the Admiralty*. For a time he went to fight in France as a private soldier.

The extension of the war

By now the war was much nearer to earning its title of the First World War. Turkish entry meant that there was to be fighting in the Middle East between the Turks and the British. There was also to be fighting in Africa over the German colonies there. In 1915 the Japanese came in and captured the German fortress of Tsingtao in China, although they did little else of consequence. In that year, too, Italy entered the war and opened up a new front against Austria–Hungary. Thus, although primarily a European war, it was not confined to the European theatre alone.

Stalemate in the west

The Western powers were equally unsuccessful in their efforts to defeat the Germans in France and Belgium. Huge offensives were launched that gained very little ground. One new and unpleasant feature was introduced on the German side in their decision to use poison gas. It proved quite effective at first because the British and French were taken by surprise, but was later countered by the use of gas masks.

Verdun

Despite their appalling losses both sides went into 1916 convinced that victory was just around the corner. The new German Commander-in-Chief Falkenhayn had worked out a strategy based on the concept of 'bleeding France white'. The idea was to attack some vital point in the front that the French could not give up and 'suck in' all their reserves in men and material. The defeat of France, Falkenhayn believed, would force Britain to make peace. The place he picked to carry out this exercise was the old historic fortress town of Verdun. Up to a point his plan worked quite well. French reserves were sucked into Verdun and they did suffer heavy losses. But German losses were equally severe and in the end the battle for Verdun cost both sides over 200,000 men. Even by the standards of the First World War this loss rate was far too high.

The Somme

One effect of Verdun was to place a much heavier burden on the British army to the north. The French badly needed someone else to take the strain off their army, and the British commander Sir Douglas Haig was willing to oblige. By 1916 his army had grown to a million men, a tremendous increase in the tiny force of 80,000 that Britain had been able to send to France in 1914.

Haig chose the River Somme as the point to launch his offensive, and it began after several delays on 1 July 1916. Unfortunately, the delays had forewarned the Germans, and the attack was a catastrophe. On the first day alone 60,000 British casualties were suffered, but the offensive dragged on. Haig had given his word to the French and would not give up. The only favourable aspect of the battle was that once again German losses were nearly as high. Somehow the amazing spirit of the 'Tommies' kept them going amid all these disasters. They sang famous songs like this:

> We are Fred Karno's army
> the ragtime infantry
> We cannot fight, we cannot shoot
> What bleedin' use are we.
> And when we get to Berlin
> the Kaiser he will say
> 'Hoch, hoch, mein gott
> What a bloody awful lot
> Are the ragtime infantry'.

They needed a sense of humour for 1916 was a terrible year for all the belligerent countries.

The war at sea

While great armies slogged it out on the European continent, a different kind of war was being fought on the high seas. There were none of the great naval battles that might have been expected, although some small actions were fought. In 1914 the Royal Navy destroyed the German Pacific squadron in the Battle of the Falkland Isles, and the Germans responded by bombarding the east coast of Britain. Their great high seas fleet, however, remained blockaded in Kiel Harbour until 1916. Then the German admirals decided to risk confronting the Royal Navy, and a great engagement was fought at Jutland. The result was really a draw. The Germans sank 100,000 ton(ne)s of British shipping and lost only 60,000 of their own. They also suffered only 2,000 casualties compared with 6,000 in the Royal Navy. The British performance was unimpressive, as Admiral Beatty underlined in his famous comment 'There's something wrong with our bloody ships today.' But they did not need a clear-cut victory because of their superiority in numbers. The German Fleet went back to Kiel and stayed there until the end of the war. Jutland had, therefore, changed nothing, and the British blockade of Germany continued. Germany's only answer was to wage an increasingly ruthless U-boat campaign in an attempt to starve out the British by crippling their vital overseas trade. In 1917 they came very near to success but the German decision, at the end of 1916, to sink all ships on their way to Britain was to prove a fatal one as you will see later in this chapter.

New leaders

By the end of 1916 the war had been going on for $2\frac{1}{2}$ years, and a new spirit of ruthless determination began to appear in all the countries involved. This was reflected in several changes of leadership in that year. In Britain the cautious Asquith was replaced as Prime Minister by David Lloyd George. He approached the war in a different way from his predecessor. Conscription was introduced, women were mobilized for the war effort and the production of munitions greatly increased. For the first time a total war economy was in operation in Britain.

In Germany, too, there were changes. The discredited Falkenhayn was sacked and replaced by the partnership of Hindenburg and Ludendorff. These two men became the war-lords of Germany between 1916 and 1918 with limitless powers. They rarely bothered to tell the Kaiser or civilian politicians what they were doing.

The war-weary French were also to find a tougher, more combative leader for 1917 in the veteran politician Georges Clemenceau. He was not against shooting traitors, like the spy Mata Hari, or silencing defeatist talk.

1917–the turning point

At the end of 1917 it seemed that it was the central powers that were winning the war and the *Entente* powers that had lost it. This proved to be an illusion because black as it was for Britain and France, the scales had really turned decisively in their favour during that year.

The end of tsarism

To understand why this was the case we need to turn first to Russia and look back into its history. We have already seen that in 1905 Tsar Nicholas II granted his people a parliament or duma, but that it was allowed no real say in the running of the country. The middle class, therefore, had little influence in government but the peasants and town workers had even less. An attempt was made by the tsarist government to transfer the ownership of land to peasant families, but nothing was done to improve conditions in the factories and workshops. The years just before the First World War were therefore characterized by a series of serious strikes in places like the Lena goldfields. There was increasing resentment of the royal family and its privileges, and in particular of the Tsarina* and her friend Rasputin (Fig. 2.2). The

Fig. 2.2   Gregori Rasputin, the Tsar's 'holy man'.

Tsarina was hated partly because she was foreign (she was nicknamed 'the German woman'), but also because of her tendency to rely on favourites for advice. Rasputin, meaning the 'disreputable one' in Russian, was an outstanding example of such favouritism. He was able by some mysterious means to counteract her son's haemophilia* and therefore could do no wrong. In the end Rasputin's privileged position led to his death in quite extraordinary circumstances in December 1916. He ate a large quantity of poisoned cakes with no apparent ill effects and was finally murdered with a volley of pistol shots from badly-scared opposition noblemen! Nicholas himself was a weak ruler dominated by his wife. It was very much a case of the wrong man in the wrong place at the wrong time. The war gave the Tsar a respite because most Russians rallied around the war effort against the hated Germans. It was not to be long though before the strains of the war began to show on Russian society. In 1916 the Stavka or high command had found in General Brusilov a man who could win battles, although he had no magic formula for success. He avoided the massive artillery bombardments that were so typical of the war and mounted smaller local attacks. These tactics were very effective against the Austrians, but Brusilov did not have the strength to defeat the Germans too. By the end of 1916 the morale and discipline of the Russian army was starting to break down. Without the loyalty of his troops Nicholas II could not hope to survive.

The March Revolution

The winter of 1916–17 was a very cold one in Petrograd, and there were serious shortages of food. The garrison was also unreliable, and the situation was ripe for revolution. When it came in March 1917 it seemed to catch everyone by surprise, as indeed the 1905 revolution had done. The Tsar was absent at the front, and the Bolshevik* leader Lenin had almost given up any hope of political change in Russia. But change had come, and in a matter of days the Tsar was forced to abdicate in favour of the provisional government under the liberal Prince Lvov. Russia, it seemed, was on the road to Western style democracy, and the new government was determined to carry on the war as before. This proved to be a fatal mistake, which was to push Russia in a completely different political direction.

Lenin's return, April 1917

In the long run the man who gained most from the policy of the provisional government was Vladimir Ilich Ulyanov, known as Lenin. He saw that the continuation of the war would provide the opportunity to impose a Marxist solution on Russia's problems.

Marxism

What was Marxism? To explain this it is necessary to go back to the year 1848. It was in that year that Karl Marx and Friedrich Engels published their famous *Communist Manifesto*, which contained some new and revolutionary proposals:
1. that all human history was 'the history of class struggle'.
2. that the dominant class was the capitalist class, i.e. the factory owners, bankers and landowners. Capitalism, Marx and Engels said, was based on the exploitation of the working class, which they called the proletariat.
3. It was inevitable that the workers would rise up and destroy capitalism and take power for themselves. They would then take control of 'the means of production'. This system would be called socialism.

The last sentences of the manifesto read: 'Workers of the World unite. You have nothing to lose but your chains.' It had a tremendous appeal to working-class people throughout Europe, but not in Russia, or so Karl Marx thought. Most Russians were peasants and Marx believed they were too conservative to want to overthrow capitalism. Lenin disagreed; he realized that the peasants and Russia's small proletariat could work together.

'Bread, land, and peace'

Before he returned to Russia in 1917 Lenin had already worked out his tactics. He ordered the Bolsheviks not to co-operate with the provisional government. Instead they were to infiltrate the soviets or workers' councils which had sprung up all over Russia. 'All power to the soviets,' Lenin cried, in contrast to the other Left-wing parties, the Mensheviks* and the Social Revolutionaries who believed in working through the new Constituent Assembly (Parliament). He also had a keen appreciation of what the Russian people wanted; an end to the war, more food and a proper land settlement. His years in exile had not been wasted, and he would take no opposition from other party members. The party would strike when the iron was hot, and their chance came in the autumn of 1917.

Fig. 2.3   Red Guards prepare to attack the Winter Palace in Petrograd, November 1917.

The Bolsheviks in power

By then, the provisional government, now led by Alexander Kerensky, was to be in a hopeless position. The government had gained a temporary advantage in July when a premature uprising by the Bolsheviks in Petrograd had failed (Lenin had been forced to flee to Finland). But in that same month Brusilov's last big attack had also failed and the army became a disorganized rabble. Kerensky's authority was further undermined by his feeble reaction to an attempted *coup** led by the former Tsarist general Kornilov. While the government dithered, the Bolshevik Red Guards mobilized, and Kornilov's offensive failed when striking railway workers refused to transport his soldiers to the capital. Lenin saw his opportunity. He accused Kerensky of 'Bonapartism' (i.e. trying to set himself up as a military dictator), and returned to Petrograd to reorganize his party. Although other Bolsheviks like Kamenev and Zinoviev had doubts, Lenin persuaded the party leadership to strike, and on 4 November 1917 the Bolsheviks seized control of Petrograd (Fig. 2.3) and Moscow. The almost bloodless *coup* was supervised by Lenin's new ally Leon Trotsky, a recent convert to Bolshevism. The only people the provisional government could find to fight for them were some officer cadets and a regiment of women soldiers!

The effect of the Bolshevik victory

Russia now had a government that was determined to pull out of the war and eventually did so (see p. 31). Long before this happened the Russian army had ceased to take any active part in the war and the Germans were able to switch troops from the eastern to the western theatre. This could have been disastrous for Britain and France, had not the loss of Russia as an ally been balanced by the gain of another, even more powerful one.

The entry of the United States, April 1917

From 1914–16 the American people had watched the European war with interest, but with a sense of detachment. They had no desire to become involved, and their President Woodrow Wilson had been re-elected in 1916 because he had promised to keep them neutral. Three factors combined to make the Americans change their minds:

1. *The German decision to adopt 'unrestricted submarine warfare' in 1916.* American opinion had already been outraged by the sinking of the *Lusitania* in 1915 with the loss of many American lives.
2. *The Zimmermann Telegram.* The American government had a copy of the telegram sent by a

German foreign office official Zimmermann to Mexico City. It showed that the Germans were encouraging Mexico to try to reconquer territories like New Mexico and Arizona long lost to the United States.
3. *Alleged German sabotage.* There was evidence that German agents inside the United States were deliberately sabotaging American industries and disrupting the communications system.

Faced with this, President Wilson had little option but to declare war on Germany on 3 April 1917 (Fig. 2.4). The great wealth and industrial strength of the USA was now at the disposal of the *Entente* powers. The question at the end of 1917 was whether American intervention would come too late to save them.

The French army mutinies

It was already clear that American help would be badly needed in the west. In May 1917 there were serious mutinies in the French army after the failure of yet another ambitious offensive. At one point about half the French army was involved in the mutiny, although by some miracle the Germans never found out about it. Troops began to 'baa!' like sheep and refuse to go up to the front, while officers were lynched. Only the devoted leadership of General Pétain nursed the French army back to health. For a long time afterwards it could not be used as an offensive force.

Germany's last offensive, 1918

The British had hung on grimly during 1917 throughout a series of terrible battles around Ypres in Belgium. But they were stretched to the limit, and the German leaders decided to risk everything in a last big attack before the Americans could arrive in strength.

Ludendorff called this the *Kaiserschlacht* (Emperor's battle), and it began on 21 March 1918. At various points along the Allied line the Germans made attacks against the British and then the French. The Germans made important gains, and almost captured the vital railway junction of Amiens, but eventually, in July, the attacks petered out (Fig. 2.5). Ludendorff's attacks had been crude, but time was against his armies throughout. The Allies survived, and they decided to co-ordinate their armies under the command of Marshal Foch. His attacking

Fig. 2.4   An American army recruiting poster of the First World War.

Fig. 2.5   British troops advancing through France in July 1918.

philosophy now found a more appropriate field for action. In August the Allied army, reinforced by the Americans under Pershing, went over to the attack, supported by great numbers of tanks. On 8 August, 'the black day' for the German army as Ludendorff called it, the British won an important victory, and gradually the Germans were pressed back. They fought grimly all the way so that the retreat never became a rout.

The collapse of the central powers

Germany's allies collapsed like a pack of cards. Austria–Hungary under its new Emperor Karl had wanted peace since 1916 and after suffering a shattering defeat at Vittorio Veneto on the Italian front in October 1918, agreed peace terms at the beginning of November. Bulgaria had already done so on 29 September having been undermined by an Allied push northwards from Greece. Turkey had also made peace. Its armies had been destroyed by Allenby in Palestine and the guerrilla tactics of Colonel T. E. Lawrence in the Arabian desert. There seemed little else left for Germany except to make peace as well. The civilian population was already starving as a result of the Allied blockade.

So it was that at the eleventh hour on the eleventh day of the eleventh month of the fourth year of the war the fighting stopped. Germany was granted an armistice* by the Allied powers prior to the signing of a peace settlement.

The cost

The loss of life suffered in the fighting was enormous. Table 2.1 will give you some idea of the scale of the slaughter.

Table 2.1 Number of troops killed, 1914–18

Country	No. of men killed (approx.)
France	1,500,000
Germany	1,700,000
British empire	1,500,000
Russia	5,000,000
(withdrew from the war March 1918)	
USA	115,000
(entered the war April 1917)	

The effect

At this level the First World War was terrible enough. But the nature of the fighting especially on the western front left dreadful scars in soldiers' minds. They remembered the pointless charges with the bayonet against barbed wire and machine guns that rarely gained more than a few hundred yards of ground. Rain, mud, rats and lice made life in the trenches a misery for the average soldier. Here is just one soldier's eye witness account from the 1917 Battle of Passchendaele, generally regarded as one of the worst battles of the war.

Going up to the line for the first time my first indication of the horrors to come appeared as a small lump on the side of the duckboard [wooden planks used to cover the muddy ground]. I glanced at it, as I went past, and I saw to my horror, that it was a human hand gripping the side of the track – no trace of the owner, just a glimpse of a muddy wrist and a piece of sleeve sticking out of the mud. After that there were bodies every few yards. Some lying face downwards in the mud; others showing by the expressions fixed on their faces the sort of effort they had made to get back on the track. Sometimes you could actually see blood seeping up from underneath. I saw the dead wherever I looked – a dead signaller still clinging to a basket cage with two dead pigeons in it, and further on, lying just off the track, two stretcher-bearers with a dead man on a stretcher. There were the remains of a rations party that had been blown off the track. I remember seeing an arm, still holding on to a water container. When the dead men were just muddy mounds by the trackside it was not so bad – they were somehow impersonal. But what was unendurable were the bodies with upturned faces. Sometimes the eyes were gone and the faces were like skulls with the lips drawn back, as if they were looking at you with terrible amusement. Mercifully a lot of those dreadful eyes were closed.[2]

The shape of things to come

The First World War was also a war of rival technologies. Both sides invented new weapons, such as poison gas and tanks, while others, like the submarine and the aeroplane, were perfected. There were Zeppelin* raids on London, and Paris was bombarded by long-range artillery. Above all there was the staggering, ruinous cost of modern war: Great Britain spent £22 million on the first two weeks of the third Battle of Ypres to fire four million rounds of ammunition. The days when wars were fought in distant places by soldiers alone were gone forever, and the thought of another conflict terrified everybody. Surely, they hoped in 1918, it would be 'the war to end wars'.

First World War timeline

1914

August–September	Battle of the Marne.
1915	Gallipoli landings.
1916	
February	Germans attack Verdun.
1 July	Battle of the Somme begins.
1917	
April	USA enters the war.
May	French Army mutinies.
November	Bolshevik Revolution.
1918	
March	New German offensive in the West.
	Russia leaves the war.
July	Defeat of German offensive.
	Large American reinforcements in Europe.
29 September	Bulgaria makes peace.
31 October	Turkey surrenders
3 November	Armistice between Austria–Hungary and the Allies.
11 November	Ceasefire on the western front.

Keywords

admiralty: the government department in charge of the navy.

tsarina: the Russian empress.

haemophilia: a blood disease common in nineteenth-century European royal families.

Bolshevik: meaning 'majority' in Russian – a Russian communist in the early twentieth century.

Menshevik: meaning 'minority' in Russian – a Russian socialist in the early twentieth century.

coup (d'etat):   seizure of power by force.

armistice: a temporary peace agreement between countries.

Zeppelin: German airship.

Questions

Extract 2.1

The United States declares war on Germany, 3 April 1917

One of the things that has served to convince us that the Prussian autocracy was not and could never be our friend is that from the very outset of the present war it has filled our unsuspecting communities and even our offices of government with spies and set criminal intrigues everywhere afoot against our national unity of counsel, our peace within and without, our industries and our commerce. Indeed it is now evident that its spies were here even before the war began; and it is unhappily not a matter of conjecture but a fact proved in our courts of justice that the intrigues which have more than once come perilously near to disturbing the peace and dislocating the industries of the country have been carried on at the instigation, with the support, and even under the personal direction of official agents of the Imperial Government to the Government of the United States. Even in checking these things and trying to extirpate them we have sought to put the most generous interpretation possible upon them because we know that their source lay not in any hostile feeling or purpose of the German people towards us (who were in no doubt as ignorant of them as we ourselves were), but only in the selfish designs of a Government that did what it pleased and told its people nothing. But they have played their part in serving to convince us at last that that Government entertains no real friendship for us and means to act against our peace and security at its convenience. That it means to stir up enemies against us at our very doors the intercepted note to the German minister at Mexico City is eloquent evidence.

1. This statement was made by the US President. Name him.   1
2. Who was the German official who sent the 'intercepted note'?   1
3. Give three examples of things that made the US government believe that Germany had 'no real friendship, for it.   6
4. Name the two men who were in charge of German war policy.   2
5. What long-term effect did American entry have on the war?   5
6. Who was the commander of the US forces in Europe in 1918?   1
7. Why do you think the German leaders risked bringing the USA into the war by their dangerous policies?   4

20

3 The Lost Peace

Europe in 1919 was in an exhausted condition. For four years a terrible war had involved most of its peoples and brought about a massive destruction. The memory of it was to dominate the next twenty years, and it is important that we understand the feelings of the time. One soldier spoke of those who had suffered and died: 'Nothing but immeasurable improvements will ever justify all the waste and unfairness of this war. I only hope that those who are left will never, never forget at what sacrifice these improvements have been won.' The man who wrote this letter was called Norman Chamberlain and he sent it to his cousin Neville, later to be a British Prime Minister.

On the one side, therefore, there was sadness at the loss of friends and relatives, but on the other, fierce hatred of the enemy. This xenophobia* showed itself in strange ways. In Britain the Royal Family had to change its name, and people threw stones at dachshunds in the street. In the USA German *sauerkraut* had to be renamed 'liberty cabbage'. Today this may appear ridiculous, but in 1918–19 such events reflected the atmosphere of the time.

It would be difficult for the peacemakers to work in an environment free of feelings of hatred and revenge.

Wartime diplomacy

One problem facing national leaders during a war is the shape of the peace settlement after it (assuming they win it of course!). This was particularly true during the First World War. Various attempts were made to end the war, notably by the former British Foreign Secretary Lord Landsdowne in 1916. But usually the terms were too high, and as the war dragged on neither side was in a mood to compromise. We will see later how harshly the Germans treated defeated Russia at Brest–Litovsk in March 1918 (see p. 31). They also had plans for the permanent occupation of northern France and Belgium.

The British wanted to destroy German naval power and share out their enemy's colonial empire with the French. France wanted, as you have seen, to regain the provinces of Alsace and Lorraine lost in 1871 to Germany. It also wanted to obtain compensation for the damage done by German forces in the northern provinces of France.

Ironically, the man who had most influence on the shape of the eventual settlement was the American President, Woodrow Wilson (Fig. 3.1). In many ways, though, it was a good thing. This was because the United States was the last major power to enter the war and therefore able to see the issues in a more detached way.

Fig. 3.1   Woodrow Wilson.

Wilson's Fourteen Points

By the autumn of 1918 Germany's military leaders realized that the war was lost. They decided to approach President Wilson in the hope that he might offer more lenient peace terms than Great Britain and France. Wilson's response was to put forward his famous Fourteen Points. Of these the most important were Point 1 which demanded 'open diplomacy' (no more secret treaties) and point 5 which demanded a 'free open-minded and absolutely impartial adjustment of all colonial claims'.

In Point 8 the US President promised that the provinces of Alsace and Lorraine, which had been lost to Germany in 1871, would be given back to France. Point 13 asked for access to the sea for a new Polish state, and Point 10 promised 'autonomous development' for the peoples of the Austro–Hungarian Empire, i.e. the right to rule themselves.

Most important of all was Point 14 in which Woodrow Wilson suggested the need for an international organization 'for the purpose of affording mutual guarantees of political independence and territorial integrity to great and small states alike'. This idea for an international peace-keeping body was to form the basis of the new League of Nations. We shall be looking at the League later.

The armistice

On 11 November 1918 Germany's leaders finally agreed to give up the struggle. Austria, Bulgaria and Turkey had already asked for peace. Wilson's Fourteen Points were to form the basis of the settlement with the defeated powers. For the moment a ceasefire was enforced.

The treaty makers

Before discussing the details of the peace treaties some attention needs to be paid to the men who made them.

Woodrow Wilson, US President (1913–21)

Woodrow Wilson was an unusual man in many respects. He had spent most of his life in universities, only coming to politics at a late stage. After a spell as Governor of New Jersey he was picked by the Democratic Party to run for President in 1912. Because of a split in the opposing Republican Party

Wilson won. He was a man of peace who was re-elected in 1916 because he promised to keep his country out of the war in Europe. When forced to enter the war in April 1917 Wilson did so in an idealistic spirit. America would fight, he said, 'to make the world safe for democracy'. Inexperienced in European politics, perhaps a little naive, Woodrow Wilson found it hard to deal with the problems facing him on the other side of the Atlantic after the war. His greatest contribution was to sponsor the infant League of Nations.

David Lloyd George, British Prime Minister (1916–22)

Unlike Wilson, the British leader was a natural politician. Beginning as a fiery Welsh radical, Lloyd George went on to hold office as Chancellor of the Exchequer. He deserted his Liberal party leader Asquith in 1916 to become Prime Minister in a coalition government with the Conservatives. Lloyd George was a shrewd, realistic statesman who saw the flaws in the Versailles Settlement. Strong anti-German feeling in Britain, however, made it hard for him to follow a moderate policy. The Prime Minister had worked hard to get everyone involved in the war effort. Now it was difficult for him to counteract the feeling that Germany ought to be 'squeezed until the pips squeak'.

Georges Clemenceau, French Prime Minister (1917–20)

Clemenceau, nicknamed 'the Tiger', was not a man who found that his mood differed greatly from that of his fellow countrymen. Already a veteran politician in 1917, Clemenceau was called in at a time of national crisis in France. At the peace conference his task was to get the best settlement for France that he could. To achieve this Clemenceau was prepared to use ruthless methods. In order to persuade Wilson of the rightness of the French cause he took the American leader on tours of ruined villages in northern France. France had suffered most heavily from the Great War and it was something that Clemenceau would not let the other Allied statesmen forget.

These then, were the men who were to dominate the peace conference when it met at Versailles (Fig. 3.2). The 'Big Three' as they are often called were accompanied by the leaders of the smaller nations involved. Some, like the Italian leader Orlando, played a significant, although not a major role.

The Versailles Treaty

*Fig. 3.2   The treatymakers (from left to right):
Orlando, Lloyd George, Clemenceau and Wilson*

As we have seen the Treaty dealing with Germany was signed at the Palace of Versailles in June 1919. It can be divided into several sections:

1. *Territorial clauses* (Fig. 3.3).
(a) Germany was to lose all its colonies in Africa and the Pacific.
(b) Alsace–Lorraine was to return to French control.
(c) France was to have access to the Saar coalfield.
(d) A special 'corridor' through German territory was to be created to give Poland an outlet to the sea.
(e) The port of Danzig was to come under League of Nations control, although the Poles could use the port facilities.
(f) Eupen–Malmedy was to be given to Belgium (after a plebiscite).
(g) North Schleswig was to go to Denmark (after a plebiscite).
(h) The city of Memel was to be given to Lithuania.

2. *Military clauses.*
(a) A demilitarized zone* was to be created in the Rhineland.
(b) Allied troops were to be stationed there, but no German military forces.
(c) The German Army was to be reduced to 100,000 men.
(d) Germany was to hand over its navy to Great Britain.
(e) Germany was to have no submarines or military aircraft.

Fig. 3.3   German territorial losses, 1919.

(f) Limits were to be placed on the number of German warships.

3. *Reparations**   The Allied powers were also determined that Germany should pay for the cost of the war. The job of working out the level of reparations was given to the Allied Reparations Commission. It completed its task in 1921 and the amount fixed for the Germans to pay was the huge one of £6,600 million! Additional demands were made in respect of coal, iron ore and other materials.

The War Guilt clause

You may think that the treaty settlement was harsh enough, but the Allied powers were still not satisfied. They also wanted Germany to admit its responsibility for starting the war. A serious attempt was made to put the German Emperor William II on trial, but he fled to Holland. When the Dutch refused to give him up the plan to try the German leaders was dropped. The question of responsibility remained, and here we need to return to the events of 1914.

The Allies believed that Germany should bear the major blame for the war because it was Germany that had violated Belgian neutrality and had encouraged its ally Austria–Hungary to attack Serbia.

Convinced that their case was unanswerable, they therefore insisted that Germany should sign the so-called 'War Guilt' clause. This clause, Article 231 of the Versailles Treaty, placed the blame for the First World War squarely on Germany's shoulders.

The German reaction

The German people were outraged when they read the peace terms. Particular criticism was directed at the War Guilt clause. Many Germans believed that it was Tsarist Russia that should take most of the blame because Russia had mobilized* its army first. The Versailles Treaty was described as a *diktat** or dictated treaty, and there was talk of refusing to sign it. Another factor was the widespread belief that Germany had not really lost the war, but had been 'stabbed in the back'. Two points need to be remembered here:

1. The collapse of Germany and its allies came very quickly between September–November 1918.
2. No Allied troops were actually on German soil when the ceasefire was agreed.

It was therefore easy to believe in the 'stab in the back' legend, blaming traitors inside Germany for its defeat.

Ironically, the phrase 'stab in the back' was first used by a British general, but it was later to be a powerful weapon in the hands of German nationalists as we shall see.

For the moment the Germans had no real choice except to sign the Treaty of Versailles. Ludendorff and Hindenburg, the generals who were really responsible for Germany's defeat, knew this perfectly well. Refusal meant an Allied advance into the heart of Germany. But who would sign the infamous *diktat*? With some difficulty the Germans rounded up a delegation: it is significant that Ludendorff and Hindenburg wanted nothing to do with it. The main responsibility fell on a civilian politician Erzberger. Two years later the unfortunate Erzberger was to be shot down in the Black Forest by Right-wing extremists. Some Germans were never to forgive those men who had the courage to come to terms with Germany's defeat.

Some contemporary views about Versailles

The Germans were not alone in their criticism of the settlement. On the Allied side, too, many had reservations about the severe nature of the treaty. Here are some examples of contemporary comment:

> This treaty ignores the economic solidarity of Europe, and by aiming at the economic life of Germany it threatens the health and prosperity of the Allies themselves . . . – *John Maynard Keynes*, a member of the British delegation, and later a famous economist.

> You may strip Germany of her colonies, reduce her armaments to a mere police force and her navy to that of a fifth rate power; all the same in the end if she feels that she has been unjustly treated in the peace of 1919 she will find means of exacting retribution from her conquerors. – *David Lloyd George*, British Prime Minister.

Some years later a little known South German politician was to write: 'Peace treaties whose demands are a scourge to nations not seldom strike the first roll of drums for the uprising to come.' His name was Adolf Hitler.

The final verdict?

It is easy with the advantage of historical hindsight* to criticize the Treaty of Versailles. Why, we ask, did the Allied statesmen impose such a severe settlement on Germany? It should have been obvious that the harsh terms were only storing up trouble for the future. However, certain factors need to be remembered:

1. A costly, bitter war had been going on for four years. It was unlikely, therefore, that the Allied leaders could have imposed a lenient settlement – even if they had all wished to do so.

2. German complaints were justified, but some attention has to be paid to their plans. The evidence suggests that if Germany had won the war it would have been just as severe in its treatment of the Allied powers. Germany's treatment of defeated Russia at Brest–Litovsk in March 1918 is a good example.

3. The alternatives to the Versailles settlement were not all that obvious. Germany could have been completely occupied, as it was to be in 1945. But this solution also created problems that remain today.

Try then to put yourself in the place of the 'Big Three' in 1919. Historians have been trying to do this for sixty years with varying results.

The associated treaties, 1919–20

Versailles dealt with the former German empire, but it was, in fact, one of several treaties.

A series of settlements broke up the old Austro–Hungarian Empire which had included most of central and eastern Europe. The Habsburg family had ruled this empire since 1438, and its disappearance from the map marked a turning point in European history. The treaties of Saint Germain and Trianon disposed of the old Habsburg lands.

Saint Germain

This created the new states of Czechoslovakia and Yugoslavia. Austria became a small independent country with Vienna as its capital.

Interestingly, Article 80 of the Versailles Treaty also prevented the German-speaking Austrians from uniting with Germany. Parts of the old Austro–Hungarian empire were given to other powers: Galicia went to Poland; Transylvania to Romania; Istria, Trentino and South Tyrol to Italy.

Trianon

This treaty reduced the size of the old Kingdom of Hungary. From 1867–1918 the Habsburg Emperor Francis Joseph (1848–1916) and then his nephew Karl had been crowned as King of Hungary. After 1919 the Hungarians lost this privileged position and became a small independent country like Austria.

Neuilly

A third treaty dealt with Bulgaria, which had been an independent kingdom before the First World War. But in 1915 it joined the war on the side of Germany and Austria–Hungary. Bulgaria's reward was to lose territory to both Yugoslavia and Greece.

These treaties also insisted on reparations being paid to the victor powers. What effect did the treaties of Saint Germain, Trianon and Neuilly have on Europe?

1. The great Habsburg Empire was gone forever.

2. The balance of power* in central Europe had been completely changed. Two new states, Czechoslovakia and Yugoslavia, had been created. An old one, Poland, had been freed from foreign occupation.

3. Two large dissatisfied powers, Germany and Russia, bordered on these new countries. Such countries were often called 'revisionist' – meaning that they would like to change the map of Europe to their own advantage.

Sèvres

One great empire remained, that of Turkey. It, too, had entered the war in 1915 on the Austro–German side. Its empire in the Near and Middle East was eagerly dismantled by Britain and France: Cyprus went to Britain; Rhodes and the Dodecanese islands to Italy; Eastern Thrace to Greece. The Turkish lands in the Middle East were to be placed under the League of Nations mandate system.

The League of Nations

Earlier in this chapter we saw how President Woodrow Wilson called for 'a general association of nations' to preserve the peace. This concept was built into all the treaties drawn up after the First World War, by means of the League of Nations Covenant. Under the terms of the covenant all the signatory powers agreed 'to promote international co-operation and to achieve international security by the acceptance of obligations not to resort to war, by the prescription of open, just and honourable relations between nations.'

The main task of the League of Nations, was, therefore, to preserve the peace by outlawing war as a method of obtaining national objectives. If a member state did use force against another then Article 16 of the covenant stated that all other members would unite against her and break off all trading and diplomatic relations.

Membership

In theory the League opened its membership to all countries, although there were important exceptions. In practice membership was limited to the USA, Europe, Latin America, the British dominions, Japan, China and a few small independent states, such as Ethiopia and Liberia.

It should be remembered that in 1919 a large part of the world was divided into colonial empires. Britain, for example, ruled over a quarter of the earth's surface at that time.

The membership of the League was, therefore, much smaller than the modern United Nations.

Organization

The League headquarters was in Geneva. It was to have a secretariat, for the office work, headed by a Secretary-General. The membership operated at two levels:

1. *The League Council.*   This consisted of all the great powers and four representatives of the smaller countries – these changed round from time to time.
2. *The League Assembly.*   All member states were represented on this body. The League began with forty-two member states. A two-thirds majority vote was needed to admit new members.

The idea behind this two-tier system was that the Council could be used to deal with sudden world crises, as bringing together the League Assembly could be a clumsy business.

Agencies

Apart from the major role of keeping the peace the League had many other jobs that were carried out by agencies.

1. *Permanent Mandates Commission.*   It looked after the colonies of the defeated powers, Germany and Turkey. The colonies of these countries were given under a 'mandate' to one of the Allied powers (Fig. 3.4): Syria went to France; Palestine to Britain; German South-West Africa to South Africa; German East Africa to Britain.

The mandated territories were to be ruled by these countries under the League of Nations Covenant until they were thought to be ready for self-government.

2. *Permanent Court of Justice.*   This was set up in The Hague in the Netherlands. It could deal with legal disputes between member states.
3. *International Labour Organization* (ILO).   It

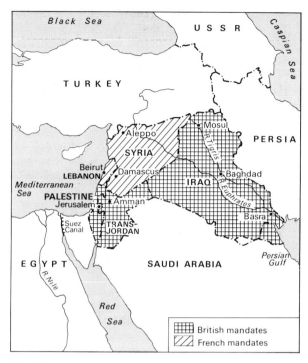

Fig. 3.4   League of Nations mandates in the Middle East.

was designed to act as 'a watchdog' over working conditions, salaries and workers' rights in the League's member states.

4. *The Nansen Agency.*   This dealt with the resettlement of refugees. Many people had lost their homes as a result of the First World War.

Nansen was a famous Norwegian explorer who became involved in this work.

Other agencies dealt with such matters as drugs, white slavery, prisoners of war and financial loans.

Weaknesses

The League of Nations had some notable successes in its early days as we shall see in the next chapter. But its long-term effectiveness was weakened by some basic flaws:

1. The League appeared to be a kind of 'winner's club'. Germany and its allies were not allowed to join until later. Soviet Russia did not join until 1934. So great was the fear of Bolshevism that the USSR had not even been invited to the Versailles Conference.
2. The USA refused to join the League in 1920, even though it was Woodrow Wilson's idea.
3. Under the League Covenant all decisions taken by the Council and Assembly had to be unanimous. In

effect, this gave every country a veto. Decision making was, therefore, made difficult.

4. The League had no army. The French leader Clemenceau wanted some provision for a League army, but the idea was opposed by the British and Americans. Clemenceau dropped the idea in exchange for a defensive alliance with Great Britain and the USA.

From its birth in 1919 the League of Nations was gravely weakened by the absence of certain great powers and its lack of real 'teeth'. It was able to deal with disputes between the smaller powers, and there were to be some notable successes in the 1920s. In 1921, for example, Sweden obtained the Aaland islands from Finland, and in 1925 the League was able to stop the Greek attack on Bulgaria. Such triumphs for peacemaking had, however, to be set against the failure to stop Czechoslovakia from seizing the coalmining area of Teschen, or Lithuania's annexation of Memel. It was unfortunately these events which were to point the way to the League of Nations's sad failure in the 1930s. It could deal with quarrels between small states, but those between great powers were another matter.

Wilson's failure

You may be surprised to learn that Woodrow Wilson had been unable to persuade his own people to join the League. After all, the basis for the whole idea had been provided by his famous Fourteen Points in 1918, and the absence of the USA from the League probably ruined its chances of success. When the Americans rejected membership on 19 March 1920 the task of enforcing the League's provisions fell almost entirely on Britain and France. As later chapters will show they proved incapable of carrying out this task. Why did the Americans turn against Wilson and the League? Several factors are relevant:

1. From independence in 1783 until 1917 the USA had always avoided involvement in European politics. To many the terms of the Versailles Treaty, which America also refused to ratify*, seemed to be just another example of squalid European power politics. Versailles and the League were a package that the majority of Americans did not want.

2. Woodrow Wilson had grown out of touch with American politics. The Republican Party opposed his foreign policy, and even some of his fellow Democrats thought he had become too arrogant.

3. Wilson's health collapsed under the strain of a campaign to persuade the American people to accept his brainchild, the League. Edmund Ions tells us that 'Wilson wandered like a ghost in the White House,

unable to work because of the excruciating pains in his head'.[1] A few days later in October 1919 he suffered a stroke that left him partly paralysed. He could not lead the fight against the opponents of Versailles and the League. When the American Senate voted against the treaty Wilson remarked bitterly: 'They have shamed us in the eyes of the world.' He died in 1924 and, therefore, did not live to see the collapse of his dreams about international peace in the 1930s.

We may perhaps agree with this comment on Wilson's career: 'He failed, and the story of his failure was one of the major tragedies of this century. If he had not failed, and if he had lived to carry on his policies or command them to a successor, the Second World War might well have been avoided.'[2]

Jan Smuts, the South African leader, gave a kinder verdict on the American President: 'It was not Wilson who failed . . . It was the human spirit itself that failed at Paris.'

Keywords

xenophobia: hatred of foreigners.
demilitarized zone: an area where one or more countries cannot station troops.
reparations: compensation in the form of enforced payments of money or goods to another country.
mobilize: put the armed forces into a state of readiness for war.
diktat: German word meaning an enforced or imposed peace settlement.
hindsight: looking back in time.
balance of power: a condition in which no country or group of countries is stronger than any other.
ratify: to accept a treaty or agreement, usually by a parliament.

Questions

These questions are based on Chapters 1–3. Select ONE of the possible answers in each case.

1. The man responsible for the German invasion plan in 1914 was:
(a) von Moltke.
(b) Kaiser William II.
(c) Hindenburg.
(d) Bismarck.
(e) Schlieffen.

2. Two eastern provinces were involved in a European diplomatic crisis in 1908. They were:
(a) Alsace and Lorraine.
(b) Galicia and Transylvania.

(c) Bosnia and Hercegovina.

(d) Bosnia and Macedonia.

(e) Serbia and Istria.

3. The general who was going to 'bleed France white' in 1916 was:

(a) Ludendorff.

(b) Conrad.

(c) Haig.

(d) Falkenhayn.

(e) Tirpitz.

4. 'War in Balkans' and 'Suffragette killed by King's horse'. These headlines apply to the year:

(a) 1913.

(b) 1909.

(c) 1914.

(d) 1918.

(e) 1912.

5. In a crisis in 1905 the Kaiser reminded another European country that he knew 'the road' to its capital. The country and capital were:

(a) Britain and London.

(b) France and Paris.

(c) Russia and St Petersburg.

(d) Serbia and Belgrade.

(e) Austria and Vienna.

6. On 1 July 1916 the British army launched a major offensive on:

(a) the Marne.

(b) the Aisne.

(c) the Rhine.

(d) the Somme.

(e) the Scheldt.

7. 'Son of a landowner.' 'Exile in Zurich.' 'Smuggled home in a German train.' This man was:

(a) Pilsudski.

(b) Rasputin.

(c) Marx.

(d) Kerensky.

(e) Lenin.

8. The man who predicted that the story of the twentieth century would be the story of 'the colour line' was:

(a) W. E. B. du Bois.

(b) Mahatma Gandhi.

(c) Friedrich Engels.

(d) Cecil Rhodes.

(e) Benjamin Disraeli.

9. All the following were motives for imperialism EXCEPT:

(a) the need for markets.

(b) religious zeal.

(c) feelings of racial superiority.

(d) desire for national prestige.

(e) the wish to help the working class.

10. 'They have shamed us in the eyes of the world.' The 'they' referred to is/are:

(a) the House of Commons.

(b) the German Foreign Office.

(c) the American Senate.

(d) the Russian duma.

(e) mutinous French troops.

11. J. M. Keynes said that 'the economic solidarity of Europe' was threatened by the Treaty of:

(a) Brest–Litovsk.

(b) London.

(c) Trianon.

(d) Versailles.

(e) Lausanne.

12. The state that did NOT join the League of Nations until 1934 was:

(a) Germany.

(b) Russia.

(c) USA.

(d) Japan.

(e) Italy.

13. Which TWO of the following were decisive in bringing about German defeat in the First World War? (Select your answer from (i)–(v).) They were:

(a) the sacking of Falkenhayn.

(b) American entry into the war.

(c) the French defence of Verdun.

(d) the British naval blockade.

(e) the collapse of Austria–Hungary.

(i)   (a) and (b)

(ii)   (b) and (c)

(iii) (b) and (d)

(iv)   (c) and (d)

(v)   (d) and (e)

14. Read the following extract from a speech by Lloyd George and fill in the blanks with the two-word combinations offered: 'You may strip Germany of her . . . reduce her armaments to that of a mere police force and her . . . to that of a fifth rate power.'

(a) Emperor and navy.

(b) colonies and navy.

(c) army and Parliament.

(d) coal and empire.

(e) pride and industry.

15. The headquarters of the League of Nations was in:

(a) New York.

(b) The Hague.

(c) Rome.

(d) Geneva.

(e) Oslo.

4 Europe in the 1920s

Germany, 1919–24

The immediate postwar period in Germany was one of chaos and disillusionment. The shock of defeat in the Great War was combined with resentment against the severe treatment of Germany in the Versailles Treaty. As we have seen, many Germans found it difficult to accept that they had been defeated at all.

The Weimar Republic

One immediate need was to replace the old monarchy by a new form of government. The Hohenzollern family had ruled Germany from 1871–1918. They were to be replaced by a republic*, which was to be responsible for signing the peace treaty with the Allied powers. This republic took the name of the small town of Weimar in Saxony. It was there that the new constitution was drawn up.

It had several provisions which need to be remembered:

1. Elections were to be carried out by a system called *Proportional Representation*. Each party received seats in parliament according to the number of votes it received (unlike the British system of 'first past the post', i.e. the party that gets the most votes wins).
2. The head of state was to be the President. He was to be elected directly by the German people and hold office for seven years.
3. All men and women over the age of 20 years were to have the vote in parliamentary elections. Rather strangely the new parliament kept its old name of Reichstag or Imperial Parliament. There was, of course, no longer an Emperor.
4. A special article in the constitution, Article 48, gave the President the right to rule without the Reichstag in emergencies.

In many ways the Weimar Constitution was democratic and fair, but it proved to have some major weaknesses. The most serious ones were all related to the four provisions of the constitution already mentioned.

The new system of Proportional Representation meant that every party, however small, had deputies (M.P.s) in the Reichstag. It is difficult to form a strong government when there are eight or nine parties in parliament.

The election of the President by universal suffrage*, although apparently a good idea, proved to be a disadvantage. It allowed the great war hero Paul von Hindenburg to be elected in 1925. Hindenburg was anti-democratic in his outlook and proved to be a bad choice.

The emergency decree law Article 48 was misused by Hindenburg between 1930–33, who ruled without the support of the Reichstag.

Another point to remember is that many of the men who held important posts under the old Emperor William II, judges, civil servants and army officers, stayed on under the republic. They had no great love for it and hoped to undermine it.

Left versus Right

From 1919 onwards the biggest party in the Reichstag was the Social Democratic Party under Ebert. But they never had an absolute majority over all the other parties. To rule Germany they had, therefore, to form coalitions* with other parties, such as the Catholic Centre Party and the Nationalists. This made life difficult enough, but the troubles of the Weimar government did not end there. Extreme parties appeared on the Left (the communists) and the Right (the National Socialists or Nazis). The communists thought that the government was too conservative, while the Nazis thought they were traitors to the German cause. In the background was the vast problem caused by the Allied demand for reparations.

For the first five years of its life the Weimar Republic had to struggle hard to survive. It was a period marked by armed uprisings and economic crisis.

Fig. 4.1   Rosa Luxemburg in 1919.

The Spartakist Bund

The first signs of trouble came from the communists. Two of their important leaders, Karl Liebkneckt and Rosa Luxemburg, known as Red Rosa (Fig. 4.1), had formed the Spartakist Bund or league. It was named after a slave who had led a revolt against the Roman Empire. In 1919 the league seized power in Berlin and set up a communist government. It didn't last long. The government under Ebert called in Right-wing ex-soldiers or *Freikorps** and they crushed the communists. Luxemburg and Liebkneckt were murdered before they could be brought to trial. Their belief in a workers' state frightened middle-class people in Germany.

Bavaria, 1919

In the South German state of Bavaria another communist leader Eisner also tried to seize power. He too was defeated by the *Freikorps.*

The Kapp Putsch, 1920

Having survived attacks from the Left, the Republic now had to face a threat from the extreme Right. Many former army officers and other Right wingers could not accept the new democratic Germany. They despised the 'November criminals', the men wrongly blamed for agreeing to the armistice of November 1918. The Right wingers found a leader in a civilian, Wolfgang Kapp, who hoped that the small, regular German army would help him. Kapp and his supporters staged a revolt or putsch* in Berlin in 1920. But on this occasion the Right-wingers ran into a strong display of working-class solidarity. Berlin workers went on strike and paralysed the city. It also became clear that the Army Commander Hans von Seeckt would not support the revolt either. Within a few days it collapsed.

Right-wing bias in the law courts

The treatment of the Kapp conspirators proved to be far more lenient than that of the communists. Of twenty-two political murders committed by the Left between 1919–23, ten of the murderers were executed and eighteen imprisoned. But of 354 Right-wing murders, 326 remained unsolved and the twenty-eight people who were sentenced served an average of four months. The old imperial judges preferred the Nationalists to the Leftists and gave the former extremely light sentences.

The Beer Hall Putsch, November 1923

Right- and Left-wing agitation lessened after 1920, but did not disappear. Political murders were common; that of Erzberger in 1921, for example. The humiliation of reparations and the presence of Allied troops on German soil increased the desperation of the nationalists. In Bavaria such feelings centred around the new National Socialist or Nazi Party and its leader Adolf Hitler. Although Austrian by birth, Hitler had become a fanatical German nationalist. He persuaded the well-known war hero Erich von Ludendorff to join the Nazis, hoping that his support would win over the local army chief. Hitler and Ludendorff planned their putsch for early November 1923. It began in a melodramatic manner, with Hitler firing a pistol into the ceiling of a local beer hall. His Nazi brownshirts arrested the Bavarian Prime Minister and the army commander, but then allowed them to escape. A Nazi march through the city of Munich (Fig. 4.2) was broken up by a volley of shots from a police unit. Ludendorff marched on through the police lines, but the Nazis broke and ran. According to one story Hitler fled from the scene carrying an injured child! Some days later he was arrested in the house of a friend.

The Hitler trial

The authorities in Bavaria did not dare to challenge Ludendorff, but they put Adolf Hitler on trial. From start to finish it was a farce. Hitler was allowed to

Fig. 4.2 Nazis march through Munich during the Beer Hall Putsch.

make political speeches and shout down witnesses. In the end he received a five-year sentence, which was extremely lenient considering that he had aimed to overthrow the German government in Berlin. He in fact served only nine months of this sentence. Hitler used the time to write his book *Mein Kampf* (*My Struggle*). By the end of the year 1924, he was out of prison and able to resume political activity.

Peacekeeping after the world war

The developments in Germany were carried out against a background of confusion elsewhere. Allied attempts to crush the new Bolshevik government in Russia dragged on until 1921 (see Chapter 5). One of its side effects was a war between the Soviet Union and Poland in 1920–21 that resulted in a victory for the latter. The Bolshevik government was increasingly isolated from the other European powers because of the fear it aroused.

The Treaty of Rapallo, 1922

The Soviet Union's response was to draw closer to the other 'black sheep' in the European family, Weimar Germany. While the Western allies haggled about reparations, Russia and German delegates met secretly at the Italian town of Rapallo. Diplomatic relations* had already been re-established at Brest–Litovsk, and this treaty contained an important secret clause. In exchange for training facilities in the Soviet Union, the Germans agreed to help train the new Red Army. Not surprisingly the British and French were furious when they found out about this secret agreement.

Italy and Yugoslavia

Although Italy had finished on the winning side in the First World War, it was not satisfied with the arrangements made at Versailles, nor its associated treaties. Before long Italy belonged to the group of 'revisionist' powers – Germany, Hungary, Austria, Bulgaria and Turkey – that had grievances against the peace settlement. One particular Italian complaint concerned the towns of Trieste and Fiume which had been given to the new state of Yugoslavia. Some extreme Italian nationalists took matters into their own hands and seized Fiume. Their leader was an eccentric poet called Gabrielle d'Annunzio. He and his followers were expelled from Fiume after a few weeks, but the episode showed Italy to be a potential troublemaker in the 1920s. By 1924, in fact, both Trieste and Fiume had reverted to Italian rule.

The problem of reparations, 1923–4

Central to the problem of keeping Europe stable and peaceful after 1919 was the question of reparations. The huge sums owed by Germany were needed partly because Great Britain and France had borrowed large amounts of money from the United States to pay for the First World War. The Western Allies therefore put more pressure on Germany to pay. Successive German governments complained bitterly about the level of payments required, and in 1923–4 the situation reached crisis point. The Germans defaulted on payment of a consignment of telegraph poles, a seemingly trivial matter. But the French Prime Minister Raymond Poincaré decided that the Germans needed to be taught a lesson. In January 1923 French and Belgian troops entered the Ruhr, the heart of Germany's industrial area. They did so against British opposition and Prime Minister Stanley Baldwin refused to support the French action.

The French believed that they could make the Germans co-operate by the use of armed force. They

Fig. 4.3   One result of inflation: laundry baskets had to be used to collect the extra money needed from the bank to pay wages.

were wrong. Instead German workers followed a policy of passive resistance, refusing to work in the mines and factories. French strong-arm tactics caused riots and demonstrations. In Essen French soldiers shot demonstrating workers, so uniting all Germans in hatred of the occupying force. In the end even Poincaré was forced to accept that the occupation of the Ruhr had failed to obtain its objective. Other events in Germany made the message clear. Under the pressure of reparations payments and the virtual close down of the Ruhr the economy collapsed. The mark became virtually worthless: millions of marks were needed to pay for cigarettes or even a loaf of bread (Fig. 4.3). What life was like in Germany in those days you can learn by reading the following of a young English tourist called Anne Parris at the time.

Over 55 years ago, when 15 years old, I was sent on holiday to visit my mother's people in Schleswig-Holstein. My father gave me a little over £1's worth of German marks for expenses, which he had obtained from Thomas Cook's in London.

This was just before a League of Nations plebiscite awarded the northernmost part of the principality to Denmark. It coincided with what I have since read described as a 'gigantic confidence trick' when the then German government succeeded in stopping run-away inflation, more or less immediately, by reducing the value of a billion old marks to just one, government guaranteed, new mark or Renten Mark.

I understood little of all this at the time. All I knew was that my father gave me a 20 billion mark note which he told me was worth exactly £1. There were also a few notes of lower value and some loose coins; these were largely made of aluminium.

I was instructed to take this money at once to Uncle Louis, who was a clerk in the town hall in Tondern, a border town, which later became Danish after the plebiscite. This was in case some of the notes had been withdrawn from circulation in between my father's transaction with Thomas Cook and my arrival in Schleswig-Holstein. In fact, some of the smaller denominations had been withdrawn, but at least my 20,000,000,000,000 mark note was still valid.

In due course I had to catch a train from the country town of Niebüll to travel about 15 miles [24 km] or so to the present day border town of Flensburg, where my mother used to go to school. At the booking office, which did not open until shortly before the train was due to arrive, I put my 20 billion mark note down on the pay place and with the little German language at my command, said 'Flensburg bitte'.

A worried clerk refused to take it, not knowing if it was still valid. The only other money I had was the loose coins. I emptied these out of my purse on to the counter, and the booking clerk, with the help of an impatient lady behind me in the queue (the train was already arriving) counted these out between them. I was given back just one aluminium coin.

After this I decided I must take steps to get this 20 billion marks exchanged for the new marks as soon as I got to Flensburg. This was quite an adventure for me, as I had never been in a bank before, even in England. I have wondered since that my father allowed me to travel alone at such a young age in such circumstances. In those days, perhaps, things were safer then now, and one did not foresee difficulties even for girls travelling alone.

Outside Flensburg railway station I eventually found myself in a busy street and was thankful to see a policeman I could ask for directions. 'Bank bitte,' I said. He was obviously amused.

Bowing gracefully to each bank in turn and with a gesture of both hands, he said 'Bank. Bank. Bank' about six times. I was in a street full of banks; they seemed to be all round me. I turned to the nearest.

Unable to understand the notices on each little cubbyhole, I went to the nearest one, held up my 20 billion mark note, and said 'Bitte in klein Geld' (literally, 'please in small money'). It had taken me some time to work out this phrase in a foreign language. I was given 20 small white notes of the new Renten Mark, worth one shilling each. Relieved of anxiety, I found my way with ample time to the steamer and paid my fare for the trip down the fiord to Glücksburg. Here my cousin Leni would meet me with her husband to take me to their farm in the horse and trap.

This childhood experience has etched the horror of inflation on my mind.

My schoolteacher aunt who lived in Wuppertal Barmen, used to rush out to shop as soon as she was paid on Friday to buy food. By Saturday morning the prices would have risen extortionately. To try to counter inflation, as it was impossible to save, she bought good furniture for her flat, which . . . would keep its value.[1]

Anne Parris refers to a Renten Mark or new mark. This was introduced in 1924 when the old money system had to be replaced. This fixed the value of the new mark at twenty to £1.

The Treaty of London, 1924

With British help a compromise was reached. The new German Prime Minister Gustave Stresemann agreed to call off the German campaign of non-co-operation in the Ruhr. In exchange Franco–Belgian troops would be withdrawn.

The Dawes Plan

Something more important emerged from the meetings however. Anxious to recoup the money they had given to Great Britain and France, the Americans were also looking for a solution. Their President Calvin Coolidge summed up the United States's attitude in a terse phrase: 'They hired the money didn't they?' Even Coolidge now realized that the Germans needed help if the whole reparations system was not to collapse altogether. The solution fell into two parts:
1. The USA would make large loans to Germany.
2. Germany would be given longer to pay.

The plan took its name from one of the American representatives General Charles Dawes. Four years later the Young Plan was to extend the period of German payments to 1988! In return the German Rhineland was to be evacuated by Allied troops in 1930, five years earlier than planned.

The 'New Turkey', 1919–24

One of the defeated powers that appeared to benefit from the experience was Turkey. Throughout the nineteenth century the Turks had maintained an increasingly feeble grip on their empire in Europe and the Middle East. The Russian Tsar Nicholas I had referred to Turkey in a famous phrase as 'the sick man of Europe'. Punished for its alliance with Germany by the Treaty of Sèvres, Turkey then fell victim to Greek expansionism. In 1920 the Greeks seized Smyrna and seemed poised to take over the whole of Asia Minor. That they did not was largely the work of one man, Mustapha Kemal, a former Ottoman soldier. Kemal organized the Turks so effectively that the Greek attack was repulsed. The Allied powers, who had given the Greeks every encouragement, were reluctantly forced to accept the new situation.

The Treaty of Lausanne, 1923

The revised settlement gave Turkey the whole of Asia Minor, Istanbul and eastern Thrace. A new feature of this settlement was that it provided for an exchange of population between Greece and Turkey. This was to be supervised by the League of Nations.

Kemal's reforms

Once Turkey's international position was secure, Kemal turned to domestic reform. The last of the Sultans, Muhammed VI, was deposed, and a republic proclaimed in 1923. Further reforms were designed to modernize the Turkish state and reduce the influence of the Muslim religion. Civil servants had to wear Western dress, the fez* was abolished, as was the wearing of the veil by women. In the closing years of his life Kemal took the title *Atatürk* meaning 'Father of the Turks'. The changes he made in Turkish society were to have considerable influence on the rest of the Muslim world.

The Western powers considerably underestimated the force of Turkish nationalism when they imposed the Treaty of Sèvres. One clause of this treaty also caused needless offence throughout the Muslim world by abolishing the office of caliph. This was normally held by the Turkish sultan and was the highest religious post held by a Muslim. It was widely believed that in agreeing to the abolition of the caliphate, Lloyd George had broken a pledge given to Muslim leaders. Whatever the truth of the matter, the behaviour of Britain and France was based on an assumption of the permanence of European dominance. How this power began to decline will be the theme of Chapter 6.

Keywords

republic: state without a monarch.

universal suffrage: the right of all adults to vote.

coalition: joining together of political parties in order to form a government.

Freikorps: groups of demobilized German soldiers with Right-wing sympathies.

putsch: German word for a takeover of power by force.

diplomatic relations: recognition of another country's government leading to an exchange of ambassadors.

fez: a hat worn by Turkish males.

5 The USSR and the Communist World Movement

When the Bolshevik party overthrew the provisional government in November 1917 it found itself in a precarious position. All that had really happened was that the party seized control of the big urban centres like Moscow and Leningrad, the new name for Petrograd. Elsewhere control was exercised by anti-Bolshevik forces.

The consolidation of power, 1917–18

In these circumstances Lenin's main objective was to survive, and to do this he took steps to eliminate all opposition. When in November the elections to the Constituent Assembly only returned just over a hundred Bolshevik deputies, he authorized its abolition. Seeing that this action alone would not defeat the opposition Mensheviks and Social Revolutionaries, Lenin set up a secret police organization of his own: the Extraordinary Commission for Combating Counter-Revolution and Speculation (Cheka), which was placed under the command of Dzerzhinsky. 'Under the name Cheka this Soviet secret police soon became the symbol of terror such as the world has never seen.'[1] It was to be the forerunner of the Committee of State Security (KGB) of today. If the opposition parties could not accept the new state of affairs, then Lenin said their place was in prison. The Cheka did not shrink from more brutal counter-measures, and when Fanya Kaplan tried to murder Lenin in August 1918, 700 oppositionists were shot.

The external enemies . . .

Such problems were insignificant compared with the major external threat facing the Bolshevik government in 1918, for it was born into a hostile world, and one that was prepared to work actively for its downfall. All the major powers had their own reasons for wanting to crush Bolshevism.

France

The French were angered by Russia's sudden withdrawal from the war and wanted a government in power that would bring Russia back into it. France had also loaned the former Tsarist government large sums of money, which the Bolsheviks refused to pay back.

Britain

The British government was equally keen to overthrow the Bolsheviks and bring the Russians back into the war. Some members of the government, like Churchill, were also fiercely anti-Bolshevik because of the party's Marxist ideas. He saw himself as the leader of some sort of crusade against Bolshevism, but the official line was that put forward by Foreign Secretary A. J. Balfour in December 1918:

'We have constantly asserted that it is for the Russians to choose their own form of government; that we have no desire to intervene in their domestic affairs; and that if, in the course of operations essentially against the Central Powers, we have to act with such Russian political and military organizations as are favourable to the *Entente*, this does not imply that we deem ourselves to have any mission to establish or disestablish, any particular system among the Russian people.'

Lenin and Trotsky did not of course believe this version of Britain's actions in Russia, but it remained the official explanation.

The United States

By 1918 the American position, after some early doubts, was clear cut: Bolshevism was a virus that must be purged at once. Secretary of State for Foreign Affairs Robert Lansing had no doubt that

Russia was 'a seething cauldron of anarchy and violence. I can conceive of no more frightful calamity for a people than that which seems about to fall upon Russia.' He used his influence with President Woodrow Wilson to persuade him to intervene in Russia.

Japan

The Japanese had done little fighting in the First World War, although they had joined the Allied side in 1914. Their main interest in intervention was to obtain a toehold in the vast Russian province of Siberia.

Germany

Last, but by no means least, were the Germans. Until March 1918 the Bolshevik government was still in a state of war with Germany, which put forward very harsh peace terms. Trotsky, as Foreign Minister, adopted a policy of 'no peace, no war' at the negotiations. This meant dragging out the peace talks in the hope that the Germans might be defeated in the West. Trotsky also believed that a German attack on defenceless Russia would arouse outside sympathy. He was wrong, and the German leaders tired of shadow-boxing. In February 1918 they ordered their troops to advance, and it soon became clear that the Bolshevik government would have no option but to sign the peace treaty.

When it was signed at Brest–Litovsk, its terms were harsher still, depriving Russia of a third of its territory and industrial capacity. Only Lenin's resignation threat persuaded the other Bolshevik leaders to accept the treaty. The only consolation for the Bolsheviks was that by the end of the same year Germany, too, would be forced to admit defeat.

. . . and the internal ones

The White Russians

It was also Allied policy to assist anti-Bolshevik forces inside Russia, usually called the Whites. The White Russians were really united by only one thing, hatred of the Reds or Bolsheviks. It was not clear with what they would replace Lenin's government, although some undoubtedly favoured a restoration of the monarchy. Such niceties did not greatly interest the Allied powers, which were only too willing to assist them. As early as December 1917, the White Russian Commander-in-Chief Alexeyev re-

ceived a large sum of French money and a promise of military assistance.

Ramshackle White armies appeared in various parts of Russia under leaders like Kolchak, Denikin, Wrangel and Yudenitch. Fig. 5.1 shows their base of operations.

The nationalities

Like the United States of America, Russia is a vast land with a great mixture of peoples. Not all of them were enthusiastic about being ruled from Moscow or Leningrad. The revolutions of 1917 seemed to give a long awaited opportunity to break away from such control, and it was seized by the Cossacks and the Ukrainians. They set up their own independent republics, although promising support to the White generals. The White leadership certainly made a serious blunder in 1918 by saying that Russia must return to its 1914 frontiers. This would put an end to

Fig. 5.1   The Russian Civil War, 1918–21.

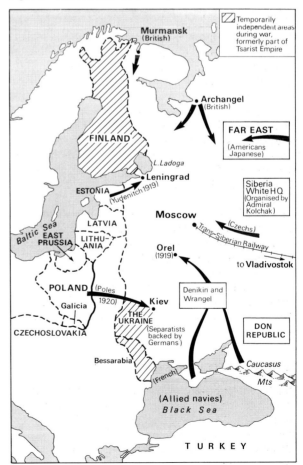

the newly-won independence of the Ukrainian and Cossack peoples.

The Romanov family

Another peril facing the Bolsheviks was the survival of the royal family in exile. Powerless they might be, but the Tsar and his family could be a focus for opposition to the regime. In 1918 they were all shot in the cellar of their house in Ekaterinburg. To this day no one is sure whether it was Lenin or the local Bolshevik commander who authorized the executions. For many years a story persisted that one of the Tsar's daughters, the Grand Duchess Anastasia, had survived the massacre, but this has now been discredited.

The civil war

The years 1918–20 were, therefore, years of survival, resulting ultimately in the defeat of the anti-Bolshevik forces. On paper this result seemed unlikely because at one point, in the autumn of 1918, the infant USSR almost disappeared from the map altogether. It was, in fact, little bigger than the kingdom inherited by the notorious Tsar Ivan the Terrible in 1533. The reasons for the eventual Bolshevik victory are complex.

1. The Allied powers were not really dedicated to the destruction of the Bolsheviks. The terrible losses in the First World War meant that there was little enthusiasm for a new and bloody war in Russia. When Allied troops landed they tended to stay near their bases. Their main interest was to secure important arms dumps near places like Murmansk. Little real effort was made to work out a common strategy with the White generals. The Allied leaders were happy to let others do the fighting, including the Czech Legion, a force of escaped Czechoslovak prisoners of war anxious to win support for their own national independence. Another factor was the state of Left-wing opinion in Britain and France. In Britain for example, the Trade Union Congress* organized a 'Hands off Russia' campaign.

2. The Whites were poorly led, and their offensives were poorly co-ordinated. For most of the Civil War period their leader Admiral Kolchak was too far away from the frontline in Siberia. White soldiers also alienated the peasants by committing numerous atrocities.

3. In Leon Trotsky, the Bolsheviks had found an able organizer and general. He created the Red Army (Fig. 5.2) and made good use of former Tsarist army officers like Tuchachevsky. To ensure the political

reliability of the soldiers, special commissars or agents of the government were attached to all units.

4. Foreign intervention aroused both resentment and national feeling in Russia. It did the White leaders little good in the eyes of their own people to be associated with rapacious foreigners like the Japanese.

The end of intervention

By 1921 all the various foreign armies had been withdrawn from the Soviet Union. Their intervention left a bitter legacy of hatred and mistrust. It is important to remember this because it goes some way towards explaining the Soviet Union's present suspicion of the West.

Fig. 5.2   Leon Trotsky, the creator of the Red Army, was later to be exiled from the Soviet Union in 1929 and murdered by a Stalinist agent in 1940.

Fig. 5.3   Red Army soldiers move across the ice in a surprise attack on the naval base at Kronstadt.

The Kronstadt mutiny, 1921

The difficulties facing the Bolshevik government were far from over, however, and in 1921 it received a particularly severe shock. The sailors from the Kronstadt naval base had played a vital rôle in the November Revolution. It was these same sailors who in 1921 staged a serious uprising against the new government. They were disillusioned with Lenin's policy of war communism* which had involved the seizure of food from the peasants by force.

In the crisis the Bolshevik leaders showed a streak of ruthlessness. Trotsky sent the Red Army over the ice to seize the naval base (Fig. 5.3) and the ring-leaders were shot.

The New Economic Policy, 1921

The Kronstadt mutiny had a decisive effect on Lenin's thinking. He realized that war communism, adopted in an emergency situation, was no longer the right policy. Famine stalked the countryside and hundreds of thousands were dying of starvation. Those peasants who had food supplies hung on to them to force up prices. Lenin was flexible enough to see that this could not continue, and he admitted this in a speech in October 1921: 'The system of distribution in the villages and the immediate application of communist methods to the towns held back our productive forces and caused the great economic and political crisis we met in the spring of 1921.'

Lenin's use of the world communist* is significant. It was soon to replace Bolshevik in the party title. The change of direction came in the New Economic Policy (NEP) announced by Lenin in 1921. It had two main characteristics:

1. The state was to control heavy industries, such as coal, iron ore, shipping, but also transport and foreign trade. More significantly, some private enterprise was to be allowed in the form of small businesses.

2. Attempts to coerce the peasantry were to stop. The peasants could have some land of their own and sell the food grown for profit.

Lenin called this system 'state capitalism'*, but it was never meant to be anything more than a stopgap. It was really a compromise between state ownership of production and private enterprise or capitalism. The important thing to remember about the NEP was that Lenin never intended it to be permanent; he always believed that full-scale communism would come about in the near future.

Communism as a world movement

Lenin also believed that revolution in Russia was only the beginning. The NEP was adopted, he said, because 'only through an understanding with the peasantry can the socialist revolution be saved, *until revolution has broken out in other countries* [author's italics]'. It should be remembered that no communist, least of all Karl Marx, expected a revolution in backward Russia. It was the industrialized countries, France, Britain and Germany, that were expected to be the key to communist success. Without revolutions in those countries Lenin and Trotsky thought that Soviet communism must fail too.

At first things looked promising. We have seen how Left-wing movements opposed intervention in the Russian Civil War in Britain and France. In Germany the communists staged attempted *coups* in 1919. In Hungary Bela Kun and his supporters actually succeeded in forming a government for a short time. A Communist party appeared in China in 1921, the same year that the British Communist Party was founded. But events outside the Soviet Union flattered to deceive. The German Communist Party was crushed, as was Bela Kun in Hungary. The middle classes in central Europe were terrified by the Bolshevik menace and lent their support to Right-wing militarists. Briefly, too, the flame of revolution flickered in Britain, generally regarded as unpromising ground by Lenin and his colleagues.

In 1919 there was trouble on Clydeside, and a soviet was formed by Belfast workers. The police went on strike in Liverpool, and Lord Curzon was alarmed enough to ask in the Cabinet for a special minister to co-ordinate resistance 'to the spread of Bolshevism in this country'. The Clydeside Marxist leader John MacLean, an Honorary President of the First All Russian Congress of Soviets, stated his belief that capitalism was 'the most infamous, bloody and evil system that mankind has ever witnessed. I am . . . the accuser of capitalism dripping with blood from head to foot.'

MacLean was absent on 'Bloody Friday', 31 January 1919, when a pitched battle took place in the city between the police and demonstrating workers. The Riot Act was read and a radical leader called Willi Gallacher punched the Chief Constable. Gallacher was arrested, but was later elected as a Communist M.P. in 1945. Manny Shinwell was also arrested – he became a Labour Cabinet Minister, although he was never in the radical tradition of men like MacLean and Gallacher. The local soldiers were locked into Maryhill barracks, and until his death in 1961 Gallacher was convinced that 'if the troops had come out there would have been big doings in Glasgow that night'.

Gradually the tumult died away, although the crisis showed only too clearly that there was a wide gulf between the working class and the Lloyd George government. In a Cabinet report of January 1919 Conservative leader Bonar Law is quoted as saying: 'There was no doubt that many people attributed the present industrial unrest to the lack and poor quality of beer.' Lenin and his government became con-

vinced that Britain was a hopeless cause, an opinion that was strengthened by the behaviour of Labour Party and trade union leaders during the 1926 General Strike. Britain, said the Russian leader scathingly, was 'the only country in the world with a bourgeois working class'.

The subject colonial peoples of Africa and Asia appeared to offer more promising material for revolution. Lenin certainly thought so. In 1920 he called for a 'close alliance of all national and colonial liberation movements with Soviet Russia'. A meeting was convened at Baku, but it accomplished little. The Japanese party was not represented at the conference and it was virtually wiped out in 1929 by police action. Elsewhere the picture was just as disappointing. In India the communists were outshone by the Congress Party in the drive for *swaraj* or independence. In Indonesia a communist rebellion was bloodily crushed in 1926.

Only China provided an example of apparent success, for the Communist Party had merged into the larger Kuomintang or Nationalist movement. Co-operation with the Nationalist government continued until 1927 when the picture changed dramatically. General Chiang Kai-shek, until then regarded as a friend of the communists, suddenly turned on them. Thousands of communists were massacred in Shanghai, and the leaders fled into the countryside. Chiang's Russian mentors were also forced out of the country as the general apparently forgot about his Russian training. Diplomatic relations between China and the USSR were broken off, and the outlook for communism there seemed bleak.

The Polish war, 1920–21

Only in one instance did the new Soviet state try to export revolution by force of arms. Even then it was a campaign that followed an attempt by the Poles to annex the Ukraine. Poland and Russia were ancient enemies, and the Polish leaders thought that the chaos of the Civil War period provided an opportunity too good to miss. Their army seized Kiev, but its success was short-lived. Tuchachevsky revitalized the Red Army and in 1920 drove the Poles back to the gates of Warsaw. This should have been the signal for which the Polish workers were waiting, but they were strangely apathetic. The Polish army was reorganized by Pilsudski and French assistance brought about a decisive Russian defeat. Lenin was bitterly disappointed, but should he have been?

The historian E. H. Carr comments on this important turning point:

The Russian peasant who supplied the manpower of the Red Army, while stoutly defending the revolutionary cause in his homeland had not stomach for a fight to transport revolution to other countries. The peasant now beginning to revolt against the miseries and the devastation which were the aftermath of the civil war, was recalcitrant to hardships sustained in the name of international revolution.[2]

After seven years of war and hardship the people were tired and in no mood for foreign adventures however essential to the cause of world revolution.

Splits and conspiracies

Lenin kept hoping, and he gave full support to the Comintern or Communist International. This was the international wing of the Soviet Communist Party, which had the job of encouraging workers' revolutions everywhere. Lenin's old friend and colleague Zinoviev (Fig. 5.4) was put in charge. His task was a difficult one because everywhere the communist movement was plagued by splits and disagreements. In Germany in 1920 the Communist Party broke away from the majority Social Democratic Party. The French communists split with the socialists and the Italian communists did likewise. In the capitalist countries the Comintern faced a wall of mistrust, encouraged by Zinoviev's fiery speeches. In 1924 the *Daily Mail* accused him of plotting a communist revolution in Britain. The accusation was untrue but the 'Zinoviev Letter' cost the Labour Party the 1924 election (Fig. 5.5). Anti-communist hysteria reached a peak during the Palmer raids in the United States (see p. 61). Only in 1934 did the United States government agree to grant diplomatic recognition to the USSR.

The Soviet Communist Party continued to pay lip service to the concept of international revolution, but it was the pragmatists who were to win the day.

Keywords

Trade Union Congress: the governing body of the British trade union movement.

war communism: a system combining worker occupation of factories with seizure of food supplies in the countryside.

communist (formerly Bolshevik): one who believes in the creation of a socialist society.

state capitalism: a compromise between private ownership and government ownership, as in the New Economic Policy.

Fig. 5.4   Gregori Zinoviev, head of Comintern.

Fig. 5.5   The 'Zinoviev Letter' lost the Labour Party the general election. (Look at the questions on this cartoon on p. 46).

VOTE FOR MACDONALD AND ME

6 Europe and a Wider World

After the First World War, as before it, two great imperialist powers, Britain and France, dominated the world. Although their control appeared absolute, there were significant stirrings in Africa and Asia, as yet barely appreciated in London and Paris.

The politicians in these capitals were too busy reconciling themselves with Germany, via the Treaty of Locarno of 1925 and Germany's entry into the League of Nations in 1926, to pay much heed to the 'colour line'. Full German membership of the League was a triumph for Anglo-French diplomacy, but it meant little to people at home.

Great Britain, 1919–29

Immediately after the war, Lloyd George spoke of making the country a 'land fit for heroes', but the great sacrifices of the war proved to be in vain and never in the interwar period did unemployment drop below the one million level. Worse still, such workers lacked the safety net provided by the welfare state of today.

The miners

An early example of government attitudes was afforded by its reaction to the Sankey Commission of 1919 which had been set up to look into the question of state ownership of the mines. The commission was in favour of this, but the Lloyd George government rejected its conclusions and ended state control of the pits in 1921. At the same time, the miners, supported by the dockers and transport workers, were in dispute with the coalmine owners. This Triple Alliance eventually collapsed, and on 15 April, 'Black Friday', these men were forced to go back to work. But the problem had merely been postponed, not solved.

The end of Lloyd George, 1918–22

In 1918 Lloyd George was the 'man who won the war', but his image as the angel of victory was soon tarnished. He had split his own Liberal Party in 1916 when forming a coalition government with the Tories, and in 1918, he added insult to injury. Liberals who supported Lloyd George in the so-called 'khaki election' received a 'coupon' to rubber-stamp their election. Conservatives would not stand against Liberals with the coupon. The remaining Liberals were defeated at the polls, but this only left an opening to the Left to be filled by Labour.

The Prime Minister mishandled the Irish crisis (see p. 38), and also wrongly backed Greece against Turkey in the Near East. By 1922 his political reputation had been severely shaken and was not helped by rumours of sexual and financial scandal.

The Tories were thoroughly disillusioned, and in October 1922, at a famous meeting of backbenchers at the Carlton Club, Lloyd George was disowned. Despite all his powers as an orator and his great political gifts, Lloyd George was never to hold office again. He was succeeded by Bonar Law, a man of modest talents but frail health, who rapidly gave way to Stanley Baldwin (1923–9).

The first Labour government

Baldwin was fortunate in making his most serious political blunder early in his career, for in 1923 he decided to hold an election on the issue of Free Trade. This decision was, to say the least, premature as Free Trade remained the sacred issue of British politics for at least another decade.

The result of the election was indecisive. The Tories remained the largest party with 287 votes, but Labour and Liberal combined could outvote them. The Liberal leaders, Lloyd George and Asquith, therefore decided to allow Labour to take office under Ramsay MacDonald. But the two parties were uneasy

Fig. 6.1 Labour Party rally at Crewe during the General Strike of 1926.

partners, and MacDonald's government only stayed in office for nine months during 1923–4. Its nine-month tenure of office is remembered chiefly for Wheatley's Housing Act and the controversy surrounding the Zinoviev letter (see p. 35).

The General Strike, 1926

It was during Baldwin's second government that the nine-day General Strike took place, and, as in 1921, its centre point was the mining industry. Competing coal imports from Germany had brought no reply from the owners, other than to cut wages and lengthen the working day. Once again a commission of enquiry was appointed, this time headed by Lord Samuel, a Liberal. It recommended a smaller wage cut and the modernization of the industry. By this time, however, the miners were in fighting mood. They demanded: 'Not a penny off the pay, not a minute on the day.' By 26 April, the coal owners had locked them out of the pits, and the TUC were reluctantly forced to declare a General Strike as from 3 May 1926 (Fig. 6.1).

Baldwin's tactics

In the tense atmosphere of the time, Baldwin's tactics were straightforward: 'We must wait for the strike to wear itself out.' This common sense contrasted strongly with the shrill hysteria of Churchill's *British*

Gazette and the pro-government line of Sir John Reith's infant BBC. Baldwin understood the basically conservative nature of the TUC leadership who were finally frightened by Mr Justice Astbury's ruling that the General Strike was 'illegal and contrary to the law'. Men like MacDonald, Bevin, J. H. Thomas and Snowden were not the stuff of which revolutionaries were made. On 12 May the TUC called off the strike, leaving many rank-and-file traditionalists feeling bitter and betrayed. So were the miners, who under their leaders Arthur Cook and Herbert Smith, carried on their struggle for another seven bitter months before being forced to return to work by starvation and lack of means.

Results of the strike

At the time, the General Strike seemed a traumatic and indeed almost revolutionary event. Its results did not prove it to be so.

Parliament passed the 1927 Trades Disputes Act, making all general and 'sympathetic' strikes illegal. Civil servants were not allowed any links with either the Labour Party or trade unions.

On the surface, industrial relations became more peaceful because of the strike since no year up to 1939 saw the loss of more than 10 million days to strikes. This, though, had more to do with fear of mass unemployment in the 1930s, and the traditional class bitterness remained.

Labour soon recovered from the humiliation of 1926 and returned to office again between 1929–31. Unfortunately for them, this period coincided exactly with the Wall Street Crash and the orthodox economics of Chancellor Snowden, who had little idea of how to deal with its effects (see Chapter 9). It was the misfortune of Left-wing governments in Britain, France and Spain that their periods in office were times of financial slump.

Ireland

As we have seen Ireland was one of the major issues that brought down the Lloyd George government. The Irish Question had, in fact, dominated the later half of the nineteenth century. Its solution appeared likely to result in civil war in 1914 (see p. 2), but the question of independence remained. It was clear that the Ulster Protestants would never accept Home Rule if this meant domination by the Catholic South. Hopes that the South might remain part of the United Kingdom were hopelessly jeopardized by the British handling of the 1916 Easter Revolt in Dublin. The leaders of the Irish Republican Brotherhood, Pearse, Connolly and others, were shot, thus creating another series of martyred Irish patriots to add to the existing long list.

The effects of this blunder were seen in 1918 when Sinn Fein*, the Irish Nationalist Party, won most of the seats outside Ulster. They then refused to take up their seats in Westminster, and demanded independence for Ireland. The Lloyd George government rejected this demand, and in 1918 a savage war began between the British army and the Irish Republican Army (IRA), the military wing of Sinn Fein.

What followed was one of the least creditable pages in modern British history. The War Office enlisted the infamous Black and Tans, irregular troops who took their name from their black tunics and tan trousers. Many of them were little better than gaolbirds, and they were given free rein in the Irish countryside. The IRA replied in kind and for three years shootings, burnings and lootings were commonplace.

By 1921 Lloyd George realized that further fighting would be futile, and an Irish delegation came to Downing Street to talk to him. What happened next has remained a matter of controversy ever since, for many Irish Republicans claim to this day that Lloyd George tricked the leaders of the delegation. It is certainly true that de Valera, the President of the provisional Sinn Fein government, rejected the agreed terms out of hand.

Fig. 6.2   Ireland in 1922.

The Anglo–Irish Treaty, 1921

The treaty had three main parts:
1. The twenty-six southern counties were to become independent as the Irish Free State. This included two Ulster counties (Fig. 6.2).
2. The other six counties of Ulster were to remain part of the United Kingdom and to continue to send representatives to the Westminster Parliament.
3. Provision was made for a boundary commission to deal with the required territorial revisions. There was also to be a Council of Ireland to discuss the question of eventual unification of north and south. This is an important point. The division between the six counties and the Irish Free State was not expected to be permanent.

The Civil War, 1921–2

The controversial nature of the treaty was, in fact, to be responsible for another round of the Irish tragedy. Those men who accepted the setting up of the Free State, like Michael Collins and Arthur Griffiths, found themselves fighting former colleagues who did not. Collins died in an ambush while the Free Staters executed the Republican hero Erskine Childers. The struggle was short but bloody, and resulted in a Free State victory. It left a permanent mark on the politics of independent Ireland, for the supporters of Collins formed the Fine Gael* Party and his opponents led by de Valera founded Fine Fail*. Not until 1926 did Fine Fail agree to sit in the Irish Parliament or Dáil. Some IRA members were never to accept the permanent division of their country.

India

Ireland was Britain's oldest colony. Its most important was India where British influence had been dominant since 1763. Indian nationalists had been watching events in Ireland with interest, although they were not, at that time, pressing for complete independence. Since 1885 nationalist hopes had been spearheaded by the Congress Party, but it had remained loyal to the British Crown in the moment of crisis. In 1914 the party declared its support for Britain's war against the Central Powers, and thousands of Indian soldiers were to lose their lives on the western front. In exchange for this demonstration of loyalty the Congress leaders expected some concessions, but they were to be disappointed. When nothing was forthcoming from Westminster, they decided to take matters into their own hands, and in 1916 the party conference demanded dominion status for India. This meant equivalent status with the white dominions of Australia, New Zealand, Canada and South Africa, which all had self-government within the Empire.

This new position was not accepted by a man, newly returned to India, who was to play the dominant role in the struggle for Indian independence.

Gandhi

In many ways Gandhi was an unlikely hero: the English educated lawyer who spent many years of his life in South Africa. Throughout his political career Gandhi was convinced that the British were a 'righteous people' who could be persuaded to accept the justice of the Indian cause. For this reason, he always advocated *satyagraha* or non-violence as a means of obtaining political objectives.

He had first used these tactics in South Africa, but when he returned home in 1915 such an approach did not accord with the mood of the moment. Congress rejected Gandhi's scrupulous loyalty to a war-torn Britain, but his moment was soon to come.

British concessions

The British administration, for its part, temporized. In 1917 Edwin Montagu, the Secretary of State for India, visited the country and subsequently put forward some reform proposals. Usually known as the Montagu–Chelmsford reforms (1919), they provided for Indian representation on a Council of State and a Legislature. The reforms did not satisfy the Congress Party because they were hedged about with qualifications. The Viceroy, who represented the British Crown, still had control over defence and foreign affairs, and the vote was only given to property owners.

The Amritsar Massacre, 1919

Indian disappointment contributed to a restless and violent mood in the country, but it was only one factor in the situation. Equally important was sectarianism that resulted from ill-feeling between the Muslim and Hindu communities. The outnumbered Muslims were always suspicious about Hindu intentions, and this was something that the British and the Congress Party leaders tended to forget. In 1919 such fears were the occasion for serious Muslim rioting in Calcutta because the Montagu–Chelmsford reforms did not make special provision for the minority.

At the same time Gandhi proclaimed a civil disobedience day for 6 April 1919, the first of his big non-violent campaigns. On 13 April 1919 a large crowd of Gandhi's supporters gathered at the town of Amritsar where there had already been some disturbances.

In circumstances which have never been satisfactorily explained, the local British commander Major-General Dyer ordered his men to fire on the crowd: 379 people were killed and 1,200 wounded. The event caused profound shock throughout India, and its effects were magnified by British insensitivity. The commission of inquiry seemed, to Indian eyes, to go out of its way to whitewash the British authorities. It merely described the Amritsar Massacre as 'unfortunate'. The treatment of the local population afterwards was equally insulting. Failure to bow to a British officer became a flogging offence, as did refusal to sell milk.

In the circumstances, it is not surprising that the Indian reaction was violent. Even Gandhi declared that co-operation was not possible with 'this satanic government', while Nehru, the first Prime Minister of independent India, wrote that the event 'filled him with bitterness'. This change of attitude was reflected at the Congress Party Conference in 1920, when the party decided to campaign for *swaraj* or complete independence.

Gandhi and Nehru

Throughout the 1920s and 1930s, the Congress movement was to be dominated by two men, Gandhi and Nehru, the son of one of the founder members of the party (Fig. 6.3). Although the British persisted in viewing Nehru as a dangerous extremist, he was, in fact, extremely dependent on the older man. In background, he was totally different, coming from a rich family in the northern city of Allahabad and completing his education at Eton and Oxford. But he proved to be a great asset to the Congress Party, not least because of his international contacts. In 1920 Nehru attended the Congress of Oppressed Nationalities in Brussels, and in this capacity he met people like Madame Sun Yat-sen (see p. 44), George Lansbury, the Labour politician, and the Vietnamese Nguyen-Ai-Quoc, later to be famous at Ho Chi Minh. Nehru's contacts with the British Labour Party were to prove especially helpful, even if in a moment of frustration he once called their leaders 'sanctimonious and canting humbugs'.

He also visited Moscow in 1927, and wrote later that the visit had 'helped me to see history and current affairs in a new light'. In no sense though was Nehru ever a Marxist.

At home he found some discontent with Gandhi's leadership, reliant as it was on fasts and days of protest. The British authorities soon learnt that arresting Gandhi was counterproductive because it only increased his popularity and authority with the people. Elements in the Congress Party led by Subhas Bose found Gandhi's non-violent tactics increasingly unappealing. Bose went so far as to describe him as an 'old, useless piece of furniture'.

There were squabbles too with the Muslim League about the allocation of seats in any Indian Parliament. The League demanded one third of the seats and when this was refused their leader Jinnah described it as 'the parting of the ways'. Gandhi and Nehru still persisted in their underestimation of the religious question.

The Gandhi–Irwin conversations, 1931

Before such tensions could break up the independence movement, an important breakthrough took place. It owed much to the good personal relationship between Gandhi and Lord Irwin, the new British Viceroy, and their historic conversation

Fig. 6.3   Nehru and Gandhi.

in 1931. As a direct result of this, the Viceroy recognized the Congress Party as the representatives of the Indian people, and the way was prepared for a Round Table Conference later that year.

The Round Table Conference, 1931

This took place in London, and was attended by both leaders of Congress and the Muslim League. The major question on the agenda was India's future development and the constitutional arrangements. Unfortunately, it was soon destroyed by Gandhi's attitude on the question of the Untouchables, the lowest caste in the Hindu caste system. These people, who made up about 30 per cent of the Hindu population, were a group apart. They did all the dirty jobs that higher castes rejected and were avoided by all the other sectors of Hindu society. The shadow of an Untouchable would make another Hindu unclean, but the British wanted to make special provision for them in an Indian Parliament. Gandhi refused to accept this, saying that the Untouchables, 'the Children of God' as he called them, should obtain seats inside the general Hindu provision. When the British would not give way, he walked out of the Round Table Conference. This tactic only played into the hands of those British politicians like Churchill who were totally opposed to constitutional change in India. He referred to Gandhi in sneering terms as a 'naked fakir' but many other Conservatives, like Baldwin, were more sympathetic.

In the short term, however, the British reacted strongly to the collapse of the Round Table Conference. In January 1932 Congress was declared an illegal organization and its leaders imprisoned. Demoralized and divided as it was, the party seemed to be in real danger of collapse. It was largely saved from this by the efforts of Nehru, because Gandhi went into semi-retirement and in 1934 abandoned his campaign of civil disobedience.

The Government of India Act 1935

Meanwhile, the British government moved at its own pace towards a solution of the Indian problem, culminating in the 1935 Government of India Act. This had three major elements:
1. The administration of Burma was to be wholly separate from that of India.
2. India was to have a federal system with separate provincial governments elected by the people. There was to be a special arrangement to include the Indian princes who were not under direct British rule. The provincial governments were to control matters like health and education.
3. The Viceroy would retain certain reserve powers, leaving him in control of foreign affairs, security and defence.

The Act caused further division in the Congress Party. The Right wing favoured power-sharing with the British, whereas the Left, under Nehru, did not. Nevertheless, the elections in 1937 confirmed the political domination of Congress. It had an outright majority of the vote in five provinces, and was the largest single party in three others. In comparison the Muslim League did badly, which allowed the Congress leaders to continue to ignore the religious question. Already Jinnah was highlighting the dangers of Hindu domination under the new Act, and once again alarming rumours began to spread under the slogan 'Islam* in danger'. Girls were to be forced to learn to dance and all schools were to be turned into Hindu temples! If such stories seem surprising now, they reflected the fundamental religious divide in Indian society.

The Middle East

Another area of British responsibility lay in those Middle Eastern lands previously ruled over by the Ottoman Turks. Here, as you will see, British diplomacy found itself in a muddle, although some of the blame must rest on the French, too. For in their anxiety to defeat the Turks, the British had made three separate, and contradictory, agreements.

The MacMahon Pledge, 1915

This pledge was made to the Arabs of the area now called Saudi Arabia, and virtually assured them of independence. You may remember that the British government also sent out Colonel T. E. Lawrence to assist them (see p. 15).

The Sykes-Picot Agreement, 1916

This Anglo-French agreement divided the former Turkish lands into spheres of influence. Palestine and Trans-Jordan were in the British sphere, while France laid claim to Syria and the Lebanon. The terms of this agreement were kept secret.

The Balfour Declaration, 1917

This was the most controversial and significant of the three because it introduced an outside agent into the area. It arose from the anxiety of the Allies to win the financial support of wealthy American Jews. Some of them, notably Chaim Weizmann, were Zionists*, and therefore committed to the idea of a separate state for the Jewish people. You should remember here that ever since AD 70 when the Romans crushed the Jewish revolt, the Jews had lost their original homeland in Palestine. Weizmann was able to persuade the British government to look favourably on Jewish aspirations, and in 1917 the Foreign Secretary, A. J. Balfour, made the following very important declaration: 'His Majesty's Government view with favour the establishment in Palestine of a National Home for the Jewish people.'

The declaration went on to safeguard the rights of the existing Arab population, but they had not been consulted beforehand. On the other hand, the declaration said nothing about setting up a Jewish state; it merely sanctioned Jewish settlement in Palestine. Unfortunately, the British decision opened the way for developments that could never have been foreseen in 1917.

It also rather predictably aroused the anger of the Palestinian Arabs as they watched the increasing flow of Jewish immigration. In 1917 there were only 60,000 Jews resident in Palestine but under the British mandate the number rose steadily. Between 1923–32, 84,454 Jews went to Palestine, and the number rose in spectacular fashion after Hitler came to power in Germany.

As the British government became aware of Arab anger, it made some efforts to cut back the level of Jewish immigration. After a serious Arab revolt in

1936, a 1939 white paper placed a limit of 75,000 persons per year on Jewish immigration until 1944, and thereafter no immigration was to be allowed without Arab agreement. Such proposals were, of course, made without knowledge of Hitler's death camps, and their discovery made the operation of this policy impossible.

Britain's African Empire

The famous poet Rudyard Kipling once described the British Empire as 'the empire on which the sun will never set'. An American wit once countered this by saying that this was because God never trusted the British in the dark! Whatever the eventual fate of the Empire in the 1920s, British sway in Africa was absolute. They and the other European colonial powers ruled over almost the entire continent. There seemed to be little sign of an African nationalist movement as such, and self-government was only conceded to the whites of southern Rhodesia under the 1923 Constitution, an odd arrangement, which was to store up trouble for the future, as we shall see. It also ignored a striking imbalance in population: 1,400,000 blacks in 1941 to only 69,000 whites.

The greatest apparent changes came in the dominion of South Africa where the Dutch-speaking Afrikaner settlers were rapidly recovering from their defeat by the British in 1901. The Afrikaans language had been accorded equal status, but there was still considerable discrimination in favour of English speakers. It was this that fuelled the rise of the Nationalist Party with its commitment to white superiority. Jan Smuts, the great wartime leader, led the United Party which paid lip service to the concept of racial equality, but by the 1930s minor legislation was being introduced that penalized the black and Asian communities.

Obsessed as they were with European and Far Eastern security, it is hardly surprising that successive British governments appeared to pay little attention to their African colonies.

France

As you have seen, the major worry of the French government after the First World War was security, but also the reconstruction of their war-devastated country. France was less dependent on foreign trade because of its large agricultural sector, but like other European governments, it adopted a policy of tariff protection.

Politics in the 1920s

Politics in the 1920s and early 1930s were dominated by four men, Clemenceau, Poincaré, Briand and Barthou. The former disappeared from politics after a misguided bid for the Presidency in 1920, the latter was tragically assassinated in 1934. Poincaré was the 'tough' man of French politics, who sent French troops into the Ruhr in 1923, and held a second term as premier from 1926–9. The franc was revalued while the younger Briand took over control of foreign policy. Once Poincaré had retired, however, the instability of French politics became clear as a type of political musical chairs became commonplace.

Political scandals, like the infamous Stavisky Affair of 1934, in which the suicide of a small time crook, Stavisky, disclosed links with government ministers and forced the resignation of Prime Minister Chautemps, were highly damaging. It was a fatal year in which Barthou was shot by a Croatian terrorist, whose real target was the King of Yugoslavia, and the small French Fascist groups attempted a *coup*. In a sense the Republic never recovered, for the government feared Fascist groups, such as the *Croix de Feu*, was terrified at the prospect of war and willingly followed the Chamberlain policy of appeasement (see Chapter 11).

The French Empire

The French Empire, too, had its problems notably in North Africa. In 1921 the Riff tribesmen of Morocco under Abd el Krim staged a revolt, which the French only put down with difficulty. At the time, it was widely believed that the Italian dictator Benito Mussolini (see Chapter 7) had been behind much of the trouble. In Syria, too, the French were confronted by a nationalist revolt in a territory that they held under a mandate of the League of Nations. General Sarrail bombarded Damascus in 1925, but still the revolt dragged on. In the end, the French were forced to give a guarantee of ultimate Syrian independence in 1936.

From reading about the French and British Empires you may gain the impression that there were no stirrings along the lines suggested by W. E. B. du Bois (see p. 2). But this would be a false idea.

On the surface the Anglo–French empires held absolute sway, but underneath the black Africans were feeling the need for freedom. Education, as is so often the case in independence movements, was the key and a small number of black men and women were leaving the secondary schools and getting an education in Britain or the USA. They returned home to Africa, as Oliver and Atmore tell us, 'young and inexperienced', but yet not given 'the merited status' they thought their educated deserved.[1]

In West Africa, which was the first area to be in close contact with the Europeans, small associations sprang up among the professional classes. In 1918, for example, the lawyer J. C. Casely Hayford founded the National Congress of British West Africa, and this spread to Nigeria in 1920. Their main demand was that Congress should take part in the government of Nigeria and the Gold Coast. When it was (predictably) rejected, the local associations concentrated on their own affairs, but they did exist and provided a basis for future political movements.

In French West Africa, a similar pattern began to emerge when in 1917 the 80,000 Senegalese elected Blaise Diagne to the Chamber of Deputies in Paris. He became Under-Secretary of State for Colonies in metropolitan France, and encouraged other Senegalese to join French political parties. From 1936, when a Left-wing goverment was elected in France, their supporters could get government appointments, especially in education, in the colonies. Large numbers of French West Indian subjects also began to become involved in French Left-wing politics.

The different ways in which the British and French colonies were to develop was already apparent in the 1920s. But there was also a common bond. French and British West Indian students were firm adherents of Pan Africanism, what Marcus Garvey was to call the 'back to Africa' movement. Other influential figures in the movement were Edward Blyden and W. E. B. du Bois himself. When du Bois wrote his prophetic words about the 'problem of the colour line' he could not have foreseen the difficulty of the struggle that lay ahead. But that struggle had begun.

To being with, in the West Indies, there were two clear divisions:
1. The English speakers backed the Pan-African movement, as did the West Africans.
2. The French-speaking West Africans joined West Indian French speakers like Aimé Casaire with his belief in the doctrine of Negritude (awareness of being black). This placed more emphasis on black culture and language.

Throughout its long history, Africa had been divided by a mass of languages and dialects. This process was now to repeat itself under the colonial empires. Some had a wider vision not dominated by language. In Nigeria, for example, Ladipo Solanke founded the West African Students Union in 1925. In 1935 African nationalism was fired by Mussolini's attack on Haile Selassie of Abyssinia, 'the lion of Judah' and the representative of the oldest royal family in Africa. This attack in fact coincided with the return of Nnamdi Azikiwe from his studies in the USA. It was he who launched the first popular press in the Gold Coast and Nigeria. More significantly, in the long run, it was also Azikiwe who was responsible for sending more students from Nigeria and the Gold Coast abroad to study. One of these youthful scholars was Kwame Nkrumah, later to be President of an independent Gold Coast (see p. 187).

Like most political movements, the Pan-African one had its teething troubles, notably when Azikiwe's National Council of Nigeria and the Cameroons split away from Obafemi Awolowo's Action Group after 1945.

The basis of the trouble, as so often in African politics, was tribalism. The first named group was largely Ibo; Awolowo's supporters were mostly Yoruba. Such tribal divisions were to lead Nigeria to tragedy in the 1960s (see p. 188).

East Africa

What of East Africa during this period of growing black consciousness? In part, the African attitude was dictated by their colonial masters, who blocked black land settlement around areas such as Mount Kenya. The attitude of the British government was made clear in 1923 when it declared that in Kenya it regarded itself as 'exercising a trust on behalf of the African population'. Ironically, this statement was made in response to complaints by Indian settlers who wanted representation in the government, but who were tartly told that black interests must be 'paramount'.

So in Kenya, Asian settlement made white–black relations even more complicated. It did not, though, affect the growth of black political association that was based on the dissatisfaction of the majority Kikuyu tribe with its economic circumstances. Members of the tribe were forced to squat on European farms or become agricultural labourers. When Thuku tried to protest, he was exiled, and Jomo Kenyatta became Secretary of the Kikuyu Central Association. Then he too left to study in Great Britain in the 1930s. This was untypical, however, as the veneer of European civilization made little impact in East Africa, and economic issues dominated. A characteristic of the Kenyan movement was the series of disagreements between Kenyatta and Thuku, which followed the latter's release from prison. Throughout the 1930s, Kenya, according to Oliver and Atmore, was the 'most troubled' of the British African colonies because it was the so-called 'trousered blacks' who offered leadership, not the old-fashioned chieftains.[2]

Elsewhere the heavy hand of Portuguese colonialism in Angola and Mozambique and Belgian colonialism in the Congo stifled the aspirations of the African people.

Important dates in the growth of black nationalism

1917   Blaise Diagne elected to French Parliament.
1920   Hayford founds National Congress of British West Africa.
1922   Henry Thuku exiled to north-west Kenya.
1925   Ladipo Solanke sets up West African Students Union.
1931   Thuku released.
1935   Mussolini attacks Abyssinia.
       Azikiwe returns from the USA.

China

One of Napoleon Bonaparte's more celebrated remarks was 'let China sleep', and for centuries, its contacts with the outside world had been minimal. This was partly a matter of geography, but also a consequence of the Chinese attitude to foreigners. When King George III of Britain asked the Emperor Chien Lung for closer trading and diplomatic links with his country, he replied tersely: 'The Celestial Empire ruling all within the four seas . . . does not value rare and precious things . . . we have never valued ingenious articles nor do we have the slightest need of your Country's manufactures'.

The Chinese emperors, whose dynasties stretched back thousands of years before Christ, regarded other races as barbaric, an opinion that was not altered by their first contact with Europeans. In 1860 China received a rude shock when a British and French expeditionary force captured Peking and forced the Manchu emperor to flee. The immediate result of this was to make them even more xenophobic than before, but equally unwilling to change. Their rigid system of government and administration, based on the teaching of the ancient philosopher Confucius, made them cultured, but inflexible, in their attitude to the modern world. But the series of Opium Wars in the latter half of the nineteenth century forced at least some Chinese to take the European powers more seriously and see that modern weapons were necessary if the country was not always to be at the mercy of foreigners.

The Boxer Rising, 1899

In the end, the foreigners were to win the day, but not before the conservatives in China made their biggest attack on what they called 'the foreign devils' in the Boxer revolt of 1899. The Boxers were a secret society who went to extreme lengths to destroy any traces of Western influence – they took their name from their preoccupation with the martial arts. For a while, encouraged by the old Empress Tsu Hsi, the Boxers laid siege to the foreign legations* in Peking, but their success was short-lived. A mixed force of French, British, Japanese, Germans and Americans marched on Peking and defeated them. The Boxer leaders were executed and the foreign powers demanded their pound of flesh from the Manchu emperor.

The 'Open Door'

This new regime allowed the foreign powers a commercial toehold in China through control of its major ports – thus the British obtained Hong Kong and the French received Kwangchowwan.

This humiliation made some younger Chinese take an interest in Western culture as well as Western technology. Then came the Chinese Revolution of 1911, which deposed Pu Yi, the last of the Manchu.

Sun Yat-sen

The revolutionaries were led by Dr Sun Yat-sen, a Christian, who had visited America and Western Europe and believed in democracy. Their aim was to set up a constitutional state based on a study of the USA and France, the two republican countries most favoured by Chinese intellectuals.

The dictatorship of Yuan

Others had less noble ideals, and one of them was Yuan-Shih-k'ai, the former Manchu Commander-in-Chief and first President of the Republic. Although Yuan was prepared to depose the Manchu, he wanted the throne for hinmself. He therefore tricked Sun Yat-sen into resigning in exchange for obtaining the support of the army. Sun was then forced into exile, and for four years (1912–16) China was dominated by Yuan's dictatorship. His anxiety to remain in power, however, was to prove his undoing.

There were several reasons for Yuan's downfall, one

Fig. 6.4   Execution in a war-lord's capital.

of which was his own shifty and treacherous character which did not inspire confidence. His own generals also preferred a weak central government, which would not interfere with their own freedom of action. Most crucial of all was the attitude of Japan, which did not want a strong China on its doorstep. In May 1915 Japan submitted the notorious Twenty-one Demands to China, the acceptance of which would virtually have made the latter a Japanese puppet state. Yuan's failure to reject them out of hand dealt a fatal blow to his prestige. In 1916 he quietly disappeared from the scene, an event that was followed by internal chaos, which was to last until 1925.

War-lordism

This was the heyday of the war-lords (Fig. 6.4), regional military bosses who controlled large tracts of land like medieval barons. The central government in Peking became virtually irrelevant.

An attempt to restore the Manchu dynasty in 1917 failed dismally, but Chinese nationalism had been awakened by the behaviour of the foreign powers. When, in 1919, the German colony of Shantung was given to Japan there was a revolt, and the Chinese delegation at Versailles refused to sign the treaty. Strong pressure from students and urban workers at home forced the government to adopt this strong position.

Only the USSR at this stage had friendly relations with the Chinese government, and in 1920 it agreed to give up its claims to northern Manchuria. This was part of Lenin's policy of 'no annexations', and received a favourable response in China. A comparison was made between Soviet behaviour and that of the 'capital imperialists'*, Britain, France, Japan, and the United States. As a result of this, Soviet influence in China became increasingly important.

The Kuomintang

The new Soviet alliance allowed the discredited republicans to make a comeback. Sun Yat-sen returned from exile and founded his Kuomintang or Nationalist Party. This was a broadly based movement that included the Communist Party. Its distinguishing feature was extreme nationalism, as exemplified by Sun's protégé, the young Russian-trained general Chiang Kai-shek (Fig. 6.5).

Sun died in 1925, and Chiang became leader of the new republic. Like his mentor, he was a strong Chinese nationalist, and in his book *China's Destiny*, he placed all the blame for the country's ills on the foreign powers.

Fig. 6.5   Chiang Kai-shek.

Fig. 6.6   Chiang Kai-shek's northern expedition, 1926–7.

Such arguments were given greater appeal by such episodes as the massacre inside the International Settlement in Shanghai. There on 28 June 1925 nationalist disturbances resulted in the shooting of fifty-two people by British and French police. Even the peasantry were involved in the new feeling of national consciousness.

The great northern expedition 1926

In this atmosphere Chiang was able to unite all sections of Chinese society in his northern expedition against the war-lords (Fig. 6.5). All their strongholds were captured, and for the first time since 1912, the country was really unified. Unfortunately, Chiang's extreme anti-communism was soon to destroy this achievement by involving his government in the prolonged struggle against the Chinese Party (see p. 34).

China exhibited its own unique features during this period, but developments there, as in other areas, showed that the days of the European colonists were numbered.

Keywords

Sinn Fein: Gaelic word meaning ourselves alone.

Fine Gael: meaning United Ireland Party – the pro-treaty party.

Fine Fail: meaning soldiers of destiny – the anti-treaty party after 1921.

Islam: the Muslim religion.

Zionist: a member of a movement believing in a separate Jewish state.

legation: a group of diplomatic representatives.

capital imperialists: a reference to the Western capitalist powers, which also had the largest colonial empires.

Questions (based on Chapters 5 and 6)
Fig. 5.5 on p. 35

1. Who was the MacDonald referred to in the cartoon?   1
2. The election in the cartoon took place in 1924. How did the 'Zinoviev Letter' affect the election result?   1
3. Name the leader of the successful party in this election.   1
4. The election was to be followed within two years by a major industrial disturbance in Britain. Outline the causes and results of this dispute.   6
5. Name the foreign leader who said at the time of the dispute that Britain's working class was 'bourgeois'.   1
6. Some years before this leader introduced a new economic policy in his country. Explain what this meant.   4
7. The new economic policy followed a period of civil war in that country. Name THREE leaders of the anti-government forces involved in the war.   3
8. Give THREE reasons why foreign powers felt that they needed to intervene in this war.   3
                                                        ——
                                                        20

7 Fascism

During the period between the two world wars, an important political movement appeared. Though largely a European phenomenon, its influence was to be felt throughout the world. It was called Fascism.

What Fascism meant

The world Fascism comes from the Latin word *fasces*, a bundle of rods, symbolizing power, carried before a Roman magistrate. From the beginning the movement had strong associations with armed groups and violence. It had certain clear characteristics:

1. *Anti-communism.* Fascism was a Right-wing reaction against communism. Where communist parties appeared, Fascist movements were usually formed to counteract the 'Red menace'.

2. *Extreme nationalism.* Another characteristic of Fascism was its belief in the virtues of nationalism, which manifested itself in various ways. Two aspects of this were hatred of foreigners or xenophobia and a build-up of military strength in the country concerned. This amounted to jingoism, i.e. a belief that your country is always right and other countries are always wrong.

3. *Racism.* Most Fascist movements took their dislike of foreigners to more extreme lengths. They isolated and picked on certain groups within their own society. These people might be Jews, blacks, Catholics, the sub-normal, gypsies, or indeed almost anyone. They had one thing in common, they were soft targets for ignorance, hatred and prejudice. Race was usually the basis for such campaigns, but not always, as we shall see.

4. *One-party rule.* Fascists rejected democracy; they believed in the need for strong and often brutal government. There was no room in their scheme of things for freedom of discussion or opposition. The Fascist state was, therefore, under the control of one party which, in turn, was dominated by a strong, dynamic leader. In Germany the Fascists talked of a Führer* principle or leader concept. The leader would work with other Fascist party members, but he would make all the important decisions. His toughness, virility and decisiveness were all important parts of the Fascist myth. '*Ein Reich, Ein Volk, Ein Führer*' ('One Empire, One People, One Leader') sang the Nazis in Germany. This slogan summed up the Fascist philosophy.

Totalitarianism

One word often used to describe Fascist regimes is totalitarian. It means a regime where all aspects of daily life are under the control of one party and no opposition is tolerated. It should be remembered, however, that other non-Fascist regimes, such as Stalin's in Russia, could also be described as totalitarian.

Fascism as a world movement

We mentioned earlier that Fascism began in Europe, but then spread elsewhere. This is an important point. Although it made its greatest impact in Italy and Germany, Fascism had an influence on the political life of many countries. In the United States, the Ku Klux Klan and German American Bund can accurately be described as Fascist movements. In Latin America Perón's regime in Argentina had many Fascist characteristics. In Britain Sir Oswald Mosley formed the British Union of Fascists in the 1930s. There were blueshirts in the Irish Free State, Rexists in Belgium and the Cross of Fire in France. Throughout the interwar period Fascism was one of the two dominant political movements in the world. The other, of course, was Marxism or communism.

Italian Fascism

The first country where Fascism was to make an

impact was Italy. Within four years of the end of the Great War, the first Fascist regime was to be established there. How did this come about?

To answer this question, we need to examine postwar Italian society.

Italy, 1918–22

Italy emerged from the war in disillusioned mood, and reference has already been made to its bitter reaction to the Versailles Peace Settlement (see Chapter 2). But other forces were also at work which produced the instability on which Fascism was to thrive. Some were especially important:

1. *The foundation of the Italian Communist Party in 1921.*   This alarmed the upper and middle classes in Italy. They feared that communist takeover of power would mean the loss of their wealth and property.
2. *The attitude of King Victor Emmanuel III.*   He was a monarch of Right-wing attitudes (as was the Queen Mother) who sympathized with many of the things for which the Fascists were soon to stand.
3. *The weakness of the Italian governments of the day.*   They were unable to control the Right- and Left-wing extremists who fought each other in the streets and created an atmosphere of fear and anxiety.
4. *The attitude of the army.*   Many of its officers and men had anti-democratic tendencies and were no great supporters of the Italian Republic. This was especially true of crack troops like the blackshirted *arditi*, hundreds of whom now put on the black Fascist uniform.

One piece only of the jigsaw remained, the strong dynamic leader (or Duce* as the Italians called him) who would seize the opportunity offered to the Fascists. His name was Benito Mussolini (Fig. 7.1).

Mussolini's background

Mussolini was born in 1883, the son of a blacksmith As a young man he wanted to be a teacher, but an interest in politics took him into journalism.

Surprisingly, at this stage of his life, Mussolini was a socialist, and became for a time the editor of the party newspaper *Avanti!* ('Forward'). He broke with the party over the question of Italian entry into the First World War, which he strongly supported. Then, after service with the Italian army, Mussolini returned to political life as a convinced nationalist and opponent of Bolshevism. In 1919 he founded the *Fascio di Combattimento* (Fascist fighting units) which in 1921 became the *Partito Nationale Fascista* (National

Fig. 7.1   Benito Mussolini the orator.

Fascist Party). Many disillusioned ex-soldiers and nationalists joined, although in the first instance they looked to Gabrielle D'Annunzio, the hero of Fiume, for leadership. Mussolini handled this situation cleverly, for while he copied the poet's style of leadership (the *stile fascista*), he kept D'Annunzio and his Fiume expedition short of funds.

'The intrepid one', as Mussolini called D'Annunzio, was deserted by his followers who swelled the ranks of the Duce's blackshirts. These blackshirts provided Mussolini with a private army, and carried out the dual task of protecting him and doing daily battle with the communists.

The rise of Fascism

Everywhere, political conditions seemed to favour the Fascists. In 1920 there were a series of sit-down strikes in the factories of northern Italy, and the socialist unions imposed boycotts* on the *agrari* (rich landowners and farmers) of the Po Valley. Both the industrialists and the landowners looked to the

Fascists for help, and money poured into party funds. The opposition appeared to be impotent, as the Socialist Party split into a communist and moderate wing in January 1921, and the Catholic *Partito Populari* (People's Party) was only united by its opposition to the anti-clerical Liberal Party.

Mussolini, for his part, made two effective moves. First of all, he renounced his youthful republicanism, which had offended the King, and then he gave up his anti-clericalism*, which pleased the newly elected Pope Pius XI.

This political instability was compounded by an economic crisis. In two years, 2,500,000 demobilized soldiers were thrown on to the employment market with predictable results. The unemployment figure, which stood at 90,000 in July 1920, had reached 500,000 by the end of 1921. Over the same period, the cost of living had risen by more than 50 per cent.

In desperation, the Liberal Prime Minister Giolitti tried an old prewar trick of trying to buy votes. In May 1921, he invited the Fascist deputies into the government bloc in parliament, hoping that by doing this he would be able to tame the Fascist 'wild men'. This was a complete failure, and the rampages of the blackshirts continued throughout the countryside. These were the men who have justly been described by the Italian historian Carocci as 'a mixture of idealists, spoilt brats, misfits, and hooligans',[1] but their hour of triumph was near. Neither of the two big parties, the socialist or the *Populari*, could form a stable government, and both King and propertied classes alike were terrified of Bolshevism. It was evident also that turbulent political conditions would not allow the weak Italian economy to recover.

Mussolini in power, October 1922

By October, Mussolini felt confident enough to challenge the government: 'Either the government will be given to us or we shall take it.' He began to lay plans for a march on Rome. In the capital itself there was panic. The Prime Minister, Facta, threatened to kill himself, but then advised that the whole country be placed under martial law. But the weak King, Victor Emmanuel, refused to sign the decree, or rely on the support of loyal troops under Marshal Badaglio. Instead, on 29 October 1922, he sent Benito Mussolini a telegram inviting him to become Prime Minister of Italy. The next day, Mussolini arrived in Rome by train to accept the appointment, although at that time his party only had thirty-five parliamentary deputies and 300,000 members. More importantly, however, as you have seen, the Duce had won the support of the real power centres in Italian society. His triumph was complete when the legions of blackshirts were allowed to march in celebration through the streets of Rome. (An interesting event at this time was a mysterious fall from the balcony of his house, which prevented Mussolini's rival D'Annunzio from taking part in the so-called 'March on Rome'.)

Making Italy Fascist

When he became Prime Minister, Mussolini said that his aim was to 'make Italy Fascist'. But for the first two years he had to move carefully. The Fascists were in a coalition with the *Populari* and they had little popular support. At this stage the Duce was heavily dependent on the support of the King and his generals. Some things he could do, such as placing a ban on the Communist Party, but he was not really master of his own house. Then came the crisis that nearly brought Mussolini's career to a premature end.

The Mattcoti murder, 1924

Giacomo Matteoti was a well-known socialist deputy and opponent of Fascism. His speeches in parliament irritated Mussolini, and eventually the blackshirts decided to take matters into their own hands. Matteoti was kidnapped in Rome and bundled into a car. Some days later, his body was discovered outside Rome. In the circumstances, it was not surprising that Mussolini was blamed for the murder. Whether he ordered it is still uncertain, but there were widespread demonstrations against the government. Mussolini, for one, lost his nerve, but his opponents failed to press home their advantage. Instead, they decided to boycott parliament, and Mussolini recovered his confidence. Assured of the King's support, he made a brash speech in January 1925 taking full responsibility for the murder. His opponents failed to take up the challenge; they were never to get another opportunity.

Consolidation and reform, 1925–9

Having secured his power base, Mussolini went on to impose his style of Fascism on the Italian people. Special courts were set up to deal with the opponents of the regime and a rigid censorship was introduced. One one occasion, a man was imprisoned for calling the Duce 'the big cheese'! As a former journalist, Mussolini was well aware of the value of propaganda to his regime. Great efforts were put into prestige projects, and Mussolini was always there to give the right example. When he began the 'Battle for Wheat', the photographers were there to take pictures of Il Duce working, stripped to the waist, in the cornfields. Slogans like 'Mussolini is always right' were a characteristic of this period. Foreigners were impressed, too: Mussolini, in the famous phrase, 'made the trains run on time'. The reality was a little less impressive.

Mussolini did have some successes: grain production did increase and he was responsible for draining the Pontine Marshes outside Rome. But Italy remained a very poor country throughout the Fascist era. The average Italian worker only earned a third of the wages of his opposite number in Britain, for example. The boasting of the Fascist government concealed the fact that there was a gross imbalance of wealth between poor, underdeveloped, agrarian, southern Italy and the rich, industrial north. Long after Mussolini was dead, Italian governments were still struggling with the same problem.

His over-ambitious foreign policy also put undue strain on the weak Italian economy. The Mediterranean Sea, Mussolini said, would become 'an Italian lake'. He was fond of talking about the 'eight million bayonets' which would restore the ancient glories of the former Roman Empire. It was no accident that Fascist banners and insignia bore a strong resemblance to those of ancient Rome.

The Lateran Treaty, 1929

Mussolini's most lasting achievement came in an unlikely area. It was he who solved the 'Roman Question', which had perplexed Italian governments since 1870. When, in that year, Italy became a united country, the Pope lost all his lands in central Italy. Rome, in fact, became the capital of the new Italian kingdom. This new situation was not accepted by the Roman Catholic Church. Successive Popes refused to recognize the Italian government or meet its representatives. Mussolini saw the obvious advantages of coming to terms with the Church, which still had great influence over the Italian people, the bulk of whom were Catholics. On the other side, Pope Pius XI seemed ready for compromise. He described Mussolini as 'a man whom Providence has caused us to encounter', and approved of the regime's stand against communism. The Church also had financial difficulties which Mussolini was prepared to help resolve.

The result of negotiations between the Pope and the Fascist government was the Lateran Treaty of 11 February 1929. By its provisions:
1. the Pope was to control an area of 44 hectares (109 acres) inside the city of Rome. This mini-state was to be quite independent. It exists today and is called the Vatican State;
2. Catholicism was recognized as the official religion in Italy;
3. the Pope recognized the Italian government and the House of Savoy as the ruling royal house;
4. the Pope was to receive £30 million (2 billion lire) to compensate him for the lands lost in 1870.

The Lateran Treaty was a great triumph for Mussolini. It gave the Fascist regime the stamp of respectability. It also solved the most persistent problem the new Italian state had faced.

Relations between the government and the Church were not, however, entirely smooth. Mussolini wanted all Italian youth to join his Fascist youth movement. He therefore authorized the closure of all the offices and halls of Catholic Action – the Catholic youth movement. Pope Pius XI reacted sharply. He issued an encyclical* condemning Mussolini's action and attacking Fascism for trying 'to monopolize completely the young, from the tenderest years up to manhood and womanhood'. The effect of this condemnation was weakened though by the Pope's refusal to denounce Fascism. Some historians criticized Pius XI for showing excessive sympathy for Fascism. It is only fair to point out that the Pope never condoned Mussolini's rather feeble attempts to introduce anti-Jewish laws in 1938. The legislation was ineffective, and Pius XI came to regret his former co-operation with Mussolini. In his last illness, he expressed his sorrow that he had 'made pacts with men without Faith and without God'.

Was Fascist Italy totalitarian?

The struggle between Mussolini and the Church highlighted the weakness of the Duce's position. While the Fascist press and radio took every opportunity to remind the people of the Duce's leadership, there were important checks on his power. One was the Roman Catholic Church, an institution with great international prestige. The other was the monarchy. Victor Emanuel III had been responsible for his appointment in 1922. He was also largely responsible for his humiliating removal from power in 1943. The Duce might refer to him insultingly as 'a little sardine', but he could never forget his existence.

In a real sense, then, Mussolini's power was limited, and we cannot therefore accurately describe his regime as totalitarian.

The corporate state

Mussolini allied himself to the most powerful, conservative interest groups in Italy. It is hardly surprising, therefore, that the Fascist regime carried out policies which were against the interests of the working classes. Mussolini made much fuss about helping the workers, but the survival of the regime did not depend on them. To please the industrialists and landowners, he invented what came to be known as the corporate state. The idea was that both workers and employers would be represented in a series of corporations, which would fix salaries and prices for that industry. But there was no real equality under the corporate state. The worker could not strike, the trade unions were abolished and replaced by Fascist ones, and the labour force had no say in wage negotiations or conditions of service. This contrasted with the position of employers. They could avoid state interference by contributing to Fascist Party funds. Many were pleased, in any case, by Mussolini's repressive policy towards the work force. This lack of democracy was typical of the Fascist system.

Mussolini's achievement

It may seem strange in view of what you have just read that Mussolini retained such popularity with the Italian people. Some of his policies appear ridiculous today, such as encouraging the growth of the birth rate by placing a tax on bachelors, but there was a dramatic element in his rule which appealed to many Italians. He was an effective public speaker and his ambitious projects did something to heal wounded Italian pride after the First World War.

Until the Ethiopian War of 1935–6 (see Chapter 11), the Duce retained the tacit support of most of the Italian people. He was finally ruined by the fatal alliance with Germany, but this alliance was a logical outcome of the Duce's earlier fantasies. The power and ruthlessness of Adolf Hitler appealed to a man who lacked these attributes himself.

We can leave the final word on Mussolini to one of his former socialist colleagues: 'He is a rabbit; a phenomenal rabbit; he roars. Observers who do not know him mistake him for a lion.'

German Fascism

The rise of National Socialism, 1925–33

When we last mentioned Adolf Hitler, he was an obscure south German politician who had just emerged from prison. The four years that followed were depressing ones for Hitler and his new National Socialist Party. The recovery of the German economy was paralleled, as we have seen, by German entry into the League and an improvement in its relations with the Western democracies. Nazi fortunes reached their lowest point in 1928 when the Party received only 800,000 votes in the Parliamentary elections. There seemed little chance that Hitler would be able to seize power in Germany as his great hero Benito Mussolini had done in Italy.

The lesson of 1923

But Hitler had learnt one important lesson from the failure of the Beer Hall Putsch in 1923. Never again would he try and take power by force. Although the Nazis despised the Weimar government, they would use the weapons of democracy to overthrow it, i.e. the ballot box.

The economic crisis, 1929–33

The turning point in Hitler's career came with the onset of a second serious economic crisis in Germany in 1929. Within four years, he and his party were to be brought from obscurity to the brink of power, and the extent of the Nazi breakthrough is shown in Table 7.1.

Table 7.1 The rise of the National Socialist Party, 1928–32

Year	Votes	Seats
1928	800,000	12
1930	5,000,000	107
1932 (July)	13,000,000	230

Note the obvious contrast with the Italian situation. Hitler had a massive popular base from which to launch his bid for power. How did he achieve it?
1. The single most important factor behind Hitler's success was the economic crisis. By 1932 there were 6 million unemployed people in Germany, and the Weimar government seemed to have no answer. All the American loans, which had been the basis for German prosperity in the 1920s, had been called in as a result of the crisis in the USA (see Chapter 9).

The millions of unemployed people provided the Nazi Party with natural recruits and supporters.

Hitler, after all, was promising that he could save Germany from economic disaster, and provide them all with jobs.

2. The weakness of the Weimar regime was another factor. Particularly important during the period 1930–33 was the behaviour of President Hindenburg. He ruled through a series of favourites, Brüning, von Papen, and Schleicher, none of whom had a majority of seats in the Reichstag. This allowed Hitler to accuse the Weimar, governments of being undemocratic.

3. As in Italy, the conservative upper classes found National Socialism (the German version of Fascism) an appealing philosophy. Industrialists, such as Krupp and Thyssen, contributed a great deal of money to Nazi Party funds. This was used to finance Hitler's lavish election campaigns. Army officers were attracted to Nazi promises of rearmament. Both groups supported Hitler's anti-communist stance. So did the Prussian landowning class, the Junkers, even if they despised the social background of the Nazis.

4. The strange tactics of the German Communist Party must be taken into account. We saw earlier how the party suffered in the opening years of the Weimar Republic. It was not allowed to benefit from any lessons learnt then because of Stalin's short-sighted folly. Insisting that Fascism was the last stage of capitalism, to be followed by a communist revolution, Stalin instructed the German communists to co-operate with their natural enemies, the Nazis. After helping the Nazis in their attacks on the republic, the party was destroyed when Hitler came to power.

5. No analysis of the background to the rise of Nazism can afford to neglect the role played by Hitler himself, and his personal qualities. Firstly, he kept the party together in the difficult years between 1924–8. Secondly, he was completely single-minded in his drive for power. Those, like the Strasser brothers, who wanted real social reforms were thrown out of the party. Hitler knew such notions would offend the industrialists whose support he needed. Taking the title of Führer or leader, Hitler insisted on absolute obedience from party members.

Lastly, he had an almost hypnotic effect on the masses, and a unique ability to understand their moods. Here is an account by Albert Speer, an intelligent, educated man (later to be Germany's Armaments Minister) of the time when he first heard Hitler speak in 1930:

Hitler entered and was tempestuously hailed by his numerous followers among the students. This enthusiasm in itself made a great impression upon me. But his appearance also surprised me. On posters and in caricatures, I had seen him in military tunic, with shoulder straps, swastika armband, and hair flapping over his forehead. But here he was wearing a well-fitted blue suit and looking markedly respectable. Everything about him bore out the note of reasonable modesty. . . . Hitler's initial shyness soon disappeared; at times now his pitch rose. He spoke urgently and with hypnotic persuasiveness. The mood he cast was much deeper than the speech itself, most of which I did not remember for long.[2]

The very next day, Albert Speer applied for party membership and later became Nazi Party Member Number 474,481. He was a middle-class architect, but Hitler was equally effective with peasants, factory workers and small shopkeepers. Hitler was, in Alan Bullock's words, the 'greatest demagogue* in history'.[3] He told the people what they wanted to hear: vote for me and I will destroy communism, Versailles, the Jews, and rebuild the economy. By 1932 it seemed that the German people had accepted the Führer's message.

On the brink

Then with victory in sight, the Nazis seemed to be running out of luck. Hitler's first problem was the aged President Hindenburg, who flatly refused to appoint him Chancellor, although the Nazis were the largest party in the Reichstag. Hindenburg called Hitler 'the Bohemian Corporal' (which was odd when one remembers that he was Austrian by birth), and regarded him as totally unsuitable for the post because of his humble social origins. Then the Nazis began to suffer electoral setbacks. In the 1932 Presidential election, Hitler stood against Hindenburg and lost. This was followed by a collapse in the Nazi vote in the November Reichstag elections. The number of seats won by the party went down from 230 to 196.

Even more alarming from Hitler's viewpoint was the growing reluctance of industrialists to contribute money to Nazi Party coffers. Some at least were becoming alarmed by the brutality of Hitler's brownshirts (the *Sturm-Abteilung* (SA) or Storm-troopers), and the violent language of some of the party leadership. By the end of 1932 there seemed a real chance that Hitler and his colleagues had missed their opportunity. The mood of the time was expressed in the diary of his propaganda chief Joseph Goebbels. His entry for 5 December 1932 reads: 'We are all depressed, above all because of the danger of the whole party falling apart and all our work having been in vain . . .'[4]

The Nazis were, however, saved from their difficulties by the stupidity of others. Two men in particular were responsible for their reprieve. Franz von Papen, a former Chancellor and friend of Hindenburg was one. He was convinced that he could tame the Nazis and use them to establish himself in office. Kurt von Schleicher, the last Chancellor of the Weimar Republic, was another. Schleicher had been a master of intrigue who had used his influence as Defence Minister to bring down other governments. But his own period in office was to last barely seven weeks. His efforts to win over the Left wing of the Nazi Party failed. So did his attempts to forge an alliance with the trade unions. No one trusted Schleicher and in the background Papen was working against him. By the end of January 1933 Papen had persuaded Hindenburg that Hitler must be made Chancellor. The plan was that Papen himself would be Vice-Chancellor in the new government and control Hitler and his Nazi colleagues. He was soon to learn that Hitler was nobody's puppet.

Germany under Hitler, 1933–9

On 30 January 1933 Adolf Hitler was appointed Chancellor of Germany (Fig. 7.2). He now had the opportunity to carry out the programme outlined in *Mein Kampf* in 1924. Some of it concerned foreign policy objectives, but other parts of the programme dealt with the day-to-day running of Germany. It was more genuinely Fascist than that of Mussolini in Italy, as we shall see.

The years of waiting, 1933–4

When Hitler became Chancellor, he headed a coalition government in which there were only two other Nazis apart from Hitler himself – they were Frick, as Minister of the Interior, and Goering, as Minister without portfolio. The other eight top government posts were held by conservatives led by von Papen. This meant that Hitler was not in a position to implement policies that would arise opposition from the non-Nazis in the cabinet. Like Mussolini, in 1922–4, he would have to be careful. Again he would only contemplate moves that would have general support, such as the destruction of the Communist Party.

The Reichstag fire

He needed an excuse, and this was provided on the night of 27 February 1933 when the Reichstag building went up in flames (Fig. 7.3). The fire was a

Fig. 7.2 Hitler and Hindenburg.

Fig. 7.3 The Reichstag fire, 1933.

godsend for the Nazis, who blamed the communists for burning down the Reichstag building. No one is certain who was actually responsible for the fire, although it seems likely that Nazi brownshirts were involved (they could use an underground passage linking the Reichstag to Goering's flat opposite). At the time, the Nazis put the blame on a half-mad Dutch communist, Marinus van der Lubbe, who was found wandering in the ruins. Attempts to link leading communists to the fire failed completely, but van der Lubbe was later executed.

If the Nazis hoped that they would stampede the middle classes into voting for them, they were disappointed. In the March 1933 elections, the party only received 44 per cent of the total vote. A majority of the German people still refused to back National Socialism as a cure for all Germany's problems.

The Enabling Act 1933

Although Hitler's victory in the elections was indecisive, he was able to use the support of the Nationalist Party, which won fifty-two seats in the elections. Added to the 288 seats won by the Nazis, this gave Hitler an outright majority. This allowed the government to pass in March 1933 a Law for Removing the Distress of People and Reich, usually called the Enabling Act despite the opposition of the Social Democratic Party. But Hitler had what he wanted, emergency powers to be used without consulting the Reichstag. Before many years had passed, the Nazi leader expected to hold all the levers of power in Germany. In the meantime, a few old scores could be settled. All the Communist Party deputies in the Reichstag were sent to concentration camps, the Social Democratic Party was dissolved and the Catholic Centre Party obligingly dissolved itself. By the end of 1933, effective opposition to Hitler in Germany had disappeared.

The Night of the Long Knives, 30 June 1934

The most serious threat to Adolf Hitler's position came in fact from inside his own party. The brownshirted SA, now swollen in numbers to about 2 million, had, up to that point, been instrumental in helping Hitler to power. Their leader, Ernst Röhm, was one of Hitler's oldest colleagues, going back to the days of the Beer Hall putsch. But Röhm had his own ideas about the way the new Germany should be run. He wanted to break the long-established power and influence of the landowners and industrialists. More dangerously, he wanted his Storm-troops and the regular army to be combined under his own leadership. Hitler knew that this was something that

the army generals would never tolerate. Although Röhm himself had been an officer in the army, many of his brownshirts were little more than thugs united only by their loyalty to the Nazi Party. At first, Hitler was reluctant to deal harshly with his old friend Röhm. But Röhm refused to fall in with Hitler's demand that he be content only with the leadership of the SA and cease his criticisms of the government. By early summer 1934 the situation had reached crisis point. The army was not prepared to tolerate Röhm's pretensions, and Hitler dared not antagonize its leaders. A secret meeting, probably on the cruiser *Deutschland*, was held between Hitler and the generals. It resulted in the following agreement:

1. Hitler would push ahead with rearmament and eliminate the danger from Röhm and the SA.
2. In exchange, the generals promised that they would be loyal to Hitler and authorize a personal oath of loyalty to him.

The scenes that followed seemed more characteristic of a gangster movie than the administration of an old and civilized country. Röhm and the SA leaders were sent on leave, which they took at Bad Wansee, a lakeside resort not far from Berlin. There, during the night of 30 June 1934, a column of fast-moving cars led by Hitler himself arrived. The startled Röhm was aroused from his sleep to be told by his friend and leader: 'Ernst, you are under arrest'. He and the other SA leaders were accused of planning a putsch against the regime. Throughout Germany, the blood purge continued.

It was the chance for which Röhm's enemies in the party leadership, Goebbels, Goering and Himmler (head of the sinister blackshirts or *Schutzstaffel* (SS) had been waiting. Röhm was shot by SS men (Fig. 7.4), but other enemies of Hitler also perished during that Night of the Long Knives. They included General von Schleicher, Gregor Strasser, an old party rival, and even von Kahr, Bavarian Prime Minister at the time of the Beer Hall Putsch in 1923. Franz von Papen, who had infuriated Hitler by criticizing the Nazis some days before in a speech, was fortunate to escape with his life (although the speech-writers were shot). Foreigners were outraged by this bloody massacre, but in Germany no one protested. Reich President Hindenburg sent Hitler a telegram of congratulation, thanking him for having 'saved the German nation'. The Nazi regime had survived its greatest crisis.

Hitler becomes Führer

One stumbling block only remained, and it was swiftly removed. In August 1934, President Hindenburg died, and with him went the old Germany that

Fig. 7.4   Hitler's blackshirts, the SS.

The Latin American model

We mentioned earlier in this chapter that Fascism was largely a European movement, but that it had some influence in other parts of the world. Two South American regimes in particular have been identified with Fascism during the period after the First World War.

Vargas in Brazil

In 1930 Getulio Vargas became President of Brazil, and further strengthened his position by staging a *coup d'état* in 1937. This effectively removed all opposition, and Vargas set up what he called his *Estado Novo* or new state. Although Vargas made favourable references to Nazi Germany, it is doubtful whether his regime can really be called Fascist. He set up no political movement and in the Second World War, Brazil fought on the side of the Western democracies. By all accounts, Vargas was an amiable, easy-going dictator whose motto was 'leave things as they are to see how they will turn out'. Such an attitude had little in common with the more muscular Fascism of Europe. The Vargas dictatorship, which finally ended with his suicide in 1954, seems to have been little more than an updated version of the Latin American tradition in caudillismo (the Spanish word for dictator is *caudillo*).

Perónism in Argentina

The career of Juan Domingo Perón (Fig. 7.5) seems to have a lot more in common with the European dictators. As a young officer, Perón had been a military attaché in Mussolini's Italy, and he admired what he saw. On returning to Argentina, Perón was largely responsible for setting up a secret military society called GOU (Government, Order, Unity). Its object was to spread Fascist ideas in the Argentine army.

Perón was given his chance in 1943 when the army seized power and he was made Secretary of Labour. By 1945 Perón himself had emerged as the leader of a new style regime. It had some notable Fascist characteristics such as extreme nationalism and intolerance of any opposition. But Perónism had one very unusual feature: it was based on an alliance between Perón and the *descamisados* or 'shirtless ones', the working classes. Perón worked closely with trade union leaders to improve the workers' lot, although he was careful to retain overall control of the unions for himself. He also set up his own political

the Nazis wished to destroy. Hitler was now able to take supreme power. From being merely Führer of the Nazi Party, he assumed the title of Führer of the German people. He was now both Chancellor and President, and every German soldier took the oath of loyalty to him personally.

The totalitarian state

We spoke earlier of the concept of a totalitarian state, and Nazi Germany between 1934–45 provides a classic model of such a system. From the time of Hitler's assumption of the title of Führer in August 1934 until his death in May 1945, his power was unquestioned. There was no king or pope to worry about in Nazi Germany. In some respects certainly Hitler was inefficient, retaining the lazy habits of a frustrated youth. The historian David Irving has argued that Hitler was the 'weakest leader Germany has known this century'.[5] But this weakness concerned only Hitler's willingness to make decisions. There was no question during this time of where the real power lay for in Hermann Goering's words: 'It is the Führer alone who decides.' We will see later how this authority was used to affect the life of Germany.

Fig. 7.5   Juan Perón of Argentina.

movement and introduced a series of five-year plans to expand the economy. In other respects too Perón's regime was strongly reminiscent of Mussolini and Hitler. He married a glamorous film star Eva Duarte – regarded as a saint by the workers – and was an effective organizer of the media in Argentina. The historian Richard Collier tells us that 'mass rallies and balcony speeches were the hallmarks of the new political style'[6] – activities that invariably surround Fascist dictators.

Unfortunately for Perón, Fascism came a little too late in Argentina, for in 1945 both Hitler and Mussolini fell from power. The United States government made concerted efforts to get rid of him after 1945, and he only survived by playing down the Fascist ideals of earlier years. He fell from power in 1955 after rumours that the 'shirtless ones' were to be provided with arms to protect Perón from attack by conservative army officers!

The significance of Fascism

Careful reading of this chapter should underline the point that Fascism tended to differ sharply from country to country. Perónism in Argentina had peculiar characteristics of its own, as did Italian and German Fascism. They were essentially the by-products of the traumatic upheaval that made up the First World War. Even though Italy finished on the winning side in that war, it was still a revisionist power in the same sense that Nazi Germany was. This spirit of postwar disillusionment gave European Fascism its peculiar tinge of bitterness which was not to be found in organizations like the Perónista, the Ku Klux Klan and the German-American Bund. It is true too, that the German variety of Fascism proved itself to be the more ruthless. But it shared with its Italian cousin the promise of economic recovery, for in both countries large-scale unemployment played a significant part in the rise of Fascist parties. The Italian Fascists lacked the overwhelming popular support that Hitler obtained in Germany, which may go some way to explaining the less savage nature of their regime. The Italian blackshirts knew all about making their opponents swallow castor oil and eat live toads. They could never have conceived of the systematic evil of a concentration camp, or the vicious racism of the Third Reich.

What finally distinguished Fascism from other political ideas was its negative nature. Where Marxism had a solid set of concepts behind it, Fascism could offer little but a set of prejudices. It survives to this day, but in a discredited and weakened form, such as the National Front in Britain. The excesses of National Socialism have placed it beyond any claim to political respectability.

Keywords

Führer: a German word meaning chief or leader.

Duce: the equivalent word in Italian, and the title used by Mussolini.

boycott: a refusal to co-operate or work with; taken from an incident in nineteenth-century Ireland in which Captain Boycott's tenants refused to work for him.

anti-clericalism: opposition to the power of the Church, especially its tendency to interfere in politics.

encyclical: a written statement by the Pope, usually named after its opening phrase, e.g. 'With burning sorrow', Pius XI 1937 encyclical condemning the persecution of the Jews in Germany.

demagogue: a leader with the ability to whip up emotions and prejudices.

Questions

Extract 7.1

Hitler was driven to the Bavarian Ministry of the Interior where he leaped out of the car, followed by a rattled Gauleiter Wagner, who was also Minister of the Interior. The Führer strode into the building, the skirt of his leather coat flying, and up the stairs toward Wagner's office. As he burst into the anteroom the head of the Upper Bavarian SA started to salute but Hitler rushed at him, shouting 'Lock him up!' He began cursing all traitors in general and the SA leaders whose men had been lured to the streets of Munich by pamphlets in particular. 'You,' he yelled, 'are under arrest and will be shot!'

It was 6 am when the Führer, still in a 'terrifying state of excitement' emerged from the building.[7]

1. In what year did the events take place?   1
2. Who was the leader of the SA?   1
3. Explain why Hitler thought it necessary to arrest the 'traitors'.   3
4. What significance did the city of Munich have in the early part of Hitler's career?   2
5. In what ways did the purge of the SA strengthen Hitler's personal power in Germany?   3
6. Explain what you understand by the term 'Führer'.   1
7. Adolf Hitler was the leader of a Fascist party. What were the characteristics of this political movement?   4
8. The Nazi regime is often described as totalitarian. Why would it be inaccurate to use this term about Fascist Italy?   5

      20

8 Prohibition, Prejudice and Prosperity, 1919-29

The intervention of the United States in the First World War in 1917 marked a new phase in the country's history. Since the gaining of independence from Britain in 1783, the American people had avoided foreign entanglements, and concentrated on building up the strength of their great nation.

They survived a bitter civil war, which ended in 1865, but after it the Union continued to grow in size and strength. Immense natural resources, gold, coal, oil and iron ore, were discovered in the nineteenth century to speed on this process of growth. At the same time, the United States was attracting a vast reservoir of human resources, as the poor, the persecuted and the ambitious flooded in from every nation in Europe. Between 1880–1920, 23 million immigrants came into the country, every man and woman a believer in the 'American Dream'. Irish, Jews, Germans, Poles and blacks all were to make their contribution to the development of what, by 1900, had become the greatest industrial power in the world.

The political system

The United States was divided from Europe, both by its vast size and geographical location. It also developed a political system uniquely its own.

The Constitution

This was based on the Constitution drawn up in 1776, which allowed a President to make the decisions (the executive) and a Congress to pass the laws (the legislature). But unlike the British system, the Americans had separation of powers, i.e. the President does *not* sit in Congress and the majority in Congress can be of a different party from that of the President.

A third body, the Supreme Court, had a watchdog role. Its job was to watch over the government (President and Congress) and make sure it kept within the Constitution. The American people regard their Constitution as a sacred text and jealously guard it as such. Changing it is a long and costly process, involving a constitutional amendment, e.g. giving women the vote.

The parties

For most of its history, the United States has had two political parties, the Democrats and the Republicans. There have been others – Populists, Bull Moosers, Socialists and Progressives – but their impact has always been short-lived.

Only the two main parties have been able to put a candidate into the White House, so third parties have only really had nuisance value. However, even the Democrats and the Republicans are influenced much more by local issues than might be the case in Europe. Remember the vast size of the USA: 4,830 km (3,000 miles) from New York to San Francisco. Party lines are also much easier to cross in the United States, so it is not unusual to find a registered Republican in a Democrat government; an example would be the Republican Stimson who worked for F. D. Roosevelt.

Table 8.1 outlines the essential differences between the parties today and who supports them.

Table 8.1 The Democratic and Republican Parties

Party	Social and ethnic groups	Political divisions
Democratic	blacks, organized labour, Puerto Ricans, Irish Catholics, Jews, Southern whites.	interventionist – believe in big role for Washington; government can help with welfare programmes, etc.
Republican	big business, farmers, small-town America, White Anglo-Saxon Protestants (WASPS) in older states – Vermont, Maine, Rhode Island, etc.	states rights – keep out federal government. Prefer action be left to local enterprise.

American politics is difficult to fit into rigid categories. It would be easy to find exceptions to the general rules set out in Table 8.1. In 1956, for example, many in the white South voted for the Republican Eisenhower, while in 1932 the farmers voted for the Democrat Roosevelt!

A final point to remember is that the USA is a democracy*. A complex series of primaries or local elections is needed to put forward a Presidential candidate. Once nominated, the candidate needs a popular majority from the electorate and a majority in the electoral college.

Both the Senate or upper house of Congress and the House of Representatives are directly elected by the people, too.

Prohibition, prejudice and prosperity: the USA, 1919–29

Ill-health prevented President Woodrow Wilson from standing in the 1920 election and his replacement James Cox was defeated. His Republican opponent Warren Gamaliel Harding was a little-known small-town politician from Ohio, a product of the party machine. But Harding represented the mood of the moment which favoured a withdrawal from international involvement.

'What America needs,' said Harding in a campaign speech, 'is not heroics but healing, not nostrum but normality.' The people agreed and gave Harding 16 million votes to Cox's 9 million. Calvin Coolidge, Governor of Massachusetts, became Vice-President in the new administration.

Harding, described by Woodrow Wilson as a man with a 'bungalow mind', was President, but he made little attempt to disguise his personal weaknesses or his ignorance of public affairs. Harding preferred the company of his Ohio gang and their talent for poker

playing. When asked for his opinion on foreign policy issues, Harding used to reply: 'You and Jed Welliver get together . . . he handles these matters for me.' He was equally free in confessing his ignorance of economics, telling colleagues: 'I can't make a damn thing out of this tax problem.' But there were men of ability too in his administration, such as Andrew W. Mellon at the Treasury and Herbert Hoover as Secretary for Commerce.

Prohibition

Harding's administration coincided with the era of Prohibition, one of the strangest in American history. For fourteen years it became a criminal offence to buy, consume, or transport alcohol in any state in the Union. The Eighteenth Amendment to the American Constitution provided powers for this measure and the Volstead Act of 1919 made it law.

Such a piece of legislation now seems absurdity, but at the time various influences came together in the misguided attempt to make the United States 'dry':
1. When the United States came into the war in 1917, it was considered desirable to prevent armaments workers from drinking too much in case it interfered with production. Licensing laws were introduced to limit drinking hours, as indeed they were in Britain. Drunkenness became unpatriotic.
2. Small-town America had long been weary of the 'demon drink'. Strong religious feeling was involved as the non-conformist sects – Methodists, Baptists, etc. – had a long tradition of hostility to the consumption of alcohol. Church-going ladies banded together in anti-saloon leagues (Fig. 8.1) to denounce it and agitate for prohibition.
3. In the South, there was a racist element in the issue, for it was said that alcohol could stir up the Negro and make him question his subservient position.

Fig. 8.1   An anti-saloon league, the 'Women's Christian Temperance Union' by Ben Shahn.

Fig. 8.2   Federal agents discover illegal still for making alcohol.

4. On a practical level, drink was also denounced by the famous motor manufacturer Henry Ford as a danger to life on the roads. This was, of course, sound common sense, but it was combined with less rational arguments to persuade President and Congress alike that the American people should abstain from strong drink.

In Harding's defence, it must be said that it was Woodrow Wilson, not he, who presided over the enactment of Prohibition. The Ohio gang openly flouted the drink laws in their poker parties in the White House! So did millions of other Americans during the years of alcoholic drought, for Prohibition proved to be one of the greatest legislative disasters ever (Fig. 8.2). Even people who rarely drank in ordinary circumstances began to acquire a taste for 'hootch' as the illegal alcohol became known. Respectable citizens frequented speakeasies where they could drink the alcohol obtained for them by hoodlums. This was the heyday of the mobster in cities like Chicago, and names like Al Capone and Baby Face Nelson became household words.

Selling alcohol became big business, and with the vast profits, came protection rackets and gang warfare. Law enforcement became a lottery as gangsters bribed city authorities and made their own rules. A vivid example of what this meant came with the notorious St. Valentine's Day Massacre in 1929. On this occasion, Capone's hoodlums, disguised as policemen, machine-gunned six members of a gang headed by Bugs Moran. Capone was eventually deported on tax evasion charges, but he died a rich man.

The federal government lacked the resources to enforce the prohibition legislation. Even its most famous agents, Izzy and Mo, were hardpressed to contain the epidemic of illegal drinking after 1919. Their quickest arrest came in Pittsburgh where a taxi driver produced a bottle of whisky, on request, in only 15 seconds!

In most respects the ban on alcohol was out of keeping with the spirit of the times, which rejected pre-war inhibitions. It was the jazz age, a period of dance crazes like the Charleston and the black bottom, and the motor car gave the middle-class American much greater mobility. For young women in particular, it was an exciting time. The Nineteenth Amendment had given them a vote in 1919, and they threw themselves enthusiastically into all the exotic merry-making of the 1920s.

At the same time, writers were able to indulge in sharper criticism of American society than had ever been the case before. Scott Fitzgerald became the golden boy of American literature and Sinclair Lewis lampooned small-town America in novels like *Babbit* and *Main Street*. Most famous of all, perhaps, was the journalist and critic, H. L. Mencken. No one in the United States was safe from Mencken's witty asides, least of all the politicians for whom he had a hearty contempt.

'Democracy,' wrote Mencken, 'is the theory that the common people know what they want and deserve to get it good and hard.'

Prejudice

America's isolation and its cosmopolitan population made it easily susceptible to outbursts of extreme patriotism. The Bolshevik Revolution of 1917, a profoundly disturbing event to most Americans, provided the occasion for one of these. In 1919 a bomb blew in the door of the Attorney-General's house, and he seized on this excuse to initiate the infamous Palmer Raids. Thousands of unfortunate people, whose main crime was that they were recent foreign immigrants, were locked up on suspicion of being Bolsheviks or anarchists*. The government seemed unaware that there was any real difference, and the hysteria of the moment brought about a gross miscarriage of justice.

In 1920 two Italian anarchists, Sacco and Vanzetti, were charged with involvement in a hold-up in Lexington, Massachusetts. Friendly witnesses were to testify that neither man was anywhere near the scene of the crime, but to no avail. The politics and nationality of the two men doomed them. Trial Judge Thayer referred to the defendants as 'dagoes' and

Fig. 8.3   The Ku Klux Klan terrorized blacks in the southern states of America.

made no secret of his intention to 'get them good'. Both men were sentenced to be electrocuted, but were saved by a massive international campaign against the sentence. In the United States itself grave doubts were also expressed about the justice of the verdict. But Thayer obstinately refused to budge, and under Massachusetts law he had to move for a retrial. In 1924, after numerous appeals, Sacco and Vanzetti were sent to the electric chair.

The Red Scare came to an end in 1920 when the surviving 'Bolsheviks' were released from prison. It is interesting to note that in the 1920 Presidential election, the socialist Debs received a million votes – the Democrat Cox had only polled 9 million.

Extremism was still to show itself in other ways. In the southern States the 1920s were to mark the peak in popularity of the Ku Klux Klan (Fig. 8.3), a racist organization founded after the Civil War. Primarily aimed at blacks, the Klan also denounced Catholics, communists and Jews – anyone, in fact, who did not conform to the Klan's simplistic view of American society. Its supporters wore white gowns and hoods, and threatened its victims with fiery crosses. Its chiefs were called Kleagles and Goblins, and its leader Simmons adopted the style of Imperial Wizard. To many, the Klan seemed to be a bad joke, believing as it did that the Pope was in league with the Bolsheviks in Moscow. Others had reason to think differently, as the Klan burned their homes or murdered their relatives. The historian André Maurois believed that the Klan attracted weak minds with its childish ceremonial and uniforms.[1] But there were $4\frac{1}{2}$ million of them in 1924. Southern racism caused 130 lynchings in 1918–19, with fourteen victims burnt alive, and twenty-three days of race riots in Chicago destroyed 1000 black homes.

At an official level, the United States government was also concerned about the extent of foreign influence, and more especially about the level of immigration. In 1920 over 400,000 immigrants wanted to enter the United States, and to combat this, the Harding administration passed an immigration law in 1921. By its provisions, each European nation was given a fixed quota allowing in only 3 per cent of the number of its nationals present in the USA in 1910.

Whether such a measure was needed is debatable. It certainly made life more difficult for the governments of some of the poorer European states. At the time, the American government appeared to believe that it didn't need foreigners. This thinking also led to the adoption of a policy of tariff protection, which was, in the long run, extremely damaging.

Teapot Dome, 1923

Little else of consequence was attempted by the Harding administration, until its own excesses brought it down. In 1923 news of a major political scandal began to emerge centred on the unlikely location of Teapot Dome, Arizona, the site of a huge oil reserve. To obtain a concession there, the wealthy oil magnate Edward L. Doherty had given Harding's Secretary for the Interior, Albert Fall, $100,000. Attorney-General Daugherty was also implicated, for it was said that he had been ignoring known violations of the Prohibition law. The news of Teapot Dome is said to have killed Harding, who himself owed $180,000 to his Wall Street brokers at the beginning of 1923, and the succession fell upon Vice-President Calvin Coolidge.

'Silent Cal'

The new President was the opposite of Harding in almost every way. The nasty taste of Teapot Dome was cleared up by a commission of enquiry, and Fall and Daugherty went to gaol. The American people had confidence in the honesty of Mr Coolidge, and they were amused by his eccentricities. 'Silent Cal' was noted for sparing use of the tongue and every time he opened his mouth one wit commented 'a moth flew out'. His unhurried ways were also extended to running the federal government, for the new President was proud of the fact that every afternoon he could put his feet up on the desk and fall asleep. Coolidge turned the art of non-government into a science, and was, therefore, able to carry out silly practical jokes like pressing the bell on the White House gate to see all his staff come running!

As Governor of Massachusetts, Coolidge had a record of strike-breaking and his message for the unemployed was blunt: 'If a man is out of work, it is his own fault.' His administration was to be the golden age of private enterprise or *laissez-faire**. What the American people wanted, Coolidge remarked, was 'as little government as possible, at as low a cost as possible'. It was fortunate for him that his period in office coincided with a time of remarkable economic growth in the United States.

Prosperity

America's standard of living astonished Europeans, and by 1926 there were already 11,000 millionaires in the country.

For the first time, mass production made it possible for ordinary citizens to buy consumer goods which might earlier have been regarded as luxuries. The automobile industry, in particular, flourished, and by 1929 there were over 26 million privately-owned vehicles. Radio, too, proved to be a great invention, and so did a variety of household goods, such as refrigerators, vacuum cleaners and washing machines.

Banks and insurance companies were thriving and credit accounts became commonplace. No one foresaw the dangers in extensive use of hire-purchase facilities. There was a great deal of market sharing and price fixing in some sectors of the economy, a process which the Coolidge administration did nothing to impede. The President agreed with his Treasury Secretary Mellon that if taxation exceeded 25 per cent of income, 'it became confiscation'.

The danger in lowering taxes at any time was that, like unlimited credit facilities, it encouraged people to spend. When the means of buying increase faster than the production of things, prices must go up. Inflation was a characteristic of this period, and although many Americans prospered during the boom, others did not:

1. *The farmers.*   Between 1922–7, more than a million farmers were forced off the land. The people who fed the nation received less than 10 per cent of its income. After the First World War, farmers could not sell all the food they produced, and they also suffered from the restriction on immigration, which made labour scarce and pushed up wages.

2. *The blacks.* Although many black workers migrated to the industrial north, they were badly paid and forced to live in dismal urban slums. The open discrimination in the southern states was merely exchanged for the hidden discrimination of the north.

3. *Organized labour.* If the capitalist system, in which Coolidge believed, was to thrive, the trade unions had to be kept in their place. It became virtually impossible for unions to recruit during this time, and the Supreme Court ruled in favour of the infamous 'yellow dog' contracts. Workers could be made to sign a document promising that they would not join a union. In the 1920s the unions were unable to protect these workers, such as miners, whose employment was endangered by shifting economic fortunes.

To the acute observer, the most perturbing feature of the United States at this time was the vast inequality of wealth. In 1929 36,000 rich families had an income equal to that of the 12 million who earned less than $1,500 a year. In addition, 71 per cent of American families earned less than the $2,500 per annum needed to live decently.

The 1928 election

But on the surface everything in 'Silent Cal's' America seemed fine. In November 1924 Coolidge was elected President in his own right, comfortably defeating the Democrat John W. Davies, who was unable to make effective use of the Teapot Dome scandal.

In 1925 he announced to the world that the American people had 'reached a state of happiness rarely seen in the history of mankind'. There seemed no reason why this happy state should ever end, but in 1928 Coolidge bowed out of American politics. Instead, the Republicans chose the upright, if unimaginative, Herbert Hoover as their candidate. His opponent was Al Smith, the Governor of New York State, who suffered from two major weaknesses. He was a Catholic and a 'wet', and 1928 was a little too early for either to be acceptable. Smith was nicknamed 'Alcohol Smith' and cartoonists drew his cabinet with the Pope and twelve priests sitting in it. He campaigned on a reform programme, but the electorate remained apathetic, preferring Hoover's promise – ironic as it turned out – to banish poverty from the nation.

An age of discovery

Despite the dark clouds that hovered in the United States in 1929, this was, in many respects, an

Fig. 8.4   Charlie Chaplin.

exciting decade. From modest beginnings in Hollywood, California, the film industry became big business, and its stars, Chaplin, Pickford, Keaton and Valentino, became famous throughout the world. Most famous of all was Charlie Chaplin (Fig. 8.4), a Cockney entertainer, who moved to Hollywood and could earn the vast figure, particularly for those days, of $10,000 per week. When Charlie returned to Britain in 1921, the crowds at Waterloo Station carried him shoulder-high from the train! Alistair Cooke is almost certainly right to say: 'Throughout the 1920s and into the early 1930s, Chaplin was the most famous man on earth.'[2] He symbolized the fantasy world of Hollywood that was to cheer so many Americans in the dismal 1930s.

Radio also became a popular, well-established medium by the end of the decade. Many popular performers, like Bing Crosby and Bob Hope, were to start their show business careers in radio shows; yet the audience was still by modern standards curiously innocent. As late as 1938, thousands of Americans were driven into a state of panic by Orson Welles's radio production of H. G. Wells's *War of the Worlds*. Simulated news bulletins of a supposed Martian landing were accepted as the real thing!

Another great breakthrough came in the field of aviation. In 1927 Charles Lindbergh flew his 'Spirit of St. Louis' across the Atlantic, and became a national hero overnight. This pioneer work was to be followed by the establishment of viable commercial airways, like Pan-American, which was able to offer a rudimentary service over the Pacific by the 1930s.

Uncle Sam's backyard

In Chapter 3 we saw how anxious the American government was to recoup the loans made to the Allied governments in the 1914–18 war. Its other major foreign preoccupation was Latin America, 'Uncle Sam's backyard'. Since 1822, when President

Monroe had warned the European powers not to interfere there, this area, with all its turbulent politics, had been regarded as the special preserve of the United States.

Before the First World War, President Theodore Roosevelt spoke of the need to 'speak softly and carry a big stick' (Fig. 8.5), and to a considerable degree this motto describes US relations with the twenty Latin American republics in the twentieth century. It was certainly true of Cuba where the USA had helped to expel the Spanish in the war of 1899. In return, the Americans insisted on adding the so-called Platt Amendment to the Cuban Constitution which gave them 'the right to intervene in Cuba to secure the lives and property of Americans'. United States marines were in fact sent into the island between 1906–9 and again in 1917. They also went into the Central American Republic of Nicaragua in 1926, when a government was established there which Washington regarded as unacceptable.

Fig. 8.5   *The United States in central America.*

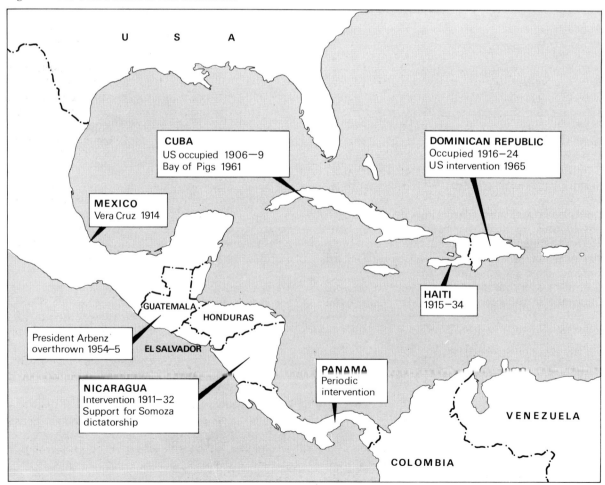

The assertive nature of American policy did much to account for the Latin American detestation of the 'gringo' (foreigner) and his interference in their affairs (although President Franklin D. Roosevelt did attempt to improve the relationship by means of his 'Good Neighbour' policy in the 1930s).

But this is only one of the themes which has run through the history of Latin America in this century.

Poverty is certainly another, and is largely the result of the uneven distribution of land throughout the subcontinent. At the end of the nineteenth century 80 per cent of all land in Latin America belonged to only 10 per cent of the people, and the domination of great landed families has remained a characteristic of its society until the present day. In Chile there were 600 great families, in Peru forty, in Argentina 2,000, but everywhere the picture was the same. The people who worked the land, the peons or peasants, remained in desperate ignorance and poverty throughout the period up to the Second World War.

Great inequalities of wealth were combined with a dangerous tendency to rely on one product to pay for the needs of the Latin American states. In Cuba, the commodity was sugar, and the island was badly hit by the great economic crisis that followed the Wall Street Crash of 1929. This was because American sugar beet growers demanded protective tariffs to keep foreign sugar out of their markets. The economy of Ecuador was equally dependent on the cocoa crop which was devastated in the 1920s by a plant disease called Monila. A switch was then made to banana growing, but over-dependence on this crop was to prove just as dangerous after the Second World War.

The case of Chile was somewhat different. The country's greatest asset was its nitrate deposits and between 1880–1920, production ran at a level of approximately 200,000 ton(ne)s per year. Demand was especially heavy during the First World War, because nitrates are needed to make explosives. Then, however, synthetic* nitrate production in Europe brought about a catastrophic collapse. There was a partial recovery in the 1930s, but the fortunate Chileans also had valuable copper deposits on which to rely.

Political developments

Latin America has long been famous for its rapid changes of government, and this was certainly a feature of its history in the interwar period. In Ecuador alone, during the so-called 'Waltz of the Presidencies' (1931–5), there were four different Presidents, but as we saw in Chapter 7 the subcontinent also had its own peculiar brand of dictatorship.

In Cuba, the economic crisis of 1929–33 brought down the dictator Machado, but others followed him. Real power, however, rested with the commander of the army, Fulgencio Batista, who managed to get himself elected President in 1940 (thus underlining the persistent and crucial role of the military in Latin American politics). The pattern elsewhere was similar, with Cerro and Benavides ruling in Peru, and General Carlos Ibáñez del Campo coming to power in Chile in 1927. But whereas the Peruvian dictators outlawed the reformist American Popular Revolutionary Alliance (APRA) and imprisoned its great leader Haya del Torre, Ibáñez appeared to be the people's man. He obtained a large working-class vote, and embarked on an ambitious public works programme, causing one contemporary historian to describe him as 'a forerunner of Perón'.[3] But, like Perón, he became increasingly authoritarian and was overthrown in 1931 (although like the Argentine dictator he returned to political power after 1945).

Chile therefore proved to be part of the general pattern, but it was also an exception, for in 1938 a Popular Front government was elected. The communist movement was strong in the country and it united with other Left-wing parties around the slogan 'Food, a roof, a shirt'. There was strong resentment in Chile's working class against both American exploitation of the copper deposits, and the rich absentee landowners who preferred life in the capital Santiago to their estates. The Popular Front government was to remain in power for some years, but the Right triumphed again in 1948 when the Communist Party was banned under a law 'for the defence of democracy'.

This then was the southern neighbour of the United States, an area of extremes of wealth and poverty and turbulent politics. The men in Washington could never be sure how the twenty Latin American republics would order their affairs, however much they might try to influence events themselves.

Keywords

democracy: the government of a country by the people, usually through representatives elected by them.

anarchist: literally meaning a believer in no government, but really someone wanting no strong central government.

laissez-faire: a system of government based on the idea of 'leaving things alone', especially in economic matters. As little government interference as possible is perhaps the best explanation for this French phrase.

synthetic: artificial substitute.

9 Capitalism in Crisis

In the last chapter you saw how, during the 1920s, the United States became a very prosperous society. You also saw that not all Americans shared in this general prosperity and how this situation was largely ignored by succeeding administrations.

Hoover's administration, 1929–33

The high point of the postwar boom came in the presidency of Herbert Hoover, who took over from President Coolidge in March 1929. The new President used slogans like a 'car in every garage' and 'a chicken in every pot', to underline his belief in America's God-given right to prosperity. In 1929 alone, $11,000 million in new securities went on to the stock market. Then suddenly disaster came with the collapse of the Wall Street stock market on 23 October 1929, Black Thursday. Shares changed hands at bewildering speed, firms went bankrupt, speculators killed themselves and the economic bonanza was over (Fig. 9.1).

The causes of the slump

Why did all this happen so quickly? The speed of the crash was in itself deceptive because the underlying causes went back much further. As with many historical problems, there has been a good deal of controversy about the more important causes, but the following are some of the relevant factors:
1. During the First World War, the United States had greatly increased its industrial capacity to provide both itself and its allies with munitions and other supplies. Farmers were also encouraged to grow more food. Technical inventions enabled American industry and agriculture to produce more. After the war, demand for all this extra food and supplies disappeared.
2. Industrialists forced up prices and profits to benefit themselves. At the same time, they held down wages so that the workers could not afford the new mass-produced consumer goods, e.g. cars, telephones, refrigerators, etc. Instead, the extra cash from production profits went into overspeculation in stocks and shares.
3. At the same time, the United States government followed a policy of tariff protection* to keep out cheap foreign goods. Foreign countries hit back by placing tariffs on American goods and making them more expensive to buy. The important point about this was that American domestic and foreign markets were growing *smaller* throughout the twenties.
4. An important point about any capitalist system is that it relies on credit, so that the amount of money in use at any one time is actually far greater than the amount of money in the banks at that time. Stability is maintained as long as everyone has faith in the banking system, but when this is lost, the whole system can suffer a serious crisis of confidence.

In October 1929 the American business community went through just such a crisis of confidence with near fatal consequences. The whole philosophy of self help and the American dream made it doubly difficult to face up to the severity of the problem and deal with it adequately.

One commentator has summed up the brittleness of the American position: 'The stock market crash swept away the stilts upon which stood this Brighton Pier of an economy.'[1]

What the slump meant

At the time of the Wall Street Crash, President Hoover asked for patience. He was confident that 1930 would see a 'turnround' of the economy. But the turnabout never came.

Between 1929–32 industrial capacity dropped by a half. Only 12 per cent of steel plants were still operating in 1932, and by 1933 the unemployment figure had reached 13 million. The American people, plunged into a dark night of despair, found their feelings epitomized in the song 'Buddy, can you spare a dime?'

Fig. 9.1   Car for sale. The Wall Street Crash ended the age of prosperity and heralded the depression.

Hoover's countermeasures

In this desperate crisis, Herbert Hoover was out of his depth. The President had a fine record in government, but he was paralysed by his own beliefs. *Laissez-faire* meant leaving the economy to run itself without government interference, but the circuits had apparently blown. All Hoover could do was apply a few traditional remedies.

Government aid was made available through a Reconstruction Finance Corporation to help state governments deal with unemployment. But it was only tinkering with the system. Budget balancing* was tried, in the hope that curbing federal spending might help. It was the opposite policy that was required. Even the old policy of tariff protection was reactivated in the Smoot–Hawley Act of 1930. An America needing larger markets found itself even more firmly bound behind a wall of tariffs.

Only on the long drawn out question of reparations did Hoover prove effective. In 1931 he declared a moratorium* on foreign debts for a year, in effect giving whole debtors a year extra to pay. Within a short period, in fact, the whole reparations system collapsed under the weight of its own futility and the international economic crisis.

Crisis around the world

The crisis that began on Wall Street in October 1929, rapidly affected the whole industrialized world. It was very much a case of 'when America catches a cold, Europe sneezes', and it was the weakest links in the chain that felt the strain first. In 1931 Austria's leading bank, the Credit Anstalt, was forced to close, and its failure was followed by that of other Austrian banking houses. Germany, so recently rescued from hyperinflation, immediately suffered from the cancellation of American loans on which she had relied since 1924. Unemployment shot up to 6 million and the dark shadow of National Socialism loomed over the political scene.

Britain

The second Labour government under Ramsay MacDonald had barely established itself in 1929 when it was confronted by the most severe crisis the country had known. Like the Hoover administration across the Atlantic, the Labour government had little idea of how to combat the depression. It tried budget cutting through the May Committee of 1931, which recommended that the salaries of teachers and civil servants be cut. This was too much for many Labour Cabinet ministers who resigned in protest, forcing MacDonald to call an election. His solution to the crisis was a coalition of all parties in a National government, but most of his colleagues rejected such a concept. The election gave the National government a huge majority, but Labour turned its back on MacDonald for the rest of his political career.

The new government proceeded with great caution. In September 1931 Britain went off the gold standard – the fixed value of the pound sterling against that of gold. This move was long overdue, as the value of the pound had been artificially high throughout the 1920s, making British exports far too expensive. In 1932 tariff protection was introduced. Duties of 10 per cent, and then 20 per cent, were placed on foreign goods, but imperial preference was applied – such duties were not imposed on goods from the Empire. A series of small measures, such as the Special Areas Act of 1934, were introduced to help the depressed areas of the north, but generally these had little effect. The setting up of the Unemployment Assistance Board (UAB) in the same year provided more effective aid to those out of work. But the poking and prying of the Means Test officials, whose job was to check the available means of the unemployed, embittered a whole generation of British workers.

Yet remarkably, although unemployment ran at a level of 3 million in 1933 (one worker in four was unemployed), not a single life was lost through political agitation. Neither the communists, nor Sir Oswald Mosley's British Union of Fascists could take advantage of a potentially revolutionary situation. The most lasting achievement of Mosley's blackshirted thugs was to see the enactment of the Public Order Act (1936) banning the use of political uniforms. In the long run, there were serious pointers in the thirties towards long-term economic weakness in Britain. In 1938 there was a £70 million deficit on the balance of payments*, and unemployment was still at one million as late as 1940.

The old traditional industries of the north-east and north-west were in decline, a trend that was overlooked in a prosperous south-east only marginally affected by the depression. The profound experience of the depression years separated north from south, and working class from middle class. Its special wretchedness was described by the novelist Walter Greenwood in *Love on the Dole*, an account of one unemployed man's life. 'He was standing there as motionless as a statue, cap neb pulled over his eyes, gaze fixed on pavement, hands in pockets, shoulders hunched, the bitter wind blowing his thin trousers tightly against his legs. Waste paper and dust blew about him in spirals, the papers making harsh sounds as they slid on the pavements.'[2]

France

The scale of the problem facing the French government was smaller and the effects of the slump less dramatic than in Britain, Germany and the United States. Initially, two things favoured the French:
1. The balance between industry and agriculture in the country. This meant that France was more dependent on domestic rather than foreign markets. So it was correspondingly less affected by the dramatic slowdown of international trade after 1929.
2. They had built up large reserves of gold before 1929.

For these reasons the effects of the depression were most serious in the political, rather than the economic area. On 6 February 1934 a concerted effort was made to overthrow the parliamentary system by the Fascist leagues. A night of rioting in Paris resulted in six deaths and many injured, and filled successive French governments with a fear of a Fascist *coup d'état*. In the short run, it also united the Left and brought it the electoral victory of 1936. The socialist Blum became Premier and introduced much needed social reforms, such as the right of workers to paid holidays. So great was the hatred of Blum's Popular Front government in Rightist circles that the fashionable slogan of the day was 'Better Hitler than Blum.'

If politics predominated, it would be wrong to ignore the economic crisis which also confronted France. While it is true that unemployment remained low, the French obsession with gold was ultimately a double-edged sword. Other countries abandoned the gold standard*, leaving French exports too expensive for the world market. It was the unlucky Blum who was eventually forced to devalue* the franc in 1937. The defeat of the Popular Front government was followed in 1938 by the introduction of new deflationary* policies by the Finance Minister Paul Reynaud.

Life in Nazi Germany

In Chapter 7 we saw how a Fascist regime was established in Germany in 1933. Like the other advanced countries, however, it had to deal with the side-effects of the slump, and it was this very slump which had helped to put Adolf Hitler in power.

Just as Mussolini regulated the work force through his corporate state, so Hitler, too, deprived the German workers of their rights. Free trade unions were abolished, and all workers had to join the Nazi Labour Front run by Robert Ley. Part of their wages went in contributions to the Labour Front, and they were forced to contribute to *Winterhilfe* (Winter Relief), a fund under Goebbel's control. It was supposed to help the homeless and destitute during the winter.

There is no evidence that Hitler was ever influenced by Keynesian ideas (see p. 76), but the methods used to revive the German economy were certainly similar:

1. *Public work schemes*, i.e. building roads, bridges, clearing swamps, etc., in fact, anything that would provide work. A famous by-product of this policy was the construction of the autobahn or motorways. Germany was the first European country to have such a system.
2. *Rearmament.* The appearance of armaments factories provided extra jobs.
3. *Conscription.* This was introduced in 1935, and many young men were called up. This took hundreds of thousands of unemployed men off the streets, and stimulated demand for goods.

To persuade the Germans to accept their loss of freedom, the Nazis also offered them what has been called 'bread and circuses'. Just as the old Roman emperors tried to please the mob by increasing the bread ration and throwing Christians to the lions, Hitler offered his workers holidays in the sun. Cheap holiday cruises to Majorca were part of this fairly transparent attempt to bribe the workers, as was the promise of a Volkswagen. Each worker was to pay into a fund which would entitle him to a 'People's Car', and Goering would build a special factory to produce them. But the workers never got their Volkswagens! Instead, the money was spent on armaments.

By August 1934 Hitler had made himself supreme master of Germany. No one dared challenge his authority, and his minion Joseph Goebbels, the Minister of Propaganda and Enlightenment, began the process of taking control of the hearts and minds of the German people.

It was a process carried out with the utmost efficiency. The books of anti-Nazi authors were burnt and the music of Jewish composers, like Mendelssohn, banned. Foreign films could not be shown, although we know that Hitler and Goebbels secretly admired Hollywood movies like *Gone With the Wind*! Film, radio and newspapers were used to seal off the German people from the outside world. The result of all this, the American journalist William Shirer wrote later, was 'to afflict the German people with radio programmes and motion pictures as inane and boring as were the contents of daily newspapers and periodicals'.[3]

How could this happen? This is not an easy question to answer, but remember that the older German had lost everything in the inflation of 1923–4. Then came the crash of 1929–32 and the mass unemployment that followed. Men of this generation were grateful to Hitler for giving them work. For the young, he was a romantic adventurer, leading the Reich to ever greater heights of glory.

The Hitler Youth

The Führer was only too aware of the need to win over German youth. 'This new Reich,' he boasted, 'will give its youth to no one.' It soon became clear what this meant. By 1936, all youth movements had been abolished except the Nazi Hitler Youth (Fig. 9.2), and children were taught only by reliable party members.

To a background of summer camps, cold showers and physical jerks, the children of Germany learnt to worship their Führer and accept his cranky racial theories. Girls had a special organization of their own, for at the age of fourteen, they joined the pompous-sounding League of German Maidens, to learn about the need to keep fit and become good wives and mothers.

The sinister side to all this was contained in the National Socialist *Little Song Book*, which contained the following verse:

> So stand the storm battalions
> Ready for the racial fight
> Only when the Jews lie bleeding
> Can we really be free.

Such an upbringing could only breed hatred and fanaticism. By 1945 members of the Hitler Youth were betraying their own parents to the authorities for criticizing their beloved Führer.

The police apparatus

The rigid control of the German population demanded extensive police powers, and the country was criss-crossed by a web of police authorities that did not always co-operate one with the other. There was the *Geheime Staats Polizei*, the secret state police, set up by Goering in 1933, and better known as the Gestapo. Then came Himmler's blackshirted SS, the brownshirts and Heydrich's *Sicherdienst* (SD) with its job of spying on all German citizens. The military had their own special intelligence service called the *Abwehr*, but in 1936, all police forces were placed under the control of the sinister Himmler. Even party members were not safe from the spying activities of such men whose job it was to make sure that 'the law and the Führer are one'.

Fig. 9.2 Hitler Youth salute their Führer.

The Jews

Adolf Hitler had nothing but contempt for religion, describing the Protestant Churches as 'insignificant little people who sweat with embarrassment when you talk to them'. A few Protestant clergymen, like Pastor Neimoller, opposed him, but his megalomania ended in the setting up of a Reich Church. The swastika and *Mein Kampf* were to replace the cross and the Bible in this negation of religion which was but one step away from the final horror.

However, Hitler's fanatical anti-Semitism was racial rather than religious, and realized itself in an attempt to dehumanize the whole Jewish race in Europe. In *Mein Kampf* he had written: 'Wherever I went I began to see Jews, and the more I saw, the more sharply they became distinguished in my eyes from the rest of humanity.'

Why did Adolf Hitler hate the Jews so much? This is a very difficult question to answer, but historians have made some suggestions:

1. Hitler, as a failed artist and scholar, may well have been jealous of the Jews who dominated Vienna's art life.

2. There was probably an element of sexual envy in his attitude because his book is full of references to innocent German maidens seduced by evil Jews.

3. In some real sense Hitler believed in a Jewish-Communist conspiracy, which had brought down Germany in 1918 and destroyed its economy. The Jews must, therefore, be repaid in kind.

This pattern of revenge was to emerge in the early 1930s (Fig. 9.3).

The Nuremberg Laws of 1935 These deprived the Jews of their German citizenship, and forced them to wear the Star of David. They had to use special shops, restaurants and bars. Only during the 1936 Berlin Olympic Games was the anti-Jewish propaganda toned down, but the arch Jew-baiter Streicher still warned the people that 'the sun will not shine again for the people of the earth until the last Jew has died'.

The Crystal Night Economic revenge was a special part of Hitler's strategy, because the Jews were famed (in popular myth) for their wealth. The murder of a German diplomat, von Rath, in Paris in November 1938 by the Jew Gryspan, provided a perfect opportunity.

An anti-Jewish campaign was carefully whipped up by Goebbels throughout Germany, and the reflected glass panes of broken shop windows in the snow gave the campaign its German name, the *Kristallnacht* or 'Night of the Crystals'. In Berlin alone, 191 synagogues were burnt and thirty-six Jews killed, while a further 20,000 were taken away to concentration camps. Their property was promptly confiscated by the state, thus setting an example for future Nazi pillaging.

You may wonder why foreign politicians did not protest against such atrocities. Some did, like American President Roosevelt who said that he 'could scarcely believe that such things could happen in the twentieth century'. Such comment from the 'Jew Roosevelt' was ignored by the Nazi leadership. They knew that the broad mass of the German people had little sympathy for the plight of the Jews. In fact, their sufferings were only just beginning, and Roosevelt had severe economic problems of his own to deal with in 1938 (see p. 76). His methods were to highlight the differences between the democratic and the totalitarian state in this time of economic crisis.

Italy

In Italy, too, the depression took its toll, if more slowly than for its industrialized neighbours. The American immigration laws of 1921 and 1924 had already closed off one traditional escape route for the poor southerner. Now Italian industries began to suffer from the protection policies of its trading partners. The Duce's appetite for foreign adventures was certainly increased by perilous economic conditions at home.

Eastern Europe

The little states of eastern Europe could not escape unscathed. In Czechoslovakia, the rundown of manufacturing industry caused unrest in the German-speaking Sudetenland and increased tensions in the new state.

The agricultural-based economies of Poland, Hungary and Romania were vulnerable to the harsh economic climate and easily pressurized by a powerful, re-emergent Germany.

Trade deals were made very favourable to the Third Reich, whereby German-manufactured goods were exchanged for foodstuffs. It was no accident that in these circumstances, unpleasant local versions of Fascism appeared, the Scythe Cross in Hungary and the Iron Guard in Romania.

Latin America

In the interwar period, the world economy was dominated by the United States and the countries of western Europe. Their difficulties were, therefore, reflected in the areas where they had economic influence.

In Latin America as a whole, exports to Europe fell by over a half between 1929–32. The flow of foreign

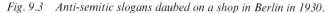

Fig. 9.3   Anti-semitic slogans daubed on a shop in Berlin in 1930.

capital, largely from the USA and Britain, dried up after 1930, a position worsened by growing competition from other areas of the world. Brazilian rubber, for example, was now in direct competition with British Malaya.

To protect themselves, the Latin American countries had to make individual agreements. Thus Argentina, alarmed by Britain's abandonment of free trade in 1931–2, sought agreement with Britain. Under the terms of the Roca–Runciman Pact of 1933, Argentina could continue her vital meat exports to Britain. In exchange, the British received preference in the Argentine market.

Generally though, the 1930s marked the end of the prosperity that Latin America had enjoyed after the First World War.

Africa

The African continent, at this time, was still, of course, under the control of the European colonial powers. But many African labourers lost their jobs in the backwash of the economic disaster and saw their standards of living suffer. The outstanding exception was South Africa, saved from recession by her control of the gold market. Economic strength in the Union was combined with a rising force of Afrikaner nationalism, largely unnoticed outside the country.

Australia

Elsewhere the tide of depression flowed on. A Labour government in Australia could not prevent a 30 per cent unemployment rate by 1933, and its tax cutting policies could not keep it in office. Left-wing attempts to use the machinery of capitalism to regulate the economy proved as ineffective as Right-wing attempts to do so.

The USSR

Ironically, the other major exception to the prevailing picture of economic collapse was the Soviet Union. Sealed off from the capitalist world by its ideology, the Soviet Union concentrated on its attempt to build up the socialist motherland. The story of this attempt will form the subject of the next chapter.

Roosevelt and the New Deal, 1932–6

On the opposite side of the world the United States,

the centre of the capitalist system, continued its battle with the economic crisis.

We have seen how Herbert Hoover was unable to put forward a really effective economic policy, and by the closing months of 1932, the President's popularity had sunk to a very low ebb. The shanty towns in which the unemployed lived were nicknamed Hoovervilles, and out-of-work army veterans marched on Washington. The 'Bonus Army' was driven out of Washington on Hoover's instructions, an unhappy sight that did little for Hoover's declining prestige. Millions of tramps or hobos roamed the country taking free rides on the railways. Their defiant slogans, including 'Hallelujah, I'm a bum', reflected both the desperation and the wasting energy of a generation of young Americans. In Los Angeles, the cutting off of electricity and gas supplies forced people to cook over wood fires, and in Pittsburgh, shop girls would work for as little as $3 a week. Savings disappeared, mortgages were stopped. On the farms, the recession forced families to move from Oklahoma (hence the name 'Okies') to California in the ceaseless search for work. There was too much cotton and too many pigs. The pigs were slaughtered and the cotton was ploughed under. The farmer's agony was movingly portrayed in John Steinbeck's novel, *The Grapes of Wrath*. The American people began to believe that prosperity would never return.

The 1932 election campaign

They could not know that relief lay just around the corner, although it came from an unlikely quarter. A man crippled by polio, from one of America's most aristocratic families, was to provide the leadership that the crisis required. His name was Franklin Delano Roosevelt (Fig. 9.4).

A relative of President Theodore Roosevelt, Franklin Roosevelt was a Democrat and a former candidate for the Vice-Presidency of the United States. From 1928–32 Roosevelt was Governor of New York State, one of the most important political posts in the USA. But he reached this position against the odds for a severe attack of poliomyelitis in the early 1920s had threatened to end his career in politics. Only his own determination and the encouragement of his wife Eleanor kept him going. This remarkable recovery brought FDR – as he came to be known – the Democratic nomination for the Presidency in 1932. In accepting it, Roosevelt used a memorable phrase: the American people, he promised, were going to have a 'New Deal'. Quite what this New Deal would mean, FDR did not specify, but this did not matter. By November 1932 the electorate was thoroughly disillusioned with Hoover and the Republican Party.

Fig. 9.4   Franklin D. Roosevelt.

In the Presidential election Hoover was routed, receiving only 15,700,000 votes to FDR's 22,800,000. For five months, however, Hoover remained in the White House as a lame duck President. In those days, the new President only took office in March. Hoover tried to get FDR to work with him against the depression but the President-Elect kept his cards close to his chest. He did not want the odium of association with the discredited Hoover. To many, the new President remained a figure of mystery; others, like the famous commentator H. L. Mencken, dismissed him as a nonentity.

The First 100 Days and after

On 4 March 1933, a cold blustery day, Franklin Roosevelt drove to his inauguration with a grim-faced Hoover. No one quite knew what to expect, but the effect of FDR's oratory was immediate.

'First of all,' he said, 'let me assert my firm belief that the only thing we have to fear is fear itself.' The President sensed that the crisis facing his administration was primarily one of confidence. The American man in the street wanted an assurance that Washington really cared about his plight and a promise of firm action.

Both these FDR provided. One of his earliest innovations was the 'fireside chat', a series of radio talks bringing him into direct contact with the people.

The contrast with the tight-lipped Hoover was clear to all.

More significantly, FDR initiated a great series of reforms to deal with the economic crisis. Many of them were passed by Congress during FDR's famous First 100 Days in the White House. The lights burned late in the White House as his brains trust, bright young people recruited from industry and the universities, worked on the legislative programme. Dozens of laws were enacted during FDR's first two Presidential terms, so we can only select some of the more important ones to study here, but even this limited selection of New Deal legislation should give an impression of the scale of change in the Roosevelt years.

Emergency Banking Act 1933

This provided many banks on the point of collapse with federal funds to keep them from failing.

Agricultural Adjustment Act (AAA) 1933

This Act paid farmers to reduce production, and tried to encourage the use of modern farming methods.

Homeowners Loan Corporation, 1933

Without the help of the Homeowners Loan Corporation many Americans would have been unable to pay their mortgages.

Civilian Conservation Corps (CCC), 1933

Tree planting and swamp clearance enabled many unemployed men to find work.

Works Progress Administration (WPA), 1935

As the CCC provided work in the countryside, so the WPA provided employment in road, school and hospital building.

Social Security Act 1935

This Act introduced old age pensions and provided federal funds for the handicapped.

National Industrial Recovery Act 1933

This set up the National Recovery Administration (NRA) which encouraged codes to fix wages, hours and prices. The symbol of the NRA was the Blue Eagle and any firms willing to co-operate were allowed to display this sign.

Wagner Act 1935

The National Labor Relations Act or the Wagner Act, as it became known, encouraged trade union membership and outlawed the notorious yellow dog contracts which had offered employment only on the promise of not joining a union.

The Tennesee Valley Authority (TVA)

An additional measure was perhaps the single most famous piece of New Deal legislation. It concerned the development of the Tennessee River Valley by a special authority set up by the federal government.

This spectacular achievement really represented action in four separate areas at once:

1. *Conservation.*   The Tennessee River was dammed to prevent it from periodically flooding the surrounding area.
2. *Employment.*   The scheme provided extra work for the unemployed.
3. *Modernization.*   The TVA provided hydro-electric power for the surrounding area.
4. *Federal enterprise.*   The TVA provides an excellent example of direct federal action involving the territory and population of seven states. In 1931 Hoover had vetoed Senator Norris's Bill to set up the TVA. FDR showed how federal power could be used in an effective and constructive way.

Prohibition Repealed, 1933

Early in his period of office, FDR did something else to cheer the American people by instructing Congress to repeal Prohibition. This was done by means of the Twentieth Amendment, and one of the most unsuccessful laws in history disappeared forever.

Opposition to the New Deal

Roosevelt's massive reform programme aroused considerable opposition in various parts of American society.

The Republicans

The Republican Party, which represented the wealthy and privileged, soon indicated its distaste for what it regarded as socialist policies. Such massive federal intervention in the economy flew in the face of American tradition. In 1935 former President Hoover sneered that only four letters of the alphabet were not being used in New Deal legislation. FDR was outraging all the economic orthodoxy to which the Republican Party clung.

The Supreme Court

FDR could defeat his Republican opponents at the polls, but the Supreme Court represented a far more doughty opposition. It was packed with old, conservative justices who viewed Roosevelt's progress with the gravest suspicion. In 1935 they ruled NRA to be unconstitutional in the famous 'sick chicken' case. The Court believed that the firm Schecter Brothers, which was accused of selling inferior chickens to its customers, was outside the jurisdiction of the federal government. In 1938 the Court went on to rule the AAA unconstitutional, forcing extensive changes in its structure. FDR hoped to replace the unsympathetic justices with men more amenable to his views, but he was unable to do this.

Kingfish and the Radio Priest

The New Deal also faced more eccentric, individual opposition. One of its most abrasive opponents was Huey 'Kingfish' Long, the Governor of Louisiana, a man who had rode to power on the votes of poor rural voters. Initially, Long had supported the New Deal, but he objected to federal attempts to make him accountable for expenditure. There were well publicized rows with Roosevelt, and ultimately Long refused to allow any New Deal programmes to operate inside his state. 'Ole Kingfish' had Presidential ambitions himself and he launched a 'Share Our Wealth' scheme. It was all rather vague, involving an attempt to redistribute national wealth and establish a minimum wage. 'Every man a king,' sang Long's supporters, but by now there were doubts. The state legislature was packed with Huey's supporters, and there were rumours of bribes and intimidation. The bubble finally burst in September 1935 when Huey Long was shot down by an embittered former supporter outside the Louisiana State House.

Even more bizarre was the career of Charles Coughlin, the 'Radio Priest'. Like Huey Long, Coughlin began as a supporter of FDR, coming to prominence as the result of a series of radio broadcasts.

'Modern capitalism,' Coughlin warned his audience, 'is not worth saving,' but his new found fame went to his head. Ignoring warnings from his Catholic superiors, Father Coughlin became more and more Right wing. He formed his own quasi-Fascist party, and took to referring to the New Deal as the 'Jew Deal'. After some years of Jew-baiting and increasingly wild language, Coughlin finally obeyed his bishop and became silent.

There were others, too, like Francis Townsend with his equally strange plans to use the economic power of the old, and Charles Lindbergh who lost the admiration of many by openly praising the Fascist dictatorships in Europe.

Even those disposed to take a favourable view of the Roosevelt administration had their doubts. Commenting on the allocation of $500 million to WPA boss Harry Hopkins for unemployment relief in 1935, the *Washington Post* said: 'The $500 million granted to Harry Hopkins for direct aid to the States will not last a month if Harry Hopkins goes on at the pace he set yesterday spending more than $5 million in his first two hours.'

Hopkins's answer to this was: 'I shall not last six months here, so I might as well do what I please!' Nevertheless, the press comment reflected an anxiety that the administration was moving too quickly, and losing touch with America's traditions. But the people were grateful, and they showed it. In the 1936 Presidential election, FDR defeated the Republican Alfred Landon by the wide margin of 28 million votes to 17 million. Only two states in the Union did not give the President a popular majority. The New Dealers had done enough to deserve a second chance.

Did the New Deal work?

In the short run, the answer must be yes because the initial New Deal legislation did raise living standards. Farmers' income for example rose from $2,285,000 at the end of 1932 to $2,993,000 by the end of 1933. It is also true that by 1936 the national income had risen by 25 per cent on the 1933 figure – although it was still $40 billion below that of 1929. Unemployment also showed a sharp downwards movement (Table 9.1).

Table 9.1 Unemployment in the USA, 1933–6

Year	No. of unemployed
1933	12,830,000
1934	11,340,000
1935	10,610,000
1936	9,030,000

But this was only one aspect of the legislation. In the countryside the programmes of crop destruction and the slaughter of livestock were unpopular. Neither did the attempt to reduce the amount of land under cultivation prove totally successful: smaller farmers and labourers just lost their livings altogether. Then came the natural disaster of the 'Dust Bowl' (Fig. 9.5) in the farm states of Kansas, Colorado and Oklahoma. Fierce storms blew away the top soil, ruining many farmers overnight and driving them westwards to seek employment.

Fig. 9.5 A farmer and his sons run for shelter during a dust storm.

Table 9.1 reveals that the New Deal did not solve the employment problem in the United States. Only rearmament and the coming of the Second World War could do that. In 1937 the administration performed a U-turn by cutting back expenditure on relief for the unemployed, but this had such disastrous effects that in the following year the programmes were reinstated.

There were some important gaps in the New Deal, too. No significant civil rights legislation was passed, so the black man was still being treated like a second-class citizen. Education was another neglected area, and the United States still had no proper health care provision fifty years after such a scheme had been started in Germany.

The significance of the New Deal

Despite this, the New Deal was still a tremendous dividing line in American history. Patrick O'Donovan believes that Roosevelt 'destroyed for ever the American Faith in the sanctity of non-interference'.[4] He certainly showed the American people that unfettered capitalism was not enough. Roosevelt himself went further; he believed that the preservation of democracy went hand-in-hand with economic security. In a radio broadcast in 1938, FDR examined the lesson of the depression years:

> We in America know that our democratic institutions can be preserved and made to work. . . . But in order to preserve them we need . . . to prove that the practical operation of democratic government is equal to the task of protecting the security of the people . . . The people of America are in agreement in defending their liberties at any cost, and the first line of the defense lies in the protection of economic security.

In 1937 and 1938 Roosevelt's dislike of Fascism was tempered by the existence of the Neutrality Acts forced on him by an isolationist Congress. But when the crisis came again in December 1941, the United States was on a sounder economic footing and able to act as 'the arsenal of democracy'.

The lesson of Wall Street

We saw earlier in this chapter that the Wall Street Crash in 1929 sparked off a truly international crisis. Its memory has continued to haunt the collective memories of the industrialized countries ever since. The experience also brought about some new thinking on the economic management of such crises.

Keynes

One man in particular, the British economist John Maynard Keynes, had taken in the lesson of 1931–2 as governments floundered in their attempts to raise tariffs and cut public spending. In 1936 Keynes published one of the most influential books of the twentieth century, *General Theory of Employment, Interest and Money*. In it, he put forward several ideas of startling unorthodoxy:

1. In an economic crisis, the government should not stand idly by, waiting for the economy to right itself. It should intervene in a big way, getting into debt if need be. Keynes called this principle 'deficit spending'.
2. The government should make work for the unemployed by starting public work schemes, such as road and bridge building. Once the workers were receiving wages again, they could use their earnings to get the economy moving.
3. Keynes said that even private firms should receive government subsidy* in times of economic hardship. They would be allowed to borrow government money at specially low rates of interest.

In reading about the New Deal you should be able to see that FDR was actually putting Keynesian ideas into operation, although there is no real evidence that he was influenced by the economist's book. In a different way, for quite different motives, Hitler was using Keynesian techniques in Germany.

More recent history has suggested that Keynesian methods cannot provide the whole answer to a severe slump, but his book revolutionized the theory of economic management. Fearful of a return to the dole queues of the 1930s, the governments of the industrialized countries would never, in the years after 1945, dare to revert to the old classic *laissez-faire* theory of the 1920s.

Keynes pointed the way to the mixed economy, which became so common after the Second World War, i.e. some state-owned industry and some private enterprise. For a long time, too, he underwrote a general commitment to the theory of full employment or jobs for all.

In 1919 Keynes had warned that the abuse of state power could ruin the economy of Germany. In 1936 he was able to show how state intervention could be an actual necessity.

Keywords

tariff protection: placing duties on goods from foreign countries.
budget balancing: when the government tries to

stop borrowing and runs the country so that money coming in equals money being spent.

moratorium: a pause or waiting period, particularly a legal authorization to delay payment of a debt.

balance of payments: the amount of goods and services a country sells abroad compared with the amount it buys from foreign countries.

gold standard: a monetary system in which the unit of currency is equivalent to a specific amount of gold. In theory, coins or paper notes can be changed into gold at the bank.

devalue: when a government deliberately reduces the value of its money compared to foreign currency, e.g. cutting the number of dollars to the pound sterling.

deflation: opposite of inflation. A decrease in the amount of money in circulation when, for example, the government makes money harder to borrow and reduces its own spending.

subsidy: financial help.

Questions

Extract 9.1

Part of an address made by a politician to the Commonwealth Club, San Francisco, in his first campaign for the Presidency, 23 September 1932

Every man has a right to life; and this means that he has also a right to make a comfortable living. He may by sloth or crime decline to exercise that right; but it may not be denied him. We have no actual famine or dearth; our industrial and agricultural mechanism can produce enough and to spare. Our government, formal and informal, political and economic, owes to everyone an avenue to possess himself of a portion of that plenty sufficient for his needs, through his own work.

1. Name the Democratic candidate who made this speech.   1
2. What famous phrase had this man used when he accepted the Democratic nomination for the Presidency?   2
3. What special factors in the USA at that time made it hard to earn a 'comfortable living'?   4
4. What former political position had the candidate held just before he became a Presidential candidate?   1
5. Who was his opponent in the election?   1
6. Give TWO examples of measures later passed to improve the 'industrial and agricultural mechanism'.   4
7. Give THREE examples of men or organizations who opposed the new policy outlined in the extract.   3
8. How successful were the measures introduced after the election campaign of 1932 in solving the ills of American society?   4

   ——

   20

10 Stalin's Russia

The struggle for power, 1922–4

In Chapter 5 we saw how Lenin steered the Soviet Union through some desperate times and established the communist regime in something like security. The last two years of his own life were clouded by ill health that ended with a second fatal stroke in 1924. It was obvious, therefore, from 1922 onwards, that Lenin's death was imminent, and the men around him became involved in a fierce struggle for power. All of them were members of the Politburo*. They were:

Trotsky, the Commissar for War;
Zinoviev, the Leningrad party boss and organizer of the Comintern;
Stalin, General Secretary of the party;
Kamenev, Moscow party boss.

Of these four men, Leon Trotsky was the most gifted and Lenin's most likely successor. He had created the Red Army, and was also a brilliant writer and thinker. On the other hand, Trotsky was a Jew, and he had not become a member of the Bolshevik Party until just before the revolution. His cleverness inspired envy, rather than admiration, and his control of the army aroused the fear that he might use it to establish himself in power. In Lenin's view, Trotsky had 'too far reaching a self confidence', but he also had strong reservations about his main rival, Joseph Stalin. In his political testament, published after his death in 1924, Lenin wrote: 'Stalin is too rude, and this defect, which is tolerable in the intercourse between us Communists, is intolerable in the person of the General Secretary.'

Stalin was a man of only average intellectual powers, but he was an extremely able organizer and was quietly working his supporters into important positions. Zinoviev and Kamenev (Fig. 10.1) were old colleagues of Lenin, but made the mistake of underestimating Stalin. They resented the influence that the newcomer Trotsky had established over their leader and failed to note the General Secretary's talent for backstairs intrigue. When Lenin died in 1924, these three men were to work together to destroy Trotsky and make it impossible for him to inherit Lenin's position and power.

Lenin's achievement

The latter's death robbed his party of a truly great leader and of one of the outstanding figures of the twentieth century. He had nursed the USSR through its most turbulent years, although it is doubtful if he would have approved of much that was to follow.

Fig. 10.1   Kamenev had been Commander-in-Chief of the Red Army 1919–24.

Stalin: 'man of steel'

When the leadership discussed Lenin's last will and testament, it was in an atmosphere of acute embarrassment. Both Trotsky and Stalin had to listen to their dead leader's criticisms. But the General Secretary was far better able to take advantage of the confused situation following Lenin's death.

He had been born Joseph Djugashvili on 21 December 1879, but later took the revolutionary name of Stalin, 'man of steel'. The young Joseph was intended for the priesthood, but he was thrown out of the seminary because of his political activities in Georgia where he grew up. A minor figure at the time of the 1917 Revolution, Stalin worked his way to the top of the Bolshevik Party, sharing the bad times and the good. He was in no way outstanding, as his biographer Isaac Deutscher says: 'What was striking in the General Secretary was that there was nothing striking about him. His almost impersonal personality seemed to be the ideal vehicle for the anonymous forces of class and party. His bearing seemed of the utmost modesty. . . . Himself taciturn, he was unsurpassed at the art of patiently listening to others.'[1] This patience was unusual among talkative, argumentative people like the Russians, and it was an attribute that proved most dangerous to his rivals. The silent, pipe-smoking Comrade Stalin did not seem to be a danger to anyone.

Trotsky's fall

Helped by Zinoviev and Kamenev, Stalin slowly eroded his rival's power base, using, for this purpose, an argument about the future development of the USSR. Trotsky talked of the need for 'permanent revolution', meaning that revolution in Russia must coincide with revolution in the other advanced countries. Lenin believed this too, as you have seen. Stalin realized that such talk was worrying for a tired generation of communists, and put forward his own doctrine entitled 'Socialism in One Country'. The emphasis, he said, should be placed upon building up the industrial and military strength of the USSR, at that time the only socialist country in the world. This had more appeal to party members, although the real difference between the two men was slight. Both believed in the need to spread communism from a strong base in Russia.

The important point was that Stalin deliberately exaggerated such differences. He accused Trotsky of being a 'panicmonger' and a 'pessimist', and as we have seen, Trotsky was not over popular with the rank and file. In January 1925 he resigned from his post as War Commissar, so giving up his most

powerful asset. This was followed by removal from the Politburo, expulsion from the party and, in 1929, exile from the Soviet Union altogether. Stalin's triumph was complete, but he was assisted by the curiously passive behaviour of his rival. Why did Leon Trotsky not fight back during those years? He, after all, was the man who had planned the Red Army's campaigns in the Civil War. This is a difficult question to answer, but the key to it seems to lie in Trotsky's absolute loyalty to the party. He himself said: 'The party in the last analysis is always right, because the party is the single historic instrument given to the proletariat for the solution of its fundamental problems'. As the party was always right, it could require a member to give up his offices and point out the error of his ways. It was strange that Trotsky identified the will of the party with that of Joseph Stalin. It did him little good. Wherever Trotsky went, to Turkey, France, or Mexico, Stalin's hatred pursued him. His children died in mysterious circumstances, and eventually in 1940, the Stalinist agent Mercador drove an ice-pick into the back of his skull. Trotsky's admirers have always believed that he would have proved a less brutal and more effective ruler of the Soviet Union. Obviously, we can only speculate about this but no one can doubt that his later years were a tragic waste of many talents.

Right versus Left

Before the discredited Trotsky had been sent into exile, Stalin had begun another campaign against Zinoviev and Kamenev. Like the struggle with Trotsky, it was to be fought on two levels, the personal and the political. Both men were senior to Stalin in terms of party experience, and both were advocates of a policy of rapid industrialization and collectivizing the farms. This meant ending the New Economic Policy (NEP), and because of the radical nature of their plans, Zinoviev and Kamenev were known as Left Bolsheviks. On the Right were Bukharin, Rykov and Tomsky, all veteran Bolsheviks who wished the NEP to continue indefinitely.

Industrialization, Bukharin believed, could proceed at 'a snail's pace'. Stalin, rather typically, was not openly associated with either group, although before 1928 his sympathies seemed to lie with the Right Bolsheviks. He used them as allies against Zinoviev and Kamenev, who were accused of holding unorthodox opinions and stripped of their important posts. Only then did they realize what sort of man they were dealing with. Stalin, whispered Kamenev, was like a new Genghis Khan*.

Stalin's rule ~~From~~

The Soviet economy

By 1928 his position as the new leader was established, but he immediately had to face another serious economic crisis. It was a repetition of the crisis of 1920–1 when the peasants were hoarding grain to force up prices and not releasing supplies to feed the big towns. The kulaks* or richer peasants were at the forefront of this action because they had grown prosperous under the NEP.

In this crisis, Stalin acted with almost reckless courage. It was clear that something radical had to be done, but no one was prepared for the pace of change that Stalin demanded which was far in excess of anything that Zinoviev and Kamenev had suggested.

The first Five-Year Plan, 1929–33

The USSR was to be developed in a series of Five-Year Plans and the NEP was to be abandoned forthwith. The first Five-Year Plan would concentrate on two main areas of development:

1. *Agriculture.* The emphasis was to be on collectivization and a great increase in production.
2. *Industrialization.* This was to concentrate on heavy industry, iron, steel, coal, etc.

Unfortunately, the production targets set by Stalin were totally unrealistic. When Bukharin, Rykov and Tomsky would not go along with the new radicalism, they, too, were discredited and removed from the Politburo. Stalin would listen to no one at this time. His policies at the beginning of the first Five-Year Plan have been described as 'a piece of prodigious insanity'[2] and a study of some figures would appear to bear this out.

In 1928 Russian production of pig-iron was only $3\frac{1}{2}$ million ton(ne)s. Stalin demanded an increase to 10 million ton(ne)s by the end of 1930. In fact, only in 1941 was the USSR approaching this figure.

While it is true that Stalin raised tractor production from 7,000 to 30,000 machines in 1929, the peasants could not drive them (Fig. 10.2)! The worst aspects of this strange blindness were to be seen in the countryside where Stalin insisted that all the peasants be forced on to large state-owned collective farms.

Fig. 10.2   This tractor symbolizes Stalin's attempt to modernize Soviet agriculture in the 1930s.

The smaller peasants objected to this less strongly than the kulaks who had gained most from the element of private enterprise allowed under the NEP.

Infuriated by their opposition, Stalin ordered his subordinates to 'smash the kulaks'. The result was tragedy. To avoid being forced into the collectives, the kulaks slaughtered their livestock and burnt their homes. Many were shot by the army and the secret police. Countless others went to labour camps in Siberia and elsewhere. We will never know how many millions perished in these years to satisfy Stalin's ambition.

Soviet agriculture paid a very heavy price for this bloodletting as Table 10.1 shows:

Table 10.1 Livestock in the Soviet Union in 1929 and 1933

thousands

Livestock	1929	1933
Horses	34,000	16,600
Cattle	65,000	30,000
Sheep and goats	135,000	100,000

Ultimately, even Stalin had to apply the brake, although once again he put the blame on others. In his article, 'Dizziness with Success', published in 1930, Stalin blamed overenthusiastic subordinates for pushing ahead too fast. The production targets were cut back considerably and some of them were met. By March 1930 55 per cent of the peasant population, that is, about 14½ million peasant households had been collectivized, and by 1936 the figure had reached 90 per cent. Similar progress was made on the industrial front once more modest targets were set. All of which suggests that the unparalleled haste of 1929–30 was a massive blunder on Stalin's part. Quite why Stalin insisted on such unrealistic production figures is unknown. Did he, as some have suggested, suffer a nervous breakdown under the strain of the crisis?

A more likely explanation is Stalin's awareness of Soviet vulnerability to an attack from the capitalist West. The following is part of a speech Stalin made in 1931:

> To slacken the pace would mean to lag behind; and those who lag behind are beaten. We do not want to be beaten. No we don't want to ...old ... Russia ... was ceaselessly beaten for her backwardness. She was beaten by the Mongol Khans, she was beaten by Turkish Beys, she was beaten by Swedish feudal lords, she was beaten by Polish-Lithuanian Pans, she was beaten by Japanese barons, she was beaten by all – for her backwardness.

To protect the Soviet heartland, Stalin believed that he must drag his countrymen into the twentieth century by the scruff of their necks. The plans took over the man and his sense of proportion.

The second Five-Year Plan, 1934–7

In his second Five-Year Plan, Stalin put greater stress on industrial expansion, and by 1938 the achievement in this sector was considerable (Table 10.2).

Table 10.2 Industrial expansion, 1913–38

ton(ne)s

Industry	1913	1929	1938
Coal	29,100,000	40,100,000	132,900,000
Iron ore	9,000,000	8,000,000	26,500,000
Pig-iron	4,200,000	4,000,000	14,600,000
Oil and gas	9,200,000	13,800,000	32,200,000

It can be attributed to four major causes:
1. foreign technicians, especially Americans, who provided valuable advice – some Soviet technicians were allowed to train abroad;
2. large-scale imports of engineering equipment and machine tools between 1929–33;
3. short-term credits, obtained abroad, combined with an export drive, concentrating on oil, grains, furs and timber;
4. the hard work and self-sacrifice of the Soviet people.

The American John Scott who worked on the construction of the showpiece steelworks at Magnitogorsk (Fig. 10.3), wrote later: 'Men froze, hun-

Fig. 10.3   Steel mills at Magnitorgorsk, 1932.

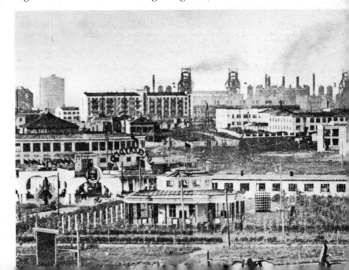

gered and suffered, but the construction work went on with a disregard for individuals and a mass heroism seldom paralleled in history.'[3]

Stalin knew how to utilize the enthusiasm of a generation of dedicated young communists. Those, like the hero Stahkanov, who exceeded production targets were suitably rewarded.

The third Five-Year Plan was interrupted by the German invasion in 1941, and changing international circumstances were reflected in the increased spending on armaments. Up to a third of the Soviet Gross National Product (GNP)* was being spent on defence.

The purges

In 1934 Sergei Kirov, the new party boss in Leningrad, was murdered in his office by an opposition communist. This simple event is generally accepted as the factor which sparked off the great series of show trials or purges between 1936–8.

The historian Robert Conquest has suggested that Stalin himself authorized the murder of Kirov because he feared his subordinate's rising popularity.[4] It was noted that at the party congress that year, Kirov had received more applause than Stalin did! The circumstances surrounding the Kirov murder were certainly odd. The assassin Nikolayev, for example, had been found by the police with a revolver, near Kirov's office shortly before the murder. Other people involved in the case also disappeared in mysterious circumstances.

Stalin's biographer Isaac Deutscher presents a more traditional, and from Stalin's viewpoint, more friendly explanation. The murder is seen not as Stalin's personal responsibility, but the trigger for the purges that were to follow.

'Stalin drew the conclusion that the time for quasi-liberal concessions was over. His victory over the opposition had been far from complete. He had only succeeded in driving discontent from the surface to the depths of political life. He would now strike deeper and harder.'[5] The real blame for Kirov's death was placed on the old Bolsheviks Zinoviev and Kamenev. But for two years Stalin played cat and mouse with the former allies of the 1920s. They had to confess to wrong thinking, but were allowed to remain free. Stalin, it appeared, was satisfied with the humiliation of his former rivals and Zinoviev's admission that the behaviour of the opposition had helped 'stimulate the degeneration of these criminals', i.e. the associates of Nikolayev.

The trial of the sixteen

The reprieve was to be short lived. In August 1936 Zinoviev, Kamenev and fourteen other leading communists were put on trial. Again foreign events may have played their part, for in March 1936, Adolf Hitler had sent his army into the demilitarized Rhineland. The looming Fascist menace may well have increased Stalin's insecurity. One thing was clear. The trial was a formality because the verdicts had been decided beforehand. The defendants were accused of a series of crimes, such as involvement in the Kirov murder and planning to 'wreck' the economy. They confessed their guilt publicly, and the notorious prosecutor Vyshinsky demanded that the court 'shoot the mad dogs'. The accused were then shot or given very long prison sentences.

The trial of the seventeen, January 1937

The destruction of the former Leftists was to be followed by another series of trials early in 1937. This time, the main defendants were Radek and Pyatakov. By way of variation they were also charged with conspiracy with Nazi Germany and Japan.

The trial of the twenty-one, March 1938

Finally it was the turn of the former Rightists, Bukharin and Rykov. Tomsky had already committed suicide. The remaining batch of prisoners also included People's Commissariat for Internal Affairs (NKVD – the new name for the secret police) chief Yagoda. He knew too much to be safe from Stalin's suspicion.

The removal of the old Bolsheviks did not satisfy Stalin's requirements. The purges were to reach right down to the bottom of the party structure. Of the members of the Central Committee of the Soviet Communist Party in 1934, 70 per cent were dead by 1938. Between 1934–8, 1½ million party members were purged.

The army purges, 1937–8

The army too was subjected to rigorous examination. The Commander-in-Chief Tuchachevsky, hero of the Civil War, was accused of planning a *coup* and shot. Three out of five Red Army marshals were purged and 40 per cent of the officer corps. The loss of all these experienced soldiers was to have grave effects on the performance of the Red Army in the early stages of the Second World War.

The psychology of the purges

Foreign observers were puzzled by the whole process of the purges, when famous communists like Zinoviev and Bukharin confessed in open court to a series of bizarre crimes. There were no outward signs of physical torture, yet the defendants showed a robot-like persistence in confessing what they had done. They did this in the full knowledge that it would not save them from execution.

We now have more information about what was happening behind the scenes at this time:

1. Stalin selected his victims very carefully for the show trials. They were, without exception, loyal communists willing to accept that their confessions would be in the interest of the party. Remember Trotsky's statement that the party was 'always right'.

2. A good deal of psychological torture was used by the NKVD. The most infamous technique used by them was called the 'conveyor belt'. A rota of interrogators would be used to exhaust the prisoner by keeping him awake at night and breaking down resistance. In the end, the prisoner would be so exhausted that he would be willing to sign anything.

3. Fear played an important part. To protect themselves, people denounced others in order to demonstrate their loyalty. No one knew when the midnight knock on the door might give warning of a visit by the secret police: 'Private loyalties and the restraints of civilized life were cast aside in a frantic attempt to avoid death or the camps.'[6]

This was a terrible time to be alive in the USSR; Stalin saw enemies everywhere. Even those who worked hard were suspect, as Stalin warned in a speech: 'The real saboteur must from time to time show evidence of success in his work, for that is the only way in which he can keep his job as a saboteur . . . We shall have to extirpate these persons, grind them down without stopping, without flagging, for they are the enemies of the working class, they are traitors to our homeland!'

Just what this meant to the ordinary Soviet citizen is demonstrated in the book *I Chose Freedom* by Victor Kravchenko:

> One morning, arriving at the plant, I found Brachko waiting for me. He was in a state of panic.
>
> 'Victor Andreyevitch,' he announced sadly, 'the Secretary of the City Committee, Comrade Filline, was arrested during the night.' Later that day Comrade Los called me. He could hardly repress a note of triumph.
>
> 'We'll have to put your case before the City Committee again,' he informed me gleefully. 'You see you were saved last time by Filline – an enemy of the people. Now we'll take care of you never fear!'
>
> My purgatory, which I had thought ended, was only beginning.[7]

Fig. 10.4   Lenin and Stalin.

Kravchenko was lucky. He survived the purges, and in 1944 defected while on a visit to the United States. Millions of others were not so fortunate.

The cult of the personality

Hand in hand with the terror of the purges went a deliberately inspired campaign of leader worship. This is often described as the cult of the personality. It meant simply that everything good in Soviet society was the work of Comrade Stalin. Pictures of Lenin always showed Stalin at his side (Fig. 10.4), and when the new history of the Soviet Communist Party appeared in 1938, his role in the Revolution was played up. All previous textbooks were withdrawn. This set the pattern throughout Stalinist Russia. Scientists were encouraged because their work could not reflect unfavourably on the regime. Some, like the famous physicist Kapitsa, were allowed to do research work abroad – he went to Cambridge to work with the famous British scientist Rutherford. Novelists, poets and historians fared less well. A few, like Maxim Gorky, seemed prepared to accept the new regime and its doctrine of 'Socialist Realism'.

This meant writing in favourable terms about contemporary Soviet life. Others could not make such a compromise and remained silent during these years. They included the novelist Boris Pasternak, the author of *Doctor Zhivago*.

A third group could not remain silent and tried to criticize the regime. One of these was the poet Mandelstam, who was sent to a labour camp in 1938 and never seen alive again. The banality* of official propaganda was scathingly described by the exiled Trotsky: 'Stalin, like Gogol's* hero is collecting dead souls for lack of living ones.'

In these circumstances, it is not surprising that little work of artistic merit survived. One of the rare exceptions was Sholokhov's *And Quiet Flows the Don*, which surprisingly escaped the censor. Even composers like Prokofiev and Shostakovich were not safe from interference. They were told to compose music that would be suitable for peasants to listen to while they were working in the fields!

Stalin's achievement

It is difficult to reach a clear-cut judgement on Stalin's career up to 1939 because of the monstrous background of the purges and the collectivization programme of 1929–30. He had made the USSR a great industrial power, but at a terrible price in human suffering. His own position as leader was unchallenged because all the men on the Politburo, Molotov, Beria, Khrushchev and Zhdanov were his

creatures. They were there because Stalin had liquidated a whole generation of party workers who were judged to be a danger to his own position. It is interesting to note the subsequent verdict on this period of Stalin's henchman Nikita Khrushchev: 'Stalin fought barbarism with barbarism but he was a great man.' His defence must rest on the recognition that he transformed Russia from being a country of wooden ploughs and famine to one of tractors and steel mills. Critics of Stalinism will always argue that the price paid for this was unacceptable. They will also say with justice that Stalin's Russia was a bleak totalitarian society that had much in common with the Nazi Germany you read about in Chapter 7.

Keywords

Politburo: the small group of communists who run the USSR (including the General Secretary and the Prime Minister).

Genghis Khan: a Mongol emperor in the fourteenth century.

kulak: the Russian word for a fist, used to describe the richer peasantry.

Gross National Product: the amount of wealth produced by any one country in a year.

banality: boring or pointless.

Gogol: a nineteenth-century Russian novelist who had written about peasant life in his book *Dead Souls*.

11 The Drift to War, 1931-9

The dragon strikes

The Japanese were not satisfied with their gains from the First World War and strongly objected to the restraints imposed on them by the Washington Naval Treaty of 1922. Chapter 9 described the side effects of the serious economic depression which struck the USA in 1929. Japan, too, was a victim of this crisis because the world-wide market for its cheaply produced goods contracted overnight.

Strike north or strike south?

The Japanese army was in a good position to take advantage of the crisis, by recruiting workers from depressed industrial areas. The generals also thought that the Japanese needed more living space, and they looked enviously at weak and backward China, especially at the province of Manchuria. The depression gave more force to the arguments of the soldiers, although Emperor Hirohito was not totally convinced. The navy preferred a strike south policy, which meant attacking the rich colonies of Britain, France and Holland in South-East Asia. But in 1931 the Chinese option seemed safer.

The Mukden Incident, September 1931

Whether Emperor Hirohito and his government would have given official permission to move against China is uncertain because the army took matters into its own hands. A bomb exploded on the Japanese-owned railway line outside Mukden. A section of the Japanese army stationed in Kwantung was responsible for this, but the Chinese were deliberately accused of responsibility. This gave the Japanese army the excuse to invade Manchuria without waiting for permission from the Japanese government in Tokyo. When Foreign Minister Shidehara heard the news, he is said to have turned ashen grey. At the League of Nations headquarters in Geneva, the Japanese delegate blamed 'military hotheads' for what had happened in Manchuria, but the troops were not recalled. The League replied by demanding Japanese withdrawal from the province, and this inflamed public opinion so much that the Imperial government could not impose its authority on the Kwantung army.

The Lytton Report

From the end of September 1931, the situation worsened. World opinion condemned Japan as the aggressor, but nothing was done to punish the Japanese. In fact, Japanese behaviour became even more brazen, and when China imposed an economic boycott, their marines were sent to Shanghai. Only Anglo–American intervention prevented further fighting between the two sides.

Then, in 1932, the League sent an enquiry team to Manchuria under the British peer Lord Lytton. Its 400-page report was issued in September 1932, and Japanese excuses were swept aside. Lytton concluded: 'Without declaration of war, a large area of what was indisputably Chinese territory has been forcibly seized and occupied by the armed forces of Japan.' Japan was now an outcast nation in the eyes of the world. But it retained the spoils of war and consolidated its position in Manchuria. The province was given the Japanese name of Manchukuo, an indication that their troops were there to stay (Fig. 11.1). An additional blow to Chinese pride was the placing of the wretched Henry Pu Yi, last of the Manchu (see p. 44), on the throne of the puppet state.

The importance of the Manchurian crisis

On the surface the Manchurian crisis may appear to have been little more than a localized squabble, but it was to cast a long shadow over contemporary world history:

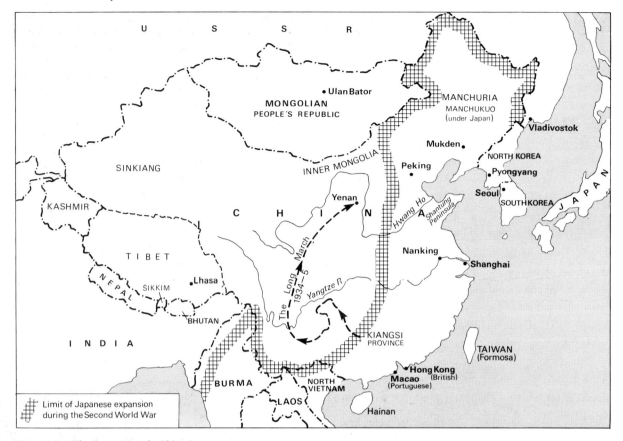

Fig. 11.1   The Long March, 1934–5.

1. *Inside Japan.*   The relative ease with which the province had been seized encouraged the sabre-rattling Japanese generals and their expansionist plans. It is difficult to argue with success, and in 1937 the army went on to attack the rest of China as well. Extreme nationalist organizations, like the Black Dragon Society, increased in popularity.

2. *The crisis was a disaster for the League.*   In the 1920s it had dealt effectively with disputes between minor powers, but in 1931–2, its inability to deal with the illegal behaviour of a great power was demonstrated to all.

3. *The success of Japan's forceful methods encouraged other black sheep in the international system.*   The 1930s were to become, in the words of the poet W. H. Auden, 'a low dishonest decade' as a result.

4. *The Manchurian episode strengthened isolationist feeling in the USA.*   When Secretary of State Henry Stimson sent out a diplomatic note on 7 January 1932 warning that the Sino–Japanese war infringed the Kellogg–Briand Pact*, it aroused little interest.

The drift towards world war had, therefore, begun with a vengeance; this much, at least, became clear to perceptive observers of the world scene.

Chiang, Mao and the Sino–Japanese War, 1930–38

The Chinese cause was not to be strengthened by the continual bickering between the communists and the Nationalist government. The communist bases were centred in the province of Kiangsi and between 1930–34, five campaigns of encirclement were launched against them by the Nationalist armies. By 1934 the situation was so difficult for the communists that they were forced to break out of the province of Kiangsi and march northwards. So began the epic 386-day 'Long March' to Yenan, the capital of Shensi province (Fig. 11.1). One hundred thousand began the journey in 1934 but only 30,000 were to survive. Night marches, river crossings and countless actions against Chiang's men meant that the surviving communists did not reach Yenan until 1936.

The march went down into history as the great epic achievement of the Chinese Communist Party, and established Mao as the leader of his party. Even he paid a price for the struggle, for in 1933 he had lost his wife Yang K'ai-hui and he composed this poem about her death:

I lost my proud poplar, and you your willow,
Poplar and willow soar lightly to the heavens of
heavens
Wu Kang* asked what he has to offer,
Presents them respectfully with cassia wine.
The lonely goddess in the moon spreads her ample
sleeves
To dance for these faithful souls in the endless sky
Of a sudden comes word of the tiger's defeat on earth,
And they break into tears of torrential rain.

The 'tiger' in Mao's life was Chiang Kai-shek, and
until their quarrel was settled, China was the helpless
victim of Japanese aggression. A freak of fortune was
to deliver the Nationalist leader into communist
hands at the end of 1936 as he travelled to the city of
Sian, anxious to talk to the former Manchurian war-
lord, Chiang Hsüeh-liang. If he hoped for a common
front against the communists, he was to be sadly
disappointed, for Chiang Hsüeh-liang promptly
placed him under arrest. Chou En-lai arrived to
represent the communists, and Chiang Kai-shek was
forced to form a common front against the Japanese,
something he should have done several years previously. The Sian meeting was to break off official
hostilities between Mao and Chiang Kai-shek until
1945, and it came not a moment too soon. In the
following year, 1937, Japan claimed that in the
Marco Polo Bridge Incident, its troops had been fired
on by the Chinese. This was used as an excuse to start
an all-out attack on mainland China, during which
Chiang Kai-shek's men left the communists to do the
brunt of the fighting. By the end of 1938, the great
cities of China, Shanghai, Peking, Nanking and
Canton, had all fallen into Japanese hands (Fig.
11.2). Meanwhile the nominal head of the Chinese
state had been forced to retreat to Chungking in the
interior.

Hitler's foreign policy: the early years

From his earliest years, Hitler had certain basic
beliefs about Germany's future. These had been put
forward in *Mein Kampf*. They were:
1. *the need to obtain* Lebensraum *or living space for
Germany in the east*. In his book Hitler wrote of

Fig. 11.2   Japanese troops seize Shanghai.

Russia: 'This colossal empire in the east is ripe for dissolution.'

The destruction of the USSR would also mean the end of Bolshevism, another of Hitler's great hates. He believed that there was a 'world-wide Jewish Bolshevik conspiracy' centred on Moscow, and the object of his life was to destroy these two evils. In the Führer's strange twilight world any methods were justified, and the people in it merely pawns. The inhabitants of the eastern lands (Russia, Poland, Czechoslovakia and Yugoslavia) were *untermenschen* or sub-human and could be used as slave labour in Hitler's 'New Order'. In his eyes, the German people were the *Herrenvolk* (master race) who were destined to rule these Slav peoples.

2. *the creation of a 'Greater Germany'*.   For centuries Germans had dreamt of a greater German empire in which all their people were brought together. In 1871 Germany became a united country, but it did so without the German-speaking Austrians inside its frontier – it is important to remember that Hitler was an Austrian who grew up in the old Habsburg Empire.

The Treaty of Versailles made matters worse, as we have seen, for Germans lived in the Polish Corridor or under the League in Danzig and the Saar. To Hitler, this was an outrage, and it strengthened his ambition to bring all the German minorities in Europe inside the frontiers of the Third Reich. Hitler believed that a nation of 80 million people would be able to dominate Europe.

You may note here a similarity with the Japanese war-lords, both they and Hitler had nothing but contempt for the lives and liberties of other races.

3. *the destruction of Versailles*.   Hitler hated the Versailles *diktat* and he realized how 'each of the points of that treaty could be branded in the hearts and minds of the German people'. Versailles would stop rearmament and hold down his brother Germans, but Hitler cared nothing for the colonial clauses. The colonies were only a bargaining counter, as far as he was concerned, to be used to embarrass Britain and France. In most respects the German dictator was a curiously old-fashioned figure in his obsession with Europe. He was, like his friend Benito Mussolini, a revisionist, but only so that the end of Versailles would allow him to continue his drive to the east. It is, in fact, possible to see Fascism as the death agony of the old European imperialism of the nineteenth century, a system in which only the techniques had changed. Can we compare Kaiser William's 'sabre rattling' with Hitler's mass rallies?

Do not, though, be deceived by this old-fashioned side to Hitler's character. Inside the romantic nationalist, there lurked a clever and ruthless statesman. All the assets that made Hitler a dynamic political leader also made him a most effective statesman. He had summed up his philosophy in *Mein Kampf* in 1924: 'When you lie, tell big lies . . . the grossly impudent lie always leaves traces behind it, even after it has been nailed down.' One of Hitler's biggest 'lies', which took several years to be 'nailed down', was that he was a peaceloving leader who wanted nothing more than justice for his country. It was one of his greatest propaganda triumphs, for it was exactly what the other side wanted to hear. No one in Britain and France could believe (until it was too late) that anyone would be insane enough to risk a repetition of the Great War.

The years of waiting, 1933–5

To begin with, Hitler moved carefully. He knew better than anyone that Germany was too weak to openly challenge its opponents. Instead he followed a policy of carrot and stick – promises of peaceful intentions in his famous peace speeches, combined with flagrant breaches of the Versailles peace settlement. It worked well because the other side became confused by Hitler's skilful footwork.

The pattern began to emerge very soon after Hitler came to power in 1933.

Germany leaves the League, October 1933

For years, the disarmament conference at Geneva had dragged on without much hope of success. Then Hitler dramatically announced that Germany had lost patience and would not disarm unless countries like France did so. In effect, the Führer argued, the Versailles Treaty had disarmed Germany and he could not continue under such 'an intolerable humiliation'. The German people agreed with him and showed it in a plebiscite. Germany walked out of the disarmament conference and the League. He was canny enough to know that Geneva was unlikely to impose economic sanctions against him.

The Polish–German Non-Aggression Pact, 1934

Shortly afterwards, Hitler made an even more surprising move, designed to quieten doubts about his long-term intentions. In January 1934 he announced that Germany and Poland had signed a non-aggression pact, a clever ploy because no one expected an agreement between these two countries. They promised not to attack each other for a ten-year period, and this seemed to confirm Hitler's claim to be a peaceloving statesman.

The other important point about the Polish–German agreement was that it was the first example of Hitler's one-by-one or bi-lateral tactics. He liked to make such agreements because they divided his enemies and broke up their alliances.

Bloodbath in Vienna, July 1934

It was not to be long, however, before Nazism showed its uglier side outside Germany, and it did so in Hitler's homeland Austria. In that country, another Nazi Party had been formed with the firm intention of seizing power from the Austrian Chancellor Dollfuss. Dollfuss himself was never a democrat, but that did not save him from a brutal end, as he was shot in his office by Nazis and left to bleed to death. This murder on 25 July 1934 infuriated Mussolini who saw himself as the protector of Austrian independence. He was particularly angry because Frau Dollfuss and her children were staying with him at the time. After describing the Führer as a 'horrible sexual degenerate, a dangerous fool', Mussolini rushed troops to the Brenner Pass*. This was a clear warning that German interference in Austria would not be tolerated, and Britain and France supported Mussolini's stance. Hitler, for once, was forced to back down, and had to hand over the Austrian Nazis responsible for the Dollfuss murder who had fled to Germany.

At this time, German–Italian relations were very bad, and an earlier meeting between the Duce and Hitler in June 1934 had been a disaster. Hitler cut a poor figure in his civilian clothes, and seemed quite overawed by the occasion. He looked, said a French journalist, like 'a little plumber'.

Stresa, 1935

His humiliation was highlighted in April 1935 when at Stresa in northern Italy, Mussolini agreed to consult Britain and France if Hitler were to interfere in Austrian affairs again. The irony was that Hitler probably did not authorize the Dollfuss murder!

The Anglo–German Naval Treaty, 1935

The apparent unity at Stresa was to be surprisingly destroyed by the British, one of the two great powers that had a vested interest in preserving the *status quo**. On 18 June 1935 the British government agreed to accept German proposals for a naval agreement, which stated that:
1. Germany could build a surface fleet equivalent to 35 per cent of Royal Navy strength.
2. the German submarine fleet could be brought up to 45 per cent of Royal Navy numbers. This British move had serious results because it was a major revision of Versailles made without consulting Britain's ally France. Hitler was delighted and described 18 June as 'the happiest day of my life'. He had always stressed the need for friendship with Britain to avoid the two-front war which had faced Germany in 1914. British motives were more complicated, and you will be able to look into them more closely later in this chapter.

Hitler introduces conscription, March 1935

The effect of the Anglo–German Naval Treaty was doubly serious in that it followed another breach of Versailles in March 1935. In that month, Hitler had announced the introduction of conscription and a peacetime army of 300,000 men. Some days earlier he had also disclosed the existence of the German air force or *Luftwaffe*. Both these acts broke the peace treaty, although Germany had, in fact, been secretly rearming since the 1920s. Neither Britain nor France took action against Hitler, and he was starting to build up a dangerous momentum.

The Ethiopian Crisis, 1935–6

For the moment though the spotlight moves away from Hitler to his fellow dictator, Mussolini, who had ambitions of his own. These centred on one of the only two independent countries in Africa in the 1930s, the old kingdom of Ethiopia: the other was Liberia. The Duce had three reasons for his interest:
1. *Historical.* He wanted to avenge the Italian defeat at Adowa in 1896, at the hands of Ethiopian tribesmen. Fascist pride could not stomach such a defeat.
2. *Military.* To demonstrate the armed strength of the new Italy.
3. *Domestic.* The world-wide depression was starting to have an effect in Italy, and the regime was becoming unpopular. Mussolini saw a chance for some cheap glory, and knew that war would be popular because many Italians felt they had been cheated at the peace conference.

The attitude of the other powers

Mussolini did not expect much trouble from Britain and France, which already had large colonial empires. But it is clear that he misunderstood likely British reaction after the talks at Stresa. In the wings was Nazi Germany, hoping to profit from any disputes between the other three powers.

Mussolini attacks, October 1935

Having convinced himself that no one would object to his plans, the Duce launched his invasion in the autumn of 1935, following a frontier incident at Wal Wal. The Italians were faced by badly armed tribesmen and expected an easy victory, but things did not quite go according to plan. The Ethiopians resisted stoutly, but more important was British public opinion, which saw the whole war as an unpleasant example of bullying. Their sympathies were also aroused by the appearance of Emperor Haile Selassie at the League Council and the news that the Italians were using gas and dumdum bullets*. But the British government wanted Italy's friendship, and Prime Minister Baldwin and his Foreign Secretary Hoare looked urgently for a compromise.

The Hoare–Laval Pact, October 1935

This search brought the British government into a most embarrassing situation over talks between Hoare and Laval, his French opposite number. In rather confused circumstances in Paris the two men made a deal that would have given Mussolini two-thirds of Ethiopia. The Duce agreed the terms, but unfortunately they were leaked to the press by some unknown party, and there was great anger in Britain. Baldwin was forced to sack Hoare.

Mussolini felt he had been tricked, and was even more outraged when Britain asked the League to apply oil sanctions against him. The French refused to agree because they saw Hitler as a much greater danger, and the plan had to be dropped. In the end, no action was taken against Italy and by May 1936, the conquest of Ethiopia was completed. The Emperor Haile Selassie went into exile in England.

The effects of the Ethiopian war were important:
1. It pushed the two Fascist dictators closer together as Hitler had said nothing about Mussolini's behaviour.
2. Ethiopia became part of Italy's African Empire.
3. The League had failed to stop Mussolini's aggression.
4. The war had, Elizabeth Wiskemann tell us, 'split the Stresa front' and freed Hitler from the fear of encirclement.[1]

Never again would the Duce be a friend of the Western democracies.

The Rome–Berlin Axis, November 1936

His new ally Adolf Hitler agreed with Mussolini on a general understanding between the two countries – although there was no military agreement as yet. This was called the Rome–Berlin Axis because the agreement spoke of 'an axis around which can revolve all those European states with a will to collaboration and peace'. This explains the references you will see to the Axis powers during the Second World War.

The Spanish ulcer, 1936–9

One thing Germany and Italy already had in common was their involvement in Spain, where a civil war had broken out in July 1936. It proved just as difficult to end as the war in the nineteenth century that caused Napoleon Bonaparte to complain of his 'Spanish ulcer'.

The background

Spain in the 1930s was a largely forgotten land that had lost its once great empire. It had a monarch, Alfonso XIII, but in the eyes of many Spaniards, he and the great landowners stood for inequality and repression. Table 11.1 helps explain this.

In 1931 Alfonso XIII was overthrown and replaced by a Republic, but matters did not rest there. In 1936 the elections were won by the Popular Front alliance of Communists, Socialists and Anarchists, who planned to introduce radical land reforms. They never got the opportunity because the same forces that had supported Fascism elsewhere now decided to overthrow the Republic. The Catholic Church, the landowners and the small Spanish Fascist Party (the Falange) all supported a revolt of Right-wing army generals led by General Francisco Franco. The rebellion began in July 1936, and before it succeeded, a million Spaniards were dead. To a considerable extent, it was a 'war between European Fascism and anti-Fascism', but still essentially a Spanish struggle. On the one side were the forces of the Popular Front, supported by the Catalans and the Basques (Fig. 11.3). Both these groups hoped that a Republican victory would mean more self-government for them. Against them was the regular army and all the forces of rich, conservative Spain. To them, the strikes, the church burnings and the chaos of the Republican years were an excuse for a return to the repression of the past. Both sides had foreign help, but the scales

Table 11.1 Distribution of land in Spain in the 1930s.

Category	Number	Percentage of total land
Large landowners	50,000	51.5
Richer peasants	700,000	35.2
Small peasant farmers	1,000,000	11.1
Poor peasants	1,250,000	2.2
Agricultural labourers	2,000,000	–
Total	5,000,000	100

Fig. 11.3   Spain in 1937.

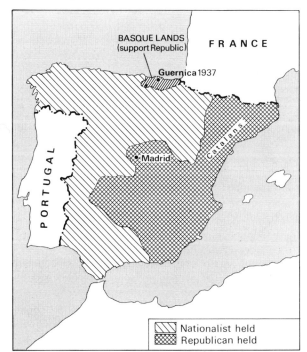

were heavily weighted in favour of the Nationalists (as Franco's supporters came to be called) (Fig. 11.4). Italy and Germany provided a great deal of military assistance to Franco, while the Republic had to rely on arms from distant Soviet Russia. Britain and France followed a rather feeble policy of non-intervention although there was striking evidence of Fascist involvement on Franco's side. In the circumstances there was only one possible result, even though Spain was the great cause for a generation of European Leftists. Welsh coal miners, Italian communists and French socialists, all fought and died for the Republic in the famous International Brigades. But the Brigades were pulled out before the end of the war, and Stalin also stopped sending aid. He was more worried about Hitler's intentions than saving the Republic.

By March 1939 the last Republican armies had been defeated, and Spain became a military dictatorship under Franco. His victory was followed by a savage purge of Republican supporters.

Fig. 11.4   *Nationalist soldiers capture Republican stronghold.*

The results of the Spanish Civil War

The Nationalist victory meant that Spain was to suffer under the dead hand of the dictator's rule until 1975. But hopes that Franco would join a Fascist bloc in the Mediterranean were to be disappointed, despite all Hitler's attempts to woo him. The Führer became so frustrated on one occasion, that he said he would prefer 'to have several teeth extracted' rather than repeat the experience. Franco remained cautiously neutral throughout the Second World War.

Nevertheless, the war in Spain did have other important consequences. The drain on Mussolini's resources – about one-third of his army fought for Franco – was to make him more dependent on Nazi Germany, and both the Fascist powers found in Spain a 'training ground' for the Second World War (the destruction of the Basque town of Guernica by German aircraft in 1937 provides a notorious example). The anti-Fascist powers, by contrast, gained little by their half-hearted support for the defeated republic.

Appeasement and what it meant

This section of the chapter deals with the reasons why the British and French attempted to appease* Hitler and Mussolini. This meant trying to reach agreement by negotiation, avoiding the use of force.

Britain

For a long time, it was fashionable to believe that Britain's appeasement policy was conducted by cowardly, short-sighted old men. This was not true. From as early as 1933, the British government knew quite a lot about National Socialism because of warnings from their Ambassador, Sir Horace Rumbold. Appeasement, then, was not based on ignorance. Neither was it the result of any sympathy for Fascist principles. There *were* people in Britain who admired Hitler and Mussolini, but Baldwin and Chamberlain were not among them.

Baldwin gave up the premiership in May 1937 to be succeeded by Neville Chamberlain, the man most associated with the appeasement policy. Chamberlain took a strong interest in the conduct of foreign policy, although he had little real experience in that field. But as a former Chancellor, he knew that armaments were costly, and Britain was still recovering from the effects of the depression.

The 'double line'

Chamberlain's policy was based on two ideas:
1. *negotiation with Germany to see what Hitler wanted;*
2. *pressing ahead with Britain's rearmament programme, especially in the air.*

Chamberlain was not keen on the idea of building up a large army and involving the country in another bloodbath like the Great War (remember his cousin's letter on p. 17). He also knew that the British people wanted to avoid war at almost any cost. So did the Dominions.

He also mistrusted the ability of the French to deal with Germany, and the good faith of the Soviet leader Stalin. Lastly, you need to remember that in the 1930s, everyone was terrified at the prospect of heavy aerial bombardment. Stanley Baldwin warned that 'the bomber will always get through' and people believed him. The prospect of massive gas attacks also caused serious alarm, and resulted in the issue of gas masks by the government – these proved to be quite redundant and were often used as lunch boxes in the war! This was why Chamberlain put forward his 'double line' in 1937: 'I believe that the double policy of rearmament and better relations with Germany and Italy will carry us safely through the danger period.'

Britain's commitments

Appeasement also needs to be placed in a world perspective. The British government's worries included not just Germany, but also Italy and Japan. The power of Italy was greatly exaggerated in Britain, but the Japanese were a serious threat in the Far East. Problems of European security often took second place to the safekeeping of the Empire.

Labour and rearmament

Inside Britain itself the situation was confused by the attitude of the Labour opposition. The party strongly opposed Fascism, but refused to support rearmament. Labour's support for the League of Nations, on the other hand, was not shared by Chamberlain and his colleagues.

France

The whole French strategy in the 1930s seemed contradictory. On the one hand, the French were constructing a massive, static defence system, the Maginot Line. On the other, they had a complex alliance system in eastern Europe. How was the French army sheltering in the Maginot forts to help its eastern allies? This was a question that few Frenchmen seemed prepared to consider. 'Je m'en fou' ('I don't give a damn') was a typical French reaction in the 1930s. It masked the nightmarish fear that France might once again be bled white as it had been in 1916. French newspapers carried headlines like 'Do you want to die for Danzig?' and few Frenchmen would have answered yes.

War or peace?

Germany's 'backgarden': the Rhineland Crisis

Early in 1936 Hitler was once again on the move; this time in the Rhineland. We saw in Chapter 3 how this part of Germany had been made into a demilitarized zone. Its status had been accepted by Germany in the Treaty of Locarno, but Hitler naturally rejected such obligations. On 7 March 1936 he sent his tiny army into the Rhineland in defiance of the Allied powers. It was a tremendous risk, as he himself recognized. He described that weekend as the 'most nerve-racking 48 hours of my life'.

But France did nothing, partly because Britain was not prepared to give any support. Britain's military chiefs did not regard the Rhineland as 'a vital interest', and the government knew that armed action would be unpopular. Germany was, in Lord Lothian's phrase, only 'going into her own backgarden'. The French leader Saurrat was facing an election, and his military chiefs showed no great enthusiasm for a tough policy.

Could Hitler have been stopped?

The reoccupation of the Rhineland has often been put forward as the moment when Hitler could, and should, have been stopped. At the time, matters did not seem quite so straightforward. The United States was known to be against even economic sanctions and the British Dominions would not fight for the Rhineland. Modern research has also shown that Germany could exert considerable economic pressure on Britain. It owed £40 million to the City of London and British firms handled 30 per cent of its oil and coal trade. Was all this to be risked for what was, after all, German territory? France had more at stake, but remembered its isolation in 1923 (see Chapter 4). Hitler had followed up the reoccupation by cleverly offering twenty-five-year non-aggression pacts to France and Belgium.

Nevertheless, the crisis was a victory for Hitler and a defeat for the Anglo–French alliance. Shortly afterwards, Belgium declared itself to be neutral, and this left the French with the difficult question of whether to extend their Maginot Line (the importance of this will be shown in the next chapter). France's little allies in eastern Europe began to have even greater doubts about French determination to stand up to Germany. Worst of all, the Führer was even more convinced of his own genius.

Hitler comes home

Adolf Hitler had always intended to bring his homeland Austria inside the frontiers of the Reich. His new friendship with Mussolini made this possible. In January 1938 Hitler summoned the Austrian Chancellor Kurt von Schuschnigg to a meeting in his mountain house at Berchtesgaden. In the interview, Hitler threatened Austria with invasion unless its government became a Nazi satellite. To his credit, Schuschnigg tried to preserve the independence of his country by holding a plebiscite on Sunday 13 March 1938. The Austrian people were to be asked whether they wanted anschluss (union) with Germany or not. Schuschnigg also tried to get foreign backing for Austria, but failed. Hitler was furious about the Austrian leader's show of independence, but he also could not allow the plebiscite to take place. The Nazis could not risk a propaganda defeat if the Austrian people voted 'No'.

So during the night of 11–12 March Operation Otto was put into operation. German troops crossed the frontier and the Nazi supporter Seyss-Inquart took over the government. Schuschnigg was arrested and sent to a concentration camp with other anti-Nazi ministers. The usual protests from London and Paris were ignored, although Hitler was about to infringe Article 80 of the Versailles Treaty prohibiting anschluss. He knew that there would be no Italian dash to the Brenner Pass as in 1934. Once in Vienna, Hitler announced Austria's union with the Reich under its old title of Ostmark – the eastern land.

He looked out in triumph over the city that had once rejected him: 'I believe that it was God's will to send a boy from here into the Reich, to let him grow up, to raise him to leader of the nation so as to enable him to lead back his homeland into the Reich.'

The people of Austria and Germany seemed to agree with him. In both countries over 90 per cent of the population voted for anschluss – only a few brave souls dared to register a 'No' vote.

The road to Munich

Fig. 11.5 will help you to guess who Hitler's next victims were to be. The fall of Austria meant the new

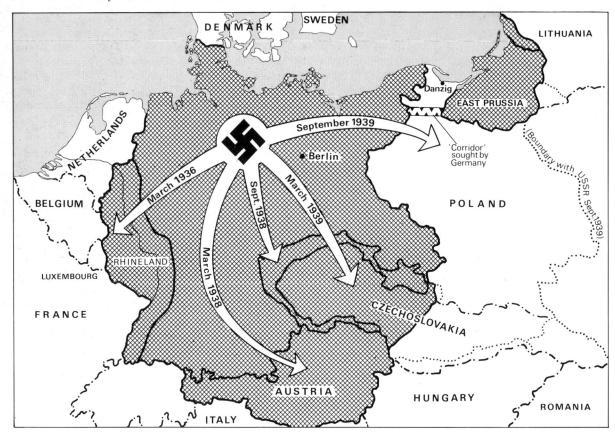

Fig. 11.5   German expansion in central Europe, 1936–9.

Czech state would be surrounded on three sides by German territory. Hitler had never disguised his loathing for the Czech's democratic system or the fact that they ruled over three million Germans. We have seen that Hitler was determined to bring all German minorities into the Reich. Rumours spread that the Czechs were about to be attacked, which resulted in a war scare in May, but Hitler was not yet ready.

A Nazi propaganda campaign was launched against President Beneš and his government, and the Sudeten German Party under Konrad Henlein was ordered to demand self-government for the German minority. So tense did the situation become that Neville Chamberlain felt obliged to intervene. First he sent Lord Runciman to make a report on the situation in the Sudetenland. He made little impression, so the Prime Minister decided to make a personal appeal to Hitler.

Berchtesgaden, 15 September 1938

Although already 69 years old, Chamberlain prepared for his first airflight to Germany. Hitler insisted on staying up in his mountain house, and reiterated his demands. Nothing less than self-government for the Sudeten Germans would do. Chamberlain did his best to comply, persuading the French also to agree. The Czech government was bluntly informed that unless it accepted the proposals 'His Majesty's Government will take no further interest in the fate of the country'. Deserted by his allies, President Beneš accepted the Anglo-French terms.

Godesburg, 22 September

Chamberlain returned to Germany convinced that the crisis was resolved (Fig. 11.6). This time he met Hitler at Bad Godesburg on the Rhine, but was amazed to learn that the Führer was now demanding incorporation of the Sudetenland into the Reich by 1 October at the latest! Polish and Hungarian territorial claims against Czechoslovakia were also to be settled. Even Chamberlain lost his temper when faced with such duplicity and flew back to London at once.

Fig. 11.6 'Still hope'. When this cartoon appeared in Punch on 21 September 1938, Chamberlain still believed that war with Germany could be averted.

Fig. 11.7 A confident Chamberlain returns from the Munich Conference.

The Munich Conference, 29 September

For a week, war with Germany seemed inevitable. Trenches were dug in Hyde Park and the fleet was mobilized. French troops went into the Maginot Line and the Czechs called up reservists. Hitler's language became even more wild as he told Beneš to 'hand this territory over to us' or face war.

Then on 28 September came what seemed to be a miracle. Hitler had agreed to a four-power conference at Munich. Chamberlain and the French premier Daladier would fly to Germany. The Duce would 'mediate' between the two sides (we now know he was secretly working with the German Foreign Office). The next day, the meeting took place, and the fate of the Czechs was sealed. Their representatives had to wait in another room, and the Russians were not invited. Under the Munich Settlement:

1. the Czech government was to evacuate the Sudetenland by 10 October. The area included the Czech frontier defences and important Skoda arms plants.

2. Polish–Hungarian claims were to be settled later. In fact, the Poles took advantage of their neighbour's plight and seized the coal mining area of Teschen.

The settlement was greeted with profound relief in Britain and France. Cheering crowds greeted Chamberlain in Downing Street when he made his famous and inaccurate comment about 'peace in our time' (Fig. 11.7). Daladier was reported to have turned up his collar as protection against the expected rotten tomatoes, but he too was greeted as a hero. Mussolini was certainly pleased that the war had been avoided, Hitler less so. Chamberlain, he complained, had 'spoiled my entry into Prague', but the German leader could afford to grumble. He had obtained the most strategically valuable part of Czechoslovakia without firing a shot.

Was Munich inevitable?

The Munich Settlement has been the subject of great controversy, both then and since. Some of the results of the settlement were undoubtedly bad:

1. Czech military power was destroyed and Stalin became even more suspicious of the West.

2. Hitler himself was convinced that the 'little worms' he had seen at Munich would never fight.

But there were also points in favour of the policy followed at Munich:

(a) Chamberlain knew that neither Britain nor its

Empire wanted war over the Sudetenland.

(b) He also knew about the weak state of Britain's defences. There were no Spitfires, no radar, and few anti-aircraft guns in 1938, and Britain needed time to rearm.

(c) The French wanted peace at almost any price; they went so far as to abandon their military agreement with the Czechs.

While it can also be argued that the Germans too gained from the breathing space, we may perhaps agree with the contemporary historian John Wheeler Bennett: 'Let us say of the Munich Settlement that it was inescapable. Mr Chamberlain had no alternative to do other than he did.'[2] Once more you must make up your own mind!

The seizure of Czechoslovakia

The day after the Munich Agreement, Neville Chamberlain visited Hitler in his Munich flat. During the visit, he persuaded the German leader to sign a declaration recognizing 'the desire of our two peoples never to go to war with another again'. Hitler had carelessly signed the document to please 'the old gentleman'. Precisely what his promises were worth became clear six months later when Hitler annexed the rest of Czechoslovakia as well. After bullying the old Czech President Hacha in Berlin, Hitler obtained permission to invade the Czech provinces of Bohemia and Moravia. German troops were supposed to be preventing a 'breakdown in law and order'. Slovakia had already declared itself independent after German encouragement. On 15 March 1939 German soldiers marched into Prague, and later in that month of March, Hitler forced the Lithuanian government to hand over the largely German city of Memel. Anxious not to be left out, Mussolini seized the tiny Balkan kingdom of Albania on 7 April. The whole system of European security seemed to be on the verge of collapse.

Chamberlain reacts

The news of Hitler's latest piece of cynical brutality brought about a complete change in British policy. Chamberlain angrily demanded whether the Czech annexation was the end of an old adventure or the beginning of a new one. It was clear that Hitler was not to be trusted, and offers of military help were made to Poland, Turkey, Romania and Greece.

Unfortunately, the effect of British toughness was spoilt by the influence of Sir Neville Henderson, Britain's ambassador to Berlin. He was so pro-German that he earned the nickname 'our Nazi ambassador'.

Saving Russia's 'chestnuts'

In the meantime, equally significant events were taking place in eastern Europe where Joseph Stalin had become increasingly suspicious of Western intentions.

Since 1934 Stalin had adopted a policy of supporting collective security and opposing Fascist aggression. This had resulted in Soviet membership of the League (1934) and defence pacts with France and Czechoslovakia (1935). Munich changed all this, and early in 1939 Stalin gave clear warning to the West that the Soviet Union must look after its own interests. In his speech to the Eighteenth Congress of the Soviet Communist Party, the Russian leader spoke of 'warmongers who are accustomed to have the others pull the chestnuts out of the fire for them'. Little notice was taken of this famous 'chestnuts' speech in Britain and France.

A second warning signal came in May when Litvinov, who had taken Soviet Russia into the League, was replaced by Molotov as Foreign Minister. Molotov was a Stalinist henchman, trained only to do his master's bidding. At last, the Western leaders appeared to wake up and press for what people like Churchill had wanted for years, firm military alliance with Russia. But the change was more apparent than real. Chamberlain remained mistrustful of the USSR and preferred alliance with Poland, which he mistakenly described as 'a great virile nation'. Anglo–French military experts also believed that the army purges of 1937–8 had weakened the effectiveness of the Red Army. These doubts resulted in only half-hearted attempts to come to terms with Stalin. The Russians, for their part, could hardly take seriously potential allies who sent second-rate diplomats to negotiate with them (and sent them by sea, a journey of three weeks!). More crucially, the Western powers could not persuade their Romanian and Polish allies to allow the Red Army on their territory.

The Pact of Steel, May 1939

Hitler, by contrast, had just made a ten-year military pact with Mussolini, and kept an eye on the protracted Anglo–French negotiations with Moscow. The pact is usually called the Pact of Steel.

The Nazi–Soviet Pact, 23 August 1939

He did not have long to wait, for by early August, Stalin was tiring of British and French indecision.

When feelers to Berlin indicated a favourable response, Stalin acted quickly. On 22 August, Foreign Minister von Ribbentrop was invited to Moscow for talks. The next day, he and Molotov signed the infamous Nazi–Soviet Pact, an event which took the whole world by surprise. For years, Stalin admitted, the two sides had been 'pouring buckets of filth' on each other. Now they were to be friends and allies, leaving Hitler free to attack Poland. The agreement stipulated:

1. that Poland was to be divided up between the two powers (this clause was kept secret);
2. neither power would attack the other for a ten-year period;
3. commercial and trading contracts were to be increased.

Hitler was jubilant and pressed ahead with his plans to attack Poland. Stalin's motives for signing the agreement are more difficult to assess. But like Chamberlain at Munich, he needed time to rearm. Fearing a Western deal with Hitler, he judged it safer to protect Soviet security. He also had to consider the attitude of Japan, which had attacked the USSR on two occasions in 1938–9.

War on Danzig

It is clear now that Hitler expected the Nazi–Soviet Pact to frighten off Britain and France and give him a free hand in Poland. For once, he miscalculated and the Munich 'worms' began to turn. The Poles, for their part, courageously refused to agree to any change in the status of Danzig or the Corridor. This resolution was strengthened by the signing of an Anglo–Polish defence agreement on 26 August 1939.

For a few days Hitler dithered, and the invasion of Poland, code-named Case White, was put off. Desperate attempts to avoid war were made by a series of mediators, including Pope Pius XII, the Queen of the Netherlands and Mussolini. They all failed, as they were bound to do, because Hitler was determined to have his war. Poland was invaded on 1 September, and appeasement had failed.

Chamberlain pushed his policy to the extreme limit by giving the Germans 48 hours to withdraw. This was too much for his critics in the House of Commons who demanded an immediate declaration of war. One irate Conservative asked the Labour leader 'to speak for England'. Eventually, an ultimatum was sent to Berlin ordering out German troops by 11 am on 3 September, and the French ultimatum was to expire at 5 pm on the same day. No reply was received, and for the second time in twenty-five years, Europe found itself at war. Chamberlain spoke of his personal regret in the House of Commons: 'Everything that I have worked for, everything I have hoped for ... has crashed into ruins.' Even on the German side there was some anxiety: 'May God help us,' said Hermann Goering, 'if we lose this war.'

Hitler's war?

In reading this section, you may have become convinced that the war that began on 3 September 1939 was indeed Hitler's war. But did Adolf Hitler have a blueprint for aggression from 1933 onwards? At least one distinguished historian, A. J. P. Taylor, has argued against this.

Put simply, the case against Hitler rests on what he wrote in *Mein Kampf* and the evidence found in captured German documents in 1945. The most famous of these is the Hossbach Memorandum, an account of a meeting between German leaders in 1937. Where most historians have accepted that Hitler planned to start a war over Czechoslovakia and Poland between 1937 and 1943, Taylor says that Hitler is merely 'talking for effect'. The existence of military plans, he believes, is only a necessary precaution, and little value is attached to the Führer's ramblings in *Mein Kampf*. You may reply that Hitler's record of aggression speaks for itself! Nevertheless, Taylor argues: 'The vital question, it seems to me, concerns Great Britain and France. They were the victors of the First World War. They had the decision in their hands.'[3] In other words, most of the blame for the war rests in London and Paris. Complicated! Certainly, but it only goes to prove that history is about argument as well as facts.

Such an argument does, however, ignore the economic and social arguments presented about Nazi policy. As Franz Neumann has pointed out, Hitler's economic plans were linked to wholesale confiscation of Jewish property, and the conquest of Europe was also backed by industrialists keen to acquire extra markets for their goods on the most favourable terms.[4]

Keywords

Kellogg–Briand Pact: signed in 1928 and after by sixty-five states. It denounced the use of war in international affairs. Sponsored by US Secretary of State Frank B. Kellogg and Aristide Briand, France's Foreign Secretary.

Wu Kang: according to ancient Chinese legend, had committed crimes in his search for immortality, and was condemned to cut down a cassia tree at the full moon. Every time he raised his axe, the tree replaced itself so he had to go on felling it for eternity.

Brenner Pass: a narrow route through the Alps marking the Austro–Italian frontier.

status quo: from the Latin, keeping things the same.

dumdum bullet: a special bullet which splinters on impact.

appease: to quiet or calm someone who is hostile.

Questions

Extract 11.1

(*A*)

I have the impression that the persons directing the policy of the Hitler government are not normal. Many of us indeed, have a feeling that we are living in a country where fantastic hooligans and eccentrics have got the upper hand.

(British Ambassador in Berlin to the Foreign Office, 1933)

(*B*)

And so we National Socialists . . . take up where we broke off six hundred years ago. We stop the endless German movement to the south and west, and turn our gaze towards the land in the East.

If we speak of soil in Europe today, we can primarily have in mind only Russia and her vassal border states.

(Adolf Hitler, *Mein Kampf*)

1. Identify the British Ambassador in extract *A*.   1
2. What phrase did Hitler use for 'the land in the East'?   1
3. Why did most foreign observers not agree with the view that the Hitler government was abnormal after 1933?   2
4. Give THREE examples of how Hitler broke the Versailles Agreement in these years.   3
5. Explain what you understand by Chamberlain's 'double line' in 1937–9.   2
6. Which of Russia's 'vassal border states' did Hitler (i) occupy in March 1939 (ii) attack in September 1939?   2
7. Explain why the USSR and the Western democracies were unable to come to terms in the summer of 1939.   3
8. To what extent do you think France and Britain were responsible for the war that began on 1 September 1939?   6
                                                           —
                                                           20

Use Chapters 10 and 11 to make up your own multiple-choice questions to ask the rest of your class next time. You cannot, of course, answer your own questions! Your teacher will help you with this.

12 The Second World War, 1939-45

The concept of *Blitzkrieg*

The war that began in September 1939 was to be a very different one from the First World War. Yet few perceived that at the beginning of the struggle. The British and French were sure that it would be a war of containment, so avoiding the slaughter of 1914–18. Their strategy was based on the belief that the German economy was weak and that it would once again be vulnerable to economic blockade. In the meantime, the French were to rely on their Maginot Line and such air and land support as the British could give them. Even on the German side many military leaders were old-fashioned in their belief that tanks and aircraft would not fundamentally change the nature of warfare.

There was one important difference. Hitler himself believed in the new methods of warfare, and he encouraged those, like Guderian and Manstein, who shared his views. This comparatively small group of men was responsible for the concept known to history as *blitzkrieg* or lightning war. The essence of lightning war was surprise and speed. The enemy was to be hit hard by Panzers* and dive bombers and not

Fig. 12.1   Instruments of Blitzkrieg: *a Junkers 87 Stuka dive bomber and a P2KW IA tank.*

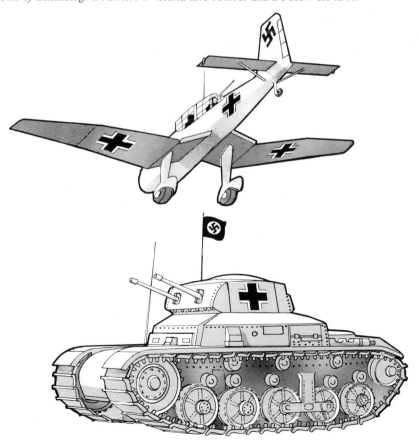

given time to reorganize defences (Fig. 12.1). Other methods, such as the dropping of parachutists, might be used to accelerate this process.

From the German point of view *Blitzkrieg* had another great advantage. If it worked, Germany would attain its objectives quickly, and there would be no need for long, drawn-out campaigns. It could not afford these because there were serious shortages of fuel and other raw materials. Although Hitler had, in fact, encouraged the belief that Germany was 'an armed camp' before 1939, this was not true. The Nazis did not have time for total rearmament, and neither did they want it.

Not until 1943–4, the historians Burton Klein and Alan Milward tell us, was the German economy put on a total war footing[1] – by then there was no choice because the country was in serious danger of defeat. Surprisingly, Adolf Hitler did not want to cut back the production of consumer goods and lose his popularity with the German people! Albert Speer writes in his memoirs: 'It remains one of the oddities of this war that Hitler demanded far less from his people than Churchill and Roosevelt.'[2]

The destruction of Poland, September 1939

The first victims of the *Blitzkrieg* were the unhappy Poles. Although their troops fought bravely, they were hopelessly outmatched. German armour smashed through their defences, German bombers destroyed their cities. The obsolete Polish air force was shot out of the sky, and the Polish armies trapped by vast encircling movements of the Panzer divisions. The Poles made the mistake of keeping most of their troops stationed in the Corridor, but this probably had little influence on the result. Cavalry were no match for tanks, as the Poles found to their cost.

Their position became even more desperate on 17 September when the Red Army entered the country from the east. Once again, independent Poland disappeared from the map of Europe. It was the victim both of its own geography and misguided policies.

The winter war, 1939–40

Stalin obtained a certain amount of security by occupying eastern Poland, but he felt uneasy. The city of Leningrad still lay dangerously close to the frontier of Finland, a former colony which had no reason to love the Soviet Union. Stalin first tried to bully the Finns by demanding cession of the Karelian Isthmus. When they refused, the Red Army attacked

their country but with minimal success. In part, this was due to the effect of the purges of Red Army officers, but the Finnish army also put unexpectedly tough resistance behind its Mannerheim Line. They had plenty of experience of fighting in the freezing, winter conditions, and not until March 1940 were the Russians able to end their resistance. This was fortunate for the Western allies who had worked out a hare-brained plan to help the Finns, thus fighting the Germans and the Soviet Union at the same time!

Ultimately, Stalin had got what he wanted, and he went on to annex the little Baltic Republics of Estonia, Latvia and Lithuania as well (August 1940).

The Phoney War, October 1939–April 1940

After the Polish campaign was over, a strange calm descended on to the western front. The French army made some feeble raids into German-held territory, and the Allied air forces dropped leaflets on Germany telling the people to surrender, but not surprisingly, this had little effect. The policy of inaction was carried to such extremes that the British Minister Kingsley Wood totally rejected the idea of bombing the Black Forest on the grounds that it was private property! Only at sea was there much activity. A German U-boat sank the *Royal Oak* in Scapa Flow. The Royal Navy responded by forcing the pocket battleship *Graf Spee* to scuttle itself in Montevideo harbour.

This strange period of non-war was called the Phoney War by the Americans, and the *Sitzkrieg* or sitting-down war by the Germans. It suited Hitler's purpose because it lulled the Western powers into a sense of false security.

Bad weather prevented a German offensive in the winter of 1939–40, and then an accident changed their invasion plans. In January 1940 a German aircraft lost its way and crash-landed in Belgium. One of the officers on board was carrying copies of the plan and did not have time to destroy them. The Belgian authorities passed on the details to the French, and it was clear that the Germans only intended to repeat their Schlieffen Plan of 1914 (see p. 8).

The Manstein Plan

This accident proved to be a blessing in disguise for the Germans who were already having second thoughts about the plan. One officer in particular, von Manstein, thought that something better than a repeat of the 1914 plan was needed. He argued for a modification of the original plan that would allow a strong thrust by tank divisions through the heavily-wooded Ardennes. Hitler strongly supported Manstein, against the advice of senior generals, and his plan was adopted.

Denmark and Norway, April 1940

France, however, was not to be the second target for the German army. Instead, acting on the advice of his admirals, Hitler invaded Denmark and Norway. They wanted the use of the Norwegian coastline for U-boat bases, and German intelligence also found out that the British were planning to mine the area off the coastline too. A more significant factor was German dependence on Swedish iron ore, which came to them via the Norwegian port of Narvik. Hitler could not see these supplies endangered by a possible Allied invasion of Scandinavia. On 8 April 1940 German naval forces set sail for Norway, and at the same time, German troops crossed the Danish frontier. On the face of it, the Norwegian expedition represented a tremendous gamble on Hitler's part. The German navy was very small, but the German forces moved too fast for the Allied governments and quickly seized the major towns of Narvik, Trondheim and Oslo. Several German warships were sunk, but the Germans had obtained their objective, the occupation of Norway. While it is true that the *Luftwaffe* controlled the skies, the Germans had also outwitted the Allies at sea, supposedly their area of strength. For the Royal Navy, the Norwegian campaign was particularly humiliating.

It had two other immediate results: the fall of the Chamberlain government in London and Allied occupation of Iceland, a Danish colony.

The Battle of France, May–June 1940

On the day, 10 May 1940, that Winston Churchill replaced Chamberlain as Prime Minister, Hitler struck in the west. The blow had long been expected, and on paper, the two sides were evenly matched (Table 12.1).

But there were two crucial weaknesses on the Allied side:
1. the inferiority of the Allied air forces, which allowed the *Luftwaffe* to play a decisive role in the land battles;
2. the Allied Dyle Plan, which was to be carried out as soon as news of the German invasion came

Table 12.1 German and Allied military forces, 1940

Military strength	Allied	German
Army divisions	136 (French, British, Belgian, Dutch)	136
Tanks	3,100	2,400
Aircraft	1,800 (600 British)	3,000

through. It involved rushing the best, motorized, Anglo-French divisions into Belgium up to the River Dyle. This made the Allied armies extremely vulnerable to a German attack through the Ardennes which would divide the forces in the north from those in the Maginot Line.

The breakout

When the Germans attacked on 10 May, their plan went perfectly. The French lines in the Ardennes were broken with ease and a flood of German tanks poured across the plains of northern France. In the north, the cities of the Netherlands were swiftly captured (although Rotterdam suffered severe bomb damage) and the Allied armies thrown back towards the Belgian frontiers. The French Commander-in-Chief Gamelin had no answer to the speed of the *Blitzkrieg*, his military thinking was still firmly grounded in the 1914–18 war. Winston Churchill was awakened early on the morning of 15 May by Paul Reynaud, the French Prime Minister, and told: 'We have lost the battle!' Churchill was thunderstruck, as he admitted later: 'I did not comprehend the violence of the revolution . . . effected by a mass of fast-moving armour.'

In desperation, Reynaud sacked Gamelin and brought in General Weygand, but it was too late. By the third week in May, German Panzers had reached the Channel coastline and the Allied forces had been cut in two.

On 27 May King Leopold of the Belgians asked for an armistice, leaving the Anglo–French troops facing disaster. Fortunately for the British, their commander Lord Gort had foreseen such an emergency and had already ordered a retreat to the port of Dunkirk. Gallant defence by the French rearguard allowed a naval evacuation to begin, but the British government did not expect to get more than 45,000 troops off the beaches. Ironically, it was Hitler who came to their rescue by ordering a 'Panzer halt' because he believed the tanks would get bogged down in the Flanders marshes and Goering's boast that the air force could finish the job. This blunder allowed 350,000 Allied soldiers to be evacuated by 4 June.

Winston Churchill warned the British people against regarding the 'miracle of Dunkirk' as a victory, but for the French, Dunkirk represented nothing more than a breathing space before the final battle. On 5 June German forces renewed their advance along the River Somme, and again, the weight of their armour was too much. France had reached, in General Weygand's words, the 'last quarter of an hour', and Britain could do no more to help its stricken ally. The resolute Reynaud was replaced as Prime Minister by Marshal Pétain who was still obsessed with his memories of the carnage in the First World War.

Italy comes in

By then, France's position had become even more precarious because of Italy's entry into the war against the Allies. The promise of colonial booty was too much for the Duce, and on 10 June his forces attacked the French along the common frontier. The inadequacies of the Italian army were glaringly revealed by its failure to make any real impression on the French defences.

The fall of France

The Germans, sweeping to victory (Fig. 12.2), regarded Mussolini's efforts with amused contempt. On 17 June Marshal Pétain asked the German government for an armistice, and this came into force on 22 June 1940. Characteristically, Adolf Hitler made the French delegation sign the armistice in Marshal Foch's famous railway carriage in the Forest of Compiègne.

Its most important terms were:
1. the occupation of northern and western France by Germany.
2. France to retain its fleet and colonies.
3. unoccupied France to be ruled by the government of Marshal Pétain.

Fig. 12.2   German troops occupy Paris on 14 June 1940.

This unoccupied area came to be known as Vichy France, after the town where Pétain based his government. The Vichy government was to earn an evil reputation for co-operating with the Nazis. But it did not have the support of all Frenchmen, for on 18 June, General Charles de Gaulle broadcast a message in London inviting all free Frenchmen to join him. This was the humble beginning of the Free French resistance movement.

Why did France fall?

The collapse of the French Republic was swift and spectacular. It is easy, therefore, to use dramatic and exaggerated language about it. The most important point to remember is that France's defeat was primarily a military one. Its generals and their methods were twenty years out of date, although the army had plenty of modern equipment. But its advantage in tanks was thrown away because they were used for infantry support rather than for rapid advance as in the German army. The speed of the *Blitzkrieg* left the French paralysed, and there were breakdowns in discipline. The British General, Alanbrooke, has left this description of the French 9th Army in the winter of 1939 – this was the army guarding the crucial Ardennes sector: 'Seldom have I seen anything more slovenly and badly turned out. Men unshaven, horses ungroomed, clothes and saddlery that did not fit, vehicles dirty, and complete lack of pride in themselves or their units.'[3]

This showed the French army at its worst, but it would be wrong to suggest that it was an accurate picture of all its units. Many French soldiers fought bravely against the enemy, none more so than the men of the 1st Army, which guarded the Dunkirk perimeter. But they were badly led and ill-prepared for the war that confronted them in the summer of 1940.

There were other factors involved, too. The Fascists opposed the war as did the communists, while government politicians bickered among themselves. Finally though, we must return to the blistering speed of the *Blitzkrieg* as the main reason for France's fall. 'It was *time* that was the vital element which – more than weapons even perhaps more than morale – France most lacked in 1940.'[4]

There was to be one last chapter in France's agony. On 3 July 1940 the Royal Navy sank part of the French fleet at Mers el Kebir after a series of misunderstandings. The British would not risk the possible capture of powerful French warships by the Nazis and felt that they had no option. To the trauma of defeat was now added the apparent treachery of an ally. 'The gratitude of "comrades in arms",' crowed the Nazi magazine, *Signal*, to mark the lowest point of the *Entente Cordiale*.

Britain's finest hour

If Mers el Kebir showed nothing else, it was that Britain would not come to terms with Hitler. He confidently expected peace overtures from the British once the Battle of France was over, an opinion that was shared by most foreigners. General Weygand believed that if Britain fought on 'in three weeks she will have her neck wrung like a chicken'. Logic pointed to German supremacy, but the British people would not accept it. They derived a strange satisfaction from being 'in the finals now', as one Cockney newsvendor put it.

So confident were the Germans that the war would be over in July 1940 that they had no real plan for the invasion of the British Isles. It had to be hastily drawn up, and was given the code name Sea Lion.

Sea Lion had two major phases:
1. the bombing and destruction of RAF bases in south-east England.
2. the landing of approximately twenty-five German divisions on Britain's southern coastline.

The German admirals, who were none too confident about getting an army across the Channel, insisted that the RAF be destroyed first. Once again, Hitler believed Goering's boasts that he could carry out this task. He gravely underestimated Britain's capacity to defend itself against aerial attack which had been greatly improved since 1938. A network of radar stations in southern England provided warning of German attacks to RAF Fighter Command. Equally important, by the summer of 1940, the RAF had the Spitfire, the fastest fighter on either side. These improvements effectively cancelled out the German advantage in numbers – 900 fighters and 300 dive bombers against the RAF's 650 fighters in mid-July 1940.

After some early harassing attacks on Channel shipping, the Germans launched their first major air offensive on 13 August 1940, Eagle Day. From the start, the *Luftwaffe* pilots were surprised by the resistance they met from an RAF fighter force that they believed to be on the verge of collapse. Nevertheless, they pressed home their attacks, and by the end of August, the leader of Fighter Command, Sir Hugh Dowding, was seriously concerned. German attacks disrupted the radar and communications system, but more seriously they were taking a severe toll of pilots who could not easily be replaced. By the first week in September, a German invasion of the British Isles seemed imminent. It did not take place for a variety of reasons.

Firstly, the *Luftwaffe* was becoming demoralized by its own losses. The much vaunted Stukas had been shot out of the skies, and daylight bombing proved impossible unless heavy fighter escorts were provided. Plane for plane, the British Spitfires and Hurricanes were proving superior to the German Messerschmitt 109 and 110*.

Secondly, the Germans made a fatal error in switching their attacks from the vulnerable RAF airfields to the centres of population like London. This was partly a result of bad intelligence, which made the *Luftwaffe* believe that the RAF was virtually beaten, but also a result of one of those freak episodes that can decide battles. On 23 August, some German bombers had strayed off course and bombed London by mistake. Churchill ordered RAF Bomber Command to retaliate, and on 25 August Berlin was raided. Hitler was furious, especially as Goering had promised the Berliners that no bombs would fall on their city. He ordered the *Luftwaffe* to switch its effort against London and on 7 September daylight raids began against the British capital. The exhausted British pilots were, therefore, given a much-needed breathing space, and all the time, more Spitfires and Hurricanes were pouring off the production lines.

Lastly, the Germans were defeated by the courage and endurance of the RAF fighter pilots, many of them very young and inexperienced. Winston Churchill summed up the British people's gratitude; 'Never in the field of human conflict was so much owed by so many to so few.'

The *Luftwaffe* made a last desperate effort to obtain control of British airspace on 15 September, but again, they were foiled by Fighter Command. The Battle of Britain, as it came to be known, highlighted some of the *Luftwaffe*'s weaknesses, as the German ace, Adolf Galland, pointed out later: 'Our range was very, very limited . . . over London for example, we could only stay ten minutes if we wanted to get back to our bases. This limited range of our fighters acting as escorts was perhaps the main factor which prevented an effective air offensive against Britain.'[5]

While true, this fact does not detract from the achievement of the 'few'. Between 12 August and the end of September 1940, they had destroyed 1,100 German aircraft (although claiming 2,700) for an RAF loss of 650 (the Germans' estimate was 3,000). In the end, these wildly exaggerated claims did not matter, for on 17 September Hitler postponed Operation Sea Lion indefinitely.

The blitz

He had failed to take the British Isles by direct assault, but was still convinced that he could break the will of its people to continue the war. London was the major target for the *Luftwaffe* in its attempt to win the war by terror. For fifty-seven successive nights, German bombers pounded the capital during what the Londoners called the blitz. The East End suffered greatly from the effects of this terrible bombing. At the same time, the *Luftwaffe* turned its attention to Britain's other major cities and ports. On 14 November 1940 the centre of Coventry was destroyed by one of the heaviest raids of the war, and 500 people died. The German bombing offensive continued into 1941, but at no time did it succeed in its object of bringing the British government to the peace-table.

A heavy price was still paid by the civilian population of the country. By the end of 1941 over 43,000 people had died in air raids.

The war in North Africa, 1940–41

Mussolini's object in coming into the war was to take over the vulnerable British and French colonies in Africa. Britain's desperate position in the autumn of 1940 appeared to present him with a great opportunity to attain his objective.

Typically, Mussolini was over-confident and wasted time allowing the British to reinforce their army in Egypt. When the Italians did invade Egypt in September 1940, they were crushingly defeated by a tiny British force under General O'Connor. In November their much-prized fleet was crippled by a surprise British attack at Taranto.

The British then wasted an opportunity by diverting troops to Greece and giving the Axis powers time to bring in German troops under General Erwin Rommel. Rommel, the 'Desert Fox', was to prove an admirable leader, and soon adapted the *Blitzkrieg* tactics of 1939–40 to the African theatre. The desert conditions were ideal for the fast-moving armoured warfare that had brought the Germans their dramatic victory in France. Rommel knew this, but his pleas for more men and material were often ignored in Berlin because Hitler preferred to regard Africa as a sideshow.

Greece and Yugoslavia

By the spring of 1941 the Führer had other worrying problems, which were largely the fault of his Italian ally. Smarting under the humiliation of the setbacks in Africa, Mussolini launched his armies against Greece. Once again, the Italian army ran into difficulties and was forced to retreat into Albania (which you will remember Mussolini had seized in April 1939). In the interim, the Greek government, fearing possible German intervention, appealed to the British for assistance. This was soon forthcoming, but also had the unwanted side effect of ensuring German involvement too. A further complication was provided by a sudden switch of sides by Yugoslavia whose co-operation was essential to get German troops to Greece. On 27 March a *coup*, led by the chief of the air force, replaced the pro-German Regent* with the young King Peter.

On 6 April the German forces invaded both countries, and the Yugoslav capital Belgrade was virtually wiped out by pitiless bombing. The German advance was so rapid that the British troops sent to help the Greeks had to be hastily evacuated to the island of Crete. Even this refuge proved to be short-lived because, in May 1941, it was captured by German airborne forces (one of the rare examples in the war of a successful, if costly, operation mounted mainly by paratroopers).

The Greek and Yugoslav peoples paid dearly for British interference in the Balkans, but the campaign certainly had one crucial result. All Hitler's other plans for conquest had to be put back by several months. We must see what these plans were.

Operation Barbarossa, 22 June 1941

Early in 1941 Hitler had effectively shelved his plans for invading Britain, although he allowed the bombing offensive against the latter to continue until May. This was because the German dictator's mind was fixed on the great project of his life, the invasion of the USSR. Despite the apparent friendliness between the two countries since August 1939, relations between Germany and the Soviet Union were slowly worsening. Hitler was angered by the annexation of the Baltic republics and the Romanian province of Bessarabia. Stalin's fears were increased by the signature of the Tripartite Pact of September 1940, which clearly seemed to be aimed at his country – the signatories being Japan, Germany and Italy. The two powers were such unlikely allies that you may think that war was inevitable. Many people believed this at the time, including the British government, which warned Stalin of Germany's aggressive intentions. Yet it was Stalin, the cunning, ruthless dictator, who seems to have ignored the evidence. To the amazement of the Germans, Soviet grain shipments continued to rumble westwards towards the Reich, while their troops took up battle stations.

Stalin was certainly concerned about his eastern frontier with Japan, but his lethargy is still difficult to explain.

The failure of the *Blitzkrieg*

Stalin's faith in Adolf Hitler ensured that the Red Army was taken by surprise when at 3 am on the morning of 22 June 1941, 3 million Germans poured across the 1,500-km (930-mile) frontier between the two states. Soviet air support was destroyed on the ground, and its command structure was in total confusion. The Panzers quickly rolled over the Soviet frontier positions as Stalin appealed desperately for help.

This was soon forthcoming from London because Churchill immediately saw that old differences must be put aside. 'If Hitler invaded Hell,' he remarked, 'I would make at least a favourable reference to the Devil in the House of Commons.'

The German High Command approached the Russian campaign in a spirit of gross overconfidence, which was heightened by the easy victories of the early weeks. The Red Army was believed to be primitive and badly led, nothing more, said a German general, than 'a pig's bladder, prick it, and it will burst'. The German plan was simple (Fig. 12.3). Three massive pronged attacks would be made against Leningrad, Moscow and the Caucasus in the south – the Germans wanted to capture the oilfields there. The bulk of the *Luftwaffe* was brought in to support the attack, and the campaign was expected to be over in eight weeks. At first, all went well, and the Germans captured big cities like Kharkov and Kursk, but the further they advanced, the more savage Soviet resistance became. Stalin, once recovered from the shock of the invasion, encouraged this resistance by referring to all the heroes of Russia's past. Even the churches were reopened and the Orthodox priests encouraged to pray for the victory of the Motherland.

The Russians were undoubtedly assisted by a confusion about objectives on the German side. Hitler could not make up his mind whether Moscow should be the main goal or not. At one point, he ordered a halt on the Moscow front, and by the time he renewed the advance, the autumn rains had come. The German divisions inched forward, but the severe Russian winter prevented them from reaching the Soviet capital. Some isolated units did penetrate the outer suburbs of Moscow, but they were driven out by workers who attacked them with any weapons they could find. For the first time the *Blitzkrieg* had failed, and never again was the *Wehrmacht* (the German armed forces) to be the irresistible force of 1939–41. This crucial failure needs further explanation:

1. *The climate.* Overconfidence made the Germans neglect to take obvious precautions. German troops

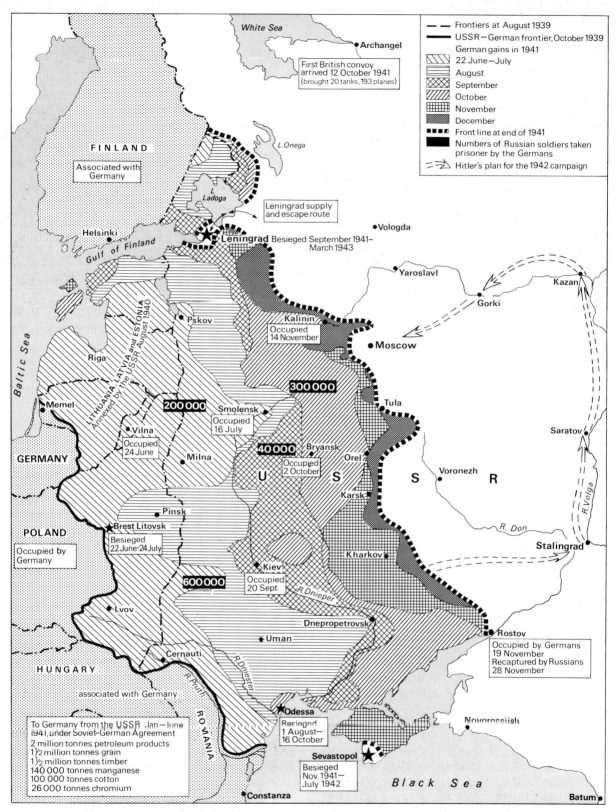

Legend:

- – – – Frontiers at August 1939
- —— USSR–German frontier, October 1939
- German gains in 1941
  - 22 June–July
  - August
  - September
  - October
  - November
  - December
- ■■■■ Front line at end of 1941
- ■■■ Numbers of Russian soldiers taken prisoner by the Germans
- ⇉ Hitler's plan for the 1942 campaign

White Sea
•Archangel

First British convoy arrived 12 October 1941 (brought 20 tanks, 193 planes)

FINLAND
Associated with Germany

L. Onega

L. Ladoga

Leningrad supply and escape route

Helsinki

Gulf of Finland

Baltic Sea

★ Leningrad Besieged September 1941– March 1943

•Vologda

•Yaroslavl

Gorki

Kazan

Pskov

Kalinin Occupied 14 November

•Moscow

Riga

LITHUANIA, LATVIA and ESTONIA Annexed by the USSR August 1940

200 000

Smolensk Occupied 16 July

300 000

Tula

Saratov

•Memel

Vilna Occupied 24 June

Milna

40 000

Bryansk Occupied 2 October

•Orel

Voronezh

GERMANY

U   S   S   R

Karsk

R. Volga

Pinsk

★ Brest Litovsk Besieged 22 June–24 July

R. Don

Stalingrad

POLAND
Occupied by Germany

600 000

Kiev Occupied 20 Sept.

R. Dnieper

Kharkov

•Lvov

Dnepropetrovsk

Rostov

Occupied by Germans 19 November Recaptured by Russians 28 November

•Uman

Cernauti

R. Dniester

HUNGARY

R. Pruth

RO MANIA

associated with Germany

Odessa Besieged 1 August– 16 October

Novorossijsk

To Germany from the USSR, Jan–June 1941, under Soviet–German Agreement
2 million tonnes petroleum products
1½ million tonnes grain
1½ million tonnes timber
140 000 tonnes manganese
100 000 tonnes cotton
26 000 tonnes chromium

Sevastopol Besieged Nov. 1941– July 1942

Black Sea

•Constanza

Batum

Fig. 12.3   The German invasion of USSR, 1941.

Fig. 12.4   A German ammunition column bogged down in mud in Soviet Russia.

were not provided with winter clothing, and Goebbels had to organize a last minute campaign in Germany to provide it. Many soldiers were to die of frostbite in temperatures as low as $-40°C$ ($-40°F$).

2. *The sheer size of the Soviet Union.*   This was a tremendous obstacle to the Germans, as it had been to Napoleon's army in 1812. A German general noted: 'We were depressed by the monotony of the landscape, and the immensity of the stretches of forest, marsh and plain.'[6] The lack of good roads in Russia turned out to be a crucial factor in slowing up the German advance (Fig.12.4). So was the German reliance on *wheeled* rather than *tracked* vehicles. As the military historian Captain B. H. Liddell Hart has pointed out, this meant that only the tanks could move around freely off the road system.[7] We have already seen that the *Blitzkrieg* could only work if the first breakthrough by the tanks was followed up by motorized infantry.

3. *The toughness of the Russian soldiers and civilians.*   The same German general commented that they 'seemed to have an illimitable capacity for obedience and endurance'.[8] But Hitler's crude racialism in ordering the liquidation of the inferior Slav peoples of the Soviet Union made his army's task more difficult. Those Ukrainians and Cossacks who welcomed the German invaders as liberators were soon disillusioned by their savage treatment at the hands of Hitler's SS. This was one of the most serious blunders made by Hitler during the war.

Stalin counterattacks, December 1941

As the Germans dug in for the winter, they were to be surprised by a sudden Russian counterattack that began on 6 December. Extra divisions brought from Siberia were led in this attack by General Zhukov. Stalin may have been able to do this because he knew that the Japanese would not now move against his eastern frontier (this information was passed on to him by the Soviet masterspy Victor Sorge in Tokyo). Only Hitler's refusal to order a general retreat saved the German army from complete disaster.

Japan strikes south, 1941–2

You read in Chapter 11 how the Japanese military leaders were divided about which direction their expansionist plans should take. While they had rapidly captured the main Chinese cities in 1937–8, the Japanese found themselves pinned down by guerrilla tactics of Mao Tse-tung. But the whole position changed with the German victories in western Europe in 1940. Britain was at full stretch in preventing an invasion, and France and the Netherlands could not really protect their colonial territories in Asia.

The Japanese took advantage of this to force the Vichy French government to allow them into Indo-China in 1940. This was to be the prelude to more ambitious projects. The main problem facing the Japanese leaders was Japan's need for basic raw materials, including oil and rubber. This made it vulnerable to economic blockade, and this was the weapon the US government used to try to prevent the Tokyo government from carrying out any further acts of aggression. An oil embargo was imposed on Japan, and relations with Washington gradually deteriorated. Until November 1941 there was still some hope that war could be avoided, but in that month, General Tojo became Prime Minister. He was the leader of the 'war party' and persuaded Emperor Hirohito that Japan should strike southwards against the European colonies in South-East Asia. To do this, the Japanese would first have to neutralize the American Pacific fleet.

Pearl Harbor, 7 December 1941

Admiral Yamamoto was given the task of planning the attack against the main US naval base at Pearl Harbor, Hawaii. He, in fact, did not believe that the Japanese could defeat the United States, but he loyally carried out the Emperor's orders. The attack was carried out by Japanese carrier-based aircraft on Sunday 7 December 1941, and it took the Americans completely by surprise. Eight American battleships and ten other warships were sunk, and over 2,000 US servicemen were killed (Fig. 12.5). It was a devastat-

ing blow, but had one fatal flaw, the American aircraft carriers were at sea and escaped destruction. They were to play a vital part in the Pacific War.

Pearl Harbor gave the Japanese Empire temporary control of the Pacific, but it also aroused the fighting spirit of the American people. President Roosevelt called 7 December 'a day that lived in infamy' because Japan had apparently attacked his country without warning (in fact, the Japanese intended to break off negotiations with the American government *before* Pearl Harbor, but there had been a diplomatic muddle). That attack allowed him to take a united nation to war with Japan. A few days later, on 10 December 1941, Hitler declared war on the USA.

Within six months, the nature of the struggle had completely changed, for Soviet and American involvement made it into a global war in a way that the First World War had never been.

Further Japanese victories

The tide of Japanese victories ran on into 1942, as the countries of South-East Asia fell before them. Their major objective was the oil-rich Dutch East Indies, but they also captured Hong Kong, Malaya, Burma and the Philippines. The British attempt to stop Japanese troops landing in Malaya failed when Japanese aircraft sank the powerful battleships *Prince of Wales* and *Repulse* on 10 December. These

Fig. 12.5   The USS Shaw *severely damaged during the Japanese attack on Pearl Harbor.*

two great ships had been sent out without any cover and were an easy target for the enemy.

Worse was to follow on 15 February, when the great naval base at Singapore surrendered to the Japanese army. This costly white elephant had not been provided with any landward defences so all its guns pointed out to sea! The Japanese attacked it from the Malay Peninsula and captured 80,000 prisoners. Its loss was a terrible blow to British prestige and was, to a large degree, the result of an underestimate of Japan's military capacity as Churchill conceded in his memoirs: 'I confess that in my mind, the whole Japanese menace lay in a sinister twilight, compared with our other needs.'[9]

American attempts to hold up the Japanese in the Philippines ended on 6 May with the surrender of their stronghold in Corregidor. The area commander General MacArthur had already left for Australia with his famous parting comment: 'I shall return.'

These Japanese victories had both short-term and long-term results. The most significant ones were:

1. the setting up of the Greater Asia Co-Prosperity Sphere, the Japanese version of *Lebensraum*. Their rule was characterized by the same cruelty and racial arrogance as that of the Germans in Europe. But they had already overtaxed their rather limited resources as we shall see.

2. the European colonial powers had suffered an irreversible defeat at the hands of an Asiatic power. 'The white man had lost his ascendancy with the disproof of his magic.'[10]

The turning point, 1942–3

In the early months of 1942 the forces of the aggressor powers seemed to be in the ascendant everywhere. No one knew then that the tide was about to turn in the most dramatic manner.

The bombing offensive

The first evidence of the turnabout came in the air battles over Germany, in which the RAF Bomber Command and the US Air Force were gaining the upper hand over the *Luftwaffe*. Although the losses were high, the continual bombardment from the skies disrupted German industry and tied down much needed aircraft. The inspiration behind this saturation or terror bombing was Sir Arthur 'Bomber' Harris. He persuaded Churchill to sanction Bomber Command's massive 1000 bomber raids against cities like Cologne and Essen in 1942. In fact, the raids were

not entirely successful and should have been replaced by the more accurate strategic bombing – aimed at essential parts of the German economy, such as the ball-bearing factories at Schweinfurt. Nevertheless, Harris's campaign showed that the balance of power in the air had changed, so that now it was Germany who was 'reaping the whirlwind'.

The Axis defeat in North Africa

The Allied air offensive had an important effect on other theatres of the war because Hitler could not provide air support for his armies. In North Africa the problem became acute, and was combined with an inability to get supplies across the Mediterranean Sea. The combined naval power of Britain and the United States was too much for the Axis powers, and Rommel was short of all the essentials of war. In the circumstances, Rommel did well, pushing the British 8th Army back to the Egyptian town of El Alamein by June 1942. But this was as much as he could do with such limited resources. In a great battle at El Alamein between 23 October and 4 November 1942, Rommel was defeated by the 8th Army, the 'Desert Rats', under General Bernard Montgomery. This defeat was crucial, but almost inevitable. Rommel's army was outnumbered by almost four to one, and the British superiority in tanks by the end of the battle was eleven to one. The German commander had already told his wife in a letter: 'I haven't much hope left.'

His fears were fully justified because four days later, the Anglo–American Operation Torch landed more Allied troops in French North Africa (Fig. 12.6). In May 1942 the remaining Axis forces in Africa were forced to surrender.

Fig. 12.6   South African troops prepare to go into action during the battle of Libya.

Fig. 12.7   The battle-torn city of Stalingrad.

Stalingrad, January 1943

The battle of El Alamein was an important Allied victory, but it was in no way decisive. The fate of the Third Reich was to be decided not in the desert, but on the Russian front. Here, too, the German forces had made great advances in the summer of 1942, advancing as far as the Caspian Sea. But they became fatally side-tracked by Hitler's obsessive desire to capture the city of Stalingrad (Fig. 12.7), which had no great military value from the German point of view. The whole of the German 6th Army, 250,000 men, was tied down in a desperate battle of attrition that reduced the city to a pile of rubble. They were then caught and surrounded by counterattacking Soviet forces. By the turn of the year, their position was hopeless, but Hitler obstinately refused to let their commander, von Paulus, break out of the siege. Yet again, Hitler was taken in by Goering's worthless assurance that he could supply the 6th Army from the air. As its numbers dwindled from cold and disease, the Führer instructed the 6th Army to 'do its historic duty to the last man'. The unfortunate von Paulus was made a field-marshal, but he could not ignore the evidence of his own eyes. On 31 January 1943 the 6th Army surrendered to the Red Army. Von Paulus and 90,000 survivors marched away into captivity.

Hitler's absurd attacks on von Paulus for not falling on his sword like a Roman general only underlined his increasing reluctance to face up to reality. His fantasies contrasted with the unwavering determination of his opponents. At the Casablanca Conference, Roosevelt and Churchill had just agreed that nothing less than unconditional surrender could be accepted from the Nazi government.

But the Führer tried one last attack on the Russian front to reverse the effects of Stalingrad. In May 1943 the Germans started a massive tank battle in the Kursk salient, but they ran out of reserves. Never again was the *Wehrmacht* to launch a major offensive in Russia. Stalingrad had been the single, most decisive battle of the war and by the end of 1943 the Germans were in a losing position (Table 12.2). Only the tenacity of the ordinary German soldier stood between Hitler and overwhelming defeat.

Table 12.2 Russian and German military strength, 1943

October 1943	Men	Tanks	Field guns
Russians	5,512,000	8,400	20,770
Germans	2,468,500	2,304	8,037

The war at sea, 1942–3

The pattern was repeated elsewhere, even at sea where the U-boats had promised so much in 1942. As late as March 1943, the submarines were able to sink forty-three Allied ships in twenty days, but that marked the peak of their effectiveness. The British discovery of centimetric radar changed the whole situation almost overnight. It allowed aircraft to pinpoint the position of U-boats in the most difficult weather conditions and destroy them. Between June and September, no Allied ships were sunk but U-boat losses were as high as 30 per cent of their effective fighting strength. The Battle of the Atlantic was as good as won when the effectiveness of the Royal Navy escort groups was added to this.

The turning point in the Pacific

Earlier in this chapter, you read about how the Japanese established their Greater Asia Co-Prosperity Area, but their ambitions did not end there. Japanese aircraft were within range of Australia's northern coastline and their land forces in a position to capture New Guinea. Japanese armies had also occupied Burma by the end of May 1942, although they had to deal with some tough defence by Anglo–Indian divisions. This proved to be the high point of their success.

In May the American navy under Admiral Nimitz foiled a Japanese expedition against Port Moresby. A month later came the decisive, and for the Japanese navy fatal, Battle of Midway. Like all the great naval battles in the Pacific, it was fought almost entirely by carrier-based aircraft, and the Americans succeeded in putting four of Japan's aircraft carriers out of action. During this battle, Nimitz had the priceless asset of knowing Japanese intentions because naval intelligence had broken their code. Japan's plans for the occupation of New Guinea had to be abandoned, and her military leaders lost the initiative.

Ringing the circle

By the middle of 1943 the Axis forces everywhere in Europe were on the retreat. The question now facing the Allied leaders was when and where to open a second front. Stalin had no doubts; he wanted an immediate assault on western Europe to relieve the tremendous pressure on the Red Army. When it was not mounted, his old suspicion of Western intentions reappeared.

Churchill, by contrast, was a great supporter of the 'soft underbelly of the Axis' theory. This meant attacking Italy, the weaker partner in the Axis alliance, an idea that left the Americans unenthusiastic. Eventually however, Churchill had his way, and in July 1943 Anglo–American forces landed on Sicily.

At first, Churchill's strategy seemed to work. By 3 September Sicily had been occupied, and on the same day, the Italian government surrendered. This followed the downfall and arrest of Benito Mussolini who had become, in his own words, the 'most hated man in Italy'. From this point, things began to go wrong for the Allies, who made the mistake of invading southern Italy rather than northern Italy, and the Germans had time to organize their defences.

A landing at Salerno on 9 September ran into fierce resistance, and it became clear that the Italian campaign was going to be a very difficult one indeed. The German leader Kesselring knew that he could expect little help from Berlin, but he made skilful use of Italy's mountainous terrain. Defensive positions like the Gustav Line greatly delayed the Anglo–American advance, so that by the end of 1943, Rome was still in German hands. An attempt to outflank the Germans by landing at Anzio was made on 22 January 1944.

The idea of landing behind enemy lines was a good one, and should perhaps have been tried earlier. But the landing failed because of the caution of the US General Lucas. He was unwilling to move inland quickly, and this gave Kesselring time to recover.

The stalemate in Italy only convinced the American leaders, Marshall and Eisenhower, that they had been right all along. Churchill continued to be enthusiastic about Italy and suggested alternative landings in the Balkans and southern France. But the Americans rightly insisted that the coastline of northern France had to be the invasion priority.

The Teheran Conference, November 1943

They were under increasing pressure from Stalin to open up a meaningful second front, and take the pressure off the Russians. When the 'Big Three' met at Teheran in November, Roosevelt gave Stalin a promise that France would be the landing target, in exchange for an assurance that the USSR would declare war on Japan as soon as Germany was defeated.

Operation Overlord, June 1944

Churchill accepted the American proposal that the invasion be launched in the summer of 1944. In the

Fig. 12.8   Wrecked landing craft and vehicles strew Omaha Beach after the D-Day invasion.

interim, the British Isles turned into a sort of floating fortress as men and supplies poured over the Atlantic.

The greater American contribution to the invasion was recognized by the appointment of Dwight D. Eisenhower as Supreme Allied Commander Europe. The operation itself was given the code name Overlord. Eisenhower had two major problems facing him:

1. to get the great invasion fleet over the Channel and ashore in France.
2. to achieve the vital element of surprise by making the Germans think the Allies were not going to land in Normandy, the real target for the invasion, but in the Pas de Calais*. If you look at a map, you will see that the shortest route across the Channel takes you to the Calais area. This was where the German High Command would expect a landing.

To land an army in France would depend on the ability to supply it efficiently, and there would be problems associated with having to capture a major French port – this could easily be wrecked by retreating Germans. To get round this problem, the Allies came up with an ingenious answer; they towed their own artificial harbours, called Mulberries, across the Channel with them. Fuel was to be pumped along the sea-bed by means of an underwater pipeline called PLUTO (Pipe Line under the Ocean).

All these inventions would have been wasted, however, if the Germans were expecting the invasion. So all kinds of ploys were used to confuse them. Dummy camps were set up facing the Calais area, and it was heavily bombed. False information was planted suggesting another landing in the Mediterranean, and so on. The effect of all this was to convince the Germans that the landing would indeed take place in the Pas de Calais. Hitler was, in any case, confident that his Atlantic Wall would defeat any attempted landing. Rommel had been put in charge of it, but the Führer studiously ignored his criticisms of the defences.

On the day, the Allied deception plan worked perfectly, and the whole vast force of 156,000 men was landed on the Normandy coast on 6 June 1944 – D-Day (Fig. 12.8). In the meantime, powerful German Panzer forces were held back in the Calais area for what Hitler and his generals believed would be the main landing. German forces were able to mount a tough rear-guard action around Caen, but the Anglo–American forces managed to break out of the bridgeheads and advance across northern France.

In August 1944 Paris was liberated by Free French forces, and General de Gaulle became head of a provisional French government.

The Bomb Plot, 20 July 1944

The spectre of defeat now faced the Third Reich, and some Germans decided that it was time to put an end to the fighting. Circles inside the army had long disliked the Nazis, and on 20 July 1944 a serious attempt was made to blow up Hitler in his headquarters in east Prussia. The attempt narrowly failed, and Hitler took a savage revenge on the conspirators and their families. Even Rommel was implicated and forced to commit suicide. The Nazi propaganda machine fabricated the story that he had died from his wounds. The Führer used his escape as evidence that his 'divine mission' should continue. His total disregard for the sufferings of the German people now became clearly apparent.

Defeat in the east

Meanwhile, the Red Army continued its relentless advance into eastern Europe. The Russian soldier was showing once more his traditional fighting qualities, but Soviet equipment in vital areas also proved to be superior. The Germans certainly had nothing to compare with the T34 tank. We have already seen how the Red Army won the gigantic tank battle around Kursk. They then moved on to drive the German forces out of the USSR altogether by April 1944 and invade Poland. By September the Red Army was in Bulgaria, Germany's former ally, and in the following month, in Hungary. Stiffer German resistance held them up around the Hungarian capital, Budapest.

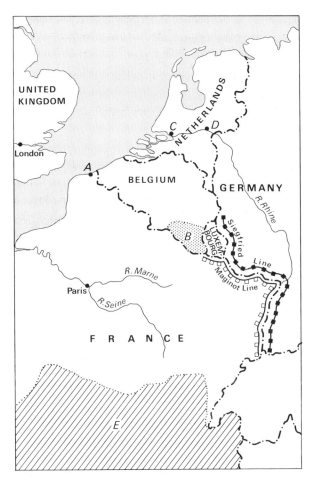

Fig. 12.9   Look at the questions on this map.

their bases in France and the Low Countries as they closed in on the frontiers of the Reich.

A more serious threat was posed by Hitler's last major offensive in the West, launched in December 1944. Surprisingly, the Germans were allowed to mount this in the very same Ardennes sector where they had attacked so effectively in May 1940. For about three weeks the Battle of the Bulge held a promise of German success, mainly because they achieved a genuine surprise. But then the wintry conditions suddenly changed to enable the Allies to use their complete mastery of the air. Ultimately, Hitler's Ardennes offensive used up valuable reserves in men and materials and hastened Germany's final defeat. By the end of 1944 the question facing the Allied leaders was no longer how but when.

Keywords

Panzer: German word for a tank.
Messerschmitt 109 and 110:   a German fighter (109) and fighter bomber (110).
regent: someone who stands in for a king or queen when they are young. In this case, the Regent was Paul of Yugoslavia.
Pas de Calais: the area around the port of Calais about 35 km (22 miles) from the English coast.

Questions

Fig. 12.9

1. What name did the Germans give to the type of warfare that allowed them to win their rapid victories in 1939–40?   1
2. Identify town A where the British army was evacuated in 1940.   1
3. Name area B where the German army made important breakthroughs in both 1940 and 1944.   1
4. Identify (i) city C, heavily bombed by the Germans in 1940 (ii) town D, the target for an Allied parachute landing in 1944.   2
5. Area E was left under French occupation in 1940. What name is usually given to the regime that ruled it?   1
6. Name the head of that government and his opponent who wanted to carry on the war from Britain and the French Empire.   2
7. Explain why the Allies wanted to seize town D in 1944.   4
8. Give at least FOUR reasons for the Allied success in the west in 1944–5.   8
   ___
   20

Hitler's last throw

The Western Allies were now confident that the war could be speedily concluded, although they suffered a setback at Arnhem in the Netherlands when an attempt to seize the Rhine bridgeheads failed.

Eisenhower continued to favour a broad advance on all fronts, whereas his British deputy Montgomery wanted to drive straight to Berlin. So intense did the debate become that everyone seemed to lose sight of the possibility that Hitler might have some shots left in his locker too!

Even in the summer the Führer still believed that he might turn the tide against the Allies. His confidence was based on the existence of two secret weapons, the V1 and the V2. The first was a pilotless flying bomb, nicknamed the 'doodlebug', the second, a genuine ballistic missile, too fast to be destroyed by Britain's air defences. By September 1944 both weapons were in use against London, but they were brought into action too late. Advancing Allied forces captured

13 From Yalta to Potsdam

Yalta

The major question at the Yalta Conference in February 1945 was the structure and organization of postwar Europe. Stalin renewed his promise to join the United Nations and come into the Japanese war. The old League of Nations was by now so discredited that all the Allied powers accepted the need for a new international organization. In exchange, Stalin was given an assurance by Churchill and Roosevelt that they accepted the special Soviet interest in Bulgaria, Hungary and Romania. Greece, as Stalin had already agreed, was to be inside the British sphere of influence. All Soviet aid to the Greek communists was withdrawn, thus contributing to their defeat in the war against those wishing to preserve the monarchy. Stalin honoured his promise over Greece, but he never allowed the promised free elections in Poland. At that time though, the Soviet leader was part of the famous 'Big Three' wartime coalition, and his two partners were still disposed to trust him.

The question of Berlin was also resolved in favour of the Soviet Union. General Eisenhower decided that it would be 'militarily unsound' to risk Allied lives in a drive for the German capital, so the job of capturing it fell to the Red Army.

By the beginning of March Anglo–American forces had reached the River Rhine, and in April over 300,000 German soldiers surrendered in the Ruhr. Their commander Model committed suicide.

Hitler's suicide

In the east the Red Army had swept out of Hungary and broken through the German defences in East Prussia. On 28 April Soviet and American forces linked up at Torgau on the Elbe (Fig. 13.1). Throughout April and into May, a great battle was fought over the bomb-devastated remnants of Berlin. Hitler's lunacy dictated that teenage boys and old men were to be forced into his Home Guard, the *Volkssturm*, to defend the Thousand-Year Reich. It made no difference to the outcome, other than to delay the inevitable. On 28 April 1945, as Russian tanks came within firing range of his underground headquarters, the Führer decided to shoot himself.

He was fifty-six years old, and his death followed that of his old friend Mussolini, who was captured and shot by communist partisans while attempting to flee into Switzerland. Hitler designated Admiral Karl Doenitz, former commander of the U-boat fleet, as the new head of state. It was he who agreed to the unconditional surrender of all German forces in Europe on 8 May 1945 – VE (Victory in Europe) Day.

Europe's dark night

The achievement of victory in Europe carried with it the discovery of unimagined horrors. As the Allied armies advanced into the heart of Hitler's Reich, they discovered the reality that lay behind the façade of boasting and brutality. In every country of occupied Europe there were concentration camps like Dachau, Belsen, Treblinka, Auschwitz and Ravensbrück, where human beings had been murdered by Hitler's SS.

Fig. 13.1   A broken bridge over the Elbe sees the link-up of Soviet and American troops on 28 April 1945.

Fig. 13.2   Victims of the concentration camp at Belsen.

The Jews

The most savage treatment, as the Nazis had always promised, had been meted out to the Jews, of whom six million perished in the death camps between 1939–45 (Table 13.1). There will always be disputes about the exact numbers involved, and we will probably never know the exact figure, but most European Jews were murdered or maltreated in the camps in a manner unparalleled in human history (Fig. 13.2). Whole famiIes were sent to the gas chambers, shot, starved or beaten to death in what the Nazis called the 'Final Solution'. Fiendish medical experiments were carried out on Jews in the interests of what Churchill called 'perverted science', and all the time, ordinary German citizens went to work, took holidays, were married and attended church on Sunday. How could this happen? Germany was after all an old and supposedly civilized country, the land of

Goethe, Bach and Handel. Albert Speer, a member of the German government, explained in his memoirs:

> I no longer give the answer with which I tried for so long to soothe the questioners, but chiefly myself: that in Hitler's system, as in every totalitarian regime, when a man's position rises, his isolation increases and he is therefore more sheltered from harsh reality; that with the application of technology to the process of murder the number of murderers is reduced and therefore the possibility of ignorance grows; that the craze for secrecy built into the system creates degrees of awareness, so it is easy to escape observing inhuman cruelties.
>
> I no longer give any of these answers.... Whether I knew or did not know, or how much or how little I knew, is totally unimportant when I consider what horrors I ought to have known about and what conclusions would have been the natural ones to draw from the little I did know. Those who ask me are fundamentally expecting me to offer justifications. But I have none. No apologies are possible.[1]

Table 13.1 Number of Jewish deaths in occupied Europe, 1939–45

Country	Jewish deaths
Poland	2,600,000
USSR	750,000
Romania	500,000
Hungary	700,000
Germany	180,000
Netherlands	104,000
Lithuania	104,000
France	65,000
Austria	60,000
Czechoslovakia	60,000

Alone among the Nazi leaders, Speer accepted responsibility for the attempt to exterminate the Jewish race. Ordinary Germans also found it difficult to come to terms with such a crime, although many thousands of them were certainly implicated in it. Throughout occupied Europe, there were anti-Semites, Fascists, or malicious neighbours who turned on their Jewish fellow citizens during those years.

You may find it hard to understand why the Jewish people went so passively to their deaths, but resistance would have been difficult. Where it did occur, the Nazi authorities reacted with characteristic savagery. In 1943 a general uprising in the Jewish ghetto* in Warsaw resulted in the systematic destruction of the whole area and the slaughter of its citizens. Some Jews lacked the will to resist, others could not believe the rumours about the concentration camps. Who can blame them for their belief that twentieth-century man was incapable of such excesses?

Just a few stories of individual heroism shine out through this fearful story. Raoul Wallenburg, a Swedish diplomat, saved thousands of Hungarian Jews by giving them Swedish passports. He was to disappear in mysterious circumstances in Budapest in 1945; probably into a Soviet prison. Anne Frank, a little Jewish girl, hid for years in a house in Amsterdam before dying in a concentration camp. Try and read her published diary if you can; it is a wonderful story of human courage and optimism in apparently hopeless circumstances.

Occupied Europe

The Jews, of course, were not alone in their sufferings,

and a general pattern emerged during the years after 1939. As they moved eastwards, the German forces, and particularly the SS, blatantly ignored the norms of civilized behaviour. Poles and Russians were regarded as sub-human, and the loss of life in their countries was immense. Twenty million Russians died in the war, together with 6 million Poles, although these figures include both military personnel and civilians. They compare with the much smaller figure of 357,000 deaths for Britain, which in itself is far lower than the loss of life in the 1914–18 War.

'The Nazis came to kill their fellow Europeans on an unprecedented scale. Their chief legacy to the continent they tried to dominate was death itself.'[2] But they did not do so unresisted. Every occupied country had its resistance forces, and only in France did the legally constituted government stay to co-operate with the Nazi administration. The men and women of the resistance movements fought a lonely and dangerous war, well away from the world of conventional warfare. Capture meant torture, imprisonment or death, yet much valuable work was done by the resistance movements. In France the Maquis* helped disrupt German communications before D-Day; in Norway the underground fighters helped to destroy the heavy water essential for the production of the German atomic bomb. Yugoslavia was a case apart because guerrilla activity prevented the Germans and Italians from ever occupying the whole country. Large Axis forces were tied down by the activities of the Yugoslav partisans led by Josip Broz, who became better known by the name Tito. The support offered by the British Special Operations Executive was very important here.

All over the continent the Nazis underestimated the resolve of the subject peoples they affected to despise.

The end in Asia

The European part of the war was over, but Japan was still undefeated in the East. We must now have a look at the war in the Asian theatre, where you may remember that the tide was beginning to turn in 1942 (see p. 111). By the autumn of 1943 the American recovery from Pearl Harbor was complete, and they planned their strategy of revenge. This was based on the idea of seizing air bases by 'hopping' from one Pacific island to the next. The Americans needed these bases for their B-29 superfortresses, which would bomb the Japanese home islands. The campaign began in November 1943 with the capture of the Gilbert Islands, which was followed by the occupation of the Marshalls early in 1944.

A two-pronged assault on the Japanese then took place. One force led by General MacArthur attacked New Guinea which had fallen by September 1944. Another led by Admiral Nimitz seized the Marianas by August. These successes put the Americans in a position to invade the Philippines and honour MacArthur's promise of 1942.

Leyte Gulf, 1944

Before doing so the Americans had to fight their last great naval battle of the Pacific War, off Leyte Gulf. It was an unusual one in that carrier-borne aircraft played only a minor role, but its effect was decisive. Admiral Halsey's fleet destroyed the last fleet Imperial Japan possessed, and made Japan's eventual defeat a certainty. Japanese desperation was indicated in this battle by their use of kamikaze* or suicide planes to sink American ships.

Iwo Jima and Okinawa

Unfortunately from their point of view, the Americans did not realize that their enemy was on the point of collapse. They stuck rigidly to their island-hopping strategy, even though it proved to be very costly. The Japanese, who regarded death in battle as a privilege, fought to the last man. The capture of the island of Iwo Jima cost 6,000 American lives, Okinawa, another 12,000. An assault on the Japanese home islands seemed likely to be a very bloody affair indeed.

The campaign in Burma

In the meantime, another war was being fought in faraway Burma by the 14th British Army, the 'forgotten army' as their commander called them. Initially, these men under General Slim had to fight off an attempt by the Japanese to invade India early in 1944. The attack collapsed around the towns of Imphal and Kohima. The end of this threat enabled Slim to launch the invasion of Burma itself. This campaign was to be linked to an offensive by Chiang Kai-shek's Chinese troops under the command of the American Stilwell.

'Vinegar Joe' Stilwell was frequently angered by Chiang's lethargy and could do little to make his army play a more positive role in the war.

All these campaigns were to be co-ordinated by Lord Louis Mountbatten who was made Supreme Com-mander of the Allied Forces in South-East Asia. His energetic leadership helped Slim's Burma offensive to push forward.

By December 1944, the 14th Army had established bridgeheads over the River Irrawaddy as a prelude to the conquest of southern Burma. Mandalay was captured in April, and in May the victorious Allied troops marched into Rangoon, the Burmese capital. The Burma campaign, fought in the most testing jungle conditions, had been concluded in only six months.

The decision to drop the atomic bomb

The island of Okinawa fell to the Americans on 21 June 1945, and it was the last major obstacle to an invasion of the Japanese home islands. But this venture was fraught with difficulties for the Allied leaders, even if Soviet Russia did come into the Far Eastern war. Wherever they advanced the Allies met fanatical Japanese resistance, and on 26 July the Imperial government ignored a demand from Roosevelt, Churchill and Chiang Kai-shek that it should surrender.

American calculations indicated that a land invasion of Japan might cost one million casualties, which was a horrific possibility after the terrible losses all the belligerent nations had already suffered. In some desperation, the Allied leaders cast about for an alternative. President Harry S. Truman, who replaced Roosevelt as President on 12 April, was the man who had to make one of the most fateful decisions in history – whether or not to use the atomic bomb (Fig. 13.3). This deadly new weapon had been

Fig. 13.3 The scientist in Sir David Low's 'Baby play with nice ball?' offers 'humanity' the chance to choose between 'life or death'. (Look at the questions on this cartoon on p. 120.)

satisfactorily tested in the New Mexico desert earlier in the year and was now ready for use.

Other factors weighed in Truman's mind, too. Some air force chiefs, like Curtis le May, believed that the Japanese economy could be hopelessly disrupted by ordinary conventional bombing. In the summer of 1945 le May reported: 'Japan will become a nation without cities, with her transportation disrupted, and will have tremendous difficulty in holding her people together for continued resistance.' This hope was countered by possible Soviet action in the Far East.

At the Potsdam Conference in July, Truman deliberately told Stalin about the existence of the atomic bomb, but the information seemed to have little immediate effect. Truman and his colleagues were worried that unless Japan was speedily defeated, Soviet influence would spread throughout South-East Asia.

In the end, Truman decided to take the decision to drop the bomb, what he himself called 'the greatest thing in history'. On 6 August 1945 a lone B-29 bomber flew from the island of Tinian to a position over the Japanese city of Hiroshima. The first atomic bomb was then detonated and 60,000 Japanese civilians died. The mission Commander Colonel Tibbets wrote later: 'Where before there had been a city with distinctive houses, buildings and everything that you could see from our altitude, now you couldn't see anything except a black boiling debris down below.'[3]

Japan surrenders

On the following day, Soviet forces crossed the frontier into the Japanese-occupied province of Manchuria. Yet still nothing definite was heard from the Japanese government. On 9 August authority was given to drop a second atomic device on the city of Nagasaki – with equally horrific results. Even then, the Japanese government was undecided, so dishonourable was the concept of defeat to their society. At this stage, Emperor Hirohito intervened in a decisive manner. After a series of cabinet meetings on August 13–14, he decided that 'the unendurable must be endured'. Japan was to surrender unconditionally to the Allied powers, and Hirohito broadcast the news to his people himself. None of them had heard his voice before, and many preferred suicide to the prospect of defeat and occupation.

On 2 September General MacArthur, acting with the agreement of the Soviet Union, accepted the surrender of the Imperial Japanese government on board the battleship *Missouri*. After almost exactly six years of fighting, the second great conflict of the twentieth century was over.

The postwar settlement

The Potsdam Conference

Before the Japanese war was over, the Allied leaders had already decided the fate of Germany. The memory of 1919 reinforced the determination to occupy defeated Germany, and the country was divided into four zones. This included a French zone of occupation, although General de Gaulle was not invited to the conference; an omission that did nothing to improve his relations with the British and the Americans. Berlin was to become a four-power city, although it was, in fact, well inside the Soviet zone of occupation. No time limit was set upon the occupation of Germany, but it was not intended to be permanent. Austria, too, was to be divided into four zones, as was its capital Vienna, and all Germany's former allies had to pay reparations to the Allied powers.

The main area of disagreement, as at Yalta, was the question of Poland. Roosevelt and Churchill had intended Poland's new frontier to be marked by the *eastern* branch of the River Neisse. Stalin, whether deliberately or not, took it to be the *western* branch of the river. By the time the conference assembled, the Poles had occupied the western lands and 9 million Germans had been forced to flee from their former homes.

New leaders

Of the Big Three who had met at Yalta in February, only Stalin remained. Truman represented the United States, and Clement Attlee was the new British Prime Minister. To everyone's surprise his Labour Party had routed the Conservatives at the polls in July 1945. The result actually came through while the conference sat and a stunned Churchill returned home as Leader of the Opposition.

The new situation certainly gave the Soviet leader an advantage, and overall, there was no doubt which great power had gained most in the closing months of the war.

'As one outcome of the war, Soviet troops were now 100 miles [161 km] from the Rhine, and occupying the whole of eastern Europe and most of the Balkans'.[4] Stalin had put Russia in a position of which tsars had dreamed, but never achieved.

The Nuremberg Trials, 1945–6

One matter on which all the Allies were agreed was

that the Nazi leadership should be brought to account for its crimes. Hitler, Himmler and Goebbels had committed suicide, but many important Nazi leaders remained alive. They included Goering, Doenitz, Speer, Kaltenbrunner (Himmler's deputy) and Hess. These men and nineteen others were put on trial and charged with:

1. conspiring to wage aggressive war against the rest of Europe;
2. crimes against humanity.

The place chosen for the trials was the city of Nuremberg where the Nazi party had held its prewar rallies. The trials lasted from November 1945 to October 1946, and involved the use of 4,000 captured German documents and the testimony of hundreds of witnesses. In every individual case, the Soviet judges voted to hang the accused, but in the end, twelve defendants only were executed. Goering cheated the hangman's noose by taking cyanide, and Albert Speer was sentenced to twenty years' imprisonment. He alone of the men on trial pleaded guilty to the charges against him.

A more serious problem concerned the smaller fry and what was to be done with them. Walter Laqueur describes the difficulties facing the Allied governments over this issue: 'The Nazi Party in Germany had counted eight million members, it included most of the higher civil servants, almost the whole business and intellectual élite*. How could a new Germany (or Austria or Italy) be built without the active co-operation of these men and women?'⁵

The sheer scale of the problem meant that denazification was bound to be incomplete. The best the Allies could do was to try and make examples of the most notorious Nazis and re-educate the German population. But many people still found the whole process unsatisfactory. Two examples underline this. In Belgium, where Fascism was a minority movement, there were 87,000 prosecutions. In Austria, with its large Nazi Party, only 9,000. Many potential war criminals, like the SS killer Adolf Eichmann, disappeared at the end of the war. Most of them went to Latin America where they found sympathetic refuges. Eichmann was to be kidnapped by the Israeli secret service in 1961, and later executed.

Another point, which was raised later, was the whole validity of the Nuremberg exercise. The idea of putting the leaders of a defeated nation on trial was a new one, although you will remember that there was talk of trying the Kaiser in 1918. But as the years went by doubts arose about the right of the Allied powers to do this. The terror bombing of Dresden in February 1945 was one of several cases cited in which Allied actions were open to serious criticism. Sensitivity in Britain on this issue was shown by the fact that the veterans of Bomber Command had no special campaign medal struck for them.

On the Soviet side, there were lingering doubts about the massacre of Polish officers in the Kattin Forest. Few people in the West believed Soviet assurances that the Nazis were responsible.

The Far Eastern settlement

In Asia, the United States government insisted that it should be the power to make the decisions. Japan was to be occupied only by American troops commanded by General MacArthur, and he was largely responsible for drawing up the country's new constitution.

Emperor Hirohito was no longer to be a god to his people but seen to be an ordinary mortal like the rest of the Japanese. He was allowed to keep his throne, but the old militaristic Japan was gone forever.

It was to have no armed forces and its old leaders like those of Germany were to be punished. Tojo, the Prime Minister at the time of Pearl Harbor, was among those hanged. A new Japan was to emerge in the postwar years, but one based on economic rather than military power (see Chapter 21).

The United Nations Organization

One last aspect of the postwar settlement needs to be examined; the setting up of a new organization to replace the old League of Nations. It was to be called the United Nations (UN) Organization, and the need for it had been agreed by the wartime allies as far back as 1943. Representatives of all the nations met at San Francisco in June 1945 to draw up the UN Constitution. In doing so, they attempted to learn some lessons from the sad failure of the old League. The UN was given powers to raise armed forces, and to encourage American participation the new UN headquarters were to be in New York City. Some of the old flaws remained, however. The League Council was replaced by a Security Council and once again, the great powers were given a right of veto. Like the League, the UN was to find it difficult to impose its decisions on the great powers (Fig. 13.4).

Nevertheless, the United Nations was to become a more effective instrument for preserving world peace than the League had been. Starting in Korea in 1950 (see p. 136) and then in the Congo, Cyprus and the Middle East, the new organization showed that it could play a valuable role in identifying, and trying to contain, aggressive behaviour within the international system. Its peacekeeping forces drafted

Fig. 13.4 'A fine team but could do with a dash of unity' by Sir David Low. At the United Nations Club there is one rule: 'All players to play together but not so as to cramp any player's style (that would be unrealistic).' (Look at the questions on this cartoon.)

troops from neutral countries, such as India, Sweden, Eire and Norway, that were ready at a moment's notice to fly off to one of the world's hotspots.

It also carried on some of the good work of the old League agencies, of which only the International Labour Organization (ILO) survived. These new agencies were:

UNESCO United Nations Educational, Scientific and Cultural Organization.

FAO Food and Agriculture Organization (pioneering new farming methods, fertilizers, etc.).

WHO World Health Organization (drugs research, disease control and notification).

UNICEF United Nations International Children's Emergency Fund.

One striking difference between the League and the United Nations was their relative size. As more and more countries obtained their independence after 1945, the UN became a truly international organization in a sense that its predecessor had never been. In its early years, the UN was handicapped by Soviet suspicions that it was a Western stooge, but its leadership has always been scrupulously neutral. Care was taken to select the Secretary-General from neutral countries, and men like Dag Hammarskjöld of Sweden and U Thant of Burma were to earn a high reputation for their work in trying to preserve world peace.

A major anomaly was corrected in 1971, when Communist China was finally admitted to the UN after years of American opposition, so that all the great powers were represented on the Security Council. In Chapter 3 we saw how several of the great powers either refused to join the League at all, or were only members for a short period. The continuous membership of the USSR and USA has been a source of strength to the United Nations in the various international crises since the end of the Second World War.

Keywords

ghetto: a special area where Jews were forced to live.

Maquis: the French resistance movement; a Corsican word meaning scrubland.

kamikaze: a Japanese airforce corps in the Second World War which crashed its aircraft into enemy targets; meaning 'divine wind'.

élite: the group in control of a profession, industry, class or government.

Questions

Figs. 13.3 and 13.4

1. Who made the decision to use the 'nice ball' in Fig. 13.3?   1
2. Name the Japanese cities against which it was used.   2
3. Name the mission commander when this weapon was first used.   1
4. What arguments were used by Allied leaders to justify the use of the atomic bomb in the summer of 1945?   6
5. Who are the four sportsmen in Fig. 13.4?   4
6. Where was the UN Charter drawn up in 1945?   1
7. State THREE important differences between the UN and the League of Nations.   3
8. Give an example of an issue where the 'team' lacked 'unity' in 1945.   1
9. Which of the men shown in Fig. 13.4 was soon replaced as leader of his country in 1945?   1

—

14 The Origins of the Cold War and the Foundation of the People's Democracies

During the Second World War there had been signs of tension among the three great wartime allies, but even in the autumn of 1945 the general feeling was still one of goodwill between the West and the Soviet Union. The exploits of the Red Army had been widely admired in Britain and the United States, and Stalin had paid grudging tribute to his Western allies.

The coming of the Cold War*

Slowly at first, but with ever quickening pace, this situation began to change. In 1945 the mood had been one of compromise, with the return of pro-German elements (from the Ukraine especially) to the Soviet Union for punishment, and Stalin's acceptance at Yalta that Greece should lie within the British 'sphere of influence'. The communists had been doing well in the civil war against the Greek monarchists, but Stalin's decision sealed their fate.

But elsewhere in Eastern Europe, the liberation from Nazi rule appeared to carry with it the acceptance of communist rule. The Red Army remained in occupation of the liberated territories, and it became increasingly clear that the local communist parties had Moscow's full backing in their drive to achieve power. In Poland, for example, Stalin went back on the promise given at Yalta that there would be free elections. At first, the Americans were inclined to take a generous view of Soviet behaviour, but others took a more pessimistic view of Stalin's long-term intentions. In March 1946, Winston Churchill, by then Leader of the Opposition in the House of Commons, made a famous speech at Fulton, Missouri. In it he said:

> From Stettin in the Baltic to Trieste in the Adriatic, an iron curtain has descended across the continent. Behind that line all the capitals of the ancient states of central and eastern Europe – Warsaw, Berlin, Prague, Vienna, Budapest, Bucharest, and Sofia, all those famous cities, and the populations around them, lie in the Soviet sphere

and all are subject in one form or another not only to Soviet influence but to very high and increasing measures of control.

The reference at that time to an iron curtain shocked many people, and to a considerable degree Churchill was pointing to a *possible* rather than an actual situation. Nevertheless, the process to which he referred was well underway, and the breakdown of the wartime *entente* was not confined to Europe alone.

Iran

As early as 1946 Stalin tried to annex the Iranian province of Azerbaijan where Anglo–Soviet troops were temporarily stationed under the 1942 Anglo–Soviet Treaty. Iran appealed to the UN Security Council and the Russians withdrew, an all-too-rare victory for the UN over a superpower. But Iran was a side-issue compared with the crucial European settlement. It is important to remember that the Soviet Union had no atomic bomb, and Stalin would not risk its security for a remote Iranian province. He seems to have been conducting a form of probing exercise, to see what gains could be made without paying too high a price.

Greece

Stalin's major objective was to obtain a dominant influence over the countries of Eastern Europe, and so compensate the USSR for its devastating losses in what Russians called the 'Great Patriotic War'. The setting up of the so-called 'People's Democracies' will form a later theme of this chapter, but we must turn now to the undoubted turning point in Soviet–Western relations after 1945, the Greek crisis of 1947. It was this crisis which is generally accepted as marking the beginning of the Cold War, i.e. the period of antagonism between the USSR and the West which was to stop short of actual war.

The circumstances were clear-cut, for on 31 March 1947, Britain, plagued by economic weakness, sent Washington a three-point note:

1. Great Britain could no longer be responsible for economic aid to Greece and Turkey.
2. The Greek economy was on the verge of collapse.
3. To maintain the Greek army in 1947 £70 million were needed.

The United States, therefore, received an ultimatum: help Greece or see it fall into communist hands. Three weeks of wrangling followed, while counteraccusations flew across the Atlantic. Then President Truman decided the Greeks must have aid if they were 'to become a self respecting democracy'. Indeed, he went further and announced what came to be known as the Truman Doctrine.

This laid down a new basis for American policy whereby the United States would 'support free peoples who are resisting subjugation by armed minorities or by outside pressures'.

Marshall Aid

This rejection of isolationism went hand in hand with a generous programme of economic aid put forward by Secretary of State George Marshall on 5 June 1947. Marshall promised that the United States would 'assist in the return of normal economic health in the world', and Western Europe quickly took up his offer (Fig. 14.1). Bevin, the British Foreign Secretary, thanked the United States for its 'inspiring lead', but the Soviet reply was frosty. The party paper *Pravda* ('Truth') called the plan an attempt to interfere 'in the domestic affairs of other countries' (see Chapter 10). Equally significant was the Soviet refusal to allow any of the other East European countries to accept aid either.

The lasting effect of Marshall Aid and the European Recovery Programme, say Waterlow and Evans, was that it was to 'divide the countries of Europe into hostile economic groups, one linked to the United States, the other to the Soviet Union'.[1] Aid, worth billions of dollars, was pumped into Europe (especially into West Germany) between 1948–52.

The people's democracies

The British withdrawal from Greece could not, of course, have proved to be so crucial, had it not been for the inroads made by communism in Eastern Europe. This could not have been done without a considerable amount of local support for the communists in these countries, and preparation for the

Fig. 14.1   Marshall Aid arrives in Europe.

postwar struggle. Thus the Polish communists had set up a 'shadow government' at Lublin in 1944, and Tito's guerrilla fighters were ready to seize power in Yugoslavia. But behind the local communist parties was the looming presence of the Red Army. A communist government was set up in Bulgaria in 1945, to be followed by Poland, Romania and Hungary in 1947.

Economic planning

Each of the people's democracies moved at a different pace from the others, although they all showed the characteristics of the centralized communist state. In Poland, land reforms were introduced even before fighting had ceased, and holdings of over 100 hectares (250 acres) were simply seized without compensation. The Poles also introduced a three-year plan of economic reconstruction in 1947, which allowed public, private and co-operative sectors to exist independently. In Bulgaria, it was a different story because most of the land was already fairly divided.

By a historical paradox, it was Tito's Yugoslavia that went furthest of all. It refused to share power with the 'bourgeois' parties and passed a constitution in 1946 that was a copy of the Stalinist model of 1936. A further decree in December 1946 gave the state full control of industry and financial institutions. Such moves appeared to be voluntary, but the shadow of a Soviet take-over by the still mobilized Red Army lurked in the background. In 1949 the Soviets exploded their first atomic bomb, but still their land forces were kept at a high pitch of war readiness.

There was, in addition, the formation of the Cominform or Communist Information Bureau, abolished to please the Western democracies in 1943, but now reintroduced. Only the Pole Gomulka had the nerve to oppose it, and he was promptly thrown into gaol.

Fig. 14.2 Klement Gottwald addresses a mass communist rally in Prague in May 1948.

Czechoslovakia, February 1948

At the start of the year 1948, only little Czechoslovakia seemed to retain the trappings of Western-style democracy.

In the event, the days of Czech democracy were numbered. In 1946 the Communists had won a small victory in the parliamentary elections, but they shared the government with the Social Democrats under Fierlinger. His party objected to the policy of craven obedience to the Communists, and in November 1947, he was removed from the party leadership. The way was now open for Klement Gottwald (Fig. 14.2), whose supporters had thoroughly infiltrated the police and armed forces. In February 1948 Gottwald, assured of Soviet support, forced the aged President Beneš to appoint a majority of Communist ministers. The anti-Communist, Jan Masaryk, son of the founder of the Czech Republic, was found dead in mysterious circumstances outside his Prague flat. He alone had the international prestige to have offered any resistance to the Communist coup. Within months, Gottwald had replaced Beneš as President of the Republic. 'It was,' he said, 'like cutting butter with a sharp knife.'

This episode gave Stalin the security zone around Soviet frontiers that he had been seeking, but his ambition did not stop there.

Yugoslavia

The people's democracies were noted in general for 'cynicism, servility, and corruption', but Stalin was to meet his match in the Yugoslav leader Josip Broz Tito, who had led his country throughout the Second World War. Germans, Italians, Četniks* and Utaša* had all gone down before the tough and courageous Yugoslav partisans, a fact that Stalin would have done well to remember. Instead, he tried his usual tactics of internal interference and infiltration, and

Soviet–Yugoslav relations grew steadily worse:
1. Yugoslavia was in dispute with Italy over Trieste, and Stalin opposed the former's claims.
2. Stalin falsely claimed that the Red Army had liberated Yugoslavia from Axis occupation.
3. Tito had evidence of secret recruitment of Soviet agents in Yugoslavia.
4. Stalin wanted to form a federation of Bulgaria and Yugoslavia, which were then to 'annex' Albania. Tito suspected that this was merely a prelude to Soviet annexation and flatly rejected it.

The USSR wanted Yugoslavia to be a pastoral* unit within the Soviet economic empire, and Tito would not settle for this. Moscow then tried abuse, calling Tito a 'Trotskyite and a Bukhavinite', but this clumsy approach failed too.

Yugoslavia left the Cominform, and the USSR tried to break the Yugoslavs with an economic blockade. Instead, the Yugoslav leader bought food and spare parts for his army from the West. Stalin had told Khrushchev in a famous phrase: 'I will shake my little finger and there will be no more Tito.' For once, he had met his match, but others were to pay the price. Tito meanwhile was given overwhelming popular support at the fifth party congress on 21 July.

The Berlin Blockade, 1948–9

In most respects, 1948 was the crucial year of the Cold War, as Allied–Soviet relations sank to a new low. Czechoslovakia and Yugoslavia were unpleasant examples of Stalinism, but they did not represent a direct attack on the postwar settlement.

Czechoslovakia proved to be the prelude to another crisis which involved all four of the major powers. Its focal point was the city of Berlin, which, you will

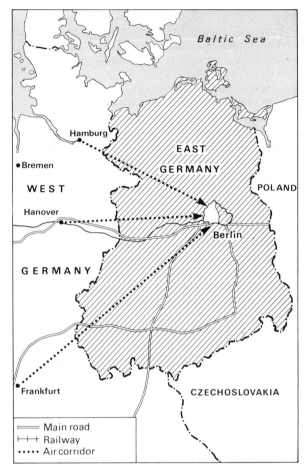

Fig. 14.3   Air, rail and road routes from West Germany to West Berlin.

Fig. 14.4   The millioneth bag of coal arrives in Berlin during the airlift of 1948–9.

recall, was made into a four-power city by the Potsdam Agreement. Fig. 14.3 shows that Berlin was an easy target for Soviet pressure because it lay many miles inside their zone of occupation. The occasion for the crisis was the decision of the three Western powers to merge their zones of occupation into one and to introduce a currency reform at the same time.

Stalin was enraged, and responded on 18 June 1948 by turning off the electricity supply and cutting off all the road and rail links between Berlin and the West. The blockade of Berlin had begun, and it was to continue for over a year.

The Western Allies responded by staging a massive airlift of supplies to West Berlin (Fig. 14.4). About 4,000 ton(ne)s of supplies were needed daily to keep the people alive but so efficient did the airlift become that by April, the figure was as high as 13,000 ton(ne)s per day. Stalin dared not close the air corridors to the West, and throughout the crisis, control towers were manned by Soviet personnel. By

April 1949 Stalin had, in any case, decided to call off the blockade. The Western allies had shown that they would honour that commitment to Berlin.

Stalinism

We said earlier that others were to pay for the defiance of Josip Broz Tito as the increasingly unbalanced dictator sought out smaller 'Titos' to punish within his satellite empire. The late 1940s and 1950s in Eastern Europe bore an uncanny resemblance to the 1930s as first one and then another notable communist disappeared from the scene.

Stalin's blood lust, wrote Khrushchev later, was the consequence of the actions of 'a profoundly sick man who suffered from suspiciousness and persecution mania'. The list makes gloomy reading:

Romania: Anna Pauker and Vasile Luce – purged May 1952.
Poland: Gomulka – arrested 1949 (but survived).
East Germany: Merkov – purged 1950.
Bulgaria: Kostov – purged 1948 (withdrew confession).

Czechoslovakia: Slansky – tried and executed 1951; Husak – imprisoned (but survived).
Hungary: Laszlo Rajk – purged September 1949.

Economic development

The parallel with the USSR did not end there because the Five-Year Plans quite often yielded spectacular results. In Bulgaria, for example, 92 per cent of peasant land was collectivized by the 1950s, but the pace was still uneven. The more individualistic Poles only collectivized 15 per cent of peasant land, and staged a revolt in 1956 for good measure.

Economic backwardness was still to remain a big issue in the 1950s, especially in Czechoslovakia, Poland and Hungary. Liberalization after Khrushchev's 1956 speech remained a false dawn, even after he was embarrassed into telling Tito in 1955: 'We sincerely regret what happened [referring to the Soviet–Yugoslav split of 1948].'

His regrets did not extend to the satellite system proper, or for popular leaders like Nagy of Hungary, who was sacked in 1955 for trying to introduce economic reforms.

The case of East Germany was rather different: firstly because of the hope of eventual reunification to which many Germans clung; and secondly, because the geographical closeness of the two states made it easy for hundreds of thousands of East Germans to flee westwards. The knowledge of superior living conditions in the West was one of the factors behind the East German workers' rising of 1953. West Germany was a bridge between the West and the Stalinist East, although for many years the West German government did not take advantage of its unique position (probably for fear of offending the Americans).

While East German leader Walter Ulbricht watched the development of Erhardt's *Wirtswunderschaft* (economic miracle) from the other side of the Iron Curtain, political realities gave him some comfort. Throughout the 1950s, West German Foreign Minister Walter Hallstein refused to have diplomatic relations with any state recognizing the German Democratic Republic. It is doubtful, in fact, whether Western Allies really wanted a powerful, reunited Germany so soon after the war.

Why Cold War?

The reasons for the start of the Cold War are complex, and historians have argued about them ever since. Some have seen it as a direct consequence of the Soviet Union's aggressive policies. Others believe (like Isaac Deutscher) that Soviet policy was dictated (i) by fear of the West, and (ii) by a desire to avoid a repetition of the terrifying slaughter of the 1939–45 war.

Here are two historians' views of the problem:
1. *The USSR was an aggressive power.*
   Was there no end to Russian demands? The admiration for Russian achievements was dimmed by fear of Soviet ruthlessness and power, and by the realization that Moscow's friends in the West would, if they could, destroy free government everywhere – *Walter Laqueur*[2]
2. *The USSR needed security from attack.*
   There are many who think that in 1945, Stalin and his hordes wanted to sweep right across Europe. In my opinion, and I am entitled to my opinion as others are, this was not the case.
   Soviet policy wanted security: the defeat of Germany, and then the building up of a ring of satellite states which would ensure Soviet Russia's security. – *A. J. P. Taylor*[3]

Cold War timeline

1946
5 March   Churchill makes his Iron Curtain speech in Fulton, Missouri.

1947
12 March   Truman Doctrine announced.
5 June   Marshall Plan announced.

1948
February   Communists in power in Czechoslovakia.
18 June   Start of Berlin Blockade.
21 July   Fifth Congress of Yugoslav Party.

1949
April   End of Berlin Blockade.

1951   Rudolf Slansky executed.

Keywords

Cold War: a hostile relationship between countries or blocs, but one that stops short of war (as in Europe in the 1940s and 1950s).
Četniks: led by Mihajlović from remnants of Yugoslav army, but anti-Communism made them unreliable allies.
Utaša: Fascist Yugoslav sympathizers giving active help to Axis forces in the Second World War.
pastoral: meaning agricultural. In this case, Stalin's plan to turn Yugoslavia into an agricultural country.

15 A World Divided

In Chapter 14 we saw how the successful wartime coalition began to break up in the years immediately after 1945. The story of how this division became a permanent feature of the postwar world will be the main theme of this chapter (Fig. 15.1).

The formation of the defence blocs

As early as 1947, Britain and France had signed the Dunkirk Treaty in an attempt to make themselves more secure in the face of possible Soviet aggression. The Berlin Blockade and the Czech crisis of 1948 extended this process to other Western countries as well. The result was the formation of the North Atlantic Treaty Organization (NATO) in 1949 with the major aim of preserving Western Europe from the danger of attack. Most of its members were European countries (Britain, France, Italy, Belgium and Holland), but Canada and the United States joined as well. Later the membership was extended to include Portugal, Greece, Turkey and eventually West Germany in 1955.

Similar anti-communist regional pacts were to be formed in other parts of the world as well. In the Middle East, the United States encouraged the formation of the Baghdad Pact in 1955 signed by Britain, Iran, Turkey, Iraq and Pakistan. In 1959 this became the Central Treaty Organization (CENTO). It was the same story in the Far East where anxiety about Chinese intentions after the Korean War brought about the formation of the South East Asia Treaty Organization (SEATO) in 1954. The member states were the USA, France, UK, Australia, New Zealand, Thailand, Pakistan and the Philippines.

The communist side was not slow to reply. In 1955 the Soviet Union engineered the formation of the Warsaw Pact which gave it a military alliance with East Germany, Czechoslovakia, Romania, Bulgaria, Poland and Hungary. Yugoslavia refused to join this organization which was clearly meant to be a reply to the earlier foundation of NATO. The tiny east

Fig. 15.1   The formation of Eastern and Western economic and defence blocs, 1947–59.

European state of Albania was also a founder-member, but withdrew in 1962 after disagreements between its leader Hoxha and the Soviet leadership. The formation of the Warsaw Pact meant that Churchill's Iron Curtain had been well and truly reinforced (see p. 121).

The emphasis of this chapter has been on the division of the world since 1945 into a rival series of blocs. The other characteristic of the time has been the growing presence of heavy armaments, and the temptation to use new and lethal methods of warfare remains. In 1952 the USA detonated the first hydrogen bomb, and was rapidly followed by the USSR in August 1953, and Britain in 1957. The Chinese were next to join the nuclear club in June 1967, and France detonated her first bomb in 1968.

The balance of power was profoundly altered once the United States had lost nuclear superiority. This altered both its defensive plans and its relationships with the communist bloc. The two superpowers were now 'eyeball to eyeball' and had a common, if understated, interest in stopping the spread of atomic weapons to smaller, less reliable states. For smaller powers, like Britain and France, having an independent nuclear deterrent such as the *force de frappe* (literally 'strike force') and RAF Bomber Command was largely a matter of prestige. They did not cause the men in the Kremlin to lose much sleep.

On a more sophisticated level, de Gaulle argued that they could not place absolute reliance on the US nuclear deterrent, and therefore needed a separate nuclear force. His argument expressed a nagging doubt that remained with the Western Europeans. Would the USA, as it had done between 1919–41, fall back on isolationism, but protected this time by a massive battery of nuclear weapons? If so, how could Western Europe defend itself? The complicated question of the arms race will receive further treatment in Chapter 24.

Economic blocs

If the motive behind the formation of the military blocs was fear, it was also important in the creation of larger economic units. The countries of Western Europe had shared a common experience of defeat and occupation between 1939–45, and they had no desire to repeat it. The urge to unite was strong, and it began in 1944 with the foundation of the Benelux Customs Union between Belgium, the Netherlands and Luxembourg. Fear of the USSR then sharpened the impetus of the movement after 1945.

Federalism and functionalism

There were two rival theories about European unity at this time.

Federalists believed that a rapid movement to complete political unification was desirable. This would result in the formation of a type of 'United States of Europe'.

Functionalists were more patient. They thought it would be more sensible to have economic union first, so destroying all barriers to trade, and then move on to political union later.

The Federalist phase, 1948–54

At first, the Federalists seemed to be making the most progress. They were encouraged by another famous speech that Winston Churchill made at Zurich in 1946, when he said that the old European hatreds should be buried forever. In 1948 the West European countries set up the Council of Europe, which was designed to be a prototype European Parliament. But it proved to be rather a disappointment, and only its Human Rights Court was to be of much significance. Nevertheless, the Federalists kept trying, and in 1954 they at last appeared to have achieved a real breakthrough. Two new multinational organizations, the European Political Community (EPC) and the European Defence Community (EDC) were to be set up to look after political and military union respectively. Unfortunately, the British refused to have anything to do with either scheme, and without them the French Parliament refused to ratify the relevant treaties. The creation of the Western European Union in 1955, with its new British commitment to the defence of West Germany, was poor consolation for the Federalists. The year 1954 marked the effective end of their movement.

The Functionalist phase, 1955–73

Even before the collapse of the EPC and EDC, the more cautious Europeans had already laid the foundations for a new approach. In 1950 the French Foreign Minister had put forward a plan for the pooling of Franco–German coal and steel supplies as evidence of the desire of the two peoples 'never to go to war with one another again'. This Schuman Plan (in fact, largely the work of Jean Monnet, later nicknamed the 'Father of Europe') was to lead to the formation of the European Coal and Steel Community (ECSC).

The Treaty of Paris, 1951

France and Germany were joined by Italy and the Benelux countries as they placed their coal and steel industries under the control of an international High Commission in Paris. Britain, though invited, refused to join the new organization. The Coal and Steel Community provided an essential base for the more ambitious project that was to come.

Fig. 15.2   Signing of the Treaty of Rome, 1957.

The Messina Conference, 1955

After the 1954 failure, the six West European countries asked the Belgian Foreign Minister Paul Henri Spaak to make a report on the possibility of further European union. Spaak's report led to the convening of a conference at Messina in Italy. This, in turn, brought about an agreement to set up a full economic and customs union of the six, known today as the European Economic Community (EEC).

The Treaty of Rome, 1957

The EEC was formally brought to life in Rome in 1957 (Fig. 15.2) and came into operation on 1 January 1958. While it aimed at full political union, it was to start by removing all barriers to trade and commerce inside the Community. Non-members would have to pay higher duties to send their goods into the EEC. Once again, the British refused to join the new Community.

European Free Trade Association, 1959

Instead, the British set up their own rival organization, the European Free Trade Association (EFTA), under the Maudling Plan of 1959. Unlike the EEC it was merely a Free Trade Area*, and did not compare with its rival in size or population. Although comprising Austria, Britain, Denmark, Norway, Portugal, Sweden and Switzerland, in fact, half its population consisted of British citizens.

The British attitude to Europe, 1945–73

Britain stays out

Why did Britain take so long to be converted to the European ideal? Several factors are worth remembering here:
1. During the war the British had not been defeated or occupied as their neighbours had been. They did not, therefore, have the same urge to unite. Winston Churchill noted this when he told de Gaulle: 'France is the tip of a continent, Britain an island, America another world.'
2. The British Empire and Commonwealth was thought to be far more important than any links with Europe. Until the late 1950s, the British still had a large Empire and felt that they had a separate imperial tradition.
3. The British government believed that it had a special relationship with the United States which was also more important than Europe. It took the Suez crisis of 1956 (see p. 158) to destroy this illusion.
4. The 1945–51 Labour government was heavily involved in a reform programme and showed little interest in organizations such as the Coal and Steel Community. Mr Attlee and his Foreign Minister, Ernest Bevin, were great believers in the Commonwealth connection, and the other members of the government were kept busy by the plans to nationalize* the railways, mines, gas, electricity, steel and the health service.

When Churchill's Conservative government took office in 1951, it proved to be equally negative where

Fig. 15.3   Macmillan calls 'Yoo Hoo! I'm back' to the Commonwealth and EFTA after de Gaulle refuses Britain's entry to the EEC in 1963.

Europe was concerned. Churchill was a great supporter of the Empire and no one really believed the new European organizations would work.

The first application, 1961

By 1961 the British government had changed its mind, and Harold Macmillan applied for entry (Fig. 15.3). The EEC was obviously a success and provided a large potential market for British exports. Edward Heath was appointed to head the team negotiating British entry into the Community. But the British had failed to allow for one thing in their calculations: the attitude of General Charles de Gaulle (President of France, 1958–69). He had not forgotten the way he claimed that France had been mistreated during the war by the British and the Americans. He also claimed that the British could not be good Europeans because of their Commonwealth links. So in 1963 the General vetoed Britain's entry into the EEC despite the fact that the other five members agreed to it.

The second application, 1967

The Conservative government was disillusioned by this failure, but Harold Wilson's Labour adminis-

tration tried again in 1967. General de Gaulle was equally stubborn on this second occasion, although he gave a different excuse for his veto. This time, he said that the British economy was so weak that it would endanger the well-being of the entire Community. Wilson's reply was to leave the application on the table, saying that Britain would 'not take no for an answer'. It had become clear that Britain could never become a member of the EEC while de Gaulle was President of France. This in itself was ironic because de Gaulle was not a true European at heart. In 1966 he took France out of NATO, and in 1965 he boycotted EEC meetings because of disagreements on agricultural policy.

When de Gaulle at last resigned in 1969, the British saw a new opportunity because his successor, Georges Pompidou, was known to be less hostile to their inclusion in the Community. Harold Wilson set the ball rolling once more in 1970, and Edward Heath completed the negotiations when he became Prime Minister after the election of June 1970.

Britain joins the EEC

In 1972 Heath signed the Treaty of Accession to the EEC, and Britain became a full member on 1 January 1973. Eire and Denmark joined at the same time, so that the six now became the nine. It might have been ten, but Norway, having negotiated entry terms, decided to stay out after a referendum. By 1981 the nine did indeed become the ten with the addition of Greece.

The EEC institutions

By 1973, then, the EEC had become a powerful economic trading bloc. How is it run? There are four major bodies involved in the day-to-day running of the EEC – or Common Market as it is sometimes called.

1. *The Commission.*   This has its headquarters in Brussels. It decides EEC policy and is run by Eurocrats or European civil servants drawn from the member states. At the top are thirteen commissioners, who each look after different areas of EEC policy, such as, agriculture, transport, foreign affairs, etc. The four big countries, West Germany, Italy, Great Britain and France, each supply two commissioners; the six small ones each send one commissioner. The commissioners are supposed to be Europeans first and French, German or Dutch, for example, second. Other people look after the special interests of the individual countries.

2. *The Council of Ministers.*   It, too, has its head-quarters in Brussels. Normally the ten Foreign Ministers sit on this council, but other ministers can also be called in in the event of an emergency. Their job is to tell the Commission what the member governments think. Since 1965, each country has had a veto which it can use to stop EEC policies it does not like. This does not help the Community much, but it is important to remember that the EEC is made up of ten countries, each with its own culture and history.

3. *The Parliament.*   This sits in Strasbourg and also in Brussels. By 1980 it had little power, although direct elections to it began in 1979. Each country has Members of the European Parliament (MEPs) with the task of representing the views of their local area. Members sit with members of similar parties from other countries, thus all the socialists sit together. The Parliament can throw out the Commission on a two-thirds majority vote, but it cannot appoint a new one, so depriving it of effective power.

4. *The European Court.*   This sits in Luxembourg, and its judges are chosen from all the member states. The court acts as a watchdog, rather like the American Supreme Court. Its task is to ensure that the EEC regulations are kept by its members. It has powers to fine governments, firms, or individuals who break them.

Common policies

When it was founded, the EEC aimed at complete political union by 1980. This did not prove possible, although it remained a stated aim of the Treaty of Rome. The Community also aimed to set up common policies in all the different areas of its life, from foreign affairs to education and welfare. By 1980 only one area had managed to provide a common approach: agriculture. The Common Agricultural Policy (CAP) sets community prices for foodstuffs and compensates farmers if the world price for a commodity, e.g. wheat, falls below the fixed EEC price. The CAP has proved to be very controversial because states with large farming sectors tend to gain far more from it than do states with small farming industries.

The Community today

At present, the EEC is in a state of transition for a number of reasons. There is considerable criticism of the CAP and the level of contributions that some EEC countries make to the Community purse. British Prime Minister Margaret Thatcher used this feeling to obtain a considerable reduction in the level of the

UK contribution in 1980. This in turn caused some irritation in France and Germany where President Valéry Giscard d'Estaing and Chancellor Helmut Schmidt resented what they felt to be her abrasive tactics. Many people in Western Europe have felt that Britain has been a troublesome member of the EEC because it lacked the true European spirit. It is certainly true that British membership of the EEC has remained a matter for dispute, even after the Labour government's 1975 referendum* which gave a 2 to 1 majority in favour of staying in.

Fishery limits have also proved to be a thorny issue between Britain and its Community partners, while the French have flouted regulations by keeping British lamb out of their markets. Community life is never likely to be peaceful, but the EEC is still very much in existence despite numerous predictions about its early disappearance! By 1980, in fact, the nine were preparing themselves for further additions. Greece, having shed itself of a Right-wing military dictatorship in 1974, was due to become a full member on 1 January 1981. Spain and Portugal were also anxious to join, both having new democratic governments in 1975 and 1974 respectively. However, an attempted *coup* in Spain in 1981 cast some doubts on the validity of its new democracy.

Associate members

Many other countries have special arrangements with the EEC to enable them to have access to its markets. All France's African ex-colonies became associate members under the Yaoundé Convention of 1963, and Britain made special arrangements for New Zealand and the West Indian Islands when it joined in 1973. Israel, India, Nigeria and Bangladesh are among other countries which have made special trading arrangements with Brussels.

Council for Mutual Economic Assistance (Comecon)

The Soviet bloc had already stolen the initiative from the West by setting up its own trading bloc in 1949. When it began, Stalin used the Council as an instrument for economic warfare against Tito's Yugoslavia. Later, however, it began to be used to strengthen the Soviet domination of Eastern Europe by dictating the flow of trade. Of the original members – USSR, Czechoslovakia, Hungary, Poland, Bulgaria, Romania and Albania – only Albania has left the organization (in 1962). East Germany also joined in 1950, as did Castro's Cuba in 1972. Although Comecon may appear to be a communist version of the EEC, it operates quite differently. The Soviet insistence that countries like Hungary and Romania are primarily agricultural producers has caused considerable resentment. In recent years, East Germany's close contacts with the West have considerably reduced the effectiveness of Soviet control over its economic policy, too.

Latin America

The sharp hostility between East and West was reflected in their military and economic agreements, but such agreements were not confined to Europe and Asia alone.

In Latin America, the impetus for economic union was also strong, developing as it did from the Economic Commission for Latin America (ECLA), set up by the United Nations in 1948 (Fig. 15.4). The grinding poverty of the sub-continent was highlighted by a rapid rise in population from 162 million in 1950 to 265 million in 1970. The ECLA response was to sponsor the economic integration of the region through the Treaty of Montevideo signed in 1960. This set up the Latin American Free Trade Area (LAFTA), an association of seven states, with the ultimate aim of creating a common market. The effect of this innovation was to be weakened by the appearance of an Andean Common Market, comprising Bolivia, Chile, Colombia, Ecuador, Peru and Venezuela, in 1969.

Keywords

Free Trade Area: a loose formation of countries agreeing to lower barriers to trade, but with no political aim, e.g. EFTA.

nationalize: to make privately owned land and industry the property of the state.

referendum: a vote by the electorate on one issue, e.g. the EEC.

Questions

Read the passage on Western Europe after 1945 and find TEN mistakes. Then rewrite the passage including the correct information.

Fig. 15.4   Members of ECLA.

In the years after 1945 Western Europe moved gradually towards unification, although the British showed little interest at this stage. Their Premier Clement Attlee commented, 'France is the tip of a continent, Britain an island, America another world,' showing that Britain preferred its Commonwealth and American links. The six decided to move ahead without Great Britain, and in 1950 Charles de Gaulle, 'the father of Europe', was largely responsible for the setting up of a coal and steel community. Then, in 1956, came the meeting at Rapallo which put forward the idea of an economic and customs union or EEC. This was agreed by the Treaty of Paris of 1957 and came into operation on 1 January 1958. Six countries joined (West Germany, Benelux, France and Switzerland) and the new organization proved to be a great success. Britain set up a rival organization, the EPC, but this had none of the economic power of the EEC. British Prime Minister Harold Macmillan decided to apply to join the EEC but de Gaulle rejected his application in 1964. In an angry reply, Macmillan said: 'We will not take no for an answer.' It was left to Labour Prime Minister George Brown to try again in 1966–7.

16 Asia in Transition

China: from war to revolution

We saw in Chapter 6 how Chiang Kai-shek turned on the Chinese Communist Party and waged a pitiless campaign of extermination against it. In 1945 the position was quite different. Both the Communists and the Nationalist government were taken by surprise at the collapse of Japan, but the former were in a much stronger position than they had been before the war. The years 1937–45 had given the Communists the chance to consolidate their control over the countryside of northern China, and they had not wasted the opportunity. For their part, the Nationalists were anxious to regain control of China's key northern cities.

They soon achieved their objective with American help, and US transport aircraft airlifted Nationalist troops to Shanghai, Nanking, Canton and Wuhen.

Manchuria

The northern province of Manchuria, seized by the Japanese in 1931 (see p. 85), was the key to the situation. In 1945 it had been quickly occupied by Soviet forces who showed a marked reluctance to leave. It was not until April 1946 that the Russians agreed to withdraw, but they had already made a secret deal allowing Mao-Tse-tung's Red Army into the province. They also took most of the vast haul of Japanese captured equipment, although some of it was left for the Communists.

The Hurley mission, August 1945

Events in China were closely watched by the United States government, which viewed the prospect of a communist regime in China with little enthusiasm. In the summer of 1945 President Truman sent General Hurley to mediate between Chiang and the Communists, and talks continued for two months. There was never much hope of success, and both sides proved unwilling to make the necessary concessions. Mao (Fig. 16.1) refused to disband his army, and Chiang broke an agreement to form a Nationalist – Communist coalition government. By November 1945 the Civil War, put off because of the Japanese invasion, was in full swing once again.

Fig. 16.1   Mao Tse-tung.

The sides

On paper, it was a struggle that Chiang and his Nationalist forces ought to have won quite easily. When the war began, he had about 4 million frontline troops and a good deal of modern American equipment. Mao only had one million men, and their equipment was inferior. Despite this the Red Army proved to have far more important assets.

1. It had a clearcut simple strategy laid down by Mao and based on his years of experience as a guerrilla leader: 'When the enemy advances we retreat; when the enemy escapes, we harass, when he retreats we pursue: and when he gets tired, we attack.' Operating from their secure bases in the countryside the Communists avoided big pitched battles with the enemy and only attacked when they were sure of success. The experience of the Long March had not been wasted.

2. The Red Army was superior in leadership, morale and organization. It had fought a vigorous, effective war against the Japanese while Chiang had languished in Chungking, sitting on US supplies, but putting them to no effective use.

3. Chiang overstretched his resources and often made bad military appointments, based not on ability but favouritism. The ordinary Nationalist soldier had little faith in his superiors, and this did much to increase the level of desertions as the war went on.

4. Communist control of the rural areas had a crucial effect on the Chinese economy. Because it restricted the availability of raw materials, this had an inflationary effect in the towns, forcing up prices sixty-seven times between January 1946 and August 1948 alone. From Chiang Kai-shek's point of view, this was a fatal development. He had relied through his years in power on the support of the middle class, and now he had lost it. Wages bought nothing, and those Chinese who had gold and silver hoarded it. The businessmen and shopkeepers of Shanghai would not make enthusiastic converts to Marxism, but they shed no tears for the Nationalist regime either.

5. The Communists were also active in the political area. To attract the masses of peasants, they had worked out a land reform programme, promising to confiscate the property of China's landlord class. In May 1943 Mao offered an alliance to third parties which also opposed the Nationalists, and this proved to be a considerable success. Although there were only three million party members by the end of the Civil War, many millions of other Chinese were sympathetic to the Communist cause.

Mao's victory

By 1948 the two sides were equal in terms of numbers, but the initiative lay with the Red Army. The decisive battle came in October, in the valley of the Huai river, when the Nationalist forces were confronted in a massive conventional battle. About 300,000 Communists faced 550,000 of Chiang's men and won a convincing victory. It was clear now that the Communists would win, and in February 1949 they captured Peking and with it north China. One victory followed another as first Nanking, Chiang's capital, and then Shanghai were captured. On 1 October 1949 Mao was able to tell the world that the Chinese People's Republic had come into existence: his life's ambition was achieved. At the same time he made Peking, meaning 'northern capital', the capital city instead of Nanking with its Nationalist associations. The discredited Chiang Kai-shek was forced to leave the Chinese mainland and take refuge in the island of Taiwan, then called Formosa. It has remained in Nationalist hands ever since.

Chiang's defeat owed as much to his own vices as it did to the virtues of the Communist Party. The judgement made by General Stilwell on 'Peanut' – his nickname for Chiang! – and his regime is savage, but not inaccurate: '. . . a gang of thugs with the one idea of perpetuating themselves and their machine. Money, influence, and position the only consideration of the leaders. Intrigue, double crossing, lying reports. Hands out for anything they can get, their only idea to let someone else do the fighting.'[1] While it would be wrong to ignore Chiang's contribution to the restoration of some of his country's dignity, the idealism of Sun Yat-sen had been a long time lost on the road to Chungking.

India: the end of the British raj

The start of the Second World War found India in a restless mood. The Congress Party was unhappy with the 1935 India Act (see p. 41) and the Muslim League feared the consequences of Hindu majority rule. The British government for its part had a war to win, and the question of Indian independence took second place to this. The appointment of Churchill as British Prime Minister strengthened those forces in Britain who opposed the granting of independence, but even they could not ignore the rising tide of discontent inside the country. As early as 24 March 1940, Jinnah demanded that 'the Muslim majority areas in the north-western and eastern zones of India should be grouped to constitute independent states'. This was the famous Lahore or Pakistan Resolution which was to form the basis of the Muslim demand for a separate state. By 1942 Jinnah had succeeded in persuading the British Viceroy Lord Linlithgow to take the concept of Pakistan seriously, and it is true that the British were generally more favourably disposed towards the Muslim League than they were to the Congress Party. To some senior British civil servants in India, Congress was still 'a movement of Hindu hooliganism'.

The Cripps mission, 1942

The Congress reaction to British indifference was to step up the campaign of civil disobedience, and in the winter of 1940–41, 30,000 of its members were in gaol. Forced at last to take action, Churchill sent the Labour politician Stafford Cripps to India in March 1942 on a special mission. He was known to be an old friend of the Congress Party, but his mission was a disaster. Churchill had refused to give him any real authority and insisted that the British government retain its responsibility for defence. No state was to be allowed to opt out of the Indian union. Worse, from the Congress viewpoint, was that Cripps's proposals contained a reference to Jinnah's Pakistan option.

The failure of the Cripps mission left the British in a perilous position in India because it coincided with the early stages of the Japanese war. Already the Imperial government was playing upon Indian hopes for independence, and General Tojo coined the slogan 'India for the Indians'. Japanese promises did, in fact, succeed in winning the active support of the Congress leader Subhas Bose. We have seen, too, (p. 117) how the Japanese army launched an offensive in Assam in the winter of 1943–4.

The Simla Conference, 1945

There was some movement in Britain's policy with the appointment of Lord Wavell as Viceroy towards the end of 1943. The failure of extended talks between Gandhi and Jinnah in September 1944 convinced Wavell that he must take the initiative. In June 1945 he convened a constitutional conference at Simla, to which both Congress and the Muslim League were invited. At the conference, Jinnah bluntly demanded that the League be recognized as the sole representative of India's 90 million Muslims. Congress leaders refused to accept this demand, and the conference broke up. Wavell knew he could do nothing without the support of the League.

The 1945 elections

In the following month, Clement Attlee replaced Churchill as Prime Minister, but Nehru and the other Congress leaders remained suspicious. Nehru was entitled to some reservations, as he had spent 3,251 days of his life in British prisons. But he failed to recognize the strength of Muslim separatism, as indicated by the 1945 elections in India. In Muslim constituencies, the League polled 86.6 per cent of the vote, while in non-Muslim ones, the Congress Party received 91.3 per cent of the vote.

Cripps again, 1946

Nehru and Gandhi made another serious error when Cripps came on his second Indian mission in 1946. He proposed that the national assembly should be responsible for defence and foreign affairs, but that the Muslims should be given a considerable degree of self-government. Even Jinnah was prepared to accept this plan, which would have kept India intact, but Gandhi and Nehru would not. It seems likely that Nehru still underestimated Jinnah's strength, but his refusal allowed the Muslim leader to press his demand for a separate Pakistan.

Mountbatten and independence, 1947

By now the Labour government in Britain was anxious for a solution. Serious mutinies in the Indian navy in 1946 had convinced Attlee that the country could not be held down by force. He, therefore, announced in February 1947 that Wavell would be replaced as Viceroy by Lord Louis Mountbatten, and that independence would come by June 1948.

Mountbatten, sent to India against his will, had a reputation for speed, decisiveness and great charm. The first time he met Nehru, he told the Indian leader: 'Mr Nehru, I want you to regard me not as the last Viceroy winding up British India but as the first to lead the way to a new India.' Nehru replied: 'Now I know what they mean when they speak of your charm being so dangerous.' The two men became firm friends, and this friendship proved to be of great value in the months to come.

Once appointed as Viceroy, Mountbatten moved with great speed, actually bringing forward the date of independence to 15 August 1947. Together with his hard-working Reforms Secretary, V. P. Menon, he produced a three-stage plan:

1. Pakistan was not only to be separated from the rest of India, but was to be divided into two different sections (Fig. 16.2).
2. The Punjab and Bengal were to be divided after a

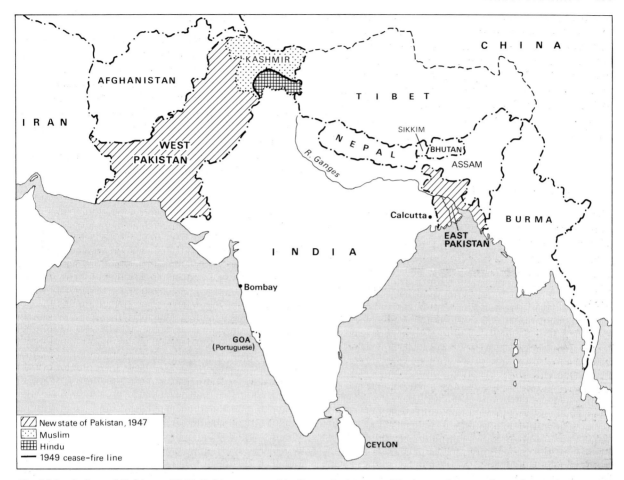

Fig. 16.2   India and Pakistan, 1947. Pakistan was a Muslim majority state. Hindus predominated in India.

Legend:
- New state of Pakistan, 1947
- Muslim
- Hindu
- 1949 cease-fire line

vote and a report by a boundary commission led by the British judge, Sir Cyril Radcliffe.

3. There was to be no special provision for the Sikh community, a special Hindu sect.

Nehru accepted the Menon–Mountbatten plan with 'no joy in my heart', as did Jinnah. He persuaded his friend Mountbatten to stay on as Governor-General and representative of the British Crown. Jinnah insisted on becoming Pakistan's Governor-General himself.

On independence day in New Delhi, Nehru told the excited citizens of the world's newest, and most populous democracy, that their moment had come. 'At the stroke of the midnight hour when the world sleeps, India will awake to life and freedom.'

Partition

The two new nations were to have traumatic birth pangs. No one had foreseen the appalling slaughter which was to take place as 4½ million Hindus moved into India and 6 million Muslims moved into Pakistan. Did Mountbatten move too fast in his desire to complete his Indian mission? Some historians have thought so, but Nehru's biographer had highlighted the surprise of the Congress leaders at the scale of the slaughter. They had, he says, 'an idealized picture of their average supporter and found it difficult to appreciate the purely animal in man'.[2]

The murder of Gandhi, 1948

The tragedy of partition was soon to be followed by another. Gandhi, who never accepted the partition of his country, had always done his best to heal its religious divisions. But on 30 January 1948, he was shot and killed on his way back from a prayer meeting by Nathuram Godse, a Hindu extremist. The death of the Mahatma, 'Holy One', was a great shock to the Indian people, who had now to face the perils of independence alone. Just what these difficulties were, we shall see in a later chapter.

Burma and Ceylon

The 1935 Imperial Act had provided a separate administration for Burma, but it, too, began to press for independence in the early postwar years. In 1946 Attlee invited the Burmese nationalist leader, Aung San, to London for talks, and it was agreed that the country should receive its independence. Aung San was assassinated in 1947, and it was U Nu who, in fact, completed the negotiations for independence which came on 4 January 1948. Mountbatten had hoped that he could keep Burma inside the British Commonwealth, but a series of misunderstandings with the Labour government prevented this. In 1949 Burma opted for the status of a republic outside the Commonwealth. Its early years were hazardous because of a revolt by the Karen tribesmen who controlled the delta of the River Irrawaddy. This was eventually crushed by General Ne Win.

The island of Ceylon had been a British colony since 1815 when it obtained its independence in 1947. Its first Prime Minister was Don Senanayoke, who led the United National Party, and he kept his country inside the Commonwealth. Immediate problems centred around the tensions between the island's two dominant races, the Buddhist Sinhalese and the Hindu Tamils, who made up about a quarter of the population. The more extreme Sri Lanka Freedom Party came to power in the 1950s and tried rather foolishly to make Sinhalese rather than English the official language. Rather predictably this led to communal rioting.

The birth of Indonesia

In 1945 the Netherlands, like the other European colonial powers, was in the process of recovering from the effects of the war. But this did not prevent an over-ambitious Dutch attempt to retain control of their previously extensive empire in the Far East. They failed to allow for changed circumstances, and were confronted by a formidable nationalist movement under Sukarno. In 1945 Sukarno was made President of the Republic of Indonesia and refused to agree to anything less than total independence. The arrival of Dutch troops in 1946 did nothing to improve the situation, and by 1949 the Dutch government was forced, reluctantly, to concede Indonesian independence. Relations between the mother country and its ex-colony remained bad though, and in 1957 Dutch property in the islands was confiscated and the owners expelled.

The Royal Netherlands government was more fortunate in the Caribbean where the break came more slowly. Surinam received its independence in 1950, and in 1954 it and the islands were grouped together as the Netherlands West Indies. They maintained, however, their association with the Dutch Crown.

Indo-China

To the north, the French proved to be just as keen to hold on to their imperial possessions in Asia. The emergence of nationalist movements in Indo-China seemed to obtain scant recognition in Paris although its immediate fate was decided at the Potsdam Conference. This laid down a temporary arrangement whereby:
1. the territory north of the 16th parallel was to be occupied by the Chinese Nationalists;
2. the area to the south was to be occupied by the British.

Real control, by contrast, lay with Ho Chi Minh and his Vietnamese nationalists, most of whom belonged to the Communist Party. At first, there seemed some prospect of agreement with the French, who had by now assumed their prewar colonial responsibilities. In October 1946 Ho visited Paris and seemed well aware of his movement's international isolation. 'It is better,' he remarked, 'to sniff France's dung, than eat China's all our lives.' Hopes of agreement were then ruined by the new French constitution, which incorporated all overseas dominions into the French Union and gave little prospect of local autonomy*. He and his colleagues felt they had been betrayed, and in December 1946 French garrisons in Indo-China were attacked. There were brief hopes of a compromise in March 1947, but a savage guerrilla war continued until the decisive French defeat at Dien Bien Phu in May 1954 (Fig. 16.3).

The Korean War

We have seen in earlier chapters how relations between the USSR and the USA worsened in the years after 1945. Bad as these relations became, however, they stopped short of war. Neither super-power was prepared to risk nuclear conflict. Churchill summed up the situation in a memorable phrase. 'Peace,' he said, 'was the sturdy child of terror.'

Fear of nuclear war did not, however, prevent the outbreak of local conflicts in which either the US or the USSR was directly or indirectly involved.

The first example of such a conflict was afforded by the Korean War which broke out in 1950.

Fig. 16.3   *French parachutists are dropped over Dien Bien Phu in November 1953.*

The background

To understand this war we need to look back to the collapse of the Japanese Empire in 1945. For nearly forty years Korea had been under Japanese rule. Now its fate lay in the hands of the victorious American and Soviet forces. Not surprisingly, the result was a compromise using the 38th Parallel*, a geographical line of latitude, to divide North and South Korea. The area to the north of this line was to be under Soviet control, the southern part would be occupied by American troops. This arrangement could only be temporary, however. What was to happen when the two great powers withdrew their troops? The Americans hoped that both parts of Korea would eventually be united under a democratic form of government. But the communist leader of North Korea, Kim Il Sung, had his own ideas. When the USA and USSR withdrew in 1948, Kim refused to take up the 100 seats provided for the North in the Korean Parliament. Bitter arguments began about the frontier dividing the two halves of the country.

The South Koreans were not blameless either. Their leader Syngman Rhee made provocative statements, saying, for example, that if 'we cannot defend democracy in a cold war, we will win victory in a hot war'. The communist North accused Rhee of sending troops on raids across the 38th Parallel.

The role of the big powers

As so often in history the truth probably lay somewhere in the middle. In fact, the squabble between the two Koreas only became of global importance because other larger countries were involved. Let us look at what these attitudes were:

1. *The USA*.   It seemed to favour the Rhee government although worried by some of the South Korean leader's warlike speeches. One important point you should note concerns a speech made by Secretary of State for Foreign Affairs Dean Acheson on 12 January 1950. In it he spoke of a 'defensive perimeter' which had to be protected as it was vital to the security of the USA, but he did not include South Korea within this perimeter. Attacks on countries outside the perimeter would have to be dealt with under the UN Charter. As we shall see, however, the USA was prepared to defend South Korea.

2. *The Soviet Union*.   Stalin supported the North Koreans, but because of Acheson's statement he may have thought that the Americans would not fight for Korea. Another factor (suggested by Stalin's biographer) is that he may have been worried by the appearance of a rival communist power, Red China. He wanted, says this writer, 'to prove himself as daring a strategist of revolution as Mao'.[3] In other words, Stalin wanted to show that he was the undisputed leader of the communist world. To

achieve this he was prepared to back Kim Il Sung.

3. *China.*   Although the communist government had only been in power for a year it showed immediate interest in the Korean question. In September 1950, two months after the war started, Foreign Minister Chou En-lai warned that China would not 'supinely tolerate their neighbours being savagely invaded by imperialists', i.e. by the USA and its allies. The importance of this statement will be established later.

4. *The United Nations.*   Strictly speaking, the UN does not count as a big power, but it did play a significant role in the war. The absence of the Soviet Union from the Security Council when the war started proved to be a crucial factor. The Russians had boycotted the UN because of the refusal to make Red China a member. This absence allowed the Americans to organize the sending of a UN Force to Korea.

Two factors need to be remembered here:

1. Russia could have used its veto to stop any UN action.

2. It suggests little co-ordination between Stalin and Kim Il Sung. If they planned the invasion together, then they made a poor job of it!

The course of the war

One fact is beyond dispute. On 25 June 1950 North Korean forces crossed the 38th Parallel and invaded the South. President Truman heard the news the same evening. He tells the story in his memoirs: 'The telephone rang. It was the Secretary of State calling from his home in Maryland. "Mr President," said Dean Acheson, "I have some serious news. The North Koreans have invaded South Korea."' Truman acted decisively in the emergency, helped obviously by the Soviet absence from the Security Council. Two days later, on 27 June, the Security Council voted in favour of taking steps to drive back the North Korean forces. A unified command structure was set up with an American general in charge. American troops were sent to South Korea at once, quickly followed by a contingent from Britain. In the end, sixteen countries were represented in the UN force. The man selected to command this hybrid army was the Second World War hero Douglas MacArthur. It proved to be a fateful choice.

At the same time, messages were sent asking Stalin to restrain his North Korean ally. It was widely, if not totally accurately, believed in the West that he had authorized the invasion. He certainly supplied the North Koreans and Chinese with weapons.

The war itself can be divided into five distinct phases which are shown on the map of Korea in Fig. 16.4.

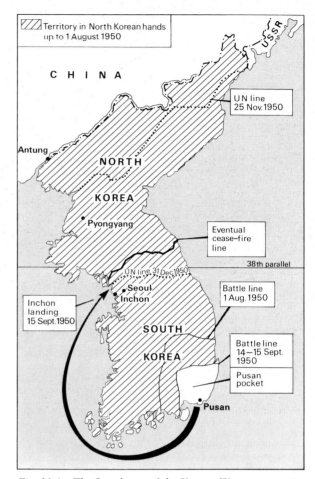

Fig. 16.4   The five phases of the Korean War.

Phase One, June–September 1950

This was a period of rapid North Korean advances so that the UN forces were forced to retreat to a small area around Pusan.

Phase Two

This was the period following General MacArthur's landing at Inchon on 15 September. United Nations troops then drove the North Koreans beyond the 38th Parallel towards the Chinese frontier (Fig. 16.5).

Phase Three

The Chinese intervened in the war on 26 October 1950. This was followed by a second UN retreat south of the parallel.

Phase Four, April–June 1951

This saw the stabilization of the front to the north of the 38th Parallel.

Fig. 16.5   *American troops moving towards the front in the Korean War.*

Phase Five

This involved a period of stalemate starting with the beginning of armistice negotiations. These were to drag on for two years.

The war ended in July 1953.

Inchon

Two important turning points can be noted. The first being the Inchon landing. This operation *behind* enemy lines was a close copy of the island-hopping technique used by MacArthur during the Second World War. Its success ensured that South Korea was saved from a complete takeover by the communist North.

Chinese intervention

The second turning point came when China intervened. This prevented a complete victory by the UN forces and brought the war to a virtual stalemate. Chou En-lai's warning (see p. 138) was not heeded by MacArthur. His orders were to avoid provoking the Chinese, but he disobeyed them. American aircraft were ordered to destroy the bridges over the Yalu River, and the Peking government saw this as an attack on Chinese security. Two hundred thousand Chinese 'volunteers' crossed the Yalu, and the Cold War grew in intensity. The Americans were accused of using germ warfare. They, in their turn, accused the communists of trying out brainwashing techniques on prisoners. Fortunately for the peace of the world, neither side wanted to see a local war turn into a general one. Peace negotiations began only seven months after the Chinese intervention, and were held at the village of Panmunjon.

The MacArthur sacking

The Chinese involvement in Korea had another famous side-effect. It became obvious that General MacArthur had been grossly overconfident in his handling of the war. When he met President Truman at Wake Island on 15 October, he was convinced that Chinese or Soviet intervention was unlikely. He proved 'to be entirely mistaken in his judgement of the war'. Worse still were MacArthur's persistent attacks on US government policy – he wanted to extend the war by bombing China itself. In the end, Truman grew tired of the man presidential advisers described as 'a son of a bitch'. He decided that MacArthur must go, reminding the American people in a speech of 11 April 1951 that 'military commanders must be governed by the policies and directives issued to them in the manner provided by our laws and constitution'. It was a courageous decision, which made the President very unpopular. The failed haberdasher from Independence, Missouri, showed himself willing and able to take on the legendary war hero. But Truman never lacked courage, his motto was: 'If you can't stand the heat, stay out of the kitchen!'

The cost

Douglas MacArthur was only one casualty of the war. Its cost in lives was infinitely higher. At least 500,000 South Koreans died and as many as 4 million North Koreans. The Americans lost 30,000 men and their allies 4,000. In addition, the whole country had been devastated by the effects of the war.

The importance of the war

What did all this destruction achieve? On the face of it, very little. Korea was, and is, still divided in two by the 38th Parallel. A demilitarized zone was also created, where disputes are still common. The communist regime remained in control in the North, as did Syngman Rhee's corrupt dictatorship in the South. But if the war did little for the Korean people, it did have great global significance:
1. Fears of communist aggression resulted in the rearming of West Germany only five years after the Second World War had ended.
2. Worries about the ambitions of Red China resulted in the setting up of the South East Asia Treaty Organization (SEATO) in 1954.
3. The war marked the emergence of Red China as an important factor in international affairs, but paradoxically the US deliberately delayed recognition of it (until 1971).
4. As you will see Korea directly influenced US domestic affairs. It provided excellent ammunition for Senator Joe McCarthy's witch-hunt against supposed communists in Washington (see p. 143).
5. The war marked the emergence of the UN as a peacekeeping agent in world affairs. In fact, Korea was unusual in that United Nations forces were clearly identified with one side.

After the war

Once the war was over South Korea lapsed back into its tradition of dictatorship and rapid economic growth. Syngman Rhee remained in power until 1960, when he was succeeded by President Park Chung-hee. Park had no pretensions to be a democrat, but the country did achieve a great deal in the industrial sector during his period in office. From 1968–78, the economy grew at a rate of more than 10 per cent each year, before South Korea began to feel the effects of another explosion in world oil prices.

On 26 October 1980 Park was shot by his Chief of Intelligence Jae Kyn. Whether this act formed part of a wider conspiracy is uncertain, but the South Korean people had already suffered eighteen years of Park's repressive rule. His death was a profound relief to many South Koreans. Widespread inflation and corruption had caused increasing discontent, especially when opposition leader Kim Yung Sam was excluded from Parliament and then sentenced to death.

Relations with the North remained poor under Park and his successor Chun Doo-hwan. The country remained firmly allied to the United States. Any future improvements in the relationship between the two Koreas appears unlikely, as Kim-Il-Sung's son and designated heir, Kim Jong-il, is reputed to be even more ruthless than his father.

Keywords

autonomy: self-government.
38th Parallel: the line of latitude or geographical line dividing North and South Korea.

Questions

Fig. 16.1

1. This Chinese leader established the People's Republic in 1949. Who was he?   1
2. Give THREE reasons why the communists won the civil war in that year.   6
3. Which city did they make the capital of the new China?   1
4. Who was China's former leader, and what happened to him?   2
5. What attitude did the USA and USSR take to the new regime?   4
6. Who thought it was 'better to sniff France's dung', and what did he mean by this?   4
7. Where and when was the French army decisively defeated in Indo–China?   2
                                                                                                      ⎯⎯
                                                                                                      20

17 The USA, the Caribbean and Latin America

The Truman Administration, 1945–52

President Franklin Delano Roosevelt died on 12 April 1945 shortly after he had begun his fourth term in office. His death was greeted with real feelings of grief in many sections of American society, but it appeared to leave a political vacuum in the country.

Truman's background

The Vice-President, Harry S. Truman of Missouri, was barely in his new post when he was thrust into the most important position in the postwar world. Nothing in his background suggested that Truman would make an effective President for he was a typical 'machine politician'. He came late to politics and had very little experience of Washington and its ways.

In this case, appearances were to prove deceptive. We have seen in Chapter 13 how Truman had taken the difficult decision to drop the atomic bomb, and he proved equally resolute in domestic affairs. One of Truman's earliest actions was to place on his desk a sign saying 'The buck stops here', and throughout his Presidency, he showed a capacity to make a stand on big issues.

The Twenty-second Amendment 1946

He was certainly never to find the management of the country easy, and from the start, he had to cope with a Republican majority in Congress. The Republican Party had regarded the Roosevelt administration as being little better than an elective dictatorship, and it was determined to curb Presidential power.

The Twenty-second Amendment to the Constitution, passed in 1946, prevented any President having more than two consecutive terms in office.

The Taft–Hartley Act 1947

The Republicans also had a reputation for being hostile to organized labour. This was confirmed by the imposition of the Taft–Hartley Act in 1947 against Truman's wishes. This Act, which followed a wave of strikes in 1946–7, stated that trade union leaders could not be communists, that there was to be a sixty-day 'cooling off' period for strikes and an eighty-day suspension of strikes likely to damage the national interest. Ironically, this allowed Truman to pose as the champion of the workers even though he had only recently taken the Mine Workers' Union to court after a six-week strike. In 1946 alone, 116 million working days were lost to strikes in the United States, three times the figure for 1945. This was a result of higher prices after the war and the resulting demand for higher wages by the unions. By contrast, the number of Americans in employment actually rose from 54 million in 1945 to 61 million in 1948. In the same period, the national income rose from $181,000 million to more than $223,000 million a year.

The 1948 election

Harry Truman had wished to complete the cycle of reforms started by Roosevelt in his New Deal, but his efforts were hamstrung by the Republican majority in Congress which set its face stubbornly against social reform. His plans to introduce civil rights reform, an area neglected by Roosevelt, also brought him into conflict with his own Democratic Party. In the run up to the 1948 Presidential election, the Southern Democrats under Senator Thurmond bolted from the party, and Thurmond himself ran as a Presidential candidate against Truman. The south, of course, was the traditional home of the segregation of and discrimination against blacks.

But this was only the beginning of Truman's difficulties, for he also lagged well behind the Republican candidate, Governor Thomas E. Dewey, in all the opinion polls. Truman's chances of victory appeared to be slight even on the eve of polling day in November. The *Chicago Tribune* was so confident that Dewey would win, it produced the headline, 'Dewey defeats Truman' (Fig. 17.1). But Truman had pitched his campaign just right, attacking the 'do nothing' Republican Congress and virtually ignoring the overconfident Dewey. He obtained 49.5 per cent of the electoral vote, and therefore, did not need the support of Thurmond and his Dixiecrats.

The President enjoyed his triumph over the pollsters and the press almost as much as his defeat of Dewey. 'Mr President,' said a sign outside the *Washington Post* offices, 'we are ready to eat crow* whenever you are ready to serve it.'

Fig. 17.1   *Truman beats Dewey despite pollsters!*

The Fair Deal

The return of a Democratic majority in the Congress also enabled Truman to carry through some of the social reforms he wanted, though in other respects, his second term was one of the most unpleasant periods in modern American history. He put forward a reform package which included civil rights measures, unemployment benefits, a housing programme, aid to farmers, price controls, federal help for education and repeal of the Taft–Hartley Act. Congress agreed to the extension of social security benefits to another 10 million people and an increase in the minimum wage. Truman was also able to push through a Housing Act which provided for the construction of about 800,000 cheap houses between 1949–55. He failed, however, to get Congress to agree to the setting up of a national health service, and it also refused to repeal the Taft–Hartley Act.

Republican gains in the 1950 mid-term Congressional elections then put an end to the Fair Deal, and the administration also had to defend itself against charges of corruption. These were minor, but did little to improve the reputation of a President and government already under serious attack in another area.

McCarthy and the second Red Scare

This concerned the administration's alleged softness towards communism. You will remember how there was a serious anti-communist campaign after the First World War (see Chapter 8) which quickly fizzled out. The anti-communist hysteria after the Second World War was to be much more sustained and important in its results. It began, it must be remembered, in the climate of the Cold War when the American people felt uncertain about Soviet intentions and there was a tendency to believe stories about spies and traitors.

Truman was not one of those Americans who believed that there was a communist conspiracy inside the United States, but even he felt obliged to take certain measures.

The loyalty oaths, 1947

One of the first actions was the insistence of the federal government that its employees took an oath of loyalty to the United States Constitution. Special boards were also set up to check on the political sympathies of federal employees. They investigated 3 million people, but only 212 were actually dismissed. Even so, serious damage had still been done to the civil rights of the American citizen.

The trial of the Hollywood ten, 1948

One industry which suffered severely from the anti-communist witch-hunt was the cinema, which certainly did have employees with Left-wing sympathies. This in itself was not surprising, because during the war, the Soviet Union had been constantly portrayed as the heroic ally of Uncle Sam. But the postwar atmosphere in the United States made the expression, indeed the holding, of such opinions unacceptable. Hollywood had become a great American institution and should not, therefore, be seen as a home for supposed communist sympathizers.

In 1948 ten Hollywood directors and scriptwriters were made to appear before the Un-American Activities Committee in Washington. This committee had been set up by Congress in 1938 to investigate anything 'that strikes at the basic concept of our Republic'. Believing themselves to be innocent until proved guilty, the accused took the Fifth Amendment and remained silent. But their constitutional rights were, in this case, violated. Some of them received prison sentences, others were thrown out of their jobs. These were the years of the Hollywood blacklist, which stopped the politically suspect from working in the film industry. Carl Foreman, the talented director, was one who was forced to seek work abroad. Even Charlie Chaplin was prevented from re-entering the USA in 1951 because he had made wartime fund-raising speeches which referred to 'comrades', proof for anti-communist fanatics that he must be in league with the Kremlin.

The Alger Hiss case, 1948

By 1948 the Republican Party too had jumped on the bandwagon. Secretary of State Marshall was described as 'a front man for traitors', and only the President himself seemed safe from accusations of being 'soft on communism'. This was the background to the notorious Hiss case, which brought to prominence a certain Richard M. Nixon, the youthful Congressman from California. It centred around the accusation by Whittaker Chambers that Alger Hiss, an official at the State Department*, had been a member of a communist spy ring in the 1930s. In many respects, Hiss stood for everything small-town America loathed: a clever, cultivated man who seemed to symbolize the liberalism of the New Deal era. After two trials and much controversy Hiss was found guilty of perjury in January 1950. He went to prison for five years and his conviction had two immediate effects:
1. It was a victory for the anti-communist witch-hunt and persuaded many people that the communists really were trying to infiltrate the United States.
2. The Supreme Court upheld the conviction of the leaders of the American Communist Party under the Smith Act of 1940. This said that it was a crime just to call for the overthrow of the United States government, even if no attempts were made to do this. The scene was set for the appearance of Senator Joseph McCarthy, the biggest witch-hunter of them all.

McCarthy's background

McCarthy, the son of Irish Catholic parents, came from the state of Wisconsin. He had seen service in the Second World War. It was typical of McCarthy to cast himself later in the heroic mould of 'Tailend Joe', the reargunner in a superfortress in its raids against the Japanese. The truth was less glamorous; the nearest McCarthy actually got to combat was target practice on Pacific islands. His capacity for invention was to prove useful later in his career.

Although elected to Congress in 1946, Joe McCarthy did not become well known until 1950 when he made his famous speech at Wheeling, North Virginia, attacking communist sympathizers in the White House and State Department. He had studied Hitler's *Mein Kampf* and certainly realized that the big lie could be an effective tactic in politics. The pattern of McCarthy's speeches emerged quite clearly at Wheeling. Pieces of paper would be waved about, and the Senator would claim that secret sources had told him the exact number of communists or communist sympathizers in the State Department: this was his favourite target. Sometimes the figure would be 205, on other occasions it was fifty-seven – cynics suggested that this was because of the fifty-seven varieties of Heinz products which made it easy to remember! Surprisingly, McCarthy's 'evidence' was rarely chal-

Fig. 17.2 Senator Joe McCarthy displaying 'evidence' during an un-American activities hearing.

lenged (Fig. 17.2). People seemed only too ready to believe his charges, and the result was tragic as many Americans were hounded out of their jobs and, in some cases, to their deaths by McCarthyite smears.

The Republican Party leaders made little effort to counter McCarthy's activities because they saw that he was a potential vote winner, and a weapon to be used against the Truman administration. In the 1952 Presidential election campaign, the Republican Eisenhower, while affecting to despise Joe McCarthy, told the nation: 'We will find the pinks; we will find the communists, we will find the disloyal.' This tacit support for his anti-communist campaign allowed McCarthy to be re-elected to the Senate, and in 1953 he was made Chairman of the Permanent Investigation Sub-committee of the Senate. This gave him the power to investigate almost any branch of the American government. His power seemed beyond challenge, and he received support from some unlikely quarters. Joseph P. Kennedy contributed money to McCarthy's crusade and Kennedy's son, Robert, worked as one of his aides. For a man who was almost unknown before 1950 and never became a leading figure in his party, McCarthy had achieved remarkable influence over his fellow countrymen.

The Army-McCarthy hearings, 1954

Then, at the peak of his power, McCarthy went too far. He tried in 1954 to challenge the US Army which was, in Larry Adler's words, as 'American as mother and apple pie'. The issue was a trivial one, centring round the conscription of one of McCarthy's aides, David Schine, into the army. McCarthy thought that Schine should be made an officer, but the army would not oblige. This incensed McCarthy, who then made some wild charges of corruption against leading army officers. He told Brigadier-General Ralph Zwicker that he was 'a disgrace to the uniform' he wore. Lacking any real evidence, but confident of success, McCarthy agreed to televised hearings of his dispute with the army. For the first time, the American people could see the Senator for Wisconsin as the bully he really was. Skilled defence lawyers exposed the emptiness of McCarthy's charges, and the great reporter Ed Murrow used the television coverage to discredit him totally. McCarthy never recovered from this defeat, and in December 1954 his colleagues in the US Senate passed a motion condemning him. Although he kept his Senate seat, Joe McCarthy was a broken man and died from alcoholic poisoning in 1957.

A discreditable chapter in American history had been closed. Its significance lay not just in the career of Joe McCarthy himself, but in the involvement of so many highly regarded Americans in his smear campaigns. Theodore Sorensen describes the involvement of Robert Kennedy, who was to be the white hope of so many liberals in the 1960s: 'The simplistic views of militant patriotism, anti-Communism, and internal security which were part of his upbringing had, in 1953, not yet been balanced by the deep devotion to Constitutional rights and civil liberties that he would ultimately hold.'[1] Joe McCarthy was a creature of his time, and that time was fearful and anxious.

The Civil Rights movement

The fall of Senator McCarthy in 1954 coincided with some important developments in the field of black civil rights. Progress here since 1945 had been disappointing, and many blacks felt frustrated and antagonized by the way they were treated by the majority white population. They were judged capable of fighting and dying for the United States, but not of exercising their political rights. Then, in 1954, came an important judgement in the case of *Brown* v. *Topeka School Board* – Brown was complaining of discrimination by the Topeka School Board. The Supreme Court justices ruled: 'Does segregation of children in public schools solely on the basis of race, even though the physical facilities and other "tangible" factors may be equal, deprive the children of the minority group of educational opportunities. We believe that it does.' This decision, however, only applied to the segregationist south.

The Supreme Court might be on the side of the black minority, but the southern state governments were not. States like Arkansas, Mississippi, Georgia and Louisiana still clung to the myth of white superiority, and it became clear that the southern blacks would have to take action themselves.

Martin Luther King

They were fortunate in finding a fine leader in the Reverend Martin Luther King (Fig. 17.3), a Baptist Minister and disciple of Gandhi. It was he who brought the Indian leader's techniques of passive resistance to the United States and organized an effective protest movement. It began in Montgomery Alabama in 1955 when a black woman, Rosa Parkes, refused to give up a seat in the whites-only section of a bus. Mrs Parkes was put off the bus, but her fellow blacks joined a bus boycott organized by King. In the end, the bus company gave way and the segregation ended. It was a small victory but an important one in the heart of the racist South.

Fig. 17.3   Martin Luther King, civil rights leader.

Little Rock, 1957

The next major crisis came when the Supreme Court ruling was put to the test in Little Rock, Arkansas, in 1957. In this instance, black students had been barred from the local all-white high school and the decision was backed by State Governor Faubus. The whole of America watched to see whether the federal government would stand firm, and to his credit President Eisenhower did so. Federal marshals escorted the students into the school, and although they went through a difficult ordeal, the point had been made. The law had been enforced, but changing the hearts and minds of southern whites was another matter.

The Washington march, 1963

After this, there was a lull in the area of civil rights, and Doctor King and his followers became restive. In March 1963 there was a great civil rights demonstration in Birmingham, Alabama, long noted for its extreme racist attitudes. The local police chief Eugene 'Bull' Connor saw in this an opportunity to put the Negro in his place. Fire hoses and dogs were used against the black demonstrators as Connor's men tried to break up the demonstration. In the end, Martin Luther King used the most potent weapon of all and sent children to break the police ranks. Even the tough Alabama policemen could not set dogs on them: the demonstrators had won. Discrimination in restaurants and cafés – the cause of the demonstration – ceased from that moment.

The victory in Birmingham was to be followed by a massive civil rights march on Washington 'for jobs

Fig. 17.4   Tens of thousands of people assembled round the Washington Monument during a mass civil rights demonstration in Washington in August 1963.

and freedom' in August 1963 (Fig. 17.4). The object was to put pressure on the Kennedy administration which had promised more than it had produced on civil rights reform.

In a great speech to 250,000 demonstrators, Martin Luther King used his gifts as an orator to the full: 'I have a dream that one day this nation will rise up, live out the true meaning of its creed: We hold these truths to be self-evident, that all men are created equal.' The speech had the desired effect, for it was soon followed by the passage of a Civil Rights Bill through Congress. This made federal funds available to help the voluntary desegregation of schools. This is where we must leave the Civil Rights movement for the moment.

The Eisenhower years, 1953–61

One side-effect of McCarthyism was that Harry Truman decided not to stand again for the Presidency. He had tired of the political pressures and the wild accusations of the Republican opposition. The new Democratic contender was Governor Adlai Stevenson of Illinois, but he had little chance against the Republican nominee Dwight D. Eisenhower. In 'Ike' the Republicans had found a certain winner with immense popular appeal that was partly a result of his wartime exploits. He won the election in November 1952, and then formed the first Republican administration for twenty years.

In action it was curiously reminiscent of the low-profile Republican administrations of the 1920s, especially in the area of economic policy. Eisenhower believed that government should interfere as little as possible in people's lives and described the New Deal and the Fair Deal as 'creeping socialism'. Some critics thought he carried this 'do nothing' philosophy too far, and he was frequently criticized for spending too much time on the golf course!

Nevertheless, he retained his great popularity with the American people and won again quite easily in 1956 against the unfortunate Stevenson who remarked ruefully: 'Who did I think I was running against, George Washington twice.' Among the significant measures passed by Congress in the Eisenhower years were the National Defence Education Act which provided student loans and more funding for science and language study, and the setting up in 1958 of the Civil Rights Commission to study racial discrimination. The Atomic Energy Act was amended to allow more research co-operation with other countries now that the hysteria about communist spies had died away. The late 1950s were a time of increasing prosperity as the United States became, in the words of the celebrated economist J. K. Galbraith, 'the affluent society'.[2] They also saw the final extension of the Union with the granting of full statehood to Alaska and Hawaii in 1959.

The 1960 election

As we have seen, the Twenty-second Amendment prevented Eisenhower from standing again in the 1960 election, and the Republican contender was Vice-President Richard M. Nixon. John F. Kennedy (Fig. 17.5), an Irish Catholic from Boston, was the Democratic choice, and the campaign was closely fought. The Democrats made great play with Nixon's past, using such slogans as 'Tricky Dicky' and 'Would you buy a used car from this man?', but it was a new political feature that may well have cost him victory in 1960. This was the series of television debates between the two contenders in which Kennedy was generally regarded as being more effective – it was said that Nixon's 'five o'clock shadow' made him look sinister and threatening!

At all events, Kennedy scraped home by the narrow margin of 113,000 votes, the closest Presidential victory in American history. At forty-three years of age, he was to be the youngest man ever to enter the White House.

The 'New Frontier', 1961–3

The Kennedy victory brought with it an immediate change in style and emphasis, which was evident in the inaugural speech of January 1961, and before it in the acceptance of the Democratic nomination. Then Kennedy had used the phrase with which his administration was most associated: 'But I tell you that the New Frontier is here whether we seek it or not ... unsolved problems of peace and war, unconquered pockets of ignorance and prejudice, unanswered questions of poverty and surplus ...'

It was a dramatic beginning, magnified by the image of the President himself and his young wife Jackie. There were comparisons between the Kennedy White House and King Arthur's Camelot, but political reality proved to be harsher. Throughout his time as President, Kennedy was to be plagued by opposition from conservative, southern Democrats and could force few of his reforms through Congress.

We have seen how a Civil Rights Bill was passed in 1963, and in the previous year, James Meredith became the first black student at Mississippi University. But this only happened after a considerable amount of pressure from the Civil Rights movement.

Fig. 17.5   John Kennedy receives a warm welcome.

The only other major Kennedy measures were the Federal Water Pollution Control Act and the Trade Expansion Act. The latter was passed in 1962 and was part of the 'Kennedy Round', an attempt to lower tariffs in the Western world.

The space race

Kennedy was always anxious that the United States should cut back the Soviet lead in the space race. American spending on the space programme was stepped up, and in 1962 John Glenn became the first American to go into orbit. Once this had been achieved, the United States began to overtake the Soviet Union in the sphere of space technology.

Dallas, November 1963

The record of the first Kennedy administration seemed likely to be disappointing, but the President felt confident that he would be re-elected in 1964. In the autumn of 1963, he planned a visit to Texas where the local Democrats had been feuding. He had been warned not to go, since Kennedy-style liberalism was unpopular in the South and a month before, Adlai Stevenson had been spat on in the street in Dallas. The President ignored the warnings and on 22 November 1963 he arrived in the city with his wife. The historian Arthur Schlesinger Jnr, who also worked in the White House, describes the scene:

> The crowds increased as they entered the city 'still very orderly but cheerful'. In downtown Dallas, enthusiasm grew. Soon even O'Donnell was satisfied. The car turned off Main Street, the President happy and waving, Jacqueline erect and proud by his side, and Mrs Connally saying 'You certainly can't say that the people of Dallas haven't given you a nice welcome', and the automobile turning on to Elm Street and down the slope past the Texas School Book Depository, and the shots, faint and frightening, suddenly distinct over the roar of the motorcade, and the quizzical look on the President's face before he pitched over, and Jacqueline crying, 'Oh, no, no . . . Oh, my God, they have shot my husband,' and the horror, the vacancy.[3]

An ex-marine Lee Harvey Oswald was accused of the assassination, although he, too, was later shot by Jack Ruby, a nightclub owner. The commission set up under Chief Justice Earl Warren in 1964 to look into the assassination stated that Oswald alone was responsible, but later investigation suggested that more than one person might have been involved.

The Kennedy legacy

Although John Kennedy died many years ago, he still retains the appeal and the charisma that he had in 1963. His main interest was in foreign policy and his legislative record is unimpressive, but the sense of nostalgia remains with the American people to this day. Is the answer, as Peter Mooney and Colin Bown suggest, that he 'symbolizes the days before the Fall – into race riots, student rebellion, Vietnam and Watergate'?[4] To answer that question you will need to read on.

Johnson and the 'Great Society', 1963–9

No man came to the Presidency in less auspicious circumstances than Lyndon Baines Johnson (Fig. 17.6). He took the oath of office in the Presidential plane, Airforce One, standing next to a distraught Jackie Kennedy, her dress still soaked with her husband's blood. Johnson told the American people, 'I shall do my best; that is all that I can do,' and he always felt that he was carrying on the work of John Kennedy and his great hero, Franklin D. Roosevelt.

The 1964 election

The early vigour of the Johnson Presidency won him the support of the American people, and he seemed likely to be re-elected in the autumn of 1964. A possibility became a certainty when the Republicans picked as their candidate Senator Barry Goldwater of Arizona, a Right winger who alarmed the electorate with his Cold War politics. Johnson won a landslide victory, receiving 61 per cent of the popular vote, and carrying forty-four states to Goldwater's six.

Johnson's reforms

Johnson proved, in fact, to be a considerable domestic reformer in his own right because he had two important advantages:
1. The memory of the dead President made Congress more co-operative when Johnson claimed to be carrying on Kennedy's programme.

2. Johnson had a great deal of experience in Congress, and he put this to good use. From 1952–60 he had been leader of the Democratic majority in the Senate and he knew all the Congressional leaders well. More use might have been made of these talents by the Kennedy people who already regarded the Texan Johnson as something of a country 'hick'. His experience as Vice-President made him wary of Kennedy aides like MacNamara, Sorensen, and Schlesinger, and the relationship with Robert Kennedy, the Attorney-General, was always a stormy one. Nevertheless unlike John Kennedy, he was able to get his reform package through the Congress.

Johnson was able to fill one important hole in the New Deal legislation by introducing free health care for the old and poor. Unfortunately, the medicare scheme did not work as well as the President hoped because of the reluctance of doctors to take medicare patients.

The Housing Development Act 1965 provided federal funds for slum clearance and house building, while the Higher Education Act 1965 also provided more money for colleges and universities.

The President's concern for the deprived areas was shown in his Poverty Programme and through the Equal Opportunity Act 1964 which set up schemes to help young people from deprived areas to receive training, higher education and employment opportunities.

The New Deal tradition was revived in his National Wilderness Act of 1964 which was designed to conserve wild life.

Black Power

The years that followed Johnson's great victory in 1964 were destined, however, to be turbulent ones. The increasing involvement in Vietnam (see Chapter 19) made Johnson unpopular in radical and student circles. At the same time, there was increasing restlessness in the black community where radical leaders were not satisfied by what had been offered in Johnson's civil rights legislation.

The 1964 Civil Rights Bill had outlawed discrimination in housing, employment and education. A second Bill in 1965 provided for supervision of elections so that blacks were not discriminated against. That progress was being made, was shown by the fact that by 1966 only 170 out of 6,000 school districts remained segregated in the USA, but the pace of change was not rapid enough. A new generation of black activists reacted strongly against what they saw as Kennedy and Johnson's tinkering with the system that oppressed them. This meant that

by the late 1960s, the black movement had moved in three separate directions.
1. There were those like Martin Luther King who still believed in a non-violent campaign of persuasion and co-operating with white liberals.
2. Others like the black Muslims advocated complete separation from the white man who was regarded as a devil. This meant setting up an alternative black society within the United States. A notable black Muslim convert was Cassius Clay, the heavyweight boxing champion of the world, who took the name of Muhammad Ali.
3. A third group, of whom the best known were the Black Panthers, advocated the violent overthrow of white society. One of their leaders, Eldridge Cleaver, summed up their attitude:

> All respect we may have had for politicians, preachers, lawyers, governors, Presidents, Senators, Congressmen, was utterly destroyed as we watched them temporizing and compromising over right and wrong, over legality and illegality, over constitutionality. We know that in the end what they were clashing over was us, what to do with the blacks, and whether or not to start treating us as human beings. I despised all of them![5]

All these groups existed in an atmosphere of racial tension in big cities like New York, Los Angeles, Detroit and Chicago. In 1965 there was a serious outbreak of rioting in Watts, the black ghetto in Los Angeles, and this formed the model for similar outbreaks during the long hot summers of the 1960s.

The murder of Martin Luther King, April 1968

A crisis point was reached on 4 April 1968 in Memphis, Tennessee. On that day, Martin Luther King, the man of peace, was shot down at a motel by a white gunman, James Earl Ray. Here it seemed was the trigger for the long-feared explosion of black violence in the great cities of America. To everyone's surprise the explosion did not come because of the dedicated work of King and aides like Andrew Young, who managed to pacify the angry blacks. In a sense, black activism had peaked although there remained much that was unsatisfactory about the position of black people in American society.

The problem of the urban ghetto remained and with it all the other problems associated with the inner-city areas. Many cities set up 'grievance response' machinery for blacks, and they began to play a greater part in both local and national politics. More black Senators and Congressmen were elected, and

this process culminated in the appointment of Andrew Young as US Ambassador at the UN in 1977. During the 1970s, too, the income of black families rose, and a genuine black middle class began to emerge. In the field of education, the federal government followed a policy of 'positive discrimination' in allowing a black quota in institutes of higher education. The question of bussing children from one area to another became controversial, and in 1972 President Nixon came out in open opposition to it. In some areas, white parents began to set up their own privately-run schools to avoid this type of government-sponsored integration.

Nevertheless, the general picture was improving and by 1972 50 per cent more black students completed high school than had done so in 1960, but it was also true that of the 10.6 million Americans who were on welfare in 1971, 43 per cent were black. As the 1970 census noted, most of these poor blacks were living in America's great urban centres. In the twelve largest American cities the black population had risen by 37 per cent between 1960 – 70. By contrast, the white population had fallen by 13 per cent. The question that remained at the end of the 1970s was whether the American Negro would get the fair deal he had been promised by the legislation of the 1960s.

The 1968 election

The year 1968 was to be a traumatic one for the United States. In April Martin Luther King died, and in June Robert Kennedy, a Presidential candidate, was shot dead in a Los Angeles hotel. The assassin Sirhan Sirhan believed him to be too pro-Israeli and the shooting took place on the anniversary of the Six Day War.

The Democratic Convention in August was a shambles as peace demonstrators fought with Mayor Richard Daley's police in Chicago before the nation's television cameras. Vice-President Hubert Humphrey was nominated, but liberal Democrats were unenthusiastic and gave their support to Eugene McCarthy and George McGovern. A bewildered country looked everywhere for reassurance and found little.

The new Nixon

This was the background to the return of Richard Milhous Nixon (Fig. 17.7) to national politics. The Nixon who narrowly lost to John F. Kennedy in 1960 and then suffered a humiliating defeat in the contest for the governorship of California in 1962, told the

Fig. 17.6   Richard Nixon, later to be the only American President forced to resign while in office.

been more interested in foreign rather than domestic affairs, and his programme seemed to offer little other than a cutback on the welfare projects and big federal spending of the Johnson period. He had campaigned on a strong law and order ticket, but his attempts to curb crime in the United States were ineffective. In 1972 alone 5.9 million crimes were committed in the country, with a murder every 28 minutes and a car theft every 36 seconds. Equally unsuccessful was Nixon's plan to pack the Supreme Court with conservative justices acceptable to the White House. The Senate refused to accept two Right-wing justices proposed by Nixon, and the Court took a liberal line on abortion and capital punishment. Government attempts to increase the number of wire tappings was also opposed.

The Nixon approach to civil rights was described by a disillusioned member of his administration as 'benign neglect'. He had never been popular with the blacks and showed little real sympathy for their problems. In office, Nixon remained what he had always been, the candidate of small-town America.

assembled press representatives that they would have 'no more Nixon to kick around'. In 1968 a rejuvenated Nixon carried off the Republican nomination in what was described as the 'greatest comeback since Lazarus'. There was talk of a 'new Nixon' although some critics still felt that this was only the product of clever advertising. Subsequent events were to prove that the old Nixon had not entirely disappeared.

In the event, the result was much closer than most people expected. Nixon's majority in the popular vote was only 499,704 and the 31,770,237 votes he obtained were actually less than he had won as the losing candidate in 1960. Many traditional Democrats had returned in the end to the party fold, although Hubert Humphrey, in fact, received 12 million votes less than Johnson had done in 1964. Another factor was the existence of a third candidate, George Wallace, renegade Democrat and former Governor of Alabama, who obtained 9 million votes.

The Nixon years, 1969–74

As Johnson served out his term, Nixon remained silent about his plans, even those concerning the Vietnam war, the most pressing problem facing the new administration (see p. 165). Nixon had always

The dollar crisis, 1971

One novel feature of the first Nixon administration was that the United States faced a serious economic crisis, the first since 1945. In 1972 there was a trade deficit of $7 billion and inflation was rising. The President reacted vigorously with a package of measures. These included devaluation of the dollar, a 10 per cent surcharge on imports, and a wages and prices freeze, the first in American history. Another controversial measure taken by Nixon was to allow the American dollar to float on the exchange market. This meant that for the first time since the Bretton Woods Agreement (1944), the dollar's value would not be pegged to the price of gold on the world market.

In the short run, the economic package appeared to work as inflation and unemployment went down, but the dollar also began to slide on the exchange market. By the mid-1970s the German mark and the Japanese yen were regarded as safer currencies for the foreign investor.

The Watergate Affair, 1972–4

By that time, in any case, the Nixon administration had been first paralysed and then destroyed by a domestic scandal of extraordinary proportions. Its key lay in the personality and past of the President himself.

The 1972 election

Richard Nixon had always been in his own eyes a loser. He had lost narrowly to Kennedy in 1960 and only just edged home against Humphrey. By nature secretive and suspicious, he was determined to win a decisive victory in 1972, and thereby ensure that he was in the White House, when the USA celebrated its 200th anniversary of independence in 1976.

Any means were justified to bring this about, and a special Committee to Re-elect the President (CREEP) was set up with a great deal of money and a 'dirty tricks' department at its disposal. Its job was to disrupt the Democratic campaign by fair means or foul, e.g. delivering Democratic laundry to wrong addresses and calling non-existent 6 a.m. press conferences for the rival party!

But then things began to get out of hand with the hiring of hare-brained agents like Gordon Liddy and Howard Hunt. On 18 June 1972 their men broke into the office of Larry O'Brien, the Democratic National Chairman, in the Watergate complex in Washington. In the process of replacing a bugging device, they were caught red-handed by the police. This seemingly trivial event was to bring down Richard Nixon and his administration.

McGovern and the Democrats

The irony of the situation lay in the fact that the Republicans did not need to act in this underhand way for the election was, in effect, won already. The radical Democrat George McGovern had won over the blacks, the students and the women's movement, but he had lost the support of more traditional Democratic voters and destroyed Roosevelt's old coalition.

By election day, McGovern was in a hopeless position and could only carry Washington DC and the state of Massachusetts. Richard Nixon took all the other states with 60 per cent of the popular vote. This time George Wallace had little effect on the result, although he amused his audiences with sarcastic references to Washington civil servants with nothing in their briefcases 'but a peanut butter sandwich'.

The cover-up

The Watergate break-in had not affected the result of the election because Nixon's White House aides had moved heaven and earth to make sure that it did not. The months that followed the massive election victory were, however, despite their efforts, to be dominated by little else. Three questions troubled the minds of the American people:

1. Did Nixon know about the break-in?
2. When did he know?
3. How deep was his involvement in the so-called cover-up? A fourth fear and worse possibility was that he had actually ordered the burglary himself!

Subsequent evidence suggested that as early as 23 June 1972, Nixon told his aide Haldeman to 'get to' the Federal Bureau of Investigation (FBI) Deputy Director Pat Gray and tell him not to 'go any further into this case period'.

The tale of Watergate remained untold until early 1973, when one of the burglars, James McCord, began to talk to the district Washington judge John Sirica, who could hardly believe the bizarre tale that he was hearing. A trail of guilt led directly back to the White House, and on 30 April 1973 Nixon announced the resignation of top aides Bob Haldeman and John Ehrlichman. It was clear that the White House staff were deeply implicated in Watergate whether the President knew about it or not.

After this, events moved rapidly. In May the Senate appointed a special Watergate Committee under the veteran Sam Ervin, and Archibald Cox was appointed Special Watergate Prosecutor by the President. Nixon pledged full co-operation to the Watergate Committee, but was then undermined by his extraordinary taste for secrecy. Routine questioning of a Nixon aide, Alexander Butterfield, on 13 July, unearthed the amazing fact that Nixon had been taping all the conversations in his office since 1969! Why the President had not already destroyed the incriminating tapes long before must remain one of the great mysteries of the whole affair. The Senate Committee then demanded that the White House tapes be handed over. Nixon refused on the grounds:
1. that they contained national security material;
2. that as chief executive he claimed the privilege of keeping his own sources of information.

This defence impressed neither Judge Sirica nor the Senate Committee. The Judge ordered the President to hand over the tapes, and again he refused. The issue went to the Supreme Court and on 12 October it upheld Sirica. When Archibald Cox agreed with them, Nixon dismissed him. Attorney-General Richardson had resigned rather than do Nixon's dirty work for him. Days before, his Vice-President, Spiro Agnew, had been forced to resign over a totally unrelated matter of taking bribes while he was holding an official position in Maryland!

Still the increasingly desperate leader clung to office, although his credibility with the American people had almost sunk to zero. Ultimately the President agreed to hand over to the new Prosecutor, Leon Jaworski, what he had refused to hand over to Archibald Cox, his predecessor.

The 18½ minute gap

At this point, it was discovered that an 18½ minute gap had mysteriously appeared in one of the recorded conversations between the President and Haldeman. While the former was notorious for his mechanical clumsiness, many suspected that it was the work of his secretary Rose Mary Woods, acting on instructions.

This was bad enough, but the tape of 23 June 1972 gave clear evidence that Nixon knew about the break-in five days after it happened, and therefore must have been deeply involved in the cover-up which followed as the Nixon men desperately tried to hide their tracks. The President of the United States was also shown in the light of a vindictive man who told his legal counsel John Dean after his 1972 victory that he wanted notes 'on all those that tried to do us in . . . They are asking for it and they are going to get it . . .' This was the Nixon who had told the press in 1962 that they wouldn't have him 'to kick around any more', and who authorized the break-in to the office of Daniel Ellsberg's psychiatrist to punish a man who had sold the Pentagon's secrets.

Nixon resigns

In the end, no one believed Nixon's assurances any more and the leaders of his own Republican Party had to tell him so. On 9 August 1974 he finally resigned, telling the American people that he was going because 'I no longer have a strong enough base in Congress'. But he had done much more than this, for the faith of people in the Presidency had been destroyed for years to come.

The meaning of Watergate

The Watergate crisis dragged on for two years and gave a severe jolt to the whole American political system, but it did show:
1. that the President was not above the law. By eight votes to none, the Supreme Court forced Nixon to hand over the tapes.
2. that the US Presidential system was a cumbersome one. Nixon had to be threatened with impeachment before he could be persuaded finally to resign. He has been the only American President to do so.
3. that the powers of the FBI and the Central Intelligence Agency (CIA) had been abused. Both organizations were used against Nixon's political enemies.
4. political immorality. The whole investigation betrayed a warped understanding of right and wrong in the White House. Other Presidents had bugged and played dirty tricks on their opponents. What distinguished the Nixon White House was its aura of vindictiveness and total ruthlessness which was derived directly from the President.
5. the importance of the press. An irony of the whole affair was the big role played by the press, especially the *Washington Post*. Nixon's White House certainly supplied them (his longstanding enemies) with plenty of material.

The final question

The question which continues to intrigue is: did Richard Nixon order his men into the Watergate complex on that night in June 1972? The answer may never be known.

Bob Haldeman, who went to prison for his part in the Watergate Affair, says in his memoirs that 'Nixon himself, caused these burglars to break into O'Brien's office',[6] while Jeb Magruder, the Deputy Director of CREEP, believes that Nixon had one fatal flaw – 'an inability to tolerate criticism'.[7]

The ex-President's memoirs contained no admission of knowledge of the burglary. Instead, Nixon contented himself with this observation: 'Later my actions and inactions during this period would appear to many as part of a widespread and conscious cover-up. I did not see them as such. I was handling in a pragmatic way what I perceived as *an annoying and strictly political problem* [author's italics].'[8]

The Ford administration, 1974–6

Gerald Ford had been an honest, if undistinguished Congressman, but honesty was a rare quality in the Nixon White House. He became an unexceptional President who tended to be overshadowed by his celebrated Secretary of State, Henry Kissinger, who had managed to survive the Watergate disaster. His most controversial decision was to give Richard Nixon a free pardon. Many people felt that Nixon, like many of his staff, including Dean and Haldeman, should have gone to gaol.

Otherwise the Ford years were characterized mainly by a rise in the cost of living at home which was due in part to the oil crisis of 1973 (see pp. 160–61). This economic decline was to give political ammunition to the Democrats who nominated the little-known former Governor of Georgia, Jimmy Carter, to run against him in 1976. Carter stood on an anti-Washington ticket, and effectively tied in the Ford administration with Watergate. Once again, though, the margin narrowed as polling day came closer, and in the end Jimmy Carter's victory margin was only to be 2 million votes.

The Carter administration, 1976–80

Jimmy Carter came to Washington on a wave of popular enthusiasm, but little else seemed to go right for him. An early blow to the administration was the enforced resignation of Bert Lance, an old friend and trusted Presidential aide, because of financial irregularities in Georgia. This was to be followed by the sacking of UN ambassador Andrew Young for failure to follow government foreign policy. Then in 1980 came the embarrassing 'Billygate' Affair when the President's younger brother Billy was found to have dubious financial connections with the Libyan government.

Carter had some worthy objectives in foreign policy (see p. 161) and some successes, but at home there was a story of unrelieved failure. A praiseworthy attempt to curb energy consumption was thrown out by Congress, and by 1979–80, the recession was beginning to take effect. Soup kitchens for unemployed car workers in Detroit did not present a good image for a Democratic President in election year. Failures in economic policy allowed Senator Edward Kennedy of Massachusetts to move ahead of the President in the opinion polls, but the President was to be fortunate on two counts. Memories of Chappaquidick in 1969 – when Kennedy's car crash had caused the death of a young secretary – had not quite disappeared from the minds of the electorate. More importantly, the holding of American hostages in Iran and the Soviet invasion of Afghanistan rallied national support for Carter. In August 1980 he retained the Democratic nomination in New York, though many delegates still favoured Kennedy. The previous month, the Republicans, stolid as usual, had rallied round the ageing ex-Hollywood film star Ronald Reagan. Reagan's film career had been mediocre, but he had been Governor of California, and the Republicans sensed the vulnerability of the Carter White House.

Reagan wins, 1980

Jimmy Carter's attempts to frighten the voters with the image of a Cold War Reagan were a total failure. Reagan won forty-four states to Carter's seven in an election affected at the last moment by further developments in the Iran hostages crisis. In March 1981, within weeks of taking office, President Reagan was wounded in an assassination attempt.

The Caribbean

The smaller states and islands to the south of the USA were in a continuous state of ferment in 1945 and the years that followed it.

The British West Indian Islands were greatly affected by the war, which gave a boost to both their morale and their economies. It enabled West Indians, in Jack Watson's words, to compare their conditions 'with those elsewhere'.[9]

One feature of this new West Indian nationalism was to create a restlessness and a willingness to move abroad.

Emigration

Such emigration was mainly to the UK as the USA placed a restriction on West Indian immigration in 1952. Labour shortages in Britain encouraged the recruitment of West Indian workers to jobs in the hospitals and transport, and by the late 1950s they were arriving at the rate of 30,000 per year. Asians also began to move in to fill vacancies in the textile industry, and this new flood of foreign workers led to growing public anxiety in Britain itself. In 1968 the ex-Conservative Minister Enoch Powell warned of 'rivers of blood' if the level of emigration continued. The speech was overemotional in tone and ignored the passage of the 1962 Act restricting Commonwealth immigration.

The 1971 census showed that there were 325,000 West Indian workers in the United Kingdom, but they were often increasingly disillusioned. A Race Relations Act did not protect them against prejudice and neither did the higher standard of living console them. The West Indian felt like a stranger in the mother country.

Why the West Indian emigrated was obvious enough; the Moyes Report of 1938 had highlighted the acute poverty in the West Indian Islands, but neither emigration nor inter-island co-operation solved the problem. Some reference should be made to institutions such as the Caribbean Development Bank set up in 1969. It was followed by the Caribbean Community and Common Market (Caricom) set up in 1973, and the Trinidad Premier Eric Williams made a generous declaration on aid. The surplus funds of Trinidad and Tobago would be used to help the whole Caribbean community. These funds were to come from its oil-rich economy. This gesture was, however, to some extent balanced by Trinidad's withdrawal from the West Indian Federation over the question of inter-island emigration.

The position of the islands was not improved by

Britain's entry into the EEC in 1973 even though the British government worked out a special deal to help the sugar crop.

Black power

Another development in the islands was the pronounced movement to the Left in the 1970s, with Michael Manley (Fig. 17.8) (1972–80) setting up a socialist government in Jamaica. His government looked east to Cuba, rather than to the capitalist West, and was copied by Maurice Bishop's government in Grenada in 1979.

The old links with other black movements also revived in the 1960s with the development of the Rastafarians in Jamaica. Distinctive in dress and hair styles, the 'Rastamen' looked to Haile Selassie and Ethiopia as their spiritual home. Their exclusive nature gave them something in common with the black Muslims (see p. 149) in the USA.

Latin America

Further south, the subcontinent followed its usual turbulent path, though still as always very much under US economic influence. Between 1949–69 the USA raised its investments in Latin America from $4,000 million to a massive $20,000 million.

The Cold War added a new dimension because the US government viewed Latin America as a breeding ground for communism. Its policy therefore varied greatly between carrot, e.g. Kennedy's Alliance for Progress, and stick, direct interference in its neighbours' affairs. Indeed Kennedy went so far as to admit in 1961 that 'foreign aid is a method by which the United States maintains a position of influence and control in the world'.

The Latin American revolt

When matters took a form Washington did not like, direct intervention was used to eject leaders, such as Arbenz of Guatemala in 1954. Lavish American aid was poured out to help repressive regimes train their police forces. It was ultimately bound to bring about a backlash and did so on two notable occasions:

1. In *Cuba*, where the squalid dictatorship of Fuences Batista had survived with gaps (notably 1944–52) since the 1940s. Batista was an open admirer of the European Fascist dictatorships, but in 1959 he was overthrown by a force of guerrillas led by the virtually unknown Fidel Castro. They had landed

Fig. 17.7   Michael Manley, the Jamaican Prime Minister, 1972–80.

in 1956 and fought a long campaign against the dictator's better-armed troops. Castroism became a potent influence, even though his lieutenant Che Guevara was killed in Bolivia in 1967 while leading an insurgent movement.

2. *Chile.*   The outstanding exception was Chile, a country with a long democratic tradition, where the Marxist Salvador Allende (Fig. 17.9) had defeated the Christian Democrat Party in 1970. Allende and his *Unidad Popular* (Popular Unity) Party wanted to create a socialist and independent society in Chile, but economic circumstances were against them.

Allende introduced land reforms and nationalized the banks, but in doing so, he frightened the middle classes who feared that they might lose their privileged position. A transport strike (almost certainly engineered by the CIA) was the prelude to a military *coup* on 11 September 1973, which 'fastened on Chile one of the bloodiest dictatorships ever to emerge in Latin America'.[10]

Salvador Allende died while trying to defend his Presidential palace, and his death was followed by a wholesale purge of Leftists. Under General Pinochet,

Chile became notorious for ruthless, authoritarian government, torture and rigid budget cutting in the economy.

Democratic Marxism had apparently failed, and the Chilean people were confronted with the type of military dictatorship to which their neighbours had become all too used.

Argentina

Cuba and Chile represented revolts against the West and its economic domination, but Argentina represented a strange 'leftover' from earlier times. You may remember here that in 1955 Juan Perón's government had fallen, and its disappearance had been followed by years of undistinguished, blundering, military rule.

Then, in 1973, the Perónista were able to bring back their leader, after Hector Campora had won the Presidential elections. Perón kept his old links with the trade unions (see p. 55), but a new radical Left had arisen with which he had few sympathies. The ruling classes feared once more that even an aged Perón might set up a 'poor man's' government. They bided their time until he died in 1974, and his widow Maria Estale de Perón was unable to cope with a series of economic crises. In 1976 another in the seemingly endless series of military *coups* removed her from office and General Vidala took over.

Fig. 17.8   Salvador Allende campaigning in Chile.

Central America moves Left

These dismal events were to some degree counterbalanced to the north by the fall of the Somoza dictatorship in Nicaragua and a Leftish revolt in El Salvador in 1980–81. The Reagan administration pumped arms into government hands, learning little, it seemed, from previous US experience in Latin America.

Keywords

eat crow: an American expression meaning to humiliate someone.
State Department: the American Foreign Ministry.

Questions

Extract 17.1

> Rightly or wrongly, I convinced myself that I was being attacked by old opponents for old reasons. I was instinctively geared to fight for my survival. After living and fighting in the political arena for so long, I was not going to give up now and leave the presidency because of something like Watergate.
>
> I would fight and do and say whatever I thought was necessary to rally my forces and maintain their confidence for this campaign.[11]

1. This is an extract from an American President's memoirs. Who is he?   1
2. What was the Watergate affair to which he refers?   2
3. What was the outcome of the 'fight for my survival', and in what year did it occur?   2
4. Name the Vice-President in this administration who was successfully charged with corruption.   1
5. The President concerned has just won a massive election victory. In what year was it held and who was his opponent?   2
6. (a) Give TWO examples of the achievements of this President in foreign affairs.
(b) Who was the American statesman associated with them?   2
7. To what political party did this President belong?   1
8. Name TWO areas in US domestic policy which were largely neglected by this President's administration.   4
9. What effect did the Watergate affair have on American political life?   5

———
20

18 The Middle East since 1945

Arab versus Jew

In Chapter 6 you saw that in 1917 the British government sanctioned the Jewish settlement of Palestine and favoured the establishment there of a national home for the Jewish people. It could not, of course, have envisaged the possibility that the leader of a supposedly civilized European country would make a systematic attempt to wipe out the Jews. In an obvious sense, therefore, Adolf Hitler changed the politics of the Middle East by leaving the British government the legacy of his death camps. Ernest Bevin, in particular, as Britain's Foreign Secretary, had to face the desperate problem created by the desire of many Jews to leave Europe forever and settle in Palestine. The restrictions of the 1939 White Paper (see p. 42) were quite irrelevant in this new and tragic situation. For Bevin knew that the Arabs were already infuriated by the presence of 608,000 Jews in Palestine by 1946, and he did not wish to offend them further.

International opinion, on the other hand, would condemn him if the British authorities turned the Jews back. President Truman had already expressed his hope that 'the British Government may find it possible without delay to lift the restrictions . . . on Jewish immigration'. But the British government did not agree and rejected a Jewish Agency request for 100,000 settlement permits in May 1946. From this point, matters went from bad to worse, as Jewish terrorist groups attacked the British occupation forces in Palestine.

On 22 July 1946 one of them, Irgun Zvai Leumi, blew up the King David Hotel in Jerusalem, in which the headquarters of the British army in Palestine were situated. Nearly 100 people died, and relations between the Jews and the British were poisoned by the resulting bitterness. Hundreds of Jewish activists were arrested by the British occupation forces although the activists' leader, Menachem Begin (later Prime Minister of Israel), escaped. The British Commander in Palestine, Sir Evelyn Barker, allowed himself to be provoked into making an infamous statement to his troops on 26 July. All Jewish shops, cafés and restaurants were put out of bounds so 'punishing the Jews in a way the race dislikes as much as any – by striking at their pockets and showing our contempt for them'.

An unedifying period followed in 1947 when the Irgun's execution of two British army sergeants sparked off anti-Jewish riots in Liverpool and Manchester. Even *The Times* was affected by the hysteria and demanded that the Irgun leaders should be 'given the same taste of British justice as were German gangsters in the war'.

Such episodes finally convinced the British government that the problem of Palestine should be handed over to the United Nations, which decided that the British mandate should be ended as soon as possible. The date fixed for British withdrawal was 1 October 1948, after which the country was to be partitioned between the Jews and the Arabs. As it turned out, the British accelerated their departure and left on 15 May with few regrets and little sympathy from the outside world. They had become the prisoners of their pro-Arab policy, although one observer, the Labour M.P. Richard Crossman, thought that Bevin himself bore much of the blame for the failure in Palestine. He wrote later: 'British policy in Palestine was largely motivated by one man's determination at almost any cost to teach the Jews a lesson.'[1]

The Arab Liberation Army

Britain's departure did nothing to solve the Palestinian problem: it merely removed the colonial power, the base of the triangle. Arab and Jew remained to nurse their ancient hatred and hostilities towards each other. Even before the British mandate ended, in January 1948, Egypt, Trans-Jordan, Iraq, Syria and Lebanon banded together to form the Arab Liberation Army, and the Syrian Prime Minister told the world that 'the people's army will soon be able to teach the treacherous Jews a lesson'. Atrocity followed atrocity, the worst being the Jewish massacre of 250 Arab villagers at Dier Yassin near Jerusalem.

In this climate of hatred, it was obvious what would happen when the British left and the Jews were expecting an Arab attack. They had considerable experience of defending their kibbutzim* in the 1930s and had a large number of British-trained army officers in their ranks.

The first Arab–Israeli War, 1948–9

On 14 May 1948 David Ben Gurion declared that the Jewish state of Israel had come into being, and he became its first Prime Minister. It was immediately recognized by the great powers, including the Soviet Union, and a Czech armaments shipment was made available to the Jewish defence organizations. Their chances of survival appeared slim, however, because they faced no less than seven separate Arab armies, each intent on 'driving the Jews into the sea'. They failed to do this and by January 1949, all the Arab forces had been driven out of Israel. For the Israelis it was very much a case of David beating Goliath, but their victory was not quite so surprising as it appeared at the time:
1. The Jews had the advantage of fighting for a cause. They knew that defeat would end their dream of a Jewish state forever.
2. The Arab armies were badly led and had no common plan of campaign. Only the Jordanian Arab Legion emerged with much credit from the fighting.

When the fighting stopped, the Middle East lapsed into an uneasy peace, with Israel surrounded on all sides by Arab neighbours determined to destroy it at the first opportunity.

The Palestinians

Most bitter of all were the Palestinian Arabs who had lost their homes in the fighting and were forced to live in refugee camps in Jordan. The UN partition plan (Fig. 18.1) had given them the worst available land in Palestine, but the war had deprived them of that as well. Half a million Palestinian Arabs remained in the camps after the 1948–9 war, a running sore in Middle Eastern politics.

Israel, for its part, remained intact, and was assured of Western support in 1950, but the overthrow of the Egyptian monarchy in 1952 placed it in an even more dangerous position. Nationalistic army officers led by General Neguib and Colonel Nasser deposed King Farouk and made their hostility to the Israelis only too clear. The new Egyptian government encouraged

fedayeen* raids into Israeli territory from the Gaza strip. By 1955 Israeli–Egyptian relations were extremely bad, and Ben Gurion warned the Egyptians that 'if acts of violence interfere with our rights on land and on the seas, then we reserve our freedom of action to protect our rights in the most effective manner'.

The Suez Crisis, 1956

The next great crisis in the area was not only to concern Egypt and Israel. It had its origins in the ambitious domestic plans of Gamel Abdul Nasser (who had replaced Neguib as Egyptian President in 1954), and his need for foreign capital. Both the USSR, on one side, and Britain and the USA, on the other, were willing to help, though each had their price. Nasser's dream was to build a great dam over the Nile at Aswan to irrigate the surrounding area and help to feed his country's growing population, but he was suspicious of foreign bankers as his biographer, Robert Stephens, says: 'He was obsessed with the fear that the country's newly won independence might be lost again through the domination of foreign creditors.'[2] In the West, such fears were likely to be seen as evidence of unreliability, especially as Nasser had bought a shipment of arms from communist Czechoslovakia in September 1955.

Fig. 18.1   United Nations partition plan, 1948.

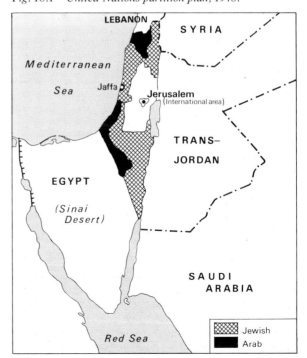

Nevertheless, Britain and the USA still promised loans of £25 million towards the cost of the Aswan High Dam project.

All seemed well, until the Americans and British abruptly withdrew from the Aswan project in July 1956. They suspected that Nasser had close links with the USSR, and the United States was angered by his decision shortly before to recognize Red China. The Egyptian leader was, therefore, left without the money to carry through his cherished plan. He was deeply angry and accused the American government of 'shamelessly' trying to undermine the Egyptian economy.

The nationalization of the Suez Canal

What then could Nasser do? Soviet money could be made available, but Nasser did not want Egypt to become dependent on foreign powers. He opted for a bolder solution. On 26 July 1956 he made a fiery speech in Alexandria in which he used the name Ferdinand de Lesseps (the man who built the canal). This was the signal for the Egyptian army to seize control of the Suez Canal, at that time the property of the Anglo–French Suez Canal Company. Its considerable revenues (Britain had obtained £3 million from canal dues in 1955) would help to pay for the Aswan Dam. Equally important, in Nasser's eyes, was the fact that nationalization of the canal would be a demonstration of Egyptian independence.

On his own admission, Nasser was surprised by the violent British reaction to his decision. Prime Minister Anthony Eden, who had negotiated the British withdrawal from the Canal Zone in 1954, was especially aggrieved, and compared Nasser to Hitler. Britain, he said, could not allow Nasser to have his 'thumb on our windpipe'. France, too, denounced Nasser's action. It already suspected him of supplying aid to its rebellious colony of Algeria. Israel, for the moment, said nothing. Last, and most important of all, was the attitude of the United States government, which had in a sense triggered the crisis. It was largely concerned about the efficient day-to-day running of the canal, but President Eisenhower was certainly alarmed by Eden's threats 'to bring Nasser to his senses'. Unfortunately, Eden and the US Secretary of State for Foreign Affairs, John Foster Dulles, did not get on well. This bad relationship caused a good deal of confusion on both sides of the Atlantic and made the British think that the Americans would support their hawkish policy towards Egypt.

The secret plan of Sèvres

This complete misunderstanding with Washington allowed the British government to hatch a complicated plot against Nasser. It was to involve Britain, France and the Israelis, who were, as always, anxious to increase their security in the area. The plan consisted of three stages:
1. Israel was to attack the Egyptians in the Sinai Desert.
2. Britain and France were to send an ultimatum to both sides telling them to withdraw approximately 16 km (10 miles) on either side of the canal – it was obvious that Egypt would refuse; it was, after all, Egypt's own territory on both sides.
3. Anglo–French troops were to land by air and sea and seize the canal.

Eden came late to the Franco–Israeli talks, and continued to talk to the Egyptians through the American-sponsored Suez Canal Users Association (SCUA). It is doubtful whether he intended to settle the crisis by peaceful means.

The Anglo–French invasion

In the end, the Israelis insisted on going ahead, and on 29 October they attacked in Sinai. Everything seemed to go according to plan, and on 5 November Anglo–French troops were parachuted into Port Said. A sea landing followed, and by 6 November it seemed that the entire canal would fall into Anglo–French hands quite easily. But then the American government made its decisive intervention in the affair and ordered Britain out. Eisenhower was infuriated by his allies' actions, which coincided with polling day in the US Presidential election. Either the British left Egypt, he threatened, or the USA would cancel a much-needed dollar loan. Faced with this ultimatum, the British pulled out, followed reluctantly, by France. A ceasefire was agreed and the Suez Crisis was over.

The significance of Suez

The most remarkable thing about Suez was that it failed to settle anything.
1. Israel gained nothing from taking part in the war. The UN forced it to return all the Egyptian land it had occupied. The Israelis vowed that next time they would look after themselves.
2. Britain and France were totally discredited in Arab eyes. The Western assumption that Nasser could not operate the canal was proven to be quite mistaken, and British trade was not disrupted.
3. Egypt suffered a considerable amount of damage because of Nasser's miscalculation about Western

reaction to nationalization of the canal. The waterway itself was forced to close for several months.
4. In the short run, the affair split the Western alliance and made it impossible to make any meaningful criticism of Soviet action in Hungary (see p. 195).

A paradox of the Suez episode was that Colonel Nasser was able to claim it was an Arab triumph, when it was really a practical demonstration of America's economic strength and of the limits of Anglo–French power in the world.

The Six Day War of 1967

We have seen that the Suez Crisis resolved nothing because the basic cause of unrest in the Middle East remained. This was the determination of Israel's Arab neighbours to destroy it. During the 1960s, this determination remained, until Arab leaders like Nasser became the prisoner of their own warlike speeches. They talked of the destruction of Israel so often that in the end they had to attack it (or would have done so had Israel not struck first). The crisis came in 1967 when Nasser appeared to be preparing the ground for another war. He made military agreements with the Syrians and the Jordanian King Hussein, and ordered the UN peacekeeping force out of the Gaza Strip and the Sinai Desert. This was followed by an even more provocative act, the closing of the Gulf of Aqaba to Israeli shipping; Egypt had never allowed them to use the Suez Canal. But Nasser was not just a reckless warmonger, and he seems to have genuinely believed that the Israelis were mobilizing for an attack on his ally Syria. There had certainly been incidents on the Israeli–Syrian frontier early in 1967.

To counter the apparent threat from Israel, Nasser moved extra forces into Sinai in May 1967, and this, in turn, alarmed the Israelis. Both Moshe Dayan, their famous one-eyed general, later Minister of Defence, and Chief of Staff Rabin advised Prime Minister Levi Eskol to strike first at the Arab armies. They did so with devastating effect early on the morning of 5 June 1967. All the Arab air forces were caught on the ground and virtually destroyed at the outset of the war – 286 out of 340 Egyptian combat aircraft were lost. So cleverly timed was the Israeli strike that it caught the Egyptian Commander-in Chief Amer in mid-air at the moment the war began! By 10 June it was all over, for without air cover, the Arab forces were no match for this Israeli version of the *Blitzkrieg*. 'Bang a tin can,' said Dayan, sarcastically, 'and the Arabs will run,' but this was unfair.

The Jordanian army at least, under King Hussein, fought bravely against the odds. But what the Arabs called the setback was to cost them dearly. In six days the whole map of the Middle East had been turned upside down:
1. Israel had taken the Gaza Strip and Sinai from Egypt. Its new frontier lay on the Suez Canal.
2. The Israelis had driven the Syrians from the strategic Golan Heights which dominated the plains of northern Israel.
3. Jordan had lost the Old City of Jerusalem and the west bank of the River Jordan.

It was an overwhelming victory, and Nasser resigned from his post as President in despair. He returned by popular demand the following day when it became clear that the people did not hold him responsible for the military disaster. In the weeks that followed, the UN passed Resolution 242 demanding that Israel return the conquered territories to the defeated Arab powers. Not surprisingly, Israel would not.

The legacy of 1967

The Middle East that we know today is still largely dominated by the effects of the Six Day War:
1. The collapse of Arab military power in that war made the Palestinian Arabs more desperate, and extreme solutions became more attractive to them. The loss of the West Bank meant that tiny Jordan had to cope with another flood of refugees into its already overcrowded camps. From such desperation was born the Palestine Liberation Organization (PLO), founded in 1964 under the leadership of Yaser Arafat, which was prepared to condone the use of terrorist methods to draw world attention to the plight of the Palestinian people.
2. The Israeli leaders seemed to become overconfident as a result of their dramatic victory. Resolution 242 was consistently ignored as Israel seemed content to rely on its military prowess.
3. The verdict of the 1967 war was bound to remain unacceptable to Syria, Egypt and Jordan. Every year that passed after 1967 without Israeli concessions increased Arab bitterness and made another war more likely.
4. The imbalance created by the Six Day War changed the attitude of other powers towards the Middle East. France's President de Gaulle became a supporter of the Arabs after 1967, and Britain moved into a neutral position after its open support of Israel in 1956. The USA alone remained as a steadfast ally of Israel.

The Yom Kippur War, 1973

In the short run, there was confusion in Arab ranks as they recovered from the shock of defeat. PLO activity increased, and guerrillas often used Jordan as a base for attacks into Israel. In September 1970 King Hussein unleashed his army against the Palestinians whom he feared were undermining the unity of his kingdom. A savage war followed, in which the Jordanian army was victorious and the PLO militias were driven out of Jordan. In attempting to heal this breach, Gamal Abdul Nasser died suddenly of a heart attack and was replaced as President of Egypt by his old friend and colleague Anwar Sadat. His appointment was to mark the beginning of a radical shift in Egyptian policy, although few would have guessed it at the time. Sadat appeared equally dedicated to the destruction of the old enemy and said that he would not rest until Sinai and Gaza were recaptured. A prolonged shooting war continued along the banks of the Suez Canal in 1971–2.

Suddenly on 6 October 1973, on Yom Kippur, the holiest day in the Jewish calendar, the stalemate was broken (Fig. 18.2). Egyptian troops poured across the Canal and attacked the Israeli Bar Lev Line on the other side. At the same moment, their Syrian allies also launched a surprise attack on the Golan Heights. This time, Jordan, which had lost so heavily in 1967, stayed out of the war.

The early stages of the war saw the Israelis in some danger of defeat, for they were taken by surprise and the Arab soldiers showed a new spirit of determination in the fighting. A massive airlift of the latest American equipment helped the Israelis to recover, but the despised Arabs had made their point. The disgrace of 1967 had been avenged even if the third week of the war found Israeli troops on the other side of the Canal and on the main road to Cairo. Once again UN and American intervention brought about a ceasefire on all fronts.

Results of the Yom Kippur War

The Yom Kippur War was, in its way, to be equally decisive in shaping the Middle Eastern role in world affairs in the 1970s. Firstly, it was a war of missile technology and so expensive for both sides that neither could take on another conflict so lightly again. Secondly, it burst the bubble of Israeli self-confidence and made them reconsider their position in the area. No longer was the Israeli army invincible and this realization caused some shock waves within the Jewish state itself. Heads rolled in the Israeli government, among them Mosha Dayan's at the Defence Ministry and Prime Minister Golda Meir's.

Most important of all was the Arab discovery of the oil weapon. It seems surprising that it had not been used before because the Middle East is the world's main source of oil. But the Western-orientated Arab states of Saudi Arabia, Kuwait and the United Emirates had been reluctant to display the collective

Fig. 18.2   Egyptian troops crossing the Suez Canal during the Yom Kippur War.

Fig. 18.3 President Sadat of Egypt addresses the Knesset during his historic visit to Israel for peace talks.

spirit needed to show the world that they meant to be taken seriously.

The Arab oil producers used the Organization of Petroleum Exporting Countries (OPEC) as the vehicle for their vengeance against Israel. Those Western countries which continued to support Israel would have their oil supplies cut off. It proved to be an effective weapon against countries like Japan, Holland and West Germany which had no domestic oil supplies of their own.

The Kissinger initiative

The volatile nature of Arab politics was soon demonstrated, after the Yom Kippur War was over, by Anwar Sadat's increasing friendliness with the USA. Soviet advisers had long since been expelled from Egypt, and it was to be US Secretary of State Henry Kissinger who played the dominant role in the diplomacy of 1973–4. 'My friend Henry', as Sadat called Kissinger, employed a technique called 'shuttle diplomacy' because of his series of one-man missions in Cairo, Damascus and Tel Aviv. Kissinger persuaded the Israelis to partly 'disengage' from the Sinai Desert and restore some of Egypt's territory.

It was obvious that the cost of modern war bore down heavily on Egypt's limited resources, but this knowledge prepared no one for the shock which came on

20 November 1977. On that day, Sadat, taking a leaf from Kissinger's book, appeared in person before the Israeli Knesset (Parliament) (Fig. 18.3) and spoke of his strong desire for peace between his country and Israel.

> It is my wish to assume responsibility for the Egyptian people and for the entire Arab nations. For I consider it my privilege and responsibility to spare the Egyptian and Arab people further suffering caused by war. I have not come to bargain for a partial peace. But lasting peace cannot be realized without a just solution to the Palestinian problem.

Sadat's initiative was followed by the exchange of ambassadors with Israel and the cession of another segment of Sinai after the Camp David Agreement of 1978, sponsored by President Jimmy Carter. But it won Sadat few friends in the Arab world which generally regarded him as a traitor. Moderate Arab leaders, like King Hussein of Jordan, were just as strong in their condemnation as the more radical governments of Syria, Iraq and Libya.

In Egyptian eyes, the settlement made sense, but Sadat seemed to get little real movement from the Israeli government. He was perhaps unfortunate that his gesture coincided with the arrival in power in Israel in 1977 of the Right-wing Likud bloc under Menachem Begin. The new Prime Minister took a hard-nosed view of the Palestinian problem and stated that 'all territory between the Mediterranean and the Jordan is Israeli territory'. Such statements were scarcely calculated to appease the Arab states any more than his constant references to the Bible as a justification for setting up Jewish settlements on the West Bank.

The election defeat of Jimmy Carter in November 1980 did little to affect the Arab–Israeli conflict because President Reagan was, if anything, more pro-Israeli than his predecessor. The US government will continue to play the role of mediator in the area unless it adopts such an anti-Arab posture that the Soviet Union seizes the opportunity to re-establish its once considerable influence there. Such an opportunity may have been created by the assassination of President Anwar Sadat in Cairo on 6 October 1981.

Nasser and Pan-Arabism

You may remember that when Mao Tse-tung came to power in China in 1949 he said that China had 'stood up'. The same feelings about the dignity of his country were present in the greatest Arab leader of modern times, Gamal Abdul Nasser (Fig. 18.4). In 1935, when he was still a schoolboy, Nasser had written: 'It seems to me that the country is dying. Despair is great . . . Who can end it? . . . Where are the men ready to give their lives for independence of the country so that the weak and humiliated Egyptian can stand up again and live free and independent? Where is dignity? Where is nationalism?'

The young Nasser felt humiliated by the way the British dominated his country and was hostile to extremist Muslim solutions put forward by groups such as the Muslim brotherhood. But he was more than just a straightforward Egyptian nationalist, for he believed in the need for a Pan-Arab movement, that is, one that would unite all the Arabs. He was also bitterly against the creation of the Israeli state and joined his school friends in a strike on the anniversary of the Balfour Declaration. For Nasser, the army was the instrument of salvation, and he was disgusted by its inept performance in the war of 1948–9. Despite this, it was a group of army officers under Neguib, Nasser and Sadat, as we have seen, which deposed the King and seized power in 1952.

Once he had removed Neguib as President in 1954, Nasser was in a position to carry out his two major aims: the modernization of his country and the forging of stronger links with the surrounding Arab states. In following this policy, he was assisted by the emergence of Ba'ath or Arab socialist parties in Syria and Iraq. By 1958 Egypt and Syria had formed the

Fig. 18.4   President Nasser of Egypt.

United Arab Republic (UAR), but it proved to be a sad disappointment. In 1961, to Nasser's surprise, the Syrians revolted, and a later intervention in the Yemen proved to be no more successful. Egypt's support of the Republicans in the Yemeni civil war was a considerable drain on the former's limited resources, and in 1965 Nasser decided to pull out. Then came the disaster of the 1967 war, and it seemed that Nasser's mission to unite the Arab world had failed. The Syrians had resented his authoritarian methods, and moderate states, like Jordan and Saudi Arabia, were suspicious of him.

Yet, with all his failings, Nasser remained 'the most progressive Egyptian ruler of modern times'. Heavy defence expenditure was a burden on the Egyptian economy but important progress had been made. The Aswan High Dam project was completed, and Egyptian oil production increased. In 1969 the country had its first trade surplus since the 1930s, and even the International Monetary Fund, that sober judge of economic health, gave Egypt the stamp of approval. Perhaps Egypt would have prospered more without Nasser's incessant wars, but his impact on the Arab world was shown by the haste with which other Arab leaders attempted to inherit his mantle.

Gaddafi and Libya

One of them was Colonel Moamar al Gaddafi, who overthrew King Idris and made himself dictator of

Libya in September 1969. Gaddafi shared Nasser's Pan-Arab dreams, but unlike his hero, was something of a religious fanatic. He approved of Sadat's expulsion of Russian advisers in 1972, but denounced his Israel mission in 1977. Increasingly bizarre behaviour patterns emerged as Gaddafi ran guns to the IRA, gave strong support to the PLO and announced the union of Egypt and Libya in April 1977. Such claims were totally rejected by Egypt and resulted in fighting along the common frontier. But the Libyan dictator would not give up, and in 1980 he announced the union of his small, oil-rich country with President Assad's Syrian Republic. This move only underlined the eccentric nature of Gaddafi's policy because Assad had signed a treaty of friendship with the USSR, the godless enemy (in Gaddafi's eyes) of the Muslim world. To make matters more complicated, the Libyan leader then proceeded to support non-Arab Iran in its war with the Iraqis in the autumn of 1980! Iran's brand of Muslim fundamentalism* seemed to have a special appeal to the Gaddafi regime. His claims to be Nasser's heir were not, therefore, taken very seriously in the Arab world.

Siddam Hussein and the Gulf War

Since the overthrow of the monarchy in 1958, the Iraqi Republic had been one of the most fervent supporters of the Arab cause against Israel and a friend of the Palestinians. It had, on the other hand, been noted for continual squabbling with neighbouring Syria, although both countries were ruled by Ba'ath socialist parties. President Hasan al Bakr was a devoted Pan-Arab, but in 1979 he was replaced as President by Siddam Hussein, who had more ambitious designs. Hussein's encouragement of a cult of the personality indicated that he saw himself as the potential leader of the Arab world. An Iraqi newspaper described him as 'the perfume of Iraq, its dates, its estuary of the two rivers, its sword, its shield, the eagle whose grandeur dazzles the heaven'.[3] Such praise encouraged Siddam to undertake a dangerous policy switch in September 1980 by attacking neighbouring Iran. The origins of this conflict were complicated and ancient:

1. There was a territorial aspect – Iraq claimed that Iran was interfering with its right to use the Shatt-al-Arab waterway (Fig. 18.5). The status of the waterway had been fixed by the 1975 Algiers Pact.

Fig. 18.5   Iran and Iraq.

2. Religious antagonism was important. Both countries had Shiite majorities, and Siddam Hussein accused the Iranian leader, Ayatollah Khomeini of inciting the Shiites* in Iraq against their largely Sunni* government (see p. 194).

3. The two countries had been enemies for a long time. The former Shah of Iran had encouraged the Kurdish minority in Iraq to revolt. It is important to remember that the Iraqis are Arabs and the Iranians are not, although both peoples are followers of the Muslim religion.

Siddam therefore had some reason to see Iran as an enemy and to expect a rapid victory after the confusion caused by the Iranian Revolution in 1979. His hopes were not to be justified because of the unexpectedly tough resistance of the Iranian forces. Instead, the war settled down into a dour slogging match around the Iranian oil towns of Kermanshah and Abadan. It also highlighted the chronic divisions of the Arab world and the instability of the Middle East. King Hussein of Jordan supported his new ally Iraq, so did the Saudis and the Gulf kingdoms. Libya, by contrast, supported the Iranians, as did Syria's President Assad. On the fringe of the conflict, as always, were the Israelis. Their attitude to the Gulf War was best summed up by a government official: 'The best outcome for Israel would be if neither side won and both exhausted their war machines for the next ten years.'

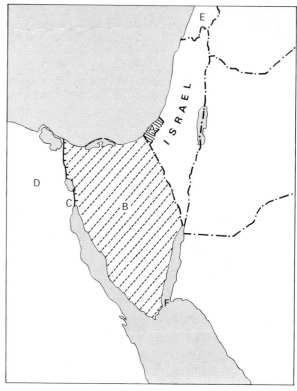

Fig. 18.6   Look at the questions on this map.

Keywords

kibbutzim: Israeli communal farm settlements.

fedayeen: Arab guerrillas, such as those who raided the Gaza Strip in the 1950s.

Muslim fundamentalism: absolute loyalty to the Muslim Holy Book, the Koran.

Shiites: those who believe in Ali as the true heir of Muhammad; found mainly in Iran.

Sunni: from Sunna the Prophet's thoughts; the more orthodox of the Muslim sects. The Prophet Muhammad (AD 570–632) was followed by three Caliphs whom the Sunni Muslims accept as his true heirs, while the Shiites do not. Sunni concentrated in all the Arab countries apart from Iran.

Questions

Fig. 18.6

1. Identify areas A and B occupied by Israel after the 1967 war.   2

2. Name the international waterway C, the target of an Anglo–French attack in 1956.   1

3. Countries D and E were opponents of Israel in 1948, 1967 and 1973. Name them.   2

4. Identify Strait F closed to Israel by Egypt in 1967.   1

5. Who were the TWO Israeli leaders who planned the 1967 war?   2

6. What TWO other areas were occupied by Israel after the 1967 war?   2

7. Explain what you understand by the term Pan-Arabism? How successful has the Pan-Arab movement been since 1952?   10
                                                                                                              ——
                                                                                                              20

19 The United States in Vietnam and Cambodia

We saw in Chapter 17 how John F. Kennedy began his Presidency in a great spirit of optimism. He said that the American people would 'pay any price . . . to assure the survival and the success of liberty'. Compare this statement with one made by an American soldier in Philip Caputo's novel about the Vietnam War, *A Rumour of War:* 'My mind shot back a decade to that day we had marched into Vietnam, swaggering confident and full of idealism. We had believed we were there for a high moral purpose. But somehow our idealism was lost, our morals corrupted and the purpose forgotten.'[1] (Caputo was a Vietnam veteran, who later covered the war as a reporter.) The second quotation tells us something about the American experience in Vietnam because for many young Americans it was to be a crusade that went wrong. Kennedy's high-flown phrases were to leave a sour taste in the mouth. To understand why we need to turn back to 1954.

The war in Vietnam

The Geneva Agreement

The peace settlement which followed the French defeat at Dien Bien Phu has been described as a watershed in the history of Vietnam. In the sense that it marked the end of French colonialism, it was. But, unfortunately, the agreement contained flaws which contributed to the tragedy that followed. There was an obvious comparison with Korea because Vietnam was also divided by a geographical line of latitude (Fig. 19.1). This time it was the 17th Parallel, but the division was only meant to be temporary. Article 7 of the Geneva Agreement stated that the Vietnamese people were to enjoy 'fundamental freedoms, guaranteed by democratic institutions as a result of free general elections by secret ballot'. These elections were to take place before July 1956 in both the North

and South. They were supposed to be the prelude to the reunification of Vietnam.

These were the weak points in the agreement:
1. It was assumed that free elections would take place.
2. It was signed only by the Vietminh and the French. Neither the Americans nor the South Vietnamese were party to the agreement.

At the time this did not seem to matter much. The Americans, after all, had refused to get involved in the French defeat at Dien Bien Phu. Ho Chi Minh was confident that the division of his country would only be a short-term solution. The Geneva Agreement

Fig. 19.1   American intervention in Vietnam, 1963–72.

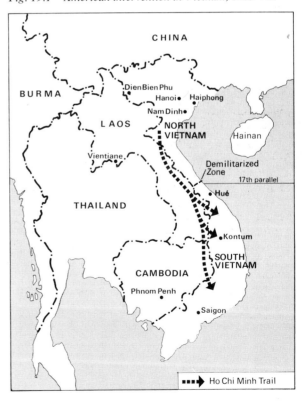

was, Ho said, 'a provisional measure aimed at the successful reunification of the country'. In other words, the communists were confident that the South (then in a state of chaos) would soon fall into their hands.

Ngo Dinh Diem

This reasonable assumption left out one important factor, the ambitions of Ngo Dinh Diem. A Catholic, educated in France, Diem returned to Vietnam in 1954. At that stage the South was technically under the rule of the French puppet Bao Dai, and he made Diem Prime Minister. As Premier, Diem's job should have been to prepare South Vietnam for free elections. But he had no intention of handing over the South to the communists. He was influenced by two factors:

1. the savage persecution of his fellow Catholics in the North (800,000 had fled to the South in 1954–5).
2. his family. One of his brothers was a Catholic archbishop and all the family were strongly anti-communist. Nepotism* was a strong characteristic of the Diem government.

To strengthen his position Diem held a plebiscite, deposed Bao Dai and made himself President of South Vietnam. He held this position from 1955–63.

The beginnings of American involvement

In 1955 Diem revealed his true colours by rejecting North Vietnamese and Soviet demands for free elections in the South. He said: 'Free elections at any time if you will guarantee that they will also be free in North Vietnam. It is obvious, however, that the communists will not carry out genuine free elections in North Vietnam and under such conditions, I cannot hold an election in South Vietnam.' Such statements pleased the Americans who were impressed by the way Diem was trying to stabilize the South. Diem seemed proof that Eisenhower's famous Domino Theory was not inevitable. They tended to overlook Diem's refusal to allow free elections in his own country. Even liberal-minded Americans like Senator John Kennedy backed Diem's position in refusing to hold an election 'obviously stacked and subverted in advance'.

The Vietcong

More important than Diem's undemocratic behaviour was the continued presence of former Viet-

minh fighters in the South. When it became clear that Diem had no intention of holding free elections these forces were 'reactivated'. For two years (1956–8) they reorganized and retrained before launching a new attack on the South Vietnamese government. Ironically, it was the latter who gave them their new name Vietcong (meaning Vietnamese communist).

At first Ngo Tinh Diem tried to disguise the level of Vietcong activity from the Americans. But he could not do so for long.

Diem's dictatorship

The appearance of the Vietcong coincided with an increase in Diem's personal power. 'Anyone,' wrote one observer, 'who did not submit to his dictatorship was persecuted, exiled, or at best, politicly extinguished'.[2] Both religion and geography played a part in Diem's policies which dangerously divided his people. Catholic Northerners seemed to be favoured over Buddhist Southerners. This antagonism had tragic consequences. A horrified world watched televised film of monks burning themselves to death in protest at Diem's policies. His apparent indifference to these suicides did nothing to enhance his popularity.

The American government viewed all this with mounting concern. It had seen Diem as a reliable bastion against communism. Instead, by the early 1960s, they found growing evidence of both Diem's unpopularity and Vietcong activity in the countryside. Under Kennedy the level of US military help was increased so that by 1963 there were about 16,000 US advisers in South Vietnam.

The fall of Diem

The situation was to change with dramatic suddenness. On 2 November 1963 Diem was overthrown by a military coup in Saigon. There is a strong suggestion that the United States government secretly approved the action of rebel army generals. He and his brother Nhu were later shot by the army. Diem's death was soon completely overshadowed by Kennedy's assassination on 22 November.

The question of responsibility

John Kennedy died at a time when American involvement in Vietnam was limited. Within five years 500,000 US combat troops were to be found fighting there (Fig. 19.2). Most of the blame for this situation has naturally been placed on President Lyndon Johnson. He, after all, was the man in charge. This leaves us with a fascinating question. Would Kennedy have pulled out US troops earlier and prevented the heavy loss of American lives? Here are two views:

1. Theodore Sorensen, a former Kennedy aide, wrote: 'It was simply not John Kennedy's nature to stubbornly throw division after division into a bloody worsening struggle without measuring the effect on our power, prestige, resources and society compared with the realistic prospects of success.'[3]

2. Hugh Higgins believes that Kennedy's speeches on Vietnam 'had the effect of moving the Vietnam war nearer the forefront of American politics and of encouraging the generals, who were adept at seizing their chances, to seek a greater share in the shaping of policy'.[4] Such differences of view demonstrate the difference in history between fact and opinion. What Kennedy would have done, if he had not died in 1963, must remain guesswork.

The outside world

Before moving on to look at the course of the war we should say something about international attitudes to it. Not surprisingly, the United States policy was fully backed by its allies, Britain, Australia and New Zealand, although the French took rather an independent line. Small contingents of Australians, South Koreans, and New Zealanders did, in fact, fight on the American side. By contrast, there was no direct involvement of the Soviet Union or China. Moscow acted as an arms supplier to North Vietnam, hoping to gain influence in the area as a result. But there was no question of direct confrontation between Soviet and American troops. China's policy, as Stuart Schram points out, was one of 'extreme prudence'.[5] As early as 1965, Mao stated that Chinese forces would not become involved in an Indo-Chinese war.

The escalation of the war, 1964–8

After John Kennedy's death the scale of the war greatly increased and became, by 1968, a major issue in US domestic politics. Why did this happen?

There appear to be two main causes:

1. Lyndon Johnson always thought of himself as carrying on the Kennedy policies – he kept on much

Fig. 19.2   American marines prepare to attack the Vietcong.

of the Kennedy team, including Defence Secretary MacNamara.

2. As you will have seen in Chapter 17, Johnson was a great domestic reformer. He was probably more interested in his 'Great Society' than foreign affairs. But he was worried about Right-wingers in Congress seeing him as 'soft' on Vietnam. As he said himself, in his usual down-to-earth way: 'They won't be talking about my Civil Rights Bill, or education or beautification [of the environment]. No. sir, they'll push Vietnam up my ass every time. Vietnam. Vietnam. Vietnam. Right up my ass.' In a sense, of course, Johnson was right, but the real attack came from the Left-wing peace demonstrators.

The Gulf of Tongking

In the meantime, the war in Vietnam reached a crisis point. The US government claimed to have evidence that regular North Vietnamese troops were fighting in the South. This was serious enough, but in August 1964 Johnson accused the North Vietnamese of attacking American warships in the Gulf of Tongking. Considerable doubt had been expressed since 1964 about the truthfulness of such claims. Reports from naval officers on the spot were confused, and months later Johnson himself said: 'For all I knew, our Navy was shooting at whales out there.'

Genuine or not, the Gulf of Tongking incident gave Johnson the powers he wanted. American opinion was outraged by the account of North Vietnamese aggression. On 7 August 1964 a resolution was put forward to allow the President to take any action, 'including the use of armed force', against North Vietnam. The Gulf of Tongking resolution was passed in the Senate by eighty-eight votes to two and in the House of Representatives by 416 votes to nil.

The bombing campaign

Once he had secured his position at home by a massive election win (see Chapter 17) Johnson authorized a new phase in the war. The Americans knew that the Vietcong in South Vietnam were receiving both men and supplies from the North. Their military leaders believed that massive bombing of the North would destroy the Vietcong's main source of supply.

On 13 February 1965 Johnson ordered the launching of Operation Rolling Thunder, all-out war against North Vietnam. The increasing scale of the bombing is shown by the fact that in 1965 the US Air Force dropped 315,000 ton(ne)s of bombs on the North. By 1969 the figure was 1,288,000 ton(ne)s. Despite American claims that only military targets were hit, there is no doubt that many thousands of innocent civilians were killed. The bombing was accompanied by the use of other weapons, such as napalm and defoliants. Crops were ruined and animal life destroyed. One American general boasted that the US Air Force would bomb North Vietnam 'back into the Stone Age'. It did not, of course, and it is surprising that American leaders ever believed that it would. They themselves had conducted elaborate surveys about the effect of saturation bombing on Nazi Germany during the Second World War. These had shown that terror bombing did not break the morale of the German people. This was also true of the North Vietnamese. Nothing the Americans could do would close down the Ho Chi Minh Trail to the South.

The war in the South

In combination with the bombing offensive went the war against the Vietcong on the ground. Like the French before them, the Americans had little difficulty in holding on to the big cities like Saigon (now Ho Chi Minh City) and Hue. The real war was fought in the countryside, and there were several reasons why the Americans and their South Vietnamese allies failed to win it:

1. The Americans faced the usual problems of dealing with guerrilla fighters. They had devastating fire power, but their enemy remained elusive. The Vietcong had deep roots among the peasantry and could easily merge into the local population.

2. There was a failure of psychology on the American side. For the ordinary Vietnamese the choice between democracy and communism was not as clear cut as Johnson and his advisers imagined. The American-backed leaders in the South, Diem, Khanh, Ky and Thieu, were little more than military dictators. Their regimes were corrupt and, as Hugh Higgins points out, strongly identified with French colonialism.[6]

3. The American campaign to win the 'hearts and minds of the people' lacked imagination and understanding. Vietnam had an ancient culture with its own beliefs and way of life and could not be bought overnight by American soldiers dispensing chewing gum and Coca Cola.

4. To Western observers the struggle appeared hopelessly one sided. The greatest military and industrial power in the world versus what Johnson called a 'little fourth rate country', North Vietnam. A journalist in 1966 noted the lavish equipment and support available to the US forces: 'Everyone of

these soldiers is inoculated against every possible disease, he gets his anti-malaria pills daily, and by deliberate exposure for two weeks has been made immune to the bacteria which attack the intestines of white people. Even their uniforms and underwear are washed twice weekly by flying laundries.'[7] They were fighting an enemy whose only defence against low-flying aircraft was the rifle (although used effectively as the Americans noted). This supposed invincibility made the Americans overconfident.

The Tet Offensive

Throughout the period 1965–8 the Americans and South Vietnamese appeared to be winning the war. Meanwhile, casualty lists continued to grow. Two thousand American dead in 1965 became 14,000 by 1968. Spending on the war ran at a level of millions of dollars a month. More dangerously, the morale of American combat troops began to crack. Drug addiction became common and 'fragging' (the use of fragmentation grenades against officers), a characteristic of front line units. The vocabulary of the soldiers, 'gooks' for the Vietnamese in general and 'head counts' for the number of Vietcong killed, showed a contempt for an underrated enemy. In another sense, it also indicated a despair about a war which could not have been won.

Still the American generals went on believing that the war was almost won; all that was needed was another 100,000 men. As you will remember there were 500,000 in Vietnam by 1968. Then, in January 1968, during the period of the Vietnamese New Year (Tet), the impossible happened. According to the computers and planners in the Pentagon*, the Vietcong were beaten, but they did not seem to be listening. Fifty thousand guerrillas attacked and occupied most of the populated areas of South Vietnam. To the acute embarrassment of the US government they even held the American Embassy in Saigon for a while. For Johnson this was to be the last straw.

By now the President had become so unpopular, he hardly dared to leave the White House for fear of meeting chanting anti-war demonstrators. Already one Democrat, Eugene MacCarthy, had declared that he would stand against Johnson on an anti-war platform, and Robert Kennedy was to follow shortly afterwards. By early spring 1968 American casualties were running at the rate of 300 a week, and the whole country was in the grip of the peace movement (Fig. 19.3). On 31 March, therefore, Johnson made on television the most fateful speech of his long political career. In it he stated his intention (i) to stop bombing the populated areas of North Vietnam, (ii) to start peace talks with Hanoi in Paris, and (iii) not to seek re-election as President in November.

Fig. 19.3   Anti-Vietnam war demonstration in New York. Among the demonstrators were thousands of veterans of the war.

Nixon and Vietnam

We saw in Chapter 17 how Richard Nixon was elected in 1968. He did this while remaining very quiet about his plans on Vietnam. As it turned out, Nixon continued for some years to behave as if it was possible to win the war. For a while the level of bombing was actually increased. On the other hand, Nixon did have one priceless advantage in dealing with the war. He had a stainless record as an anti-communist. No one could accuse the prosecutor of Alger Hiss of being 'soft on communism'! This gave Nixon more room for manoeuvre on the war than his predecessor.

In fact, Nixon even managed to extend the scale of the war. In April 1970 he allowed US troops to invade the small neighbouring (and neutral) state of Cambodia. Both Nixon and Henry Kissinger (his chief security adviser) believed that the Vietcong were using Cambodia as an important refuge and supply base. The invasion made little impact on the war. Its main effect was to cause widespread protests in the USA which ended with the shooting of protesting students at Kent State University. The lesson was not learnt, however, because in 1971 South Vietnamese troops invaded Laos as well. While there was communist activity in both these countries, it had little influence on the conflict in Vietnam.

Vietnamization

By now the ugly face of the Vietnam war was becoming more and more evident to the American people. Kennedy's crusade had turned into a 'dirty war' in which US troops were accused of behaviour more usually associated with Nazis. In 1968 an American unit massacred 500 civilians at the village of My Lai. Many Americans found the details too shocking to believe. For others the horror was not lessened by knowledge of communist atrocities.

In partial recognition of such anti-war feeling Nixon started a programme of Vietnamization*. The idea, borrowed from one of Johnson's advisers, was a simple one: gradual withdrawal of US troops combined with an expansion of the South Vietnamese army. The Americans would arm and equip this new army. They would also provide air cover. Vietnamization did not end the war, but it did greatly reduce US involvement in it. This did not apply to the war in the air, for in April 1972 Nixon actually restarted the raids on the North.

The ceasefire

Renewed bombing did not, however, bring victory.

By the end of 1972 Nixon and Kissinger knew that peace was inevitable. Very few US combat troops were left by then anyway. Prolonged negotiations with North Vietnam and the National Liberation Front (the civilian wing of the Vietcong founded in 1960) produced a ceasefire in January 1973.

America's effective defeat in Vietnam also allowed Congress to reassert itself, in the wake of a feeling that both Johnson and Nixon had deceived them about the war. In November 1973 Congress passed a law preventing the President making war without its approval, and subsequent demands for money for the Indo-China war were either rejected outright or severely curtailed.

As in 1954 it was recognized that the people of South Vietnam should be able to choose their own government. In this case a choice between President Thieu and the communist-backed Provisional Revolutionary government. The ceasefire did not affect the war between South Vietnam and the communists. It merely ended American involvement. At first it seemed that Vietnamization might work. The South Vietnamese army won no startling victories, but it appeared to hold its own. The end came with dramatic suddenness. In March 1975 President Thieu ordered his army to withdraw from the area called the Central Highlands and concentrate around Saigon. This withdrawal rapidly turned into a panic-stricken rout. By the end of the April the communists were able to march into Saigon in triumph. A fleet of helicopters removed the last of the American advisers and those South Vietnamese supporters fortunate enough to beg or bribe their way aboard.

Ho Chi Minh's dream of a unified Vietnam had come true. The attempt to prevent it had on one estimate cost 56,000 American and over 2 million Vietnamese lives.

Vietnam today

The events of 1975 did not end the problems facing that unhappy country. In 1978–9 it became involved in disputes with its communist neighbours, Cambodia and China. Peking supported the communist Khmer Rouge* in Cambodia, while Moscow supported Vietnam as it had throughout the struggle with the Americans. When Vietnamese troops invaded Cambodia, China retaliated by invading the northern provinces of Vietnam in December 1978. This invasion was limited in scope and the Chinese troops were soon withdrawn. The affair highlighted the traditional dislike between the two countries.

Fig. 19.4 The Huey Fong arrives in Hong Kong carrying 2,700 refugees from Vietnam.

The boat people

It had one sad result. Throughout the spring of 1979 the world became used to the spectacle of boatloads of refugees fleeing from their country (Fig. 19.4). To the West it seemed that the refugees (mainly of Chinese origin) were the victims of heartless racial persecution. The Vietnamese government claimed that Peking had incited the refugees to flee from their homeland. It agreed (after an international conference in July 1979) to try and regulate the flow of people.

Cambodia

The fate of Vietnam was tragic enough in the 1970s, but it paled before that of its tiny neighbour Cambodia in the same period. For many years, the Cambodians went on living a fairly peaceful existence until the American incursion of 1970 changed it from being a small neutral country into a totalitarian hell. The origins of this change, like so many others, went back to the 1950s when a radical student called Khien Samphan produced a type of blueprint for an independent Cambodia (Kampuchea).

In it, Khien made four major points:
1. Since decolonized peoples like the Khmers would be exploited by capitalists as cheap labour, they must pull out of the world system which made the rich, richer and the Cambodian poor, poorer.
2. This would mean changing the local economy.

3. The Cambodians would then have to run an agricultural society built on an old rotting capitalist one.
4. Industrialization and slow re-entry by Cambodia into world affairs would then follow.

The Khmer Rouge, led by Pol Pot, began to put this 'blueprint' into operation when they seized Phnom Penh in 1975, driving out the American-backed Lon Nol. From the capital alone 2–3 million destitute, old, sick people were driven from their homes into the countryside. One estimate was that 1,200,000 people had been slaughtered by January 1977. Two years later, Foreign Minister Sary conceded a figure of 3 million dead, although he claimed that the executions had been 'a mistake'.[8]

World opinion may have been astounded by Pol Pot's atrocities, but once the Vietnamese had seized Phnom Penh, he became the hero of national resistance, recognized by China as Prime Minister, and champion of the anti-Soviet forces in the world. In fact, Pol Pot was 'boxed in' by the Soviet–Vietnamese pact of 1978, which caused the loss of his capital and released an orgy of destruction. Rice stocks were burnt and all available machinery was smashed. This modern Luddite* then led what was left of the Khmer Rouge forces in the jungle, a fitting end for a man who had abolished towns and all education beyond the three Rs. Those who crossed the Pot regime came to an horrific end, usually battered by 'a bayonet or club, for that saved ammunition'.[9]

Pol Pot had never forgiven the betrayal of his country in the 1954 settlement or the neutralist policy followed by Prince Sihanouk in the 1960s which allowed the Vietcong hideouts in Kampuchea.

Denis Bloodworth writes: 'If Pol Pot is a monster moreover he has Frankensteins – not only in Khien Samphan and Mao, whose writings inspired him, but in Nixon and Kissinger who widened the war.'[10]

Keywords

nepotism: the tendency to favour one's relatives, by giving them jobs, etc.
Pentagon: the US Defense Department.
Vietnamization: the process of replacing US combat troops with South Vietnamese.
Khmer Rouge: the Communist forces in Cambodia (Kampuchea).
Luddite: Ned Ludd and his followers wrecked new machinery, thinking they endangered jobs, in nineteenth-century Nottinghamshire.

20 The Soviet Union since 1945

The USSR emerged from the Second World War battered, but victorious. The achievement of victory was in itself an amazing success for a country 60 per cent of which had fallen under German occupation. During the period 1942–5 industrial production increased by over 500 per cent, an average of 40,000 aircraft and 30,000 tanks being produced each year. This was one side of the picture, but there was another darker one. The Soviet Union had lost 20 million of its inhabitants and another 25 million were homeless. The fearful legacy of the 'Great Patriotic War' has remained with the Russian people ever since. Those Soviet citizens who did survive the war found that life was just as grim as it had been before 1941. Everywhere the heavy hand of Stalin dominated the life of the country, and he trusted no one. Those Soviet soldiers who had the misfortune to be taken prisoner were treated as if they were Fascist sympathizers, and the slightest indication of dissent might bring a long sentence in a labour camp. The novelist Alexander Solzhenitsyn was one man who paid such a price for a mild criticism of Stalin in a letter.

More Five-Year Plans

Economic development was to follow the prewar pattern, although recovery was assisted by systematic looting of the eastern European countries by the Soviet forces. It was certainly slowed down by Stalin's refusal to accept Marshall Aid, which meant that the USSR had to rely on its own resources. Why did Stalin turn down such valuable assistance? Almost certainly because, as Isaac Deutscher suggests, 'he could not agree to submit to the West a balance sheet of Soviet economic resources in which he would have to reveal Russia's appalling exhaustion and the frightful gap in her manpower that he was concealing even from his own people'.[1]

Despite this, the Soviet economy showed remarkable resilience, although the emphasis was once again on heavy industry. Under the fourth Five-Year Plan, 1946–50, industrial production shot up by 71 per cent on the prewar level. In the fifth plan, which ran until 1955, there was a big increase in grain production as a result of the increased size of collective farms. By contrast, production of consumer goods fell by 5 per cent in the first five postwar years. The Soviet people's living standards took second place to the needs of the state.

Repression

The Soviet people's freedom of expression and movement was controlled by Stalin's henchman Lavrenti Beria, the head of the NKVD or secret police. As his master's paranoia grew, the labour camps became more overcrowded and the likelihood of a new purge greater. Stalin had already purged the communist leaderships of eastern Europe (see Chapter 23), and in his closing years, he became obsessed by anti-Semitism. In 1953 some Jewish doctors were accused of poisoning him, but before the net could be drawn wider, the dictator died. Rumour has it that no one dared approach the dead corpse for some hours after Stalin's death, and the reaction was an understandable one. For thirty years in peace and war, Joseph Stalin had ruled his country with an iron hand, so that Russia without him was hard to imagine. The confusion of the Soviet people when Stalin died in March 1953 was best expressed by the poet Yevtushenko who wrote: 'We wept sincerely with grief and perhaps also with fear of the unknown.'[2]

The struggle for power, 1953–5

We saw, in Chapter 10, how Lenin's death in 1924 was followed by a struggle to succeed him in the Politburo. The situation in 1953 was similar, as there were several men who had claims to be the leader of the Soviet state. The most dangerous was Beria, the head of the secret police, but he disappeared in July 1953. His actual fate remains uncertain, but one account says that he was shot by his colleagues who certainly had every reason to fear his power. In the end, it was Georgi Malenkov who emerged as Prime Minister, but in no sense was he a dictator in the Stalinist mould.

Malenkov realized, rightly, that a change in the direction of economic policy was required. He intended to do this by raising the production of consumer goods and thus raising the people's standard of living. Unfortunately, his plans proved to be a little too ambitious for the time, and their failure led to his removal from the premiership in February 1955. Nikolai Bulganin became Premier, but the rising star was Nikita Khrushchev (Fig. 20.1), an agricultural expert and former wartime boss in the Ukraine. Under 'B & K', as the Western press insisted on calling them, the Soviet style of leadership appeared to be changing, with visits to India in 1955 and Britain in 1956. While it was also true that many prisoners were released from Stalin's labour camps, the change was something of an illusion. If there was 'not a clear decisive break with the legacy of Stalinism',[3] it was not surprising. All the Soviet leaders had been Stalin's men, and they dared not destroy the whole system.

Fig. 20.1   Khrushchev personified a 'new' leadership style.

Khrushchev's secret speech, February 1956

Some were prepared, however, to go further than others. Early in 1956 Nikita Khrushchev delivered a secret speech to the Twentieth Congress of the Soviet Communist Party. In it, he attacked Stalin as a 'bungler' and a 'mass murderer', implying that the purges of the 1930s were unjustified. The attack went on for five hours, and it left the delegates stunned, for Khrushchev was attacking the whole Soviet past in the person of Stalin. It was a courageous move, and a dangerous one, because not all the members of the Politburo shared his views. Some, like former Foreign Minister Molotov, tried to oppose Khrushchev's campaign of destalinization and were sacked from their top posts in 1957. By the end of that year, the rotund, extrovert Khrushchev was clearly the leading man in the Soviet government.

The Khrushchev period, 1957–64

In many respects, the period of Khrushchev's ascendancy was an improvement on anything that had gone before. More political prisoners were

released and a limited amount of criticism of the previous regime was tolerated. Khrushchev allowed the publication of Alexander Solzhenitsyn's book, *One Day in the Life of Ivan Denisovich*, and it is said that he read the manuscript himself. It has to be admitted though that the new leader was less tolerant of criticism of his government, even if he accepted attacks on Stalin.

Nonetheless, the image of the USSR under Nikita Khrushchev was generally a more favourable one. No one could imagine Stalin visiting the USA – as Khrushchev did in 1959 – and enjoying the cancan in Hollywood! There was a down-to-earth, peasant shrewdness about the new man that was undoubtedly attractive.

Agricultural reforms

Khrushchev had established a reputation as an agricultural expert, and he had ambitious plans to boost Soviet production. To do this, he needed to make the collective farms more efficient, and he attempted to do so in a number of ways.

1. *The Virgin Lands scheme.*   This plan, originally launched in 1954, aimed at reclaiming about 36 million hectares (90 million acres) of uncultivated land in Siberia. It had some success at first, but a changeable climate made good harvests a matter of luck (Fig. 20.2).

2. *Changes on the collective farm.*   After 1958, all peasants were allowed to keep or sell all the food they grew on their private plots of land. It was hoped that this change would increase the supply of food to the towns.

Khrushchev also abolished the tractor stations which had existed in Stalin's day. Their machines were sold to the collective farms. More emphasis was also placed on the use of fertilizers.

3. *Greater investment.*   Much more money was pumped into the agricultural sector. Between 1953–8, production rose by 50 per cent.

Industry

Khrushchev had also promised to raise industrial production and produce more consumer goods. More than this, he boasted that he would outstrip American production figures in both agricultural and industrial goods. To achieve this unlikely target, incentives were offered to workers, and higher wages and promotion went to those who produced more. Fibres and plastics were singled out for attention by Khrushchev's industrial programme. These efforts did have some effect as the figures in Table 20.1 show.

Table 20.1 Consumer goods produced in the USSR

Consumer goods	No. of goods per thousand of the population	
	1955	1966
Radios	66	171
Cars	2	5
Television sets	4	82
Refrigerators	4	40
Washing machines	1	77
Sewing machines	31	151

Khrushchev's fall, 1964

By the autumn of 1964, there were serious complaints in the Politburo about Khrushchev's colourful 'one-man-band' style of leadership, and his colleagues decided to remove him. When he went on holiday to

Fig. 20.2   The Virgin Lands scheme.

the Black Sea coast in October, he was voted out of his various offices and officially retired on health grounds.

In a sense, Khrushchev's extrovert personality had led to his downfall, for he was too fond of boasting about what the USSR would achieve under his leadership.

This was especially true of the agricultural sector, when in 1963 the failure of the harvest made nonsense of the Soviet leader's prediction that his country would overtake US production figures. Agriculture was Khrushchev's single most serious failure, but he had also caused some anger in ruling circles by trying to further the career of his son-in-law Adzubei. The 'hawks' in the Kremlin were angry with him for trying to cut defence expenditure, and his agricultural plans had caused him to attack heavy industry, the traditional sacred area of the Soviet economy. When these failures at home were added to criticisms of Khrushchev's handling of the Cuban Missile Crisis (see Chapter 23) and relations with China (see Chapter 23) his position can be seen to have been a vulnerable one. He never possessed the secure power base of a Stalin or a Lenin, and had also become 'a very difficult man to work with'.[4]

In one sense, Khrushchev's downfall was unique. For the first time a Soviet leader had been removed from office, not by death, exile or execution, but by the vote of his colleagues. But it was in the Soviet tradition that Khrushchev should immediately become an 'unperson'. He spent his remaining years as an ordinary old-age pensioner. When he died in 1971, no representative of the Soviet government attended his funeral. The leadership could not associate itself with the errors of the past.

The Soviet Union since Khrushchev

After Khrushchev's fall, the Central Committee of the Soviet Communist Party elected Leonid Brezhnev (Fig. 20.3) and Alexei Kosygin to be Party Secretary and Prime Minister respectively. Brezhnev had been a supporter of both Stalin and Khrushchev in turn. Kosygin had made his way up by means of his technical knowledge and his contribution to Soviet industry. These two men, who dominated the USSR into the 1970s, were to continue to carry out many of Khrushchev's policies, but usually in a less dramatic way. Alexei Kosygin resigned from his post in October 1980, supposedly on health grounds, and it seemed he would be made a scapegoat for economic problems.

Agriculture

Brezhnev was largely responsible for changes in agricultural policy, and he made the following reforms from 1965 onwards:
1. More money was invested in the agricultural programme.
2. The Ministry of Agriculture, abolished by Khrushchev, was re-established.
3. Peasants were to have larger incomes and the security of a minimum wage.
4. Local farm managers and officials were to have more freedom to adapt change to local conditions.

These reforms did have some effect as Table 20.2 shows, and with greater incentives the peasants also produced more (Table 20.3).

Table 20.2 Daily wages of peasants, 1960–75

Year	Roubles
1960	1.40
1965	2.68
1972	4.11
1974	4.50
1975	4.60

Fig. 20.3   President Brezhnev.

Table 20.3 Soviet agricultural production, 1956–75
million ton(ne)s

Crops	1956–60	1960–65	1966–70	1971–5
Grain	121.50	130.30	167.6	181.5
Cotton	4.36	4.90	6.1	7.7
Sugar beet	45.60	59.20	81.1	76.0
Potatoes	88.30	81.60	94.8	89.7
Meat	7.90	9.30	11.6	14.0

Industry

There was a similar development in industry. The latest computer technology was imported from the West, and foreign car manufacturers, such as Fiat, were encouraged to set up factories in the Soviet Union. The expansion in consumer goods production, known as 'goulash communism', continued, and more attention was therefore paid to the living standards of the Soviet people. In 1968 alone, 11 million Russians moved into new houses and flats. In contrast to the Western countries, where unemployment rose steadily throughout the 1970s, the Soviet Union was actually short of labour. Its people therefore had an economic security and freedom from want that was unique in modern Russian history.

The system of supply was far from perfect, and shortages are still a characteristic of Soviet society, but no one goes hungry. The relative inefficiency of Soviet agriculture is shown by the fact that harvest failures forced the government to buy large quantities of American grain in 1975.

Soviet society today

The USSR is a vast country with a very large population (which increased from over $226\frac{1}{2}$ million in 1964 to $255\frac{1}{2}$ million in 1976). It is dominated by the Soviet Communist Party, but only about 5 per cent of its population are actually party members. But these 5 per cent run the country and are considered to be an élite,* as Leonid Brezhnev pointed out in 1966:

> We can see party veterans, who have experienced three revolutions, communists tempered in the struggle for the industrialization of the country and the battle for the collectivization of agriculture – for the great socialist transformation of the Motherland; we see here also those who linked their lives to the party in the terrible years of the Great Patriotic War and who after the war raised up again the Soviet Motherland from ruins and ash. All of these are today actively building the communist society as members of the united army of political fighters.[5]

Brezhnev was 23 years old when the Bolsheviks seized power in Russia, but by 1980 more than three-quarters of the party membership consisted of those who had joined after 1945. They could not therefore remember the hardships of the old days, and were more concerned with the achievement of better standards of living for the Soviet people.

It is a society, too, which is increasingly better educated. Four million Soviet young people were in higher education by 1966, most of them studying scientific and technical subjects.

Opposition

As we have seen, the Communist Party membership is very small, and it is natural to ask if some Russian people oppose the party and how they show such opposition. This takes us into one of the more difficult areas of contemporary Soviet life. For as a Marxist state, the USSR is reluctant to admit its imperfections, even to the extent of denying the existence of social problems, such as alcoholism and juvenile delinquency. According to a writer in the *Soviet Weekly* the so-called 'generation gap', very much an issue in Western countries, does not exist in Russia: 'In our country the generations are not in conflict: they co-operate, and the elders hand on to the young revolutionary traditions and tasks to be done. If you were to talk to young people in the Soviet Union about a "conflict of ideas" between old and young they would think you were crazy.'[6] This account does not tally with the observations of foreign tourists, who have noted the interest shown by Soviet youth in 'degenerate' Western pop music and clothes, which are frowned on by the authorities. Some accounts tell of gangs of youths on motor bikes who roam around the woods outside Moscow, apparently rejected by Soviet society!

More serious than the quite natural clash between young people and adult authority is the treatment of political and religious opponents of the regime. Under Brezhnev and Kosygin, there appears to have been a return to Stalinist techniques of repression, although the methods are more subtle. Corrective mental treatment may now be used instead of the labour camp and a typical case is that of Leonid Plyushch (Fig. 20.4) as described by a *Chronicle of Current Events*, an underground newspaper:

> The case of Leonid Plyushch was tried by the Kiev Regional Court on 25–9 January 1973. The judge was Dyshel.
>
> The case was heard behind closed doors, with the accused not present. According to the *Chronicle*'s information, none of the officially appointed psychiatrists was present in court.
>
> The defence counsel was permitted only one meeting with his client. Plyushch was not permitted access to the case file.
>
> Nine witnesses were questioned at the trial. Among them was the man of letters Ivan Dzyuba, arrested in 1972.
>
> The court ruled that L. Plyushch was mentally ill, and that while in a non-responsible state he had committed especially dangerous crimes coming under Article 62 of the Ukrainian Criminal Code.
>
> Plyushch was charged with the following:
> 1. possessing several copies of *Chronicle of Current Events*, the *Ukrainian Herald*, and other samizdat* materials; and distributing some of them among his acquaintances;
> 2. writing seven articles of literary criticism whose content was ruled to be 'anti-Soviet', and familiarizing several acquaintances with some of these articles;

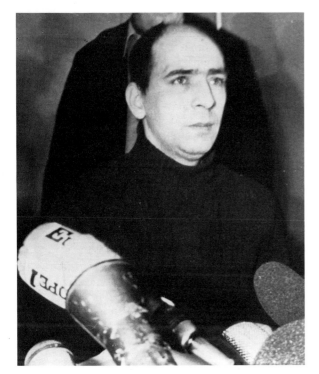

Fig. 20.4   Leonid Plyushch, the Ukrainian mathematician, who was interned for 2 years in a psychiatric hospital in the Soviet Union, giving a press conference soon after his arrival in the West.

3. signing open letters to the UN as a member of the Initiative Group; membership in the 'illegal Initiative Group';
4. 'anti-Soviet agitation' conversations with one or two of the witnesses.
   By order of the court, Plyushch was sent to a special psychiatric hospital for compulsory treatment.[7]

The Plyushch case was typical of many in the 1970s, and according to the historian Peter Reddaway, Soviet treatment of critics of the government was governed by four considerations:
1. the amount of support for the person or group in the USSR and abroad;
2. whether the foreign support might affect the well-being of the Soviet economy;
3. the actual importance of the individual or group to the Soviet economy;
4. the ability of the group or person to defend itself or himself against the Soviet authorities.[8]
   When it was judged easier to throw a dissident out of the country, this was done. Thus, in 1974, Alexander Solzhenitsyn was exiled from the USSR for the criticisms put forward in books like *The Gulag Archipelago*. But the scientist Andrei Sakharov, the father of the Soviet hydrogen bomb, was not allowed to leave.

The minorities

The people referred to above were political critics of the Soviet system. Others were persecuted for their religious beliefs. These included the Jews and the Baptists. Stalin's prejudice against the former was notorious, but the discrimination against them after 1964 was a direct infringement of the Soviet Constitution. The result was that many Soviet Jews wanted to go and live in Israel. American pressure and the desire for *détente* forced the Soviet government to agree. By 1974, 100,000 Jews had left for Israel.

Other groups were not so fortunate, and it should be remembered that the USSR consists of many different races. Only about one-half of its people are of Russian nationality, and many of the non-Russians are discontented with Soviet rule.

In Lithuania, for example, there were riots in 1972, which ended with a protesting student burning himself to death. Catholic priests were also arrested for their activities in the province. The Crimean Tartars were another minority to suffer in this way. Between 1956–74, 200 of them were imprisoned for campaigning for independence. Thousands more, who went back to the Crimea without permission, were expelled.

The Soviet achievement

All this paints a grim picture of Soviet society today, and there is much which it is right to criticize. Two additional points also need to be made:
1. Russia has no tradition of free expression as understood in the West.
2. The Soviet Communist Party believes rightly or wrongly that it represents *all* the people and that it has a duty to lead them towards socialism. No opposition to this goal can be tolerated, and the needs of the whole society must be put before those of individual people or groups.

Whether the USSR has developed the right form of socialist society is another matter. Many would argue that it has created its own privileged group of leaders who have little real contact with the peasants and factory workers they claim to represent.

The material achievements of the USSR since 1945 must speak for themselves.

Keywords

élite: in this context, the Soviet Communist Party with its job of leading the working class.
samizdat: underground newspaper or pamphlet.

Questions

Fig. 20.2

1. This man ruled the USSR from 1956–64. Name him.   1

2. In 1956 he made a secret attack on Joseph Stalin. Describe the effects of this speech in the USSR.   4

3. Give THREE reasons why this leader fell from power in 1964.   6

4. Name the TWO men who have dominated the USSR since 1964.   2

5. Give ONE example of a Soviet dissident and how he showed his opposition to the Soviet government.   2

6. Indicate TWO ways in which Soviet treatment of opposition groups has changed since Stalin's day.   2

7. What do you think has been the most important Soviet achievement since 1945?   3
　　　　　　　　　　　　　　　　　　　　　―
　　　　　　　　　　　　　　　　　　　　20

21 China and Japan: Two Economic Miracles

China since 1949

When the Communist Party came to power in China in 1949, it faced several immediate tasks. One was to restore China's prestige in the world, something which had already been partly achieved by the overthrow of the corrupt Nationalist regime. Mao recognized this when he said: 'Our nation will never again be an insulted nation. We have stood up.'

Although Mao had been a loyal Marxist all his life, his Marxism had its own specially Chinese characteristics. In 1943 Liu Shao-Chi, an old party comrade, said Mao's great achievement was to change 'Marxism from a European Asiatic form. . . . China is a semi-colonial country in which vast numbers of people live at the edge of starvation'. The task of the party, Mao said, was to swim like fish in the peasant sea, while always encouraging the revolutionary potential of the masses.

This belief caused Mao to make some controversial statements, notably the one in 1946 calling the atomic bomb 'a paper tiger'. This comment was widely misunderstood for it was the same man who said that 'power grows out of the barrel of a gun' and sanctioned the explosion of China's first A-bomb in 1964.

Mao really meant that revolution was a continuous process which could not be stopped by the existence of nuclear weapons. His thought was always unorthodox, as Schram points out, because he failed to mention 'the leading role of the proletariat'.[1] But after the shambles at Shanghai in 1927, Mao rightly saw that the peasants were the truly revolutionary force in China (see p. 34).

Sino–Soviet relations

It was this unorthodoxy which led to the ultimate split with Russia. At first, all went well. In 1950 the two countries signed a friendship treaty. Indeed, as late as 1957, Mao spoke of the need for the 'socialist camp' to have a leader which must be the USSR.

This superficial friendliness glossed over some awkward facts. Why had Stalin supported Chiang in the 1930s and in the Civil War period? Why had the Soviet armies looted Manchuria in their 1945 advance?

For ten years all this was forgotten as the Chinese copied the Soviet Five-Year Plans with their emphasis on industrial growth and collectivization. As we shall see, the failure of the 'Great Leap' owed as much to crass overambition, as did Stalin's plan of 1929–33. Then came the crashing blow as their Soviet brothers left them in the lurch (see p. 198).

The seeds of this conflict lay way back in the past, for Stalin had always feared the emergence of a powerful new socialist state on his frontiers. Mao had achieved success the unorthodox way, and he did it without the bloodthirsty purges of Stalinist Russia in the 1930s. Unlike the bureaucrats in the Kremlin, the Chinese leader always encouraged fresh thought inside his party, even if the pace of such changes often disconcerted others.

The Chinese Communist Party consolidates its power

Another problem was to establish the Communist Party as the country's effective leadership, even though it only represented about 3 per cent of the total population in 1949. 'We Communists,' said Mao, 'must be able to integrate ourselves with the masses in all things. If our party members spend their whole lives sitting indoors and never go out to face the world and brave the storm, what good will they be to the Chinese people?' But the people had to be educated to understand the party's message, and only one-fifth of them were at school in 1949. Many adults could not read and write, so the government had to mount a massive literacy campaign in the 1950s.

There were also several accounts to be settled with the supporters of the old regime, although at first the loyalty of the middle classes was accepted at face value. University teachers, managers and other professional people were kept at their posts in the period 1949–53. The significant exception to this moderate policy were the landowners who had treated the peasants so harshly in the bad old days. They were attacked as 'running dogs' of imperialism, and a big campaign was started against them. Mass trials were held, and as many as 2 million members of the landlord class may have been executed in the period 1949–51.

The Agrarian Reform Law 1950

A new land settlement was to form an essential part of the Communist Party programme, and this was implemented in 1950. The Agrarian Reform Law of that year set up peasant committees to share out the landlords' land. An estimated 54 million hectares (120 million acres) of land was redistributed in this way between 1950–52. At the same time, an attempt was made to teach the peasants up-to-date farming methods since agriculture was the basis of the Chinese economy. It had to cope with a growing number of mouths to feed. In 1949 there were 500 million Chinese, but by the late 1950s, this figure had grown to 650 million.

Co-operatives

To make the system of production more efficient, the peasants were encouraged to form co-operatives. Thirty or more families would come together and 'pool' their land, although the land would still be privately owned. By 1958 there were 750,000 of these co-operatives.

The first Five-Year Plan, 1953–7

The People's Republic of China also adopted the use of the Five-Year Plan on the Soviet model. The emphasis was to be on heavy industry, and Soviet help was forthcoming for about 150 industrial schemes (e.g. new steelworks in Wuhan and Mongolia). The two countries had already signed a friendship treaty in 1950, and the Chinese obviously relied a good deal on Soviet help.

'The Hundred Flowers' campaign, 1956–7

Mao Tse-tung always saw the development of his country on two levels: political and economic. So while his country reformed its economy, he worried lest the Communist Party became too conservative and bureaucratic*. In January 1956 Mao made a famous speech in which he said: 'Let a hundred flowers bloom . . . let a hundred schools compete [this was a reference to ancient China when there were a hundred schools of philosophy and thought].' He wanted the Communist Party to be shaken up because he said it was guilty of 'bureaucratism and mandarinism'. Students were to be encouraged to criticize their teachers, and the people could criticize the party. Such critics were not to be punished and you may not be surprised to learn that this got out of hand! In 1957 Mao had to stop the campaign, but he always kept a watchful eye on his party colleagues. In fact, his desire to prevent the appearance of élites of managers and intellectuals in the Chinese party was to be an important feature of his next reform.

The 'Great Leap Forward'

In 1958 the second Five-Year Plan was due to start, and it was to be a far more ambitious venture than the first one. There were two major aspects:
1. The industrial emphasis of the first plan was to be changed so that everyone could take part in the effort to industrialize China. Mao even encouraged peasants to set up 'backyard blast furnaces'.
2. The co-operatives in the countryside were to be replaced by a system of communes (Fig. 21.1). Private land ownership was to be abolished and the peasants were to work for the government. These communes were very large indeed, with an average of 25,000 peasants per commune. Some had as many as 50,000 peasants living on them. It was believed that these larger units of production would make agriculture more efficient.

At first, there was much enthusiasm about the 'Great Leap Forward', and some progress was made. Then the Chinese government was faced with ill luck. Bad harvests ruined its hopes of increased food production, and then the split with the Soviet Union (see Chapter 23) left it with many only partly-completed projects. The Chinese were angry and bitter about this, but they were still isolated from the West, and were thrown back entirely on their own resources. But the failure of the 'Great Leap' was not entirely due to bad luck. The leadership failed to anticipate the resentment the peasants would feel about losing their land under the commune system. They also failed to see that backyard furnaces were not an adequate substitute for modern technology. By 1961 the failure of the plan was so serious that the third Five-Year Plan had to be put back to 1966, and, as Peter Mitchell tells us, 'the euphoria of the "Great Leap" gave way to sober reassessment'.[2] Nevertheless, the failure was not total. The peasants learned

Fig. 21.1   A Chinese commune during the 'Great Leap'.

something about basic industrial techniques and their leaders learnt something about trying to run a modern economy.

The Great Proletarian Cultural Revolution

By the mid-1960s, China had recovered from the trauma of the 'Great Leap Forward' only to suffer another one. Once again, Chairman Mao decided to shake up the political establishment of the country. This time he had a major opponent who seemed to have a different conception of how China ought to be run. His name was Liu Shao-Chi.

The 'expert line'

Liu was a veteran member of the party like Mao, but he put industrialization before everything. To achieve this, he was prepared to give extra wages and incentives to 'experts' like engineers, managers and scientists.

The 'mass line'

Mao resolutely opposed this 'expert line', which he believed would set up a privileged class of people in China who would have nothing to do with the peasant masses. By 1965 he had decided that Liu and his followers should be weeded out of the party.

Liu was dismissed from his official posts in the party, and his followers were intimidated by the revolutionary Red Guards. In June 1966 all schools and colleges closed so that Chinese youth could be free to join the Red Guards campaign in the countryside. The *Thoughts of Chairman Mao*, otherwise known as the *Little Red Book*, became a type of bible for young people, and they were encouraged to believe that their leader was infallible. The Red Guards (Fig. 21.2) became more and more extreme in their behaviour, even to the extent of torturing and executing those whom they regarded as 'bourgeois revisionists' and 'capitalist roaders*'. Even the moderate Premier of China Chou En-lai, an old comrade of Mao's, was attacked during the Cultural Revolution.

Fig. 21.2   Chairman Mao encouraged Red Guard radicialism.

By 1967 everyone in the leadership had become alarmed by such excesses, and Mao ordered the People's Liberation Army to put a stop to the Red Guards' activities. In July 1968 he admitted that the Red Guards had carried their revolutionary enthusiasm too far. The cost of the Cultural Revolution was high because for two years, industry and the education system had come to a halt.

It did have some important results, especially in the education system, where Mao had criticized existent practice for he said it 'strangles talent, destroys young people'. In 1964 Mao had suggested that 'students should be permitted to doze off when a lecturer is teaching. Instead of listening to nonsense, they do much better taking a nap to freshen themselves up. Why listen to gibberish?' Such opinions would not find favour with Chinese educationalists! The Cultural Revolution forced them to change their minds by introducing new ideas. 'Open book' exams were introduced (allowing students to take books into their examinations), and there was more time available for political education.

A typical timetable for an eleven-year-old child in 1971 consisted of four periods of politics; twenty minutes' exercise; two periods of revolutionary art; six periods of maths; two periods of English; and one period of general knowledge.

Those who wished to go into higher education were not assessed purely on their academic ability. The student had to have worked on a commune or in a factory or been in the armed services, and also needed a recommendation from his/her fellow workers.

The fall of Lin Piao, 1971

Another immediate consequence of the Great Proletarian Cultural Revolution was that Mao's position in the Chinese Communist Party was greatly strengthened. Liu Shao-Chi had been removed and other old comrades, like Chu Teh, were discredited. Mao's main ally in this achievement was the War Minister, Lin Piao, who seemed to have emerged as a likely successor. But in 1971 Lin disappeared in mysterious circumstances. The Chinese explanation was that he attempted a *coup d'état* and when it failed, his flight to the USSR ended in a plane crash.

Mao's last years

The closing years of Chairman Mao were to be marked by yet another radical campaign, this time led by Mao's wife Jiang Qing, the most influential member of the 'Gang of Four' (the other radicals were Zang Chunqiao, Wang Hongwen and Yao Wenyuan). Although this period coincided with an attempt to achieve *détente* with the West (see Chapter 23), it was one of extreme xenophobia inside China. Foreign music, films and books were banned, and the ideological war against the USSR was intensified. The extent to which Mao was in control of this new campaign is uncertain, but it must have had his approval. He died in September 1976, shortly after his old friend and colleague Chou En-lai, and with his passing, a new and more moderate leadership took control of the country.

The modernizations

The Premier was Hua Guofeng, but the man with the most influence was the senior Vice-Premier Deng Xiaoping. Deng had been purged by Madame Mao, and after her husband's death, he took his revenge. The 'Gang of Four' were placed under house arrest although some of the charges against them were original to say the least: Jiang Qing was accused, among other things, of nagging Mao to death, playing poker during his last illness and watching *The Sound of Music*! All the defects in Chinese society were attributed to the Gang of Four who were put on public trial in the autumn of 1980.

Otherwise the period of Hua and Deng's domination was notable for a complete reversal of China's economic policies. Foreign technical help was actively sought, and Chinese trade missions made numerous visits to Western countries. Deng himself paid a visit to the USA as the Chinese government pushed through its new programme called the Four Modernizations (Industry, Agriculture, Science, Defence).

At the same time, there was some relaxation of the government's treatment of its critics. Wall posters, the traditional Chinese way of expressing grievances, began to appear in cities like Peking and Shanghai. By the end of the 1970s, it was permissible to suggest that Chairman Mao himself might have made policy blunders. The renewed contacts with the West in the economic field also brought about a renewal of Western cultural influence too. Western music, films, books and fashion reappeared in China as its young people revolted against the years of Maoist conformism.

The fall of Hua, 1980

By September 1980 Hua Guofeng's position had been sufficiently weakened by his links with Chairman Mao to force him to resign as Premier (although he kept his post as Chairman of the party). Deng Xiaoping also resigned, but he ensured that his supporter, the economist Zhao Ziyang, replaced Hua as Prime Minister. This was part of a general reshuffle of the Chinese Politburo designed to introduce younger and more vigorous leadership. Shortly afterwards, the long-threatened trial of the notorious 'Gang of Four' began in Peking in November. Deng, who had once been forced to parade in a dunce's cap by Madame Mao, described her as a 'very, very evil woman. She is so evil that anything you can say about her can't be evil enough.' It was clear that if Deng and Hua had not arrested the Gang of Four in October 1976, they would have fallen themselves. But the most interesting defendant was not on trial at all, Chairman Mao himself.

China's achievement

We have seen how the Chinese People's Republic has suffered several setbacks since its foundation in 1949. Its overall record still remains impressive as Table 21.1 shows.

Table 21.1 Industrial production in China, 1952–70

thousands

Industry	1952	1962	1970*
Electric power (KWh)	7,300,000	30,000,000	70,000,000
Coal (ton(ne)s)	16,500	180,000	350,000
Crude oil (ton(ne)s)	400	5,300	1,100
Steel (ton(ne)s)	1,300	8,000	1,600
Chemical fertilizer (ton(ne)s)	200	2,120	7,500

Note: *estimated figures only.

Since 1949, China has become a major industrial power and is now also a nuclear power. More importantly, the Chinese people are adequately clothed, housed and fed for the first time in their history. Many would criticize the way in which this has been attained, but even so the achievement remains a considerable one. It might have been greater still, but for the shake-ups of the 'Great Leap' and the Cultural Revolution as *The Times* pointed out: 'What Westerners would find to criticize in this method of opposing revisionism is that it is jerky: after a period of shake-up during which output declines, there is a period of smooth operation, during which it rises.'[3]

Such criticisms always need to be balanced by the memory of what the old days were like. In 1966 Sophie Knight reported on this conversation in Shanghai:

> A couple of days ago, I talked to one of the cooks in the kitchen at school. Lao Tao's parents were poor peasants. He couldn't bear the countryside, poverty, exploitation, hunger – so an uncle, a rickshaw driver in Shanghai, suggested he came to the city. When he arrived in Shanghai he got a job as a coolie too. He said in winter there was ice on the roads, and he couldn't afford a pair of shoes, so he had to run with bare feet. He was dismissed and got a job as a street-seller. He had a box in which he sold matches and candles [but] had to give most of his money to the company who sold him the matches. He said that at times he was living in a tent with ten or fifteen others, and couldn't always buy a day's bowl of rice; he occasionally ate vegetables, *never* eggs or meat.[4]

Japan since 1945

While the People's Republic continued its drive towards the creation of a perfect communist society, another economic miracle was taking place on the other side of the China Sea.

It did so in the face of defeat and occupation, for only on 28 April 1952 did the Allied occupation of the Japanese islands officially come to an end. The Americans under General MacArthur supervised the immediate postwar government of Japan and deliberately broke up the old power structure. The new constitution gave real power to the Japanese parliament and reduced Emperor Hirohito to the status of a figurehead. Japan was also only allowed a small defence force.

Land redistribution

It was also part of American policy to break the power of the landowning class by redistributing the land. No person was to be allowed to own more than 3 hectares (7 acres). Despite this restriction, more scientific farming methods allowed the Japanese to cope with a rising population (98 million by the 1960s).

The Eugenics Law 1948

This actually represented a levelling off of the population as a result of a 1948 reform. It legalized abortion and began a birth-control campaign.

Education

The schools, which had acted as a feeding ground for militaristic ideals before the war, were also carefully controlled by the Americans. Under their guidance, there was a rapid expansion of university and college places.

The economic miracle

The most striking thing about Japan in the 1950s and 1960s was its remarkable economic recovery (Fig. 21.3). In 1945 it was a devastated, defeated nation. Yet, between 1953–65, its annual growth rate averaged 10 per cent. Great industrial corporations like Hitachi became famous throughout the world, although their methods contrasted with business practice elsewhere. Japanese firms were noted for

Fig. 21.3   Japan's miracle: a Japanese electronics factory.

Fig. 21.4   Riot in Japan. Militant students clash with police in Tokyo.

their paternalism* and the close connection between workers and management. Cheap rented flats and other benefits were available for the work-force, providing they gave complete loyalty to their employers. In this way, Japanese factory workers were as closely bound to their corporations as the Chinese peasants were to their communes. Japan had a free-enterprise economy, but its industrial disciplines would have been unacceptable in most West European countries.

How did the Japanese economy achieve this remarkable growth in the postwar years? Several points need to be remembered:
1. between 1948–51 the Japanese received $2 billion in aid from the USA;
2. the hard work and co-operation of the Japanese people;
3. the fact that Japan spent virtually no money on defence;
4. the devastated state of the country at the end of the war meant that it started off with brand new equipment and rolling stock.

Political extremism

Because Japan was such a rich, materialistic society, it gave birth to various forms of political extremism (Fig. 21.4) followed by people who were bored and disenchanted with middle-class consumerism. Many Right-wingers disliked the way the USA seemed to have made Japan a puppet state by means of the Security Pact signed in 1957. This pact was renewed

in 1960, but only after serious rioting, and there were further disturbances in 1968 and 1969. A more disturbing feature from the government's viewpoint was the appearance in the late 1960s of the Japanese 'Red Army' dedicated to the overthrow of the conservative ruling classes. This was a Left-wing movement which had strong links with other terrorist groups in the world and the growing environmental lobby. Massive demonstrations against the building of a new Tokyo airport were typical of the latter's activities which obtained a lot of student support.

By the 1970s, the economic miracle had slowed down, partly as a consequence of the oil crisis of 1973. Japan had no domestic supply of oil and was therefore forced to pay the higher OPEC prices for it. Despite this weakness, its slow inflation rates and labour costs gave Japan a distinct advantage in export markets.

Relentless economic advance has led, however, to a number of political scandals like the Tanaka affair in 1979 – when a former Japanese Prime Minister was accused of taking bribes from the American Lockheed Company.

Keywords

bureaucratic: the tendency of large organizations to become too official or attached to rules.

capitalist roaders: those in China accused of following the road to capitalism.

paternalism: Japanese business organizations were noted for the firm fatherly control exercised over their workers.

22 The Emergent Nations

Much of world history since 1945 has been the story of the emergence of new independent countries free from the control of the European colonial powers and able to play their own distinct role on the world stage. This chapter is concerned with these countries.

The African continent

The Arab north (Fig. 22.1)

Chapter 18 described the development of the Pan-Arab movement and the role played by Egypt within it, although Egypt is of course an African country, too. But it has close links with the Middle East and can be justly dealt with in that context. To Egypt's west are the other Arab countries of Algeria, Libya, Tunisia and Morocco, which all obtained their independence in the years that followed the Second World War. The recent history of Libya receives some attention elsewhere (see p. 162), but it should be noted that this oil-rich former Italian colony spent the years before 1969 under the virtually feudal rule of King Idris. Its neighbour Morocco, which obtained independence from French rule in 1956, also had a monarchical form of government. Morocco's ruler in 1980 was King Hassan II, who ascended the throne in 1961. He was notable both for his dislike of democracy and freedom of expression, and his ultra-nationalist foreign policy. Claims to the Spanish Sahara in 1975 led to armed clashes with Algeria in 1976.

Algeria of all the Arab countries of North Africa has

Fig. 22.1   The Arab world in the 1960s.

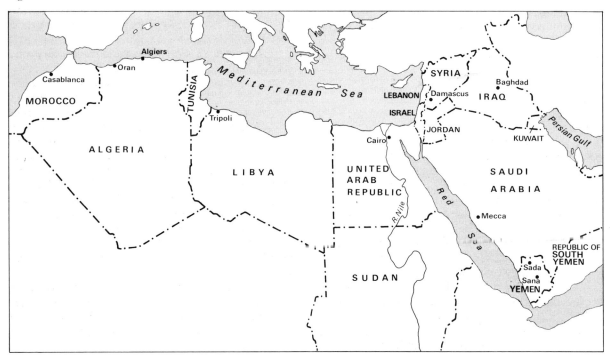

had the most difficult recent history. Starting in 1954, the Algerian people, spearheaded by the nationalist *Front de la Libération Nationale* (FLN), had to fight a bloody and long drawn-out war of independence against France, which was equally determined to hold on to its oldest colony. France even had to fight off a vicious guerrilla campaign by desperate *colons** through the *Organisation de l'Armée Secrète* (OAS). Only in 1962 did de Gaulle recognize the inevitable. The war cost many thousands of lives and left a legacy of bitterness between Algeria and France which took many years to subside. Algerian politics following independence were complicated and unusual in that the man who had led the country against French rule, Ben Bella, was deposed in 1965 by Colonel Hourai Boumedienne. Boumedienne kept Ben Bella under house arrest (from which he was only released in 1980) and set up a Left-wing government which developed close links with other radical Arab states. He died in 1979, by which time Algeria was beginning to benefit from the discovery of natural gas deposits and a more harmonious relationship with France.

This relationship also dominated the early years of independent Tunisia, Algeria's neighbour. A bloody struggle around the French naval base at Bizerta in 1962 culminated in the handing over of this last piece of Tunisian territory, but the story of Tunisian independence was a good deal less stormy than that of Algeria. Since 1955 its political life has been dominated by one man, Habib Bourgiba and his Destour Party. Although authoritarian in outlook, Bourgiba has preserved his country's independence and secured a considerable degree of economic prosperity via trading links with France and the EEC.

The west

In black Africa, it was to be the countries of the west coast with their looser tribal links which were to attain independence first. This process began with the independence of Ghana, the former Gold Coast, in 1957 which opened the floodgates for the African nationalist movements. Nigeria was to follow in 1960 and de Gaulle offered independence to all France's black African colonies which they lost little time in accepting, together with the associated status of membership of the French African Community. The sole exception was Guinea where President Sékou Touré's influence obtained a 'No' vote on the question of membership of the Community. France retaliated by withdrawing all aid to the newly independent state, but Sékou Touré replaced this with assistance from the communist bloc.

Kwame Nkrumah and Ghana

A notable figure in West Africa in these years was Kwame Nkrumah, the President of Ghana and a sponsor of the Pan-African Congress set up in 1945. This put forward the idea that all Africans are part of one racial unit and that the resources and land of the continent should be held in trust for its peoples. Nkrumah was also a founding member of the Organization of African Unity, which was set up in 1963 with the object of forming a United States of Africa.

At home Nkrumah was responsible for introducing useful projects, such as the Volta River scheme (1961), and he also promoted forestry and fishing. But there was also a less praiseworthy side to his activities. No opposition was allowed to the governing party, the Convention People's Party, and in 1959 the Preventative Detention Act allowed the imprisonment of opponents without trial. This oppression went hand in hand with expensive 'white elephants', which the Ghana economy could afford, such as the construction of underused motorways.

The promise of the early Nkrumah years disintegrated and in 1966 he was overthrown by a military *coup* while on a visit to China. He returned to Africa and lived on until 1972 vainly hoping for a recall to power, but it never came.

Ghana since Nkrumah

The new government was led by Major-General Ankrah, who speedily released all the political prisoners, but in 1969 he too fell after charges of government corruption. Once again the military were involved, but the new leader Brigadier Arifa wanted to install a civilian government. Elections were called for August 1969, and they were won by Dr Busia's Progressive Party. Busia's government faced grave economic difficulties, which it made valiant efforts to solve. The currency was devalued in 1971, and import controls were introduced in an attempt to combat runaway inflation. Sadly, however, the problem proved to be too severe for Busia, and in 1972 he was toppled by a *coup* led by Colonel Acheampong. Throughout the 1970s Ghana was plagued by economic uncertainty, and in 1978 Acheampong's regime was replaced in its turn. Yet another *coup* took place in 1979, but it had some unusual features. The leader Jerry Rawlings was only a flight-lieutenant, and he and his revolutionary council insisted on executing several members of the previous regime. Rawlings remained in power for just 112 days before handing back power to the civilian government of President Limann.

Nigeria

The Nigerian Civil War   Britain's faith in the more stable qualities of West African democracy appeared to be borne out at first by the early history of Nigeria, the largest of the black African states. From 1957–66 the country was governed by Sir Abubakar Tafawa Balewa, but in January 1966 he was overthrown by a group of army officers led by Major-General Ironsi. He was a member of the Ibo tribe, from the Christian eastern part of the country, but his regime was only to last for six months. A plan to give Nigeria a national, rather than a federal constitution, resulted in the murder of Ironsi, and his death was the signal for a massacre of the Ibo people throughout Nigeria. It was this that precipitated an Ibo revolt led by Colonel Ojukwu in May 1967. The new leader of the federal government in Lagos, General Yakubu Gowon, found himself confronted with a civil war, in which the Christian Ibos were ranged against the Muslim Hausas of the north (Gowon himself was a Muslim). The other tribes of the country, the Yoruba, the Aro and the Angas supported the Lagos government.

Although the origins of the war were largely tribal, oil, recently discovered in the east, was certainly another factor and may have encouraged Ojukwu to hold out. Russia and Britain gave strong support to Gowon's government, while France, for selfish motives of its own, helped Ojukwu. The result was disastrous for the Ibo people, and the world watched only too complacently their sufferings in the province of Biafra (Fig. 22.2).

Since 1970 the federation has remained intact, and much of the credit for this must go to General Gowon himself, who made great efforts to heal the breach with the Ibos after the civil war. He went to the Ibo territories in 1971, and tried to calm their fears of domination by making the country a federation of twelve states. On the economic front, too, there was a steady improvement in the early 1970s. Nigeria showed a healthy trading position for the first time since independence, and a big campaign was started against government corruption. Then, in 1975, Gowon was overthrown while attending the Commonwealth Conference in Kampala, and became, rather fittingly, a student of political science at Warwick University!

The country's political troubles were to continue with the murder of the new head of state, General

Fig. 22.2   UNICEF supplies food for the starving children of Biafra.

Mohammed, in 1976, but his policy of reconciliation was continued by General Obasanjo. He restored the democratic system in 1978, and in August 1979 Alhaji Shagari was elected President of the Republic.

Nigeria faced considerable economic difficulties in the late 1970s, but the discovery of oil made it potentially one of the richest countries in Africa. The experience of war and internal division have made Nigerians doubtful about grand plans for African unity, but they have at least avoided the grotesque excesses of such rulers as the self-styled 'Emperor' Jean Bokassa of the Central African Federation.

Growth and development   Nigeria, as the largest black African state, affords an interesting example of growth and development in many areas. Progress in the field of education has been particularly striking, and since the oil price rises of 1973–4 the number of students in primary, secondary and university education has risen by more than 80 per cent. In 1976 the government introduced Universal Primary Education and equal attention was paid to higher education. More than 50,000 students were enrolled at Nigeria's thirteen universities in 1978.

The east

In East Africa the colonial role was played entirely by the British who approached the subject of independence for its peoples with a good deal of caution. East Africa was poor, and the British expected the process of independence to be slower. They also did not believe in antagonizing the large European settler population by accepting the idea of one man, one vote. The idea of a multiracial constitution for the East African countries was therefore shelved, but this policy ran into serious difficulties in Kenya in the early 1950s. The majority Kikuyu tribe, led by a secret society called Mau Mau, broke into open revolt and was responsible for the deaths of many whites.

Faced with this emergency, the British government set up the East African Royal Commission. Its report of 1953 recognized that lack of land (land hunger) had driven the Kikuyu on to European farms and that the European estates contained large amounts of uncultivated land which the Kikuyu could profitably use. The commission, however, did not stop the war with the Mau Mau, and the British replied by arresting Jomo Kenyatta and other Kikuyu leaders. The rank and file were forced into protected villages, and by 1955 the revolt was broken at a cost of £20 million and 100 British lives. Two points were highlighted by the Mau Mau emergency:
1. Tribalism had a particularly strong influence in East Africa, although the British exaggerated this factor. During the emergency they only allowed African politics to function on a regional basis. The Kikuyu and Luo peoples formed the Kenya African National Union (KANU), while the Kalenjin and Bantu formed the Kenya African Democratic Union (KADU).
2. It became clear that the European settlers in East Africa could not survive without costly British military assistance.

The lesson London learnt from the Mau Mau war was to accept the principle of Kenyan independence, and in 1960 Colonial Secretary Iain Macleod began to prepare the way for this. Full independence came in June 1963, and in 1964 Kenya declared itself a Republic with Kenyatta as President. There were teething troubles in 1969 when the leading Luo political leader, Tom Mboya, was assassinated, but on the whole, Kenya has proved to be a stable and prosperous addition to the family of African nations. In 1978 Jomo Kenyatta, who had successfully healed the tribal divisions of his people, died and Daniel Arap Moi became President in his place.

The story of Kenya contrasts greatly with neighbouring Uganda which had won its independence under Milton Obote in 1962. Obote's personalized leadership style proved to be unpopular, and he was overthrown by the head of the army, Major-General Idi Amin Dada, a Muslim from the north, while attending the Commonwealth Prime Ministers Conference in 1971. Amin was to be responsible for the worst reign of terror in black African history. He personally took part in sadistic murders and beatings, and his government made Obote's reign in Uganda seem like a golden age. In the spring of 1979 his monstrous tyranny came to an end when an army of Tanzanians and rebel Ugandans invaded the country. Amin disappeared, only to re-emerge later in Libya under the protection of fellow Muslim, Colonel Gaddafi.

In the West Amin was portrayed as a clownlike, albeit sinister, figure, but it is important to remember that the British government among others was *pleased* when he seized power in 1971. The Western European craving for political stability brought about a rather patronizing attitude to Africa's political troubles. It also tended to overlook the chronic political instability of countries in western and eastern Europe in the 1920s and 1930s and the emergence of Fascist dictatorships.

Instability was not, in any case, inevitable in black Africa. Tanzania (formerly Tanganyika and Zanzibar) under Julius Nyerere opted for a socialist form of government, which he hoped would lead to an East African Federation (Fig. 22.3). Nyerere-style socialism was a development of the traditional extended family system in Africa, as he noted himself: 'In traditional society everybody was a worker. There was no other way of earning a living for the community.' But Nyerere's ideas were not popular in Kenya, and a hostile relationship developed between the two countries in the 1970s. In this climate it was not surprising that the attempt to set up an East African Community was not a success. Matters came to a head in 1977 when East African Airways was grounded because of the refusal of Uganda and Tanzania to pay landing dues to Kenya. Tanzania responded by closing its frontier with the Kenyans who then withdrew from the Community altogether.

Nyerere was also a defender of the one-party state as being especially appropriate to African conditions, arguing that African political parties 'were not formed to challenge any ruling group of our people. They were formed to challenge the foreigners who ruled over us.' Western forms of government were not then always suitable for African conditions.

Central Africa

The worst example of a colonial hand-over of power in the 1960s was that of the Belgian Congo, already notorious for King Leopold's terrible treatment of the Africans before the First World War. The Belgians were reluctant to leave, but they did so almost overnight in 1960, under American pressure. In no way were the Congolese prepared for the coming of independence, and the result was a shambles. The rich copper-mining province of Katanga attempted to break away from the central government under Moise Tshombe. He was encouraged in this separatist* attitude by Belgian industrialists. The intervention of the UN was by no means an unqualified success, and a low point was reached when federal Premier Patrice Lumumba was executed by Katangan mercenaries in 1961. Periodic fighting between Katangan and UN forces continued until 1963 when Tshombe fled to Europe. He returned to become Premier of a united Congo in 1964, but in the following year, General Mobutu overthrew him and seized power in an army *coup*. He made himself President and in 1971 changed the country's name to the Republic of Zaïre. The bloody Congolese Civil War and its grim lessons hung like a cloud over black Africa in the 1960s. The white regimes to the south saw it as a justification of their racist arguments which claimed that black Africans were incapable of ruling themselves.

Fig. 22.3   Jomo Kenyatta and Julius Nyerere discuss the possibility of an African Federation.

The south

Before the process of independence rolled along there were six separate areas of jurisdiction in the south. One bloc consisted of the British colonies of Northern Rhodesia, Southern Rhodesia and Nyasaland. The Union of South Africa made another, and the Portuguese colonies of Angola and Mozambique two more. All, in their separate ways, underwrote the belief in white supremacy and superiority.

Rhodesia and Nyasaland

Within this area, it was the blacks of Southern Rhodesia who had developed most quickly, but Southern Rhodesia was also the area where the whites had been given semi-independence from Britain under the 1923 Constitution (see p. 42). Radical African advance was to continue in the 1940s with the development of separate trade unions and a general strike in Bulawayo in 1948. The whites' response to this was to demand the consolidation of their political power, not only in Southern Rhodesia, but also in the neighbouring territories of Northern Rhodesia in Nyasaland. This was achieved when the British government agreed to the setting up of the Central African Federation (comprising the two Rhodesias and Nyasaland) in September 1953. Whatever the British government may have thought, the white settlers were totally convinced of their own superiority.

While the whites rejected the concept of black majority rule, there was also another motive behind their behaviour – the protection of their economic investments. Between 1939–53 alone the annual value of copper production in Northern Rhodesia had risen from £7m to £51m, and the settlers had no intention of allowing this wealth to fall into black hands.

The Central African Federation was to continue in existence until 1960, when the British established the Monckton Commission, which recommended that all the territories should have the right to secede* from the Federation. In Northern Rhodesia and Nyasaland events took a fairly smooth course. The former became independent in 1963 under Kenneth Kaunda, the latter under Dr Hastings Banda. Kaunda changed his country's name to Zambia, while Nyasaland became known as Malawi. Kaunda, by the 1980s, had become an elder statesman of the Pan-African movement.

In Southern Rhodesia the situation was far more complicated. This was partly because the country was a crown colony, and partly because the ratio of whites to blacks was far higher (about 1:5). This meant, as

Martin Loney points out, that 'what could be imposed on Kenyan settlers could not be imposed on Rhodesian settlers without risking a white revolt'.[1] These settlers were already alarmed by the appearance of black majority governments in Zambia and Malawi, and many of them gave their support to the extreme Rhodesian Front Party, led first by Winston Field, and then by Ian Smith (1964).

The black nationalists had founded the National Democratic Party in 1960, but in 1962 this was superseded by the Zimbabwe African People's Union (ZAPU). Both organizations were devoted to bringing white minority rule to an end. These efforts were largely directed from abroad by ZAPU leader Joshua Nkomo, a strategy which did not please those of his supporters who believed that the nationalists should be building up their strength inside Southern Rhodesia. Some of them indeed were to set up a rival organization, the Zimbabwe African National Union (ZANU), in 1963. These divisions were helpful to the Rhodesian Front government of Ian Smith, when he decided to make a unilateral declaration of independence (UDI) from Britain in November 1965 after the latter's repeated refusal to grant independence to a colony when the majority black population would be governed by the white minority. The nationalist opposition was in no position to take active measures against Smith, and the British government renounced the use of force. Inept intervention by British Premier Harold Wilson (including the attempt to impose economic sanctions) failed to persuade Ian Smith, who later declared that black majority rule would never come 'in a thousand years'. But even Smith was forced to accept the realities of politics in 1974 when the repressive Portuguese government of Caetano collapsed and its successor gave independence to neighbouring Mozambique and Angola.

In April 1980, after years of guerrilla warfare against the Smith regime, Robert Mugabe was elected Premier of the new African state of Zimbabwe. He persuaded his rival Joshua Nkomo to become Home Affairs Minister and patiently set about the problem of persuading the rival guerrilla groups to disarm.

South Africa: the white man's Laager*

The last refuge of white power and privilege was to be the Union of South Africa where the Nationalist Party defeated Jan Smuts's United Party in the 1948 elections. Under its leader Dr Malan, the Nationalist Party introduced a policy of apartheid or separate development for blacks. This was a gradual development but, in the end, segregation took in the coloured and Asian minorities as well. Apartheid meant separate education facilities, separate leisure facilities (such as different stands at football matches) and no real say in the running of the country. Since 1948 the Nationalist Party, representing the Afrikaners (White South Africans of European, usually Dutch, descent), has maintained a monopoly of power. Malan retired in 1954 and was succeeded as Premier by Johannes Strijdom, who summed up the Nationalist philosophy in the words: 'Either the white man dominates or the black man takes over.' His successor, Henrik Verwoerd, who had been imprisoned for pro-Nazi sympathies during the Second World War, spoke of the need to stop blacks seeking 'equality with the European'. He was assassinated in 1966, but this made no difference to the Nationalist hold on power. John Vorster followed him, and there was little effective change in the apartheid system.

The Bantustans   The basis of apartheid in the 1960s was the Bantustan, set up in 1962 as a result of the Tomlinson Report of 1955. These native homelands had their own assemblies, but the Pretoria government had control of foreign affairs, justice and defence. All laws had to be passed by the central government, although, in the end, the native homelands were to be self-governing and independent.

The Bantustans were, in fact, to be the linchpin of the apartheid system, but their validity had been brilliantly destroyed by B. W. Hodder.[2] He makes four essential points against the system:

1. The original absence of the Bantu from the South African lands is irrelevant because the 'very concept of land ownership' meant nothing to the African at that time.

2. Bantu homelands occupy only 13.7 per cent of the total land space of the South African Republic. Ten million Bantu live in the white urban areas and if they were to join the 8 million living in the homelands, 'conditions there would become unsupportable'.

3. Despite the promises of the Tomlinson Report, economic development in the homelands has been very slow. The homelands are broken up into 113 separate pieces, and economic reality underlined the reality of 'baaskap' (white domination). In 1973 $4\frac{1}{2}$ million whites held three-quarters of the national income, while the 20 million blacks were left with the rest.

Arguments about standards of living are, says Hodder, irrelevant. Mineral-rich South Africa was bound to supply even its blacks with a higher standard of living than the rest of the continent.

4. Apartheid cannot deal with the 2 million coloureds or 1 million Indians. They, in turn, are kept separate from white and black.

The South African movements to establish separate Bantu homelands in the Transkei (1976) and Bophuthatswana (1977) were a transparent fraud. No government in the world recognized their sovereign existence apart from South Africa. Even so, the closed minds of the white minority still gave the Nationalists an electoral majority in 1977.

The reality of apartheid   What separate development really means is felt not in the homelands, but in the black ghettos like Soweto. At any time, the black worker might be challenged by the question: 'Waar's jou pass jong – where's your pass boy?' Every year a third of a million blacks are fined or sent to gaol for various 'crimes', including going into a town to look for work without permission. Urban slums like Soweto are rigorously policed for any sign of trouble.

Opposition is difficult under such a system, and black protests were ruthlessly put down at Sharpeville in 1960 and Soweto in 1976 (Fig. 22.4). The insensitivity of the authorities was shown again in 1980 when they refused to allow black students to hold a service of remembrance for the people killed at Soweto. Anyone who protested against the system was dealt with under the Suppression of Communism Act, although most protest had nothing to do with communism and everything to do with anti-racism. While a certain amount of integrated sport had been tolerated, there is little sign that the present Nationalist government under P. W. Botha has learnt its lesson. South Africa is now virtually surrounded by black African states but its mineral wealth has made it a far stronger military power than any of its neighbours. The only hope of real change seems to lie in possible international pressure and the arguments put forward by industrialists like Harry Oppenheimer. They have said for some time that exploitation of black labour and the breaking up of black families – forcing the men to live in depressing townships like Soweto – is harmful both to social and economic life. The Afrikaner state is still capable of outrages like the murder of Steve Biko in 1978, and great power remains with the secret police organization, the Bureau of State Security (BOSS).

India and non-alignment

We have seen how India attained its independence in 1947 under Premier Nehru who went on to show that he had a special conception of India's role in the world. It would not belong to any alliance blocs but follow instead a policy of non-alignment. Nehru also felt that the Third World countries should have a special voice in global politics and he worked with the Chinese Foreign Minister Chou En-lai to set up the Bandung Conference of 1955. This conference

Fig. 22.4   Apartheid's brutal face at Soweto, the African township outside Johannesburg. A march by black students in 1976 was ruthlessly broken up by police. One hundred people died and 1000 were injured.

marked the peak of Nehru's international influence which was sadly to be decreased by the disastrous war with China in 1962 (see p. 198). The Indians also had a long-running dispute with Pakistan over the province of Kashmir which caused a great deal of animosity.

Domestic reforms

The Indian leader showed less interest in domestic affairs, although he was committed to the principle of modernizing his country. The centrepoint of such development was the series of Five-Year Plans which began in 1951, which were designed to switch India's massive reserve of manpower away from the land to its growing industrial sector (only 1 per cent of the population was working in industry at the time of independence). But to modernize itself, India needed an educated population, and a big drive against illiteracy started in the 1950s. Children under 14 years of age were to be provided with a free basic education.

In the countryside, the 'green revolution' was producing some spectacular results, as the government pioneered the use of new strains of rice and corn and also encouraged the use of fertilizers.

At the same time, Nehru began a birth control programme to try to stop the massive growth of the Indian population (this stood at 350 million in 1951 and had risen to almost 550 million by 1971). He was not very successful, but the compulsory sterilization campaign started by his daughter in the 1970s proved to be much more unpopular and controversial.

In one area, at least, Nehru was undoubtedly successful, for he did bring about a peaceful transfer of power in India. When he was struck down by a last fatal stroke on 26 May 1964 the succession to the premiership of Lal Bahadur Shastri was assured, athough he too was to die in 1966.

Indira Gandhi, 1966–80

Nehru's daughter, Mrs Indira Gandhi, then became both leader of the Congress Party and Prime Minister. She presided over the successful war against Pakistan in 1971 which resulted in the independence of East Pakistan under its new name of Bangladesh. Up to this point, Mrs Gandhi had great prestige both at home and abroad, but in 1975 she made the mistake of declaring a state of emergency and suspending parliament on the grounds that law and order was breaking down. Her opponents united against her and she was overwhelmingly defeated by

Fig. 22.5   Mohammed Reza Pahlavi, the Shah.

the Janata party in the 1977 elections. Mrs Gandhi spent some time in prison on corruption charges, but showed her power of recovery by winning the elections in 1980. The loss of her son Sanjay in an air crash then posed a question over the succession as Mrs Gandhi again showed signs of authoritarian government, a characteristic shared by Pakistan under the ultra-Muslim General Zia.

Pakistan

From its earliest days in 1947, Pakistan had suffered from disunity and a preference for army rule. General Ayub Khan's government was followed by that of Yahya Khan whose incompetence was partly responsible for the loss of Bangladesh in 1971. Seven years of civilian government under the Oxford-educated Ali Bhutto's People's Party ended when he, in turn, was overthrown by General Zia ul-Haq in July 1977. Zia was a Muslim fundamentalist whose narrow religious preoccupations made him condemn Bhutto to death for alleged involvement in a murder plot. World opinion was shocked when Zia insisted on the sentence being carried out in April 1979.

Iran

General Zia's preoccupation with the basics of the Muslim religion was also reflected in nearby Iran. In this instance, the ambitious hereditary monarch Mohammed Reza Pahlavi (1941–79) (Fig. 22.5) was so obsessed with Westernization that he lost touch with the grass roots in his country. He exiled the Shiite religious leader Ayatollah Khomeini in 1963 and pressed ahead with ambitious domestic reforms paid for by the country's oil wealth. But the bubble burst at the end of 1977 when rioting crowds demanded the return of the Ayatollah, and in January 1979 the Shah was forced to abdicate and flee from the country. He died in exile in Egypt in July 1980.

In his place, Khomeini set up an Islamic Republic and insisted on a vigorous campaign against Western cultural and economic influences. The special 'devil' denounced by Khomeini and his supporters was the United States, which was believed to have been the main prop behind the Shah's repressive regime and its secret police force Savak. This anti-American feeling resulted in the takeover of their Teheran embassy in November 1979 and the holding of fifty-three embassy staff as hostages. An American rescue mission failed disastrously in April 1980 and only strengthened the position of the Ayatollah in Iran. The issue was still unresolved when President Jimmy Carter was defeated at the polls, but by then Iran was at war with neighbouring Iraq (see p. 163).

Keywords

colons: French settlers in Algeria.
separatist: a desire to break away from central government control.
secede: to break away from or leave.
Laager: an Afrikaans word meaning camp or base.

Questions

Fig. 22.5

1. Who was the Shah, and what happened to him?   2
2. Who led the revolt against the Shah, and to what Muslim group did he belong?   2
3. Which American President became involved in Iranian affairs? How did this happen?   5
4. Give an example of another Muslim state where 'fundamentalism' is strong, and name its leader.   2
5. Give TWO other examples of Third World countries which revolted against Western influence, and describe the circumstances in which this occurred. $\frac{9}{20}$

23 Giants Dancing: the Superpowers since 1953

A recent radio series described the relationship between the superpowers in the phrase, 'giants dancing', and it is an apt description. A large part of global history since the end of the Second World War has been dominated by the stately, cumbersome dance of the superpowers, at once fearful, but respectful, of each other. In 1945 there were two superpowers, the United States of America and the Soviet Union. Today, there are three, for we must include communist China with its countless millions as another (some would argue that Japan is a potential superpower, but that must remain a question for the future).

The 'thaw', 1953–6

The year 1953 was an important year, as we have seen, for it was the year of Stalin's death and the end of the war in Korea (see p. 139). It therefore marked the beginning of a 'thaw' in the Cold War as the new Soviet leaders, Malenkov, Bulganin, and Khrushchev, showed a more friendly attitude to the West in particular and the world in general. The Soviet attitude at the Geneva Conference of 1954 (see p. 165) seemed to underline the fact that a new 'spirit' was in the air.

American–Soviet relations

Hungary, 1956

Much of this optimism was deflated by Soviet behaviour in Hungary in November 1956 when the hopes raised by Khrushchev's secret speech were brutally crushed. The Hungarian Prime Minister Imre Nagy had made two suggestions that the Russians found quite unacceptable. He proposed:
1. that Hungary should leave the Warsaw Pact;
2. the acceptance of non-communists into the Hungarian government.

Fig. 23.1   The statue of Stalin is torn down during the troubles in Hungary in 1956.

He had the full support of his people in this demand, who turned on the hated secret police and drove the Red Army out of Budapest (Fig. 23.1). It was then that Khrushchev showed his stern resolve by sending in reinforcements to crush the uprising in the Hungarian capital. Nagy was later arrested and shot, and it was clear that the wind of destalinization would not be allowed to blow through the Soviet satellite countries of Eastern Europe. It was true that there had been serious rioting in Poland in June 1956 when workers had been killed, but the reliable Gomulka had been installed by the Russians to quieten the storm and elsewhere an uneasy calm reigned. The freedom fighters of Budapest looked longingly at the skies for Western aircraft, but the USA and its allies could do nothing. They were, in any case, hopelessly divided over the Suez affair (see Chapter 18).

The Eisenhower Doctrine

President Eisenhower had angrily denounced the aggression of both the USSR in Hungary and his Anglo–French allies in Egypt in 1956. But he then proceeded to put forward a doctrine of his own which gave the USA the right to interfere in the internal affairs of Middle Eastern countries. In 1958 US marines were landed in the Lebanon to replace an anti-Western regime which the Americans disliked. At the same time, the US 7th Fleet flexed its naval muscles off the island of Taiwan as the Chinese communists appeared to threaten Chiang Kai-shek's exiled Nationalist regime.

The U-2 spy plane incident

The USSR denounced American policy in the Arab world, but Khrushchev still needed what he termed 'peaceful coexistence' with the West if he were to carry through his ambitious economic plans at home (see Chapter 20). In 1959 he visited the United States with every appearance of enjoyment, and was even seen smiling broadly at a performance of the cancan! There was to be a summit meeting with Eisenhower and Macmillan in Paris in 1960 when an unexpected event broke up the East–West dialogue. It was the shooting down of an American U-2 spy plane over Soviet territory and the capture of its pilot, the unlucky Gary Powers. Everyone knew, of course, that the United States and Russia spied on each other, but the Americans had been 'caught'! Eisenhower had no option, but to take full responsibility for the U-2 flight, and Khrushchev used the spy plane incident as an excuse to stamp out of the Paris summit. The unfortunate Powers spent two years in a Soviet prison before he was exchanged for one of their spies in 1962.

The second Berlin Crisis, 1961

The USSR was in the right over the Powers case, and this may have encouraged Khrushchev to try his luck in another area. He was also faced, at this time, with the new and comparatively inexperienced President John F. Kennedy, and Berlin was the chosen battleground. The Soviet Union had long regarded the Western outpost in West Berlin as a nuisance, and Khrushchev hoped, like Stalin before him, to pressure the Western powers out of it. He tried unsuccessfully to get Kennedy to agree to a withdrawal from the city when he met him at Vienna in 1961. When this failed, the Soviet leader backed the East German decision to build a wall between the two sectors (Fig. 23.2) in August of that year. Their leader Ulbricht was becoming alarmed at the number of East Berliners who were escaping to the West. For a short time, there was a crisis because the communist action infringed the Potsdam Agreement. American and Russian tanks faced one another across 'Checkpoint Charlie', but no one in the West wanted a fight over Berlin. Khrushchev and his allies appeared to have won that particular round.

Cuba and the Missile Crisis, 1959–62

This success may well have encouraged Khrushchev to embark on a new and more dangerous adventure on the other side of the Atlantic which brought the world to the verge of a nuclear war.

Castro's revolution, 1959

The venue was unlikely, for it was to be the small Caribbean island of Cuba which had been an American colony for part of its history. There, in 1959, the bearded revolutionary leader, Fidel Castro, had overthrown the American-backed, but corrupt, dictatorship of Batista. His island had been a playground for American gamblers and tourists, but Castro's government was to be a different matter. At first, he seemed to want good relations with Washington, but then angered the US government by nationalizing all American property on the island. The American Central Intelligence Agency (CIA) became convinced that Castro was a communist and persuaded President Eisenhower that he should be deposed. Before this could be done, Eisenhower had been replaced by Kennedy who allowed himself to be convinced of the merits of the CIA plan. The plan consisted of two parts:
1. anti-Castro Cuban *émigrés** were to be landed in Cuba;
2. following which there was to be a revolt of the Cuban people against Castro. This did not take place and the result was a fiasco as the Cuban *émigrés* were

Fig. 23.2   Tension at the Berlin Wall. Students demonstrate by the Wall to mark its first anniversary.

easily rounded up by Castro's army.

Kennedy was humiliated by this rebuff, and it is likely that observers in Moscow thought that he was a rather inexperienced American President who could easily be outmanoeuvred. Accordingly, later in 1961, the Soviet leadership took the fateful decision to place intermediate range ballistic missiles in Cuba. The Bay of Pigs landing therefore had exactly the opposite result to what was intended. Castro survived, and his ties with the Communist bloc were stronger than before, whereas the USA was made to look like a state which bullied small nations.

The discovery of the missiles

Relations between the US and Cuba were at an all-time low in August 1962, when a U-2 spy plane discovered that the Soviet Union was placing medium-range missiles on the island which were capable of hitting Washington DC. At first, Kennedy was reluctant to believe such evidence, and he was not totally convinced of Soviet intentions until 16 October when the CIA produced irrefutable proof that the Russians were building missile sites. His brother, Robert Kennedy, wrote later that 'the dominant feeling at the meeting was stunned surprise'.[1] No one had expected or anticipated that the Russians would deploy surface-to-surface ballistic missiles in Cuba.

What was President Kennedy to do faced with such a situation on an island 145 km (90 miles) from the coast of Florida? Three alternatives presented themselves:

1. He could ignore the missiles and the Russian advisers in Cuba. His own Cabinet decided that such a mild response was unacceptable.

2. He could bomb the missile sites in Cuba and risk killing the Russians and Cubans servicing them. This was the option backed by the Pentagon, but it carried with it the risk of nuclear war.

3. The Americans could blockade or quarantine the island by surrounding it with US warships. This had two advantages. Firstly, it would prevent Soviet ships bringing any spare parts for the missiles. Secondly, it would give Khrushchev and the Soviet government more time to think about whether they would fight a war for Cuba.

In the end, Kennedy decided on the blockade, and he told the American people about this in a television broadcast on 22 October 1962. In it, he called upon Khrushchev to 'halt and eliminate this clandestine, reckless and provocative threat to world peace and to stable relations between our two nations'. As Soviet ships moved towards Cuba and the waiting American cordon of warships, the situation grew ever more perilous. If the warships had fired on a Soviet vessel, then nuclear war would have been an almost certain result. For a while this seemed a strong possibility and UN Secretary-General U Thant anxiously intervened between the two sides. As late as 26 October Khrushchev reminded Kennedy in a letter: 'You have stationed devastating rocket weapons, which you call offensive, in Turkey literally right next to us.' But the Soviet leader (or those who pressed him to take a forward position in Cuba) was having second thoughts, and on 18 October he sent Kennedy two further messages, one polite and the other reminding the US government of its imperialist plots against Cuba. The milder message referred to the Soviet decision 'to dismantle the arms which you describe as offensive, and to crate and return them to the Soviet Union'. Fortunately for the peace of the world, Kennedy chose to reply to this message, and the crisis was averted. The Soviet ships carrying the offensive spare parts had already been turned back, although some ordinary merchant vessels had continued their voyage to Cuba.

The results of the Missile Crisis

Several points were agreed between Kennedy and Khrushchev:
1. The USA would leave Castro alone and cease its attempts to overthrow his government.
2. All Soviet missiles were to be sent home. In exchange, US Jupiter missiles in Turkey would also be dismantled. This was a reasonable Soviet request given the closeness of their major cities to Turkey.
3. A hot line telephone link would be created between Moscow and Washington.
4. Both sides would agree to a nuclear-test ban treaty. This was signed in 1963 by Great Britain, USA and USSR and banned the testing of nuclear bombs in the atmosphere (France and China refused to join).

Kennedy in the crisis

One of the major features of the crisis was its skilful handling by the American President. He did not boast about his victory. His Secretary for Defence, Bob MacNamara, wrote accurately: 'He demonstrated then, as I have seen him do on so many other occasions before and since, a most extraordinary combination of energy and courage, compassion and wisdom.'[2]

Cuban missile countdown, 1962

4 September	Kennedy warns USSR about possible results of placing offensive weapons in Cuba.
11 September	USSR denies existence of such weapons.
16 October	Kennedy's conversation with Bobby in Oval Office. Start of thirteen days of crisis.
22 October	Kennedy's television appearance before American people.
23 October	Row between Adlai Stevenson and Ambassador Zorin at the UN.
28 October	Khrushchev sends peace message to Kennedy.

The Sino–Soviet split, 1959–69

There was no doubt that Khrushchev suffered a setback over Cuba, and it followed another and even more historic one over China, which resulted in a definite and long-term split between the two great communist powers and was one of the reasons for the Soviet leader's fall in 1964 (see Chapter 20). The split, when it came, was not a complete surprise because relations between Peking and Moscow had been deteriorating for some years. Mao Tse-tung had not approved of Khrushchev's policy of destalinization after 1956 and neither did he believe in peaceful coexistence with the Western imperialists. Differences over foreign affairs were then compounded by some rather insensitive comments by Khrushchev about the Chinese agricultural reforms after 1958 which infuriated Mao. The split then became open when Soviet advisers were suddenly withdrawn from China in 1960. Since then Sino*–Soviet relations have been as icy as those between Stalin and the West at the height of the Cold War, and the two countries can be found on opposite sides in almost any situation. Both accuse the other of being revisionist and therefore not true followers of Marx and Lenin.

China's India War, 1962

As early as 1962, the USSR showed its disapproval of Mao by supporting India in the war over the disputed MacMahon Line. The Chinese victory over the Indians was followed by consistent Soviet support for the Delhi government in its disputes with China's ally Pakistan. In 1965 Mr Kosygin acted as a mediator in the first Indo–Pakistan War and the Russians supplied the Indian army with their latest military equipment.

Frontier disputes

China's claims against India were paralleled by its claims that the USSR illegally held Chinese territory that had been acquired by Russia in the nineteenth century. The shrill xenophobia of the Cultural Revolution (see p. 181) increased Sino–Soviet tensions, which eventually exploded in frontier fighting along the Ussuri River in 1969. Although the hostilities settled down, China still claims that Russia holds its land. Throughout the world, China contests Soviet influence and supports the enemies of Russia in the constant struggle against what the Chinese call the 'hegemonists*'. Capitalist structures like the EEC are regarded by the Peking government as being a good thing because they are anti-Soviet. The rivalry of the two communist giants could only be viewed with pleasure in the West.

The Prague Spring, 1968

Soviet difficulties in the 1960s were not limited to their disputes with China. No sooner had Mr Kosygin defused the dangerous Middle Eastern situation through his meeting at Glassborough with President Johnson in 1967 than his government was confronted by a far more serious crisis in Europe.

Once again, a Soviet satellite was becoming restless, and this time it was Czechoslovakia, which had been, in many respects, the most steadfast of Moscow's allies. The Czechs were tired not only of Stalinist-type repression, but also of the total economic failure of Antonín Novotný's government. In the early 1960s, the Czech economy was growing by a miserable 1 per cent a year. Novotný was also associated with the purging of Czech leaders, like Slansky, in 1948–9, and in January 1968 he and the other conservatives were removed from their positions on the Czech Politburo. Novotný was replaced by Alexander Dubček in his post of First Secretary to the Czech Communist Party. It was to be Dubček, from the more conservative, agrarian Slovakia, who was to be the mainspring of the series of liberal reforms that came to be called 'the Prague Spring'. For the first time, a communist government allowed free discussion in the papers and on television, and permitted its citizens to travel freely abroad. There was a genuine and intense debate inside the country about the need to bring in 'communism with a human face'. All this, as you can imagine, was very worrying for the men in the Kremlin and other ultra-conservative communist leaders like Walter Ulbricht in East Germany.

But two things need to be made clear. They underline the difference between Dubček and the tragic figure of Imre Nagy:

1. At no time did Dubček advocate leaving the Warsaw Pact. Instead he spoke of the Czech army as 'a firm link' in the alliance.

2. Neither did the Czech leader ever suggest that non-communists should be allowed into government. He was both a loyal communist and ally of the USSR. But that did not save him, as we shall see.

For six months, the Russians tolerated the new liberalism in Czechoslovakia, but they did so with growing anxiety. Then, at the beginning of August, Brezhnev and Kosygin summoned Dubček to meet them at the border village of Cierna. At the time, all seemed well as the Russians appeared to be satisfied with Dubček's assurances of loyalty. But we now know that they were, in fact, planning to remove this new and troublesome addition to the East European family.

Visits from the renegades Tito and Ceausescu of Romania (who never towed the Moscow line in foreign policy) probably did little to save Dubček. Neither did the chants of crowds in Poland calling for 'a Polish Dubček'. These simply antagonized Gomulka. The end came suddenly and dramatically during the night of 20–21 August 1968, when Warsaw Pact forces invaded Czechoslovakia. Dubček and his immediate colleagues were arrested and taken to Moscow for questioning. Their country was placed under the military occupation of the Warsaw Pact, although it was bitterly contested by the Czech people who felt their allies had betrayed them (Fig. 23.3).

Fig. 23.3   Czechs in Prague demonstrate against the Soviet occupation.

There is no doubt that the Soviet leadership was taken aback both by the slogans of 'Ivan go home' inside Czechoslovakia and the sharp international reaction. Dubious stories were circulated about West German arms shipments and Fascist *coups*, but no one was deceived. The Warsaw Pact involvement was a consequence of:

1. the sensitive geographical position of Czechoslovakia so close to the German Democratic Republic (GDR) and West Germany;
2. the fear in the Kremlin and elsewhere that Dubček-style communism might seep into the rest of Eastern Europe.

The risk was too great for the Soviet leadership, although they allowed the wretched Dubček to keep his job until January 1969. He was, by then, a sad and forlorn figure, a sop to Czech feelings until things quietened down. When they had, the Russians brought in the reliable Gustáv Husák who, ironically, was a survivor of the earlier Stalinist purge in the 1950s. Alexander Dubček now works for the forestry commission in Bratislava, while his successor still runs the grim Czechoslovakia of the 1980s.

The era of *détente*

The West condemned the Czech invasion as it had that of Hungary in 1956. Everyone realized though that the Czech people were more isolated than they had been in 1938. Their plight was to be a mere hiccup in the interlocking dance of the giant powers who made small nations weep. In the 1970s the mood changed to a demand for *détente* or understanding between the two rival power blocs.

Nixon and Kissinger

Détente was a word that was to be associated largely with two men, Richard M. Nixon, the 'Cold War Warrior' of the 1950s, and ex-Harvard Professor Henry Kissinger, his adviser on foreign affairs (Fig. 23.4). They, in turn, benefited from a peculiar set of circumstances in the early 1970s. In particular:

1. the end of the American involvement in South East Asia (see p. 165).
2. Chinese fears of the USSR dating from the frontier clashes of 1969.

These historical coincidences brought about the visits to Peking by Nixon and Kissinger in 1971–2. It also brought Red China into the UN when the USA withdrew its veto in 1971. This turnabout brought the United States government into an unusually favourable position because the Soviet Union was worried

Fig. 23.4   Richard Nixon with his adviser on foreign affairs, Henry Kissinger, who was to become the advocate of shuttle diplomacy.

about the new process of *détente* between Washington and Peking. For a long time, writers about international affairs had talked of a 'bipolar' system based on the two poles of America and Russia. Now there seemed to be a third hat in the ring.

Brezhnev replied by asking Nixon to Moscow in order to keep on good terms with the USA. Strategic Arms Limitation Talks (SALT) were started in Geneva to slow down the crippling arms race, and the USSR received a favourable trade deal with the Americans. This seemed to be a far cry from the days of Berlin and Cuba, but there were some chinks in the process of *détente*. The 1975 Helsinki Agreement emphasized the need for disarmament, but it also talked about human rights and the need for freedom of discussion. The Soviet government, however, has taken little note of this (see Chapter 20).

Afghanistan, 1979–80

The ice-breaking process of *détente* was to suffer a serious blow in December 1979 when Soviet troops invaded neighbouring Afghanistan to support the government of President Karmal. This, in itself, was not surprising because the USSR had been meddling in Afghan affairs for at least a decade, but the scale of Soviet involvement was. At least 50,000 troops were sent in, and the number was increased as Afghan resistance has grown. By the end of 1980 it was clear that the Red Army was having problems in holding down the tough Afghan tribesmen in the hills. As in 1968, the Soviet government had miscalculated, for once again there was a strong and immediate international protest. This was certainly justified since the Soviet Union was clearly operating outside its accepted sphere of influence, even if the Afghan invasion might be justified in Russian eyes by the 1968 Brezhnev Doctrine*.

On the other hand, there was an element of 'double-think' on the Western side, too. President Jimmy Carter's boycott of the 1980 Moscow Olympics caused confusion in the alliance (West Germany did not go, but Great Britain and France did), and there was a rather one-sided condemnation of Soviet, as against Chinese, policy. China's support for the odious Pol Pot regime and its invasion of Vietnam were forgotten in the rush to condemn Russia's attack on the Afghans.

The end of *Ostpolitik*?

American leaders today talk about 'linkage' (see Chapter 25) between world problems, and this is certainly true. The Afghans' resistance to Soviet domination in Asia was to coincide with another upsurge of nationalism in Eastern Europe in the late summer of 1980. In this instance, it was the Poles, angered by a series of price rises, who struck against the government of Mr Gierek. He had taken over from Gomulka in 1970 after similar protests against price rises in the cities of Gdansk and Szczecin.

The only difference between Gomulka and Gierek, said the Poles (with their wry Slav sense of humour), was that Gierek did not realize there was no difference. This Polish crisis offered a real challenge to Soviet communism when the Polish Courts ruled that the new free trade union Solidarity was not subordinate to the Communist Party. The East German government reacted by tightening travel restrictions, thus endangering Willy Brandt's policy of *Ostpolitik* (East policy), i.e. normalizing relations with the Eastern bloc, so carefully followed in the early 1970s. This had meant recognizing the East German government and accepting the new Oder–Neisse frontier between West Germany and Poland. It also incorporated a non-aggression pact with the USSR in 1970 and the Czechs thus recognizing at last the invalidity of the 1938 Munich Pact. The process continued when East Germany and West Germany were admitted into the UN as separate states in 1973. Willy Brandt won the Nobel Peace Prize in 1971, and it was he who, untainted by the war (which he had spent in Norway), performed the solemn act of homage to the Polish dead in 1970. Could this delicate mechanism be kept alive under the pressures of modern diplomacy? Both Brandt, who resigned as Chancellor in 1974, and Schmidt who replaced him, hoped desperately that it could.

Chancellor Helmut Schmidt visited Moscow in 1980 to preserve the Eastern bridge, but *Ostpolitik* was seriously endangered by the refusal of the US Senate to ratify SALT 2 and the continued Soviet presence in Afghanistan.

The West European dimension

The Federal German Republic (West Germany) feels obliged to follow US policy because of its vulnerable geographical position. Defence spending remains low, nonetheless, and the German economy gained greatly from the 'economic miracle' of the 1950s, the brainchild of Dr Erhardt. A Left-wing coalition of Social and Free Democrats has dominated West German politics since 1969, thus rejecting the Christian Democrat monopoly of the Konrad Adenauer years (1949–63).

Not so France, where the Left has been kept out of power since de Gaulle's return to politics in 1958. Despite a lapse in 1968, when de Gaulle's obsession with foreign rather than domestic affairs caused him to ignore student and worker unrest, the Fifth Republic has kept its economic and political stability. During the Presidency of Valéry Giscard d'Estaing (1974–81) an economic depression forced Premier Raymond Barre to introduce tough economy measures, but France retained its independent defence posture and remained outside of NATO. The new socialist government of François Mitterand, elected in 1981, seemed determined to continue this policy.

Britain, for its part, remained a loyal member of the alliance and spent proportionally more on defence than any of its partners. Although it began to benefit from North Sea oil during the government of Conservative Premier Edward Heath (1970–74) resources were swallowed up by the persistent problem of Ulster. British troops were forced to remain in the province from 1969 onwards. Elsewhere in the British Isles, the demand for self-government in Scotland and Wales helped to bring down the Callaghan Labour government in March 1979.

Keywords

émigré: exile from a foreign country.
Sino: meaning Chinese.
hegemonist: one who desires the dominance of one state over another.
Brezhnev Doctrine: put forward in 1968; giving the USSR the right to intervene in other socialist states.

24 The World in the 1980 s

The balance of terror

The most serious problem facing the human race in the twentieth century is the proliferation* of nuclear weapons. Since the end of the Second World War, the United States and the Soviet Union have, according to Michael Howard, 'raced neck and neck in the development of thermonuclear bombs'.[1] The formation of NATO in 1949 and the Warsaw Pact in 1955 added a further dimension to this dangerous process, as the figures in Table 24.1 indicate.

Table 24.1 The nuclear missile balance, 1978–9

Ballistic missile	NATO	Warsaw Pact
Inter-continental	1,054	1,400
Medium-range	*	722
Short-range	409	1,506
Submarine-launched	784	1,319

Note: * no figures available.
Source: The Military Balance 1978–9.

The superiority of the Warsaw Pact forces alarms Western defence leaders, but the dreadful cost which keeping those sophisticated weapons systems imposes on the economies of the countries concerned and the sheer waste of resources that goes with it should also be remembered (Table 24.2). It is not hard to agree with the recent despairing comment of a member of the Reagan administration that world governments are 'beating ploughshares into swords'.

Table 24.2 Military cost of armed forces per head of population, 1978–9

Country	Armed Forces (thousands)	Population (thousands)	Cost in £
USA	2,087	220,000	260
UK	344	56,000	120
France	513	54,000	163
West Germany	495	64,000	190
USSR	3,650	262,000	*

Note:* No figures available.

Disarmament

Over the years a number of efforts have been made to scale down armaments, even by the superpowers, but these have always foundered on the suspicion and hatred of both sides. Efforts to disarm have operated on two levels:
1. *global.* This has involved attempts by the USA and USSR to control their own armaments systems. SALT 1, signed in 1972, was such an example. Both sides recognized that there was 'no alternative to . . . peaceful coexistence'. The result of the SALT talks was the banning of the development of anti-ballistic missiles, thus reducing the anxieties of the other side. So far SALT 2 has not been signed because (i) the US Senate opposes ratification while Soviet troops remain in Afghanistan; and (ii) technical disagreements about the Soviet Backfire bomber and American cruise missile have produced a stalemate on whether these weapons should be included in the agreement.

Other global agreements have included the Test Ban Treaty of 1963 (see p. 198) and the 1968 Nonproliferation Treaty which both France and China refused to sign. Since then the sinister likelihood of catastrophic nuclear war has increased as more and more countries achieve the ability to deliver thermonuclear bombs. There are now 4 ton(ne)s of TNT (high explosive) per person in the world and an estimated 50,000 nuclear devices.

Lastly, in this context, was the Helsinki Security Conference of 1975 presided over by US President Gerald Ford and Leonid Brezhnev, with thirty-five states present. The Final Act of the conference consists of three parts: (i) methods to stop conflicts between the rival blocs happening by accident; (ii) plans for economic and technical co-operation; and (iii) an agreement about closer international contacts with special reference to human rights.

2. *European theatre.* For a long time after 1945 it seemed clear that Europe was the flashpoint for a future conflict. The crises of 1948–9, 1956, 1968 and 1980–81 only appeared to confirm this, and efforts have been made to neutralize the likelihood of Europe becoming a war zone.

Some of these attempts have been at the formal government level, such as the Rapacki Plan. This was the work of Poland's Foreign Minister in 1957, and suggested that central Europe should be made a nuclear-free zone. The idea came to nothing, even though the Austrian State Treaty of 1955 appeared to offer some precedent. Austria was prevented by the treaty from joining either alliance bloc.

Another approach is the unilateral solution as represented by organizations like the Campaign for Nuclear Disarmament (CND) in Britain (Fig. 24.1). This organization, which has had a marked revival recently, believes that Britain should set a good example by disarming, which would then allow the USSR to withdraw its rockets behind the Ural Mountains and leave Britain and Europe in peace.

The unilateralist argument can be criticized as naive and defeatist, but, as can be seen, the choice for any small European country is an agonizing one: *possible* Soviet domination versus almost certain nuclear destruction. Even the superpowers would suffer grievously in such a war, although their vast land masses would save them from total destruction.

Poverty

Other themes should be mentioned. One of these is poverty, for we live in a world where most people do not have enough to eat. Once again, statistics tell a story:

1. One-fifth of the people in the world (mostly in the northern hemisphere) have $\frac{4}{5}$ of its income.

Fig. 24.1 Members of the CND demonstrating outside the American embassy in London against nuclear weapons.

2. Approximately seven people die from hunger every five minutes.

3. One person in ten does not have enough to eat.

4. The population of the world, which was 4,500 billion in 1980, will be about 6,000 billion in the year 2000!

In answer to the question, what is being done?, the answer plainly enough is too little. For this the rich, advanced countries are largely to blame, *not* the Arab oil producers as the Western media sometimes suggest. Table 24.3 shows the foreign aid figures of the richer countries of the world as a percentage of their Gross National Product (GNP), that is the amount they earn in a year. The OPEC figures (Table 24.4) compare far more favourably.

Table 24.3 Western foreign aid contributions as percentage of GNP, 1979–80.

Country	1979	1980*
UK	0.52	0.52
France	0.59	0.59
West Germany	0.44	0.44
USA	0.18	0.19
Canada	0.46	0.47

Note: * estimated figures only.

Table 24.4 OPEC foreign aid contributions as percentage of GNP, 1979

Country	1979
Saudi Arabia	3.15
Kuwait	5.14
Iraq	2.94
United Arab Emirates	1.58
Iran	.03
Libya	.58

Source: World Bank.

The token gestures of the advanced world have greatly concerned the Brandt Commission on Third World Conditions which wants to avoid a situation in the 1980s where mankind creates 'two worlds', a poor, starving south and a rich, overfed north. A human society in which 'the rich watch the poor starving to death on TV' was how Commonwealth Secretary-General Rampal described it. Many of the suggestions of the Brandt Commission are of a strictly practical nature and appear in books like Susan George's *How the other half dies*, suggesting, for example, that 'junk' baby food should not be sent to the starving millions of Latin America.

Proper use of aid and the provision of technical experts are vital, as is education in birth-control methods and more modern agricultural techniques (Fig. 24.2).

Most important of all, perhaps, is the emphasis on a self-sufficiency which will enable the developing countries to feed themselves, instead of relying on the bottomless pit of foreign aid.

The women's movement

Everything in the last section applies to women twice over. In many Third World countries they are little more than beasts of burden producing as many children as possible. But in the West, especially in the USA and Britain, some progress has been made in the last twenty years in bettering the position of women. At least, there is now a general awareness that improvement is needed.

The importance of power sharing

In the modern world women lack a fair share of both economic and political power. They are still not in positions of power even in the advanced countries: there is no woman on the Soviet Politburo, no

Fig. 24.2　Poverty in the Third World. Agricultural techniques remain primitive.

woman has been President of the United States and only a small percentage of women have ever been elected to Congress.

Britain elected its first woman Prime Minister, Margaret Thatcher, in May 1979, but some of her policies, in particular her economic monetarism, tended to affect women adversely, partly because many of them are part-time workers. The number of female M.P.s has scarcely increased since the days of Nancy Astor in the 1920s. Although the number of women in top jobs in Britain is still relatively small, it is gradually increasing, and there are now fewer exclusively male jobs.

The record elsewhere is not much more encouraging. While it is true that Mrs Gandhi (Fig. 24.3) has had two longish spells as Indian Premier, this may well have something to do with the fact that she is the daughter of Pandit Nehru as well as with recognition of her own personal qualities. The influence of Madame Mao (later sentenced to death) was almost certainly the result of her special position and her husband's declining health.

Other women Prime Ministers have included Mrs Bandaranaike of Sri Lanka (1960–65 and 1970–77) and Mrs Golda Meir of Israel (1968–74), while Mrs Gro Harlem Brundtland became Prime Minister of Norway in 1981. Mrs Finnbogabottir was elected President of Iceland in August 1980. Madame Simone Weil completed her term of office as President of the EEC Parliament in 1982.

Economic progress has been equally disappointing. The USA still has no Equal Rights Amendment and Britain's Equal Pay Act has been found to be full of loopholes. About the former, which revived the feminist movement in the 1960s, a union secretary could still write in the next decade that 'married women refuse to join unions because their husbands – good union members – forbid it'.[2] In the USA, in 1972, only 12 per cent of women were unionized, and even in communist China, in 1955, slogans like 'Housework is glorious, too' were commonplace. Though the communist states offered more equality of job opportunity, the decision-makers are still male. Juliet Mitchell, a feminist writer, wrote of Britain in

Fig. 24.3   Indira Gandhi.

1976 that women 'were the single most impoverished social group', and this remark has a general global application.[3] It must be the task of men *and* women in the 1980s to try and reverse this trend so that historians of both sexes in a hundred years' time can tell a different tale, and one which, unlike today's, tells the story of women too.

Keywords

proliferation: spread or increase.

25 The International Political System in the Twentieth Century

A century of change

We have travelled a long way since that day in June 1914 when Gavrilo Princip killed the heir to the Habsburg throne at Sarajevo. He lived in a world of horseless carriages and primitive aircraft, while we live in an age of colour television, microchips and space probes to Saturn and beyond. It has obviously been a century of great material change, but we also need to look at the changes which have taken place in the world order.

The collapse of European power

The most striking, perhaps, has been first the breakdown and then the collapse of European colonialism. In 1900 one-quarter of the globe owed obedience to Britain; today this great empire has been virtually destroyed. France, Belgium, Holland, Spain and Portugal have also been through similar experiences (Germany, earliest of all, at the 1919 Versailles Treaty). The historian Michael Howard has suggested that one week in 1941 was crucial, when Japan attacked Pearl Harbor and Stalin launched a massive counterattack on the eastern front.[1] The US–Japanese conflict and the certain Soviet victory over Nazi Germany deprived Europe, he says, of its central position in world affairs. Instead, Europe merely became a contact point between the two great superpowers. There is a great deal of force behind this argument, but in reality the decline of the European powers was already evident in 1919, and even as far back as 1904–5.

You may recall W. E. B. du Bois's comment about the 'colour line' (see p. 2) being the dominant theme of the century. Already Asiatic Japan had defeated the Tsar of all the Russias in the war ended by US mediation at Portsmouth, New Hampshire, in 1905. The Kaiser had written to his cousin Nicholas II describing the Japanese as racially inferior 'little yellow monkeys', and yet it was mighty Russia that

had crumbled. In Africa itself, the very centre of European power, Abyssinian forces had routed the Italians at Adowa in 1896.

The significance of these events was passed over at the time, and the Versailles settlement merely perpetuated the myth of European dominance. Anglo-French power was a façade because the two strongest powers in the world had, in fact, simply opted out of European affairs after 1919. One, the USSR, was concentrating on internal reconstruction. The other, the USA, opted for 'normalcy' and a distaste for 'squalid' European power politics. The only area in which the USA took a real interest was reparations, and this attitude was maintained until Imperial Japan launched its devastating attack on Pearl Harbor.

It is therefore right that our story after 1945 should not give undue weight to Western Europe because it was essentially an area on the retreat and confused about its position in the world political system. 'Great Britain,' said Secretary of State Dean Acheson in a famous phrase, 'has lost an Empire and not yet found a role.' Britain and France found themselves in an unfamiliar and dangerous position. They wished to maintain the trappings of power, yet lacked the resources to do it. The compromise provided by RAF Bomber Command and General Charles de Gaulle's *force de frappe* (strike force) was unlikely to change this. Meanwhile, the USA encouraged European unity to reduce its own commitment to defending the continent. Britain was suspicious of organizations like the EPC and EDC lest they weaken US resolve to stay in Western Europe. The disastrous American isolationism of the 1930s always lay before European eyes.

The superpowers

In the last chapter, we saw how the build-up of nuclear armaments became a very serious problem after 1945. But this build-up has, in the main, been a by-product of the rivalry between the two major superpowers and their associated alliance systems. It is probable that if nuclear weapons had never been invented, the postwar world would still have been dominated by the struggle between the USA and the USSR and their differing political ideologies.

Decolonization

In earlier chapters, we saw how much of the story of this century has been concerned with the revolt of the non-white races against European colonialism. By the 1970s the process of freeing the Afro-Asian nations had almost been completed. Britain was still in dispute with Argentina over the Falkland Islands, and the Portuguese clung on in Angola and Mozambique – until 1974 – but the days of imperialism were over.

Once in control of their own destiny the blacks showed the same inclination to remain free and independent as their white masters had before them. This view was clearly stated on 12 January 1970 by General Gowon during his country's painful and bloody civil war: 'Our objective was . . . to assert the ability of the black man to build a strong progressive and prosperous modern nation.' The problem for the Afro–Asian nations was twofold:

1. Would they be allowed to stabilize the new states in peace?
2. Would they be able to overcome the very strong legacy of white colonialism which had left them with an élite of European educated rulers, for example, Sun Yat-sen, Nkrumah, Nehru, Banda and Kenyatta, who often had little in common with the ordinary villager or townsman? In addition, the European powers had drawn up the frontier lines of the new states, often paying scant attention to the views of the people living in the area, e.g. the 1913 MacMahon Line.

Africa offers perhaps the most interesting example of decolonization and its mishandling by the white colonialists. Several factors were forgotten by the administrators of London, Paris and Brussels in their haste to 'wind-up' the by now heavy burden of empire.

Firstly, Africa lacked a class structure and therefore found it hard to copy the largely class-based parties of Western Europe. This made a one-party state more appropriate to the development of African countries.

Secondly, where the Europeans did encourage the appearance of a multi-party system they did so on multiracial lines – as with ZAPU and ZANU in Zimbabwe. A Ghanaian paper commented: 'Party politics is too colonial, and alien a system, and kicks against Africa's natural social organization.'[2] Thus,

in 1972, Zambia became a one-party state to avoid the quarrels which a tribal-based system would bring. Such developments are usually roundly condemned in the West, but we need to think harder about the basis of the criticism.

Ethnic and religious divisions are not uncommon in the so-called 'advanced' countries either: Greek versus Turk in Cyprus (the former held down by the Turkish army since 1974); Catholic against Protestant in Northern Ireland; Walloon against Fleming in Belgium. The list goes on. . . . French separatism in Quebec, encouraged by de Gaulle in 1967, forced a referendum on the issue of a free Quebec, outside Canada, in the 1970s.

In Africa differences have tended to be tribally based; in West Europe and North America language and religion have been predominant. But is this not, we should ask ourselves, simply old wine in new bottles? It would be as well to note Hodder's comment on the true nature of African society in which the authority of 'a local village, village group, clan or ethnic group may well be far more effective and significant than the national or even regional government'.[3]

Africans, too, have begun to realize their economic power, which has also served to highlight the less generous side of imperialism: Spain hung on in the Sahara because of its rich phosphate deposits; natural gas was the lure for France in Algeria; and chrome for the whites in Zimbabwe. This new economic power, like that of OPEC in the Middle East, can bring pressures to bear on the West with regard to South Africa. Nigeria has a huge negative trade balance with Great Britain, and supplies the USA with a good deal of its oil. On a visit to London in March 1981, its President made it amply clear that Nigeria, the largest black African state, might opt to use its own 'oil weapon'. The collapse of imperial Portugal in 1974 has merely brought the economic realities of African life a good deal closer to Messrs Vorster and P. W. Botha.

In the 1960s the following rhyme used to circulate in the black ghettos of the USA:

> If you're white alright,
> If you're brown stick around,
> If you're black get back.

In the First World War black Americans felt they had won their right to civil rights, and in the Second World War 200,000 Anglo-French non-white citizens gave their lives for the mother country. When peace came, the survivors came back to demand the right to independence, bolstered by the knowledge that the non-European armies of Emperor Hirohito had dealt savage blows to European colonialism in 1941–2. In both the USA and Africa the dreams of the blacks were slow to be realized, but du Bois's prophecy pointed in the direction that the struggle would take. Even he, however, could not have foreseen the recovery of a war-ravaged Japan after 1945 and its domination of the industrialized countries of the West.

Linkage

As has already been pointed out the years immediately after the Second World War were dominated by the relationship between the USSR and USA. In Chapter 14 we saw how this relationship had broken down to such a degree that a period of Cold War followed. Then followed a period of gradual 'thaw' which culminated in the Nixon–Brezhnev *détente* of the early 1970s. Both Nixon and his chief foreign policy adviser Henry Kissinger were believers in the concept of 'linkage', i.e. all the world's trouble spots could be linked together with the Soviet–American relationship, the old bipolar system. Under this theory, therefore, America's war in Vietnam was 'linked' with Soviet involvement in the troubled Middle East, and both could be dealt with under the umbrella of Soviet–American *détente*. This theory sounds attractive in that the two great superpowers could solve all the world's problems by working together. There are two major flaws in the linkage philosophy however:

1. Nixon and Kissinger were themselves responsible for 'mending the fences' with Red China, a power which had actually fought Soviet troops along the common frontier in 1969, and was noted since the early 1960s for fanatical hostility to Moscow. Chinese policies and actions, therefore, bore no connection to linkage.

2. Kissinger's biographer David Landau points out that 'easing the threat of instant and mutual mass slaughter should not be equated with the resolution of other crises that can and must be settled without resort to inter-continental missiles'.[4] In other words, there are many smaller conflicts that cannot and should not be settled by the superpowers with their threatening battery of thermonuclear missiles and bombs. More recent history has shown that the Soviet–American giants are far from invulnerable on the world stage. The USA could not win in Vietnam, and the USSR has been ordered out of both Egypt and Ethiopia. Tiny Albania has moved first into the Soviet bloc, then come under Chinese influence and finally has chosen its own stubborn form of independence. Yugoslavia, as we have seen, broke away from Stalin in 1948, and in the 1970s a new

phenomenon called Eurocommunism was prominent. Far from following the 'Moscow line' the Italian Communist Party condemned the Warsaw Pact invasion of Czechoslovakia in 1968, as did the French. No longer then was the communist world a monolith dominated by the USSR, and neither was the USA in total control of its alliance system, having to cope with troublesome allies, such as de Gaulle.

The bipolar system was, in fact, becoming multipolar as the superpowers showed:
1. an inability to control the Middle East;
2. that limited interference in the Far East was ineffective;
3. they could not prevent the growth of rival centres of power like Japan, the EEC and China.

The world of the two giants was therefore rapidly becoming a world of multiple power centres. The USA and USSR remain the strongest military economic units by far, but they cannot order about countries as small as Egypt, Israel, Vietnam and Kampuchea. They may subvert regimes from inside, as in Chile in 1973 and Afghanistan in 1979–80, but such events are usually the result of unusual political and economic circumstances.

It would be tempting to draw a parallel with the pre-1914 world with its alliance blocs and great power wranglings. But that would be to overlook one major event, the Bolshevik Revolution of 1917, which drew one great ideology into international affairs and created a counterideology in Fascism. Whether the communists in the Kremlin plan world conquest is doubtful, but their system of ideas demands the obedience of millions.

That, together with the struggle of the non-white races, has marked a distinguishing feature of the twentieth century.

Conclusion

The world today can be called a 'global village' in a sense that was never true in 1900. We can flash messages around the globe in seconds, and the technology of the USA in particular influences the life-styles of many countries and the leisure moments of hundreds of millions of people.

It must be our hope that this technology will be used to deal with world-wide problems too.

Questions

The following questions are based on Chapters 14–24. Select the correct answer or answers in each case. You should allow yourself forty minutes to complete them.

1. 'From . . ., in the Baltic, to . . ., in the Adriatic, an iron curtain has descended across the continent.' The two cities mentioned are:
(a) Hamburg and Venice.
(b) Stettin and Lublin.
(c) Stettin and Trieste.
(d) Rotterdam and Naples.
(e) Lublin and Palermo.

2. 'SEATO Treaty signed.' 'French defeat at Dien Bien Phu.' These headlines refer to the year:
(a) 1945.
(b) 1960.
(c) 1954.
(d) 1957.
(e) 1949.

3. Which of the following Russian leaders disappeared in 1953?
(a) Stalin.
(b) Molotov.
(c) Zhukov.
(d) Beria.
(e) Bulganin.

4. The U-2 spy plane in 1960 was flown by:
(a) Lee Harvey Oswald.
(b) Gary Powers.
(c) John Glenn.
(d) Adlai Stevenson.
(e) Jim Lovell.

5. All the following were leaders of Nationalist movements after 1945 EXCEPT:
(a) Ho Chi Minh.
(b) Jomo Kenyatta.
(c) Ben Bella.
(d) Gandhi.
(e) Bao Dai.

6. Important international agreements were signed in 1963 and 1968 concerning:
(a) nuclear weapons.
(b) conservation of whales.
(c) refugee settlement.
(d) tariff levels.
(e) navigation rights.

7. A major cause of the Sino–Soviet split was:
(a) Khrushchev's policy of peaceful coexistence.
(b) Chinese criticisms of Stalin.
(c) the Soviet alliance with Yugoslavia.
(d) the Chinese invasion of India.
(e) the status of Formosa.

8. All the following Democratic politicians became President of the USA EXCEPT:
(a) John F. Kennedy.
(b) Lyndon B. Johnson.
(c) Franklin D. Roosevelt.
(d) Harry S. Truman.
(e) George McGovern.

9. Which one of the following communist leaders was imprisoned under Stalin but returned to lead his country?
(a) Ulbricht.
(b) Dubček.
(c) Tito.
(e) Husak.

10. The Berlin Wall was built in:
(a) 1948.
(b) 1954.
(c) 1961.
(d) 1956.
(e) 1953.

11. 'Rebels seize power as Batista falls.' This 1959 headline refers to:
(a) Argentina.
(b) Cuba.
(c) Morocco.
(d) Mexico.
(e) Portugal.

12. Which of the following wartime leaders still ruled their countries in 1960?
(a) Eisenhower and Churchill.
(b) de Gaulle and Nixon.
(c) Brandt and Tito.
(d) Tito and de Gaulle.
(e) Khrushchev and Chiang Kai-shek.

13. Which of the following events was crucial in the history of American civil rights?
(a) the Alger Hiss Trial.
(b) the Taft–Hartley Act.
(c) the death of Malcolm X.
(d) *Brown* v. *Topeka School Board*.
(e) the trial of the Hollywood ten.

14. 'Tailend Joe.' This nickname was once claimed by:
(a) Joseph Stalin.
(b) Joseph McCarthy.
(c) Joseph Kennedy.
(d) Joseph Godber.
(e) Joseph L. Mankowitz.

15. The Treaty of Accession to the EEC was signed for the UK by:
(a) Wilson and Brown.
(b) Callaghan and Owen.
(c) Heath and Home.
(d) Macmillan and Heath.
(e) Jenkins and Healey.

16. Which of the following sold atomic secrets to Russia?
(a) Hiss.
(b) Fuchs.
(c) Rosenburg.

(d) Acheson.

(e) Philby.

17. Chinese forces crushed a revolt in Tibet in:

(a) 1949.

(b) 1955.

(c) 1960.

(d) 1958.

(e) 1962.

18. One family has supplied two Indian premiers since 1947. It was:

(a) Gandhi.

(b) Singh.

(c) Desai.

(d) Nehru.

(e) Shastri.

19. One of the supposed reasons for Nixon's defeat in 1960 was:

(a) his Quaker religion.

(b) Eisenhower's refusal to help him.

(c) his poor showing in a television debate with Kennedy.

(d) lack of funds.

(e) the U-2 spy plane affair.

20. The recovery of the French economy after 1945 was largely the work of:

(a) Schuman.

(b) Pompidou.

(c) Faure.

(d) Monnet.

(e) Barre.

21. 'It must be the policy of the United States to support free people who are resisting attempted subjucation by armed minorities or by outside pressures.'

(i) This statement was made by:

(a) F. D. Roosevelt.

(b) Harry S. Truman.

(c) Dwight D. Eisenhower.

(e) Dean Acheson.

(ii) The statement was in response to communist activity in:

(a) Turkey.

(b) Iran.

(c) Greece.

(d) Spain.

(e) Italy.

22. Read the following two statements:

A. 'We will be unceasing in the search for peace; resourceful in our pursuit of areas of agreement even with those with whom we differ; and generous and loyal to those who join us in common cause.'

B. 'America cannot – and will not – conceive all the plans, design all the programs, execute all the decisions and undertake all the defense of the free nations of the world.'

(i) Statement A was made by:

(a) L. B. Johnson.

(b) J. F. Kennedy.

(c) Adlai Stevenson.

(d) Robert MacNamara.

(e) Barry Goldwater.

(ii) Statement B was made in 1969 on the island of:

(a) Formosa.

(b) Guam.

(c) Singapore.

(d) Iwo Jima.

(e) Ceylon.

(iii) One result of statement B was:

(a) the withdrawal of US troops from Vietnam.

(b) increased American aid to Nationalist China.

(c) the cancellation of the US space programme.

(d) the resignation of President Nixon.

(e) the sending of the 7th Fleet to the Gulf of Tongking.

23. Khrushchev's secret speech in February 1956 was important because it:

(a) ended the Cold War with the West.

(b) angered Tito.

(c) criticized Stalin's elimination of the old Bolsheviks.

(d) announced a new agricultural programme.

(e) accepted Soviet responsibility for the Second World War.

24. 'A former tank expert.' 'Lived in political exile for 12 years.' 'Withdrew his country from NATO.' These statements refer to:

(a) Basil Lidell Hart.

(b) Hans Guderian.

(c) Charles de Gaulle.

(d) General Franco.

(e) Willy Brandt.

25. Which of the following Chinese leaders disappeared in 1969?

(a) Lin Piao.

(b) Chou En-lai.

(c) Chu Teh.

(d) Chiang Kai-shek.

(e) Pu Yi.

26. Which of the following signed a treaty of friendship between their countries in 1963?

(a) Brandt and Gomulka.

(b) Adenauer and de Gaulle.

(c) de Gaulle and Moro.

(d) Macmillan and Adenauer.

(e) Kadar and Eden.

27. The treaty setting up the European Coal and Steel community in 1951 was signed in:

(a) Rome.

(b) Copenhagen.

(c) London.

(d) Brussels.

(e) Paris.

28. The Soviet invasion of Czechoslovakia in 1968 was unexpected because:

(a) Novotný was still in the Czech government.

(b) Dubček had recently met the Russians in Bratislava.

(c) weather conditions were very bad.

(d) Mr Brezhnev was expected in Washington.

(e) East Germay was threatening to leave the Warsaw Pact.

29. Which of the following has NOT been a characteristic of the USSR since 1964?

(a) persecution of the Jews.

(b) support for the Arab cause.

(c) heavy military spending.

(d) friendship with Albania.

(e) membership of the Olympic movement.

30. 'Labour camp inmate.' 'Nobel Prize winner.' 'Exile from his country.' These descriptions apply to:

(a) Jean-Paul Sartre.

(b) Boris Pasternak.

(c) Yuri Gagarin.

(d) James Baldwin.

(e) Alexander Solzhenitsyn.

31. The years 1961, 1967 and 1970 are important in British history because:

(a) they mark the dates of general elections.

(b) immigration acts were passed.

(c) the British government applied to join the EEC.

(d) defence White Papers were published.

(e) atomic power stations were opened.

32. Which of the following women has NEVER been Prime Minister of her country?

(a) Golda Meir.

(b) Margaret Thatcher.

(c) Mrs Gandhi.

(d) Simone Weil.

(e) Mrs Bandaranaike.

33. The Watergate scandal took its name from:

(a) Nixon's campaign headquarters.

(b) the US Justice Department.

(c) the Democratic Party headquarters.

(d) Martin Luther King's birthplace.

(e) Johnson's Texas ranchhouse.

34. 'Let a hundred flowers bloom. Let a hundred schools compete.' This statement by Mao Tse-tung concerned:

(a) the literacy campaign in China.

(b) the reorganization of the Communist Party in 1956–7.

(c) the closing of universities in 1966.

(d) the Sino–Soviet Friendship Treaty.

(e) the 'Great Leap Forward'.

35. A characteristic of Eurocommunism is that:

(a) it rejects state ownership of industry.

(b) it supports Peking against Moscow.

(c) it agrees with free parliamentary elections.

(d) it supports high levels of military spending.

(e) it rejects membership of the EEC.

36. The frontier between Poland and Germany after 1945 was marked by:

(a) the 38th Parallel.

(b) the Oder–Neisse Line.

(c) the Oder–Danube Line.

(d) the Polish Corridor.

(e) the Rhine–Vistula Line.

37. In 1951 an American general was dismissed for insubordination. He was:

(a) Eisenhower.

(b) Haig.

(c) Ridgeway.

(d) MacArthur.

(e) Westmorland.

Further Reading

General Books for CSE and O Level

Brian Catchpole, *A Map History of the Modern World* (Heinemann Educational Books, 1974).

R. D. Cornwell, *World History in the Twentieth Century* (Longman, 1969).

D. Heater, *The Cold War* (Oxford University Press, 1965).

Tony Howarth, *Twentieth Century History: The World since 1900* (Longman, 1979). Interesting and lively.

Ian Lister, *The Cold War* (Methuen, 1974). Useful glossary.

John Martell, *The Twentieth-Century World* (Harrap, 1980). Solid coverage.

Peter Moss, *Modern World History* (Hart-Davis, 1978). Good cartoons and illustrative material.

Richard Poulton, *A History of the Modern World* (Oxford University Press, 1981). Solid approach.

Harriet Ward, *World Powers in the Twentieth Century* (Heinemann Educational Books, 1978). Deals mainly with China, USSR and USA. Contains useful Glossary–Keywords system.

More detailed studies

Richard Collier, *From Cortés to Castro* (Secker & Warburg, 1974). Good general history of Latin America.

Robert Conquest, *The Great Terror* (Penguin, 1971). Deals with the purges from anti-Stalinist viewpoint.

Isaac Deutscher, *Stalin* (Pelican, 1966). Important biography.

M. Arnold Foster, *The World at War* (Fontana, 1976). Comprehensive history of the war.

B. W. Hodder, *Africa Today* (Methuen, 1978).

R. Ben Jones, *The Making of Contemporary Europe* (Hodder & Stoughton, 1980). General history of Europe.

Robert Kennedy, *Thirteen Days: The Cuban Missile Crisis* (Macmillan, 1969). Eyewitness account of events surrounding the crisis.

Walter Laqueur, *Europe since Hitler* (Pelican, 1972). Excellent study of Eastern and Western Europe since 1945.

Isabel Leighton (ed.), *The Aspirin Age, 1919–41* (Penguin, 1963). Very interesting collection of short articles on US history.

Peter Mooney and Colin Bown, *Truman to Carter: A Post-War History of the United States of America* (Edward Arnold, 1979). Good detailed account of recent US history.

William Shirer, *The Rise and Fall of the Third Reich* (Secker & Warburg, 1960). Eyewitness account by American journalist.

Edgar Snow, *Red Star over China* (Pelican, 1973). Written by American who became a close friend of Mao.

Albert Speer, *Inside the Third Reich* (Weidenfeld & Nicolson, 1970). Fascinating glimpse of life inside Hitler's Reich.

John Gittings, *The Chinese View of China* (BBC Publications, 1973). Very useful collection of documents.

Less detailed studies

Colin Bown and Tony Edwards, *Revolution in China 1911–49* (Heinemann Educational Books, 1974). Very well selected material on the evolution of modern China.

H. Purcell, *Mao Tse-tung* (Wayland, 1977).

John Robottom, *Modern Russia* (Longman, 1969).

B. Williams, *Modern Africa* (Longman, 1969).

B. Williams, *Modern Japan* (Longman, 1969).

References

Chapter 1

1. David Thomson, *Europe Since Napoleon* (Pelican, 1966).
2. Corelli Barnett, *The Swordbearers* (Penguin, 1966).
3. A. J. P. Taylor in *The Listener*.
4. Bernadotte E. Schmitt, *Origins of the First World War* (Historical Association, 1958).
5. Corelli Barnett, op. cit.

Chapter 2

1. Norman Stone, *The Eastern Front* (Hodder & Stoughton, 1975).
2. Quoted in Lyn MacDonald, *They Called It Passchendaele* (Michael Joseph, 1978).

Chapter 3
1. Edmund Ions, *Woodrow Wilson* (Macdonald, 1972).
2. ibid.

Chapter 4
1. Anne Parris in the *Guardian*, 27 February 1980.

Chapter 5
1. D. Shub, *Lenin* (Doubleday, 1948).
2. E. H. Carr, *The Russian Revolution from Lenin to Stalin* (Macmillan, 1979).

Chapter 6
1. R. Oliver and A. Atmore, *Africa Since 1800* (Cambridge University Press, 1967).
2. ibid.

Chapter 7
1. G. Carocci, *Italian Fascism* (Penguin, 1974).
2. Albert Speer, *Inside the Third Reich*, trs. R. and C. Winston (Weidenfeld & Nicolson, 1970).
3. Alan Bullock, *Hitler: A Study in Tyranny* (Penguin, 1969).
4. Joseph Goebbels, *Diaries*, ed. Hugh Trevor-Roper, trs. R. Barry (Secker & Warburg, 1978).
5. David Irving, *Hitler's War* (Hodder & Stoughton, 1977).
6. Richard Collier, *From Cortés to Castro* (Secker & Warburg, 1974).
7. John Toland, *Adolf Hitler* (Doubleday, 1976).

Chapter 8
1. André Maurois, *A New History of the United States* (Bodley Head, 1948).
2. Alistair Cooke, *Six Men* (Bodley Head, 1977).
3. Marcel Niedergang, *The Twenty Latin American Republics* (Pelican, 1971).

Chapter 9
1. Patrick O'Donovan in *The Observer*, 4 April 1976.
2. Walter Greenwood, *Love on the Dole* (Penguin, 1969).
3. William Shirer, *The Rise and Fall of the Third Reich* (Secker & Warburg, 1980).
4. Patrick O'Donovan, op. cit.

Chapter 10
1. Isaac Deutscher, *Stalin* (Pelican, 1966).
2. ibid.
3. John Scott, *Behind the Urals: American Worker in Russia's City of Steel* (Indiana University Press, 1973).
4. Robert Conquest, *The Great Terror* (Penguin, 1971).
5. Isaac Deutscher, op. cit.
6. Graham Stephenson, *History of Russia 1812–1945* (Macmillan, 1969).
7. Victor Kravchenko, *I Chose Freedom* (Hale, 1947).

Chapter 11
1. Elizabeth Wiskemann, *Europe of the Dictators* (Fontana, 1966).
2. John Wheeler Bennett, *Munich* (Macmillan, 1966).
3. A. J. P. Taylor, *The Origins of the Second World War* (Hamilton, 1961).
4. Franz Neumann, *The Structure and Practice of National Socialism* (Oxford University Press, 1942).

Chapter 12
1. See Burton Klein, *Germany's Economic Preparations for War* (Harvard, 1959) and Alan Milward, *The German Economy at War* (Athlone Press, 1965).
2. Albert Speer, op. cit.
3. Arthur Bryant, *The Turn of the Tide* (Collins, 1957).
4. Alistair Horne, *To Lose a Battle* (Macmillan 1969).
5. Quoted in M. Arnold Foster, *The World at War* (Fontana, 1976).
6. Quoted in B. H. Liddell Hart, *History of the Second World War* (Cassell, 1970).
7. ibid.
8. Quoted in ibid.
9. Winston Churchill, *Memoirs*, vol. 2 (Cassell, 1967).
10. B. H. Liddell Hart, op. cit.

Chapter 13
1. Albert Speer, op. cit.
2. M. Arnold Foster, op. cit.
3. Quoted in ibid.
4. Walter Laqueur, *Europe since Hitler* (Pelican, 1972).
5. ibid.

Chapter 14

1. C. Waterlow and A. Evans, *Europe 1945–70* (Methuen, 1973).
2. Walter Laqueur, op. cit.
3. A. J. P. Taylor, *How Wars Begin* (Hamish Hamilton, 1979).

Chapter 16

1. J. Stilwell, *The Stilwell Papers* (W. Sloane Association, 1948).
2. M. Edwardes, *Nehru: A Political Biography* (Penguin, 1973).
3. Isaac Deutscher, op. cit.

Chapter 17

1. Theodore Sorensen, *The Kennedy Legacy* (Weidenfeld & Nicolson, 1970).
2. J. K. Galbraith, *The Affluent Society* (Penguin, 1979).
3. Arthur Schlesinger Jr., *A Thousand Days: John F. Kennedy in the White House* (Andre Deutsch, 1965).
4. Peter Mooney and Colin Bown, *Truman to Carter: A Post-War History of the United States of America* (Edward Arnold, 1979).
5. Eldridge Cleaver, *Soul on Ice* (Jonathan Cape, 1969).
6. H. R. Haldeman, *The Ends of Power* (Sidgwick & Jackson, 1978).
7. Jeb Magruder, *An American Life: One Man's Road to Watergate* (Hodder & Stoughton, 1974).
8. Richard Nixon, *Memoirs* (Sidgwick & Jackson, 1978).
9. Jack Watson, *West Indian Heritage: A History of the West Indies* (John Murray, 1979).
10. Richard Collier, op. cit.
11. Richard Nixon, op. cit.

Chapter 18

1. Quoted in D. Leitch, *The Age of Austerity* (Penguin, 1963).
2. Robert Stephens, *Nasser* (Pelican, 1973).
3. Quoted in the *Guardian*, 1980.

Chapter 19

1. Philip Caputo, *A Rumour of War* (Macmillan, 1977).
2. J. K. Galbraith, op. cit.
3. Theodore Sorensen, op. cit.
4. Hugh Higgins, *Vietnam* (Heinemann Educational Books, 1975).
5. Stuart Schram, *Mao Tse-tung* (Pelican, 1966).
6. Hugh Higgins, op. cit.

7. Hugh Portisch, *Eyewitness in Vietnam* (Bodley Head, 1966).
8. Denis Bloodworth in *The Observer*, January 1981.
9. ibid.
10. ibid.

Chapter 20

1. Isaac Deutscher, op. cit.
2. Yevgeny Yevtushenko, *A Precocious Biography* (Penguin, 1965).
3. Walter Laqueur, op. cit.
4. Mark Frankland, *Khrushchev* (Pelican, 1966).
5. Quoted in A. Brown and M. Kaser (eds), *The Soviet Union Since the Fall of Khrushchev* (Macmillan, 1975).
6. *Soviet Weekly*, 21 April 1973.
7. Amnesty International, 1975.
8. Peter Reddaway in A. Brown and M. Kaser (eds), op. cit.

Chapter 21

1. Stuart Schram, op. cit.
2. Peter Mitchell, *China: Tradition and Revolution* (Macmillan, 1977).
3. *The Times*, 23 March 1973.
4. Sophie Knight, *Window on Shanghai* (Andre Deutsch, 1967).

Chapter 22

1. Martin Loney, *White Racism and Imperial Response* (Penguin, 1975).
2. B. W. Hodder, *Africa Today* (Methuen, 1978).

Chapter 23

1. Robert Kennedy, *Thirteen Days: The Cuban Missile Crisis* (Macmillan, 1969).
2. ibid.

Chapter 24

1. Michael Howard, *War in European History* (Oxford University Press, 1976).
2. R. Baxandall in J. Mitchell and A. Oakley (eds), *Rights and Wrongs of Women* (Penguin, 1976).
3. Juliet Mitchell in ibid.

Chapter 25

1. Michael Howard, op. cit.
2. *The Daily Times*, Accra, 2 May 1977.
3. B. W. Hodder, op. cit.
4. David Landau, *Kissinger* (Robson, 1974).

Index